P9-BJL-636

The Enjoyment of Theatre

The Enjoyment of Theatre

Kenneth M. Cameron
Patti P. Gillespie University of South Carolina

Macmillan Publishing Co., Inc.
NEW YORK
Collier Macmillan Publishers
LONDON

PN
2037
.C27

31,428

Copyright © 1980. Macmillan Publishing Co., Inc.

Printed in the United States of America

All rights reserved. No part of this book may be reproduced or
transmitted in any form or by any means, electronic or mechanical,
including photocopying, recording, or any information storage and
retrieval system, without permission in writing from the Publisher.

Macmillan Publishing Co., Inc.
866 Third Avenue, New York, New York 10022

Collier Macmillan Canada, Ltd.

Library of Congress Cataloging in Publication Data

Cameron, Kenneth M. (date)
   The enjoyment of theatre.

   Includes index.
   1. Theater.   I.   Gillespie, Patti P., joint author.
II.   Title.
PN2037.C27   792'.09   79–18216
ISBN 0–02–318360–8

Printing: 2 3 4 5 6 7 8   Year: 0 1 2 3 4 5 6

Preface

The Enjoyment of Theatre is a book whose goal is to increase the theatrical sensitivity and understanding of students in the introductory theatre course. It seeks to reach this goal by two parallel paths: through an awareness of the humanistic tradition of theatre and its place in society and through an understanding of the nature of theatre art and the work of theatre artists. Thus the book is divided into major sections, each of whose focus is a step toward the achievement of its goals: Part One, which deals with aesthetic questions; Parts Two and Three, which examine the Western theatre's history; and Part Four, which looks at the training and methods of modern theatre artists, with brief overviews of the historical background of their work.

The authors do not believe that a slavish and painstaking study of the theatre's chronology from its unknown beginnings to the present is the best way to understand its history. The authors do not believe that the theatre's history shows either progress or continuity. Therefore they feel it best to begin a study of the theatre's history with that moment that is most readily understood: the present. Part Two tries to place the student squarely in the history of his own time and then in the context of the forces that immediately preceded that time. Broadway and Off-Broadway, Absurdism and the Open Theatre, regional professional theatres and the American College Theatre Festival, all these and much more are the subjects of the first historical materials. With that information firmly in hand—with, that is, the present perceived—the introductory student can begin to look at the theatre of the past. Several basic assumptions underlie the choice of materials in the other historical chapters and in their presentation: first, that changes in the theatre are often spasms rather than organic processes; second, that a series of rolling "waves" of mainstream and avant-garde theatre characterize European and American theatre, at least since the seventeenth century; and finally, that the density of information lessens as we go back in history and that, as a result, less packed and shorter chapters are appropriate for the earliest periods.

The chapters on theatre practitioners in Part Four—the actor, the director, the designers, the playwright, and the critic—are intended to inform introductory students about theatre's people and practices rather than to teach them to become practitioners. Because we believe that an understanding of an artist's practice gives sympathy for his goals and results, we have included extensive materials on training, psychology, and methods. We must emphasize, however, that readers hoping for the advocacy of a particular method to the exclusion of others will look in vain; modern theatre people are often highly eclectic, and so we have chosen to celebrate that variety rather than to proselytize for a single approach.

Part One on the aesthetics of theatre will, we believe, reward careful study. It is intended to stimulate as much as—perhaps more than—to inform, for it deals with an area in which there are many questions and many fewer answers. The nature of theatre; its relationship to such diverse other activities as athletics, dance, film, and television; the nature of the audience and of such elements of audience perception as convention, expectation, and surprise; the nature and the elements of performance (as contrasted with drama)—these subjects and others form the basis of three chapters that will, we believe, illuminate the entire study and enliven the student's own idea of theatre.

The Enjoyment of Theatre was written by two people who, themselves, love the art and are active in it. It is their hope that the book will communicate some of that affection and that it will lead students to love the theatre as well. Some of them perhaps may want to become theatre artists themselves; others may find the pleasures of a lifetime of theatregoing. We hope that the book will serve them both well.

In an effort to facilitate readability, we have used the editorial "he" throughout the text. Its use as a referent in no way is intended to denigrate our female colleagues and students.

We should like to express our appreciation to the libraries of the University of South Carolina and the University of Rochester for their generosity and their help; in particular, we are grateful to Ms. Alma Creek and Ms. Mary Huth, and to our editors at the Macmillan Company, Lloyd Chilton and J. Edward Neve.

K. M. C.
P. P. G.

Contents

PART ONE

Theatre As Art

Chapter 1
Theatre As a Performing Art   3

Chapter 2
Theatre and the Performing Audience   23

Chapter 3
The Audience in the Theatre   47

PART TWO

The Theatre of Today and Yesterday

Chapter 4
The Contemporary Theatre: The Decades of the 1960s and 1970s   73

Chapter 5
The Modern Theatre: The Rise and Decline of Realism, 1850–1960   129

vii

PART THREE

The Theatre of the Past

Chapter 6
The Marvelous Theatre: The Rise and Decline
of Romanticism, 1750–1850   181

Chapter 7
The Golden Ages in Italy, England, and France:
The Rise and Decline of Neoclassicism, 1550–1750   211

Chapter 8
The Civic and Religious Theatre: Greek, Roman,
and Medieval, 534 B.C.–A.D. 1550   245

PART FOUR

Theatre Makers

Chapter 9
The Actor   291

Chapter 10
The Director   341

Chapter 11
The Design Team: Scenery, Lighting, and Costumes   385

Chapter 12
The Playwright and the Critic   413

Glossary   441

Bibliography   463

Index   467

The Enjoyment of Theatre

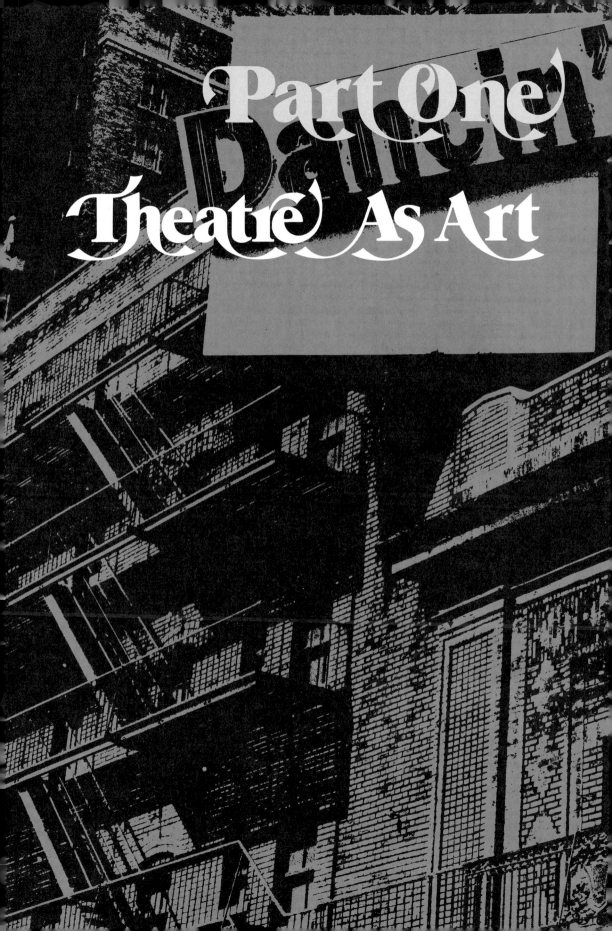

Part One
Theatre As Art

CHAPTER 1

Theatre As a Performing Art

Introduction

Broadway . . . Shakespeare at Stratford, Ontario . . . *Carousel* at a high school in Iowa . . . *Star Wars* . . . An original, student-written play at the American College Theatre Festival . . . Soap opera on television . . . *Dracula* . . . The Alvin Ailey Dance Company, with its barn-burning finale, "Revelations . . ." Women acting out their anguish for an audience of women at the It's All Right to Be Woman Theatre . . . *Il Trovatore* at New York's Metropolitan Opera . . . Two great English actors speaking mysterious, disconnected lines in a baffling scene, fascinating and confusing, on a New York stage . . . Rock concerts . . . Chicano activism in a California farm field . . . *The Fantasticks* in its twentieth year in New York; *The Drunkard* in its thousandth revival; *King Lear* in a modern setting; Greek tragedy on film; a punk rock group performing before twenty thousand people; the Dallas Cowboys performing before fifty thousand people; an urban drunk performing before ten people; a child of nine performing for himself; an actor rehearsing on an empty stage.

People speak of "performing arts."

But are all these things performances?

Or arts?

Figure 1–1. Theatre. The ancient Greek tragedy *Oedipus Rex* as performed for a modern audience by the Stratford Shakespearean Festival, 1955, using masks and a chorus. Directed by Tyrone Guthrie. *(Courtesy of the Stratford Shakespearean Festival, Stratford, Ontario, Canada.)*

They seem an odd lot—football next to dance, dance next to opera, opera next to rock, rock next to a solitary child. What they do not share with each other may be more apparent than what they do share. The expression *performing arts,* however, is used to put as many of them as possible under the same umbrella; once that is done, it becomes possible to identify smaller categories. "Performing arts," then, are many things, but things that have in common *performance* and *art.*

Performance involves the body and/or the voice to do something for somebody's enjoyment.

Art is an activity that makes (or makes up) its product for its own ends. It is also an activity that is self-contained and artificial; that is, it does not need to have any immediate use in the world. (For example, sign painting is an application of some of the techniques of an art, painting; sign-painting is an activity devoted almost exclusively to its usefulness—making signs—while painting is an art that has no *useful* product at all, although its product is often very expensive and much sought-after.)

So, the performing arts are human activities that make or make up stories or movements or sounds or combinations of those things for people's enjoyment. They are highly diverse, each appealing in very different ways to different responses.

Yet what is to be prized about the performing arts is their very diversity, their variety, and their many mutual contradictions, because human beings thrive on artistic diversity. A healthy culture (like a healthy ecosystem) is one that encourages such variety; a culturally healthy individual is one who can enjoy a variety of these seemingly polarized activities—going to a movie one night, a ballet another, a baseball game on Saturday afternoon, a symphony concert on Sunday.

Because this is a book on the theatre, it will try to separate the theatre from the other performing arts. The separation is partly an artificial one, however, because one of the outstanding qualities of the theatre is the extent to which it contributes to and draws from other arts. Even for the individual theatre artist, such contributions and borrowings are valuable: actors dance and sing as well as act; they play baseball and create films, and they are often themselves members of the audience for other arts. Theatre artists—actors, directors, designers, playwrights—move from film to theatre to opera to spectacles like political events and pageants.

Because a healthy society welcomes diversity, healthy arts are themselves diverse; because artists create in diverse ways, audiences must be able to respond in diverse ways. The performing arts, it must be emphasized, are not competitors but relatives, and audiences need to learn to appreciate the entire family. Because each member of the family is complex, however, the study of any one of them takes care and time.

This is a book about one member of that family: the theatre.

Figure 1–2. Audience Diversity. Audiences for the performing arts view theatre, athletics, film, and other activities as mutually compatible; they can watch one of them one day, another the next. *(Courtesy of the University of Rochester. Photo by Chris T. Quillen.)*

Theatre As a Performing Art **5**

Major Performing Arts and Related Activities

We have already tried to deal quickly with the terms *performance* and *art* so that the activities that can properly be called *performing arts,* and some that resemble them, can be put into a context. We also glanced at some ideas that we will have to return to later: the idea of performing *for* somebody else (the drunk on the street corner, the child by herself, the actor rehearsing) and the complicated ideas of the "usefulness" of an art and the "function" of its activity. We will come back to these matters. There is enormous overlap among the performing arts, so much so that one of them—the theatre—has sometimes been seen as an amalgam of the others; in that view, theatre itself would be the umbrella that covers the performing arts. While this idea fails as a definition of theatre, it is useful as a reminder that the theatre uses elements of other arts and that without them it would be a dull activity, indeed.

It is possible to include other arts *with* the word *theatre*—theatre dance, theatre music—so long as we remember that each art has its own special characteristics. We must not pretend that film, television, dance, opera, staged plays, mime, and athletic events, for example, are all "theatre" in a vague and general way, or we will lose the crucial distinctions among them. *The performing arts have much in common, but what they have in common does not make them identical.* To talk about them, to appreciate them, to make the most of them, we must know both what they share and what they do *not* share; then, when we understand some of their similarities and their differences, we will be able to look at one of them more closely.

What Is Film?

In the movie films, he said, we only look at what is there already. Life shines on the shadow screen, as from the darkness of one's mind. It is a big business.
E. L. Doctorow, *Ragtime*

Soft music. Low lights. People taking their seats, whispering, chuckling. Popcorn. Rattle of candy papers. The music ends; the lights go to black. "Exit" signs glow. A bright image appears on a slightly concave screen: names. Images of people and places, real people, real places, their images *big,* colorful. The images move at the same rate as real people. Loud music. Voices—the people talk. The images embody a story about people. At rare times, the speed of the images slows; once, they even freeze like a still photograph. The way that these images are presented changes, sometimes giving us very close-in pictures, sometimes very distant ones. Sometimes we are presented with images of only part of what the human eye would really see—a hand, a flower, a road. Sometimes we do not even see what the human eye might look at in the same situation; the machine that makes the images is looking at something else, and that something else becomes of great importance to us. The story continues, the images flash on.

Film is a complex form of communication relying on putting things together simultaneously and sequentially. John Harrington, *The Rhetoric of Film*

Figure 1–3. Film. From its very beginnings, as in this illustration of an early "moving picture machine," the Praxinoscope, film has held its audiences with its special appeal.

Film:

1. Uses a projected image of events, places, and people and not the events, places, and people themselves.

2. Usually presents a story and characterization.

3. Gathers its audiences into special places ("theatres") but does not allow any interplay between the audience and the images because the images have no sensitivities of their own.

4. Can be repeated identically any number of times until the film itself breaks down—but the film can be reprinted and so saved from any sign of deterioration whatsoever.

It was René Clair who pointed out that if two or three people were together on a stage, the dramatist must ceaselessly motivate their being there at all. But the film audience accepts mere sequence as rational. Whatever the camera turns to, the audience accepts.   Marshall McLuhan, *Understanding Media*

What Is Television?

[T]he audience for American television is what may be called a mass society [that] has somewhat different values and social controls from the traditional western society. In the traditional society, the upper classes set the standards of the culture and the lower classes followed along.

David Potter, in *"The Historical Perspective"*

A living-room. Few lights. Sounds from the rest of the house, from the street. Somebody passing through the room to the kitchen. A screen, twenty inches or so in its long dimension; slightly distorted sound with poor treble values. Images of real people and places, the visual quality of the images rather poor in comparison with the real people and the real places, these images being made up of moving dots. Saturated colors in rather oversimple, slightly unreal values. The images of the people are playing out a story, but one of the people in the living room does not like the story and presses a switch, and another story appears. This story seems to be preferable, but it stops and other people appear and begin to talk about automobiles. Nobody in the living room seems to care much that the images are talking about automobiles, but one of the real people leaves the room and comes back with a can of beer. The images stop talking about automobiles and the other images appear and begin to act out their story again. It is a funny story, and there is loud laughter with the funny parts, as if a big audience were sitting with the people in the living room. There is an image of a living room in the story, and it looks remarkably like the living room in which the people are sitting to watch the story. In the story living room, they even have a screen of the same sort, on which other images are being shown. They are images of a news story about a real disaster of a year before.

Time was when a person went to the movies and surrendered, knowingly, to a few hours of fantasy, the walk from home to cinema marking the transfer from world of fact to world of fiction. Now the unreal filters from the 'tube' into the home along with the real.
Daniel Shorr, "The National Seance," in Review Magazine.

Television:
1. Uses an image made up of dots on a cathode-ray-tube "screen" to create a record of events, places, and people.

Figure 1–4. Television. The audience is comfortable in its own living space; the image can be replicated mechanically. *(Photo by Augustin Aldrete.)*

2. Presents both stories with characterization and precise records of actual events or "news."

3. Does not gather its audience, but locates its outlets (the screens) in informal living spaces (living rooms, bedrooms, bars) and allows no interplay between audience and images because the images have no sensitivities of their own.

4. Can be repeated identically any number of times if recorded on film or tape; however, the commercial structure of the industry that presents television in the United States makes the frequent repetition of most programs unlikely.

The cool TV medium provides depth structure in art and entertainment alike, and creates audience involvement in depth as well.
Marshall McLuhan, Understanding Media

What Is Opera?

Without music, opera is not opera.   J. Merill Knapp, *The Magic of Opera*

A huge theatre. Elegance of decor, elegant dress on many of the audience. An entire orchestra in a pit between the audience and the stage. The lights dim; the orchestra plays—melodies, promises of what the performance to come will hold. Darkness, then stage light. A crowd in Renaissance costume, gathered before the gates of a Renaissance palace. They sing. An officer strolls among them. *He* sings. Everybody sings—nobody talks. The scene changes to a palace courtyard on a huge scale. Two women sing— glorious, soaring melodies that fill the large theatre with their timbrous voices. The audience applauds and the performance stops while the applause continues. Then the singers continue, performing a story of high passion and extreme situations—revenge, coincidence, violence. They sing in Italian, a language the audience does not understand. The story is printed in the program so that the audience will know what is going on, but most of them know the opera so well that they do not need the notes.

Our inner life . . . provides music with the form through which music expresses that life. Every contradiction ceases from the moment that the form and the object of the expression are identical.
Adolphe Appia, Music and the Art of the Theatre

Opera:
1. Uses live performers on a real stage in artificial (i.e., made-for-the-purpose) settings.

2. Uses story and characterization.

3. Gathers its audience into theatres that allow the audience to influence the performance through their reactions.

4. Can be repeated, but with the inevitable variations natural to any human endeavor: because of the production structure of commercial opera companies worldwide, however, it is extremely rare that the same singers will repeat the same opera frequently for a long time in the same theatre, and most singers take a day or two between performances.

Figure 1–5. Opera. The dominant "language" of opera gives it a unique quality among the performing arts. Here, Wagner's *Lohengrin* at the Metropolitan Opera suggests the scenic magnificence of grand opera. *(Copyright © Beth Bergman 1979.)*

    5. Uses an orchestra, typically located between the stage and the audience, and uses music as the dominant means of communication, both actor-to-actor and actor-to-audience.

> *[Opera] may be a museum piece in the contemporary world, but the true opera lover is not daunted. He is always seeking an amalgam in performance [that] will produce a miraculous result—that moment when drama, orchestra, singing, and spectacle unite to achieve what is promised by a composer and librettist of genius.*
>
> J. Merill Knapp, The Magic of Opera

What Is Dance?

> *Dancing employs rhythm in both spheres—audible and visual. It is a time–space art, and the only one.*   Agnes de Mille, *The Book of the Dance*

A theatre, a stage. Low house lights. Loudspeakers for sound. Lights to black and stage lights up: an intense blue, like sky, a picket fence, a suggestion of beach or country road or moor. Two women in very long skirts. Music through the loudspeakers. The women move to the music, their movements rhythmic, stately, visually beautiful, yet not like the movement of ordinary human beings. Their movement is to ordinary human movement what the voice of the opera singer is to the speaking voice—an extension of it, virtually another kind of reality with one foot in the mundane world. The women's bodies are disciplined and trained, even athletic. Slowly, the women grow, become ten feet tall. We understand that it must be that they are carried by other dancers who are hidden by the long skirts, but our understanding does not much change the strange and wonderful affect of their height. Two men appear. They move in the same rhythmic and beautiful way as the women, but they do not increase their height. Dwarfed by the women, they dance with and around them. There is the suggestion of a story— there is interaction among the dancers, clear suggestions that they see and respond to each other. Their actions suggest familiar human events—meeting, wooing, rejecting, loving. The men collapse; perhaps they are dead. The women's height changes. They dance together in "virtual spontaneous gesture."

The primary illusion of dance is a virtual realm of Power—not actual, physically exerted power, but appearances of influence and agency created by virtual gesture.
Suzanne Langer, *Feeling and Form*

Dance:
1. Uses live performers in a real space with artificial settings.

2. Sometimes presents stories and characters.

3. Gathers its audience into theatres and allows the audience to interact with the performance; audiences can influence the performance through their reactions.

4. Can be repeated, with the inevitable variations natural to any human endeavor.

5. Movement—both aesthetic and symbolic—is the principal means of communication, usually to musical accompaniment.

The symbol of the world, the balletic realm of forces, is the world and dancing is the human spirit's participation in it.
Suzanne Langer, *Feeling and Form*

Figure 1–6. Dance. The figures that seem to defy gravity and the spatial limits of our everyday world typify the enormous impact of dance upon its audiences. *(Photo by Augustin Aldrete.)*

What Are Athletic Events?

The battle of Waterloo was won on the playing fields of Eton.

The Duke of Wellington

A brisk October afternoon. Bright sunlight, the air cool enough for sweaters and wool jackets. An oval stadium that seats thirty thousand people; in its center, the green and grassy stretch of a football field. Food and some alcohol in the audience; color in the stands and on the field—pom-poms, pennants, young men and women in cheerleaders' uniforms, two uniformed marching bands. Two teams in differently colored uniforms. Four people in striped shirts on the field; one blows a whistle, and a ball is kicked from one end of the field toward the other. A player in blue catches the ball and begins to run; players in red wrestle him to the ground. The blue players gather together, then line up on each side of and behind the ball. One of them passes the ball backward. Players charge in all directions, blue and red mingling in fierce, violent contact. The audience cheers. The cheerleaders do somersaults and handsprings, and

Figure 1–7. Athletics. The real suspense of games, played by "heroic" performers within highly prescribed rules, gives them an immediacy that leads audiences to quick and marked responses—cheering, songs, shouts, groans. *(Courtesy of the University of Rochester. Photo by Chris T. Quillen.)*

they exhort the audience to more noise. The blue players kick the ball to the red, who move it back up the field with skill and determination. The audience becomes noisier. The red cross a white line with the ball, and a larger part of the audience make more noise than ever, tooting horns and ringing bells and shouting. Two men dressed in a horse costume canter onto the field and cavort about. The players line up again and prepare for the red team to kick the ball to the blues again.

When the One Great Scorer comes to write against your name—He marks—not that you won or lost—but how you played the game.

Grantland Rice, *Alumnus Football*

Athletics:

1. Use live performers in a real performing place.

2. Use competition instead of story; have no characterization. (However, sports audiences often create near-mythic "characters" around sports heroes.)

3. Gather their audiences into prepared—and often very large—spaces and allow the audience reaction to influence the event.

4. Can never be repeated in an identical way. The rules of sports guarantee that the *form* will be repeated, but it is in the nature of games and competitions that the outcome will always be different and will always be in doubt until the very end.

Anyone who doesn't know how to play is illiterate. . . . Sport is where an entire life can be compressed into a few hours, where the emotions of a lifetime can be felt on an acre or two of ground, where a person can suffer and die and rise again on six miles of trails. . . . Sport is a theatre where sinner can turn saint and a common man can become an uncommon hero.

George Sheehan, in *On the Run*

What Is Theatre?

The theatre is the home of the Now.

A theatre. An audience, waiting, expectant in the half-light. The accents of New York mingle with those of the Midwest and the South. Many are carefully dressed, some informally. Between audience and stage there is an orchestra pit, but there is no orchestra visible; instead, loudspeakers flank the stage opening. Darkness. Stage light. A voice, music; an authoritative man is counting a rhythm for a group of dancers. He begins to teach them a simple dance routine, then withdraws into the audience part of the theatre and directs the others through a loudspeaker. There are characterizations and a story, but the characters both talk and sing their emotions and their experiences. We learn that they are trying out for the chorus of a Broadway show. They dance. They sing. They make the audience laugh, listen, sit still with attentiveness. The sexual attractiveness of several of the women onstage is emphasized by their costumes and is part of what is sung and talked about. The language and the subject matter, by the standards of many communities, is frank, even a little shocking. But the audience responds with joyous laughter, noisy applause.

"Is this a theatre?" whispered Smike, in amazement; "I thought it was a blaze of light and finery."

"Why, so it is," replied Nicholas, hardly less surprised: "but not by day, Smike—not by day."

Charles Dickens, *Nicholas Nickleby*

Figure 1–8. Theatre. A "blaze of light and finery" when a performance is in progress, the theatre uses elements of many arts and many technologies to engage its audience. Here, one of the first electrically lighted theatres, 1883.

Theatre:

1. Uses live actors on a real stage with artificial settings.

2. Uses story and characterization.

3. Gathers its audiences into defined spaces and allows the audience reaction to affect the performance.

4. Can be repeated, but with the inevitable variations natural to any human endeavor.

> . . . can this cockpit hold
> The vasty fields of France? or may we cram
> Within this Wooden O the very casques
> That did affright the air at Agincourt?
> . . . . let us, ciphers to this great accompt,
> On your imaginative forces work.
> Suppose within the girdle of these walls
> Are now confin'd two mighty monarchies. . . .
> Think when we talk of horses that you see them
> Printing their proud hoofs i' the receiving earth;
> For 'tis your thoughts that now must deck our kings. . . .
> William Shakespeare, *The Life of King Henry the Fifth*

Some Aspects of Theatre

A comparison of these discussions of the performing arts may give the impression that there is so much overlap among them that only some mechanical differences separate them, that, for example, theatre is simply opera without the music, or that film is merely theatre recorded on strips of acetate, or that television is nothing but film made visible with electronic impulses. Such a view, however, is woefully inaccurate. It is not entirely false—the mechanical differences do have significance—but it does not begin to touch on other differences.

When an important element in a performing art changes, the art itself changes. That is, when a composer sets a play to music, he does not automatically create an opera—although he may create a very bad opera of some sort. When, however, a story from one performing art is transferred to another—as, for example, when Victorien Sardou's play was made the basis of the opera *Tosca* by Puccini—it is clear that, although the superficial elements of the versions are similar (basically the same story, the same characters, many of the same audience–actor elements that opera and theatre share) the end products are different. *Tosca* is not simply Sardou's play sung. Its internal structure is different; its emphases are different; its audience's expectations are different. For, where the theatre audience draws its pleasure from story suspense, brilliance of language, and acting performance, the opera audience draws its principal pleasure from the glory of melody and the performance of the singers.

In fact, the differences that seem to separate dance from theatre, theatre from opera, opera from film, and so on create other and more profound differences. The *fact* of film defines the difference between movies and theatre; but the *art* of film is made possible by camera work, by quick cutting, by a juxtaposition of images that is impossible in the theatre, by a disjunction

Figure 1–9. Arts in Opposition. For all their similarities, the performing arts remain distinct; here, the contest for audience between music and drama is caricatured by George Cruikshank.

(sometimes) between sound and image that is unlikely in the theatre, and so on. The very structure of a film script—the way the action moves forward—is vastly different from a play because film gives its information differently. Indeed, it is not too much to say that *the basic differences among the performing arts are founded on their differing means of communication.* Thus it is possible to have the same story at the center of a performance in each performing art, but to have the performances themselves turn out to be markedly different because of the differences in the arts. For example, Shakespeare's *Romeo and Juliet* has been a staged play, a ballet, an opera, several films, and, in an adaptation, a Broadway musical *(West Side Story).* All are significantly different, even though the Shakespearean text itself is the basis for much of the script in the film and opera versions. One of the things that happens in a case like this is that the artists themselves make decisions that select from the basic story—in this case, Shakespeare's play—those elements that will best be communicated by their art, the opera composer selecting those moments and events that are best communicated musically, the choreographer those moments and events that are best communicated in structured and pleasing movement. Another thing that happens is that each art focuses its audience's attention in a different way. The production of Shakespeare's play may lead us to watch and listen to the actor, the richness of his or her voice, and the poetic beauty of Shakespeare's verse; the opera may lead us to listen to the music instead of watching the singer or following the dramatic development of the story; the dance may ask us to watch and to respond sympathetically with our own bodies, almost forgetting story and character, which become a pretext for the movement.

It is a commonplace that good novelists rarely become good playwrights. The reason is that the requirements of the stage are simply not the same as the literary requirements of the book; a play*wright* is not necessarily a *writer.* In the same way, a good playwright might not be a good creator of opera librettos because he might not grasp the vital necessity of serving the music. A good playwright might not be a good film-script writer because he might not grasp the necessity of serving the visual needs of the camera. Often, bad films are made from good plays for this reason or because the film is shot as if it were merely a photographic record of the staged play— which is not the same as a good film.

A critic once observed that great operas were made from bad plays. The remark will not stand up to close scrutiny, but it does underscore what we have been saying about the performing arts: a story or a structure that may serve one art badly may have precisely the elements to serve another well.

Art and Life

After reading tne discussions of the art and athletic events, someone might be tempted to look at still other activities and say, "But what about rock concerts? Or the circus? Or church services? Aren't they related, too?"

Of course they are. So are many unplanned events that draw a crowd

Figure 1–10. Performers or Participants? Onlookers in New York's Central Park watch—and involve themselves in—disco roller skating. Are they really an audience? Or are they, with the skaters, all performers in a larger theatre?

and that are then affected by that crowd—an argument between two drivers whose bumpers have locked, for example, or an impromptu street dance, or a political rally, or even a classroom with teacher and students. Are not these in some sense theatre, too—or at least performance?

The answer is a very qualified "yes." While a rigid definition of the word *theatre* is no longer valid, a distinction has to be made between art—in this case, the art of the theatre—and life.

An older definition of *theatre* would include the separation of the actors and the audience, the nature of the theatre building, and the kinds of things the actors perform, and it would touch on the aesthetics of the art. The most radical contemporary definition would take account of the movement of theatre into the streets, fields, and other social centers as "street theatre," "guerrilla theatre," and even group therapy and other activities that are far from the old idea of the art. There is no point in making a definition that is so inclusive that it finally includes everything, for, when that happens, the word loses its meaning and we are left with no useful language with which to communicate.

Thus, we continue to distinguish between theatre as an artistic event and *uses* of certain elements of theatre for life events. For this reason, the argument between the two angry drivers is excluded from the idea of theatre, because it lacks the single characteristic that most separates the art of the theatre from theatrical events in life: *artistic self-awareness* or *intention;* as well, it lacks the two elements that are part of self-awareness, *preparation* and *discipline.*

By *self-awareness* or *intention,* we mean the consciousness in the performer that what he does is meant to accomplish certain ends and to have certain effects on the audience.

By *preparation,* we mean the anticipation of performing, with all the necessary training, psychological orientation, and talent.

By *discipline,* we mean the admission that performance exists for both audience and performer, and that the performer lives his life so that the performance (whether he be actor, playwright, director, or designer) will be at optimum level every time it is undertaken.

Artistic self-awareness does not guarantee that every performance will be good. It does try to guarantee that what is done will in fact be a performance and not an accident and that it will aspire to be art.

To define *performance,* then, so that it will exist within the definition of *theatre,* it should have, besides self-awareness or intention, three other elements: the *actor,* the *audience,* and the *action.*

By *actor,* we mean a performer who impersonates—that is, somebody who uses the pronoun *I* and means somebody other than himself.

By *audience,* we mean a group of people separate from the actor who are gathered together for the specific purpose of attending the event.

By *action,* we mean an invented human development within which the

Figure 1–11. The Actor. The "person who impersonates" is one of the three essentials of theatre. *Equus* at the American Conservatory Theatre. *(Photo: Bill Ganslen, San Francisco.)*

actor's impersonation functions—*not an action that is told about, but one that is embodied by the actor and seen by the audience.*

The theatre, then, is an art in which performers, by impersonating, represent or embody imitations of people in a story that is shown to an audience.

The theatre is not better or worse than other performing arts because of its special nature; it has its special attributes, from which both advantages and disadvantages inevitably spring. Its greatest advantage is *immediacy,* the sense of "nowness" that arises from theatre's *showing* of human actions rather than a telling about them. The theatre has been called "the home of the Now"; the person who said that meant that the theatre is a unique art because in it, fictional events happen with convincing truthfulness even as we watch, and they happen and are gone even as a moment exists and is gone, never to be recaptured. The audience for this "home of the Now" must pay close attention because the Now will vanish; the playwright must work with great skill to make the Now so important that audiences *must* pay attention; the actors must perform brilliantly so that the Now will be arresting, vibrant, more memorable than life. Tomorrow night, the actors will perform a little differently because they are humans and not machines; tomorrow, the audience will be different, and the rich interaction between actors and audience will change.

Because of the physical presence of the actor, the theatre presents a more immediate image of human behavior than any other art. "In person" is always a selling point for live performances; "I saw Liza Minelli *in person!*" Or, even more magically, "I sat in the first row; I was close enough to touch her!" We are human beings; we are touched, aroused, dazzled by the immediacy of other human beings. Neither the heightened intensity of portrait painting nor the close-up intensity of film can equal the impact of the live performer because we are in the theatre with those living human beings who present their stories so convincingly and entertainingly.

Perhaps, as audience members, we human beings are gossips, to put it baldly; or perhaps, as Alexander Pope had it, "The proper study of mankind is man." We remain fascinated with the humanness of being human, and theatre is the art that brings us up closest to a human activity that is rivetingly like life in its immediacy but satisfyingly unlike life in its artistic separation.

The other side of the virtue of immediacy is the partial disadvantage of *nonrecoverability.* As we have seen, film and television performances can be recovered exactly as they were made; the theatrical performance cannot. When the moment is gone, it is entirely gone. We cannot turn back to it as we turn back the pages of a book, except in memory. Nor, however, can we turn forward to see how a performance will come out, and there is a great artistic advantage (common to all the live performing arts); nor can we put the performance aside for a while and pick it up later, nor can we interrupt it (as we could, for example, with a tape cassette) and start it up again later.

Each theatrical peformance is unique. The actor is quite right when he sighs, "Ah, you should have seem me last night!" And the audience is right to gasp each time an actor makes a dizzying leap onstage; tomorrow, or even tonight, he may miss or break a leg. "What I love," one critic wrote,

Figures 1–12 and 1–13. Audience. Many factors influence the ways that audiences behave and the ways in which they get and express pleasure. Here, two comic views of "the pit" of an English theatre in 1800 (below) and 1880.

"is that at any moment I may see the leading man suffer a heart attack!"

Thus, *the theatre performance proceeds at its own pace and must be followed at that pace,* and for better or for worse, *it can be neither replicated nor repeated.*

The question of the *intensity* of the theatre as compared with the other performing arts is a very difficult one. The theatre's immediacy gives it an inherent intensity; the theatre's very nature as an art gives it an intensity far beyond that of most of life. To say, however, that a great moment in the theatre is more highly charged than one in opera or dance is not true; it is best to say that they are different. (It is significant, for example, that musical comedy succeeds partly because it uses songs at precisely those moments of greatest intensity, going to melody, harmony, and rhythm where action and speech are judged insufficient—for example, Cervantes/Don Quixote's "The Impossible Dream" in *Man of La Mancha.*) Both dance and opera seem to offer potential for greater intensity in at least some moments

Figure 1–14. Scenic Illusion. Despite limitations of space and of technology, the theatre has astonished its audience with dazzling effects. Here, a horse-race, complete with real horses, moving background, and wind.

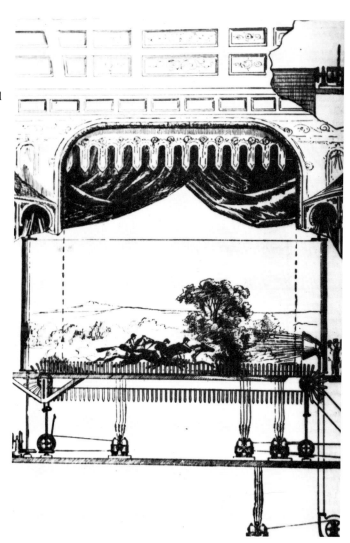

of their performances. There are few occasions when the movement of the stage actor can equal the leaps of a Baryshnikov or the catches and falls of a Pilobolus Company; there are few occasions when the voice of the actor can rival the sounds of a great soprano in *Il Trovatore.* On the other hand, there is less that either dance or opera can offer that will match the illusion of a great comic or tragic scene greatly played, when it is neither movement nor music that we follow, but convincing and immediate human action.

Another aspect of theatre that can work both for and against its effectiveness is its *scenic and spatial limitation.* Film, for example, can take us anywhere and show us actual images of distant places, even on a vast scale (the Grand Canyon, the city of Hong Kong, outer space). The theatre can give us replicas of such places but can give them only on a scale appropriate to the actors working in or in front of the scene. Too, many kinds of activity are difficult or impossible to bring on the stage—aerial dogfights, elephant stampedes, and chariot races among them. Film and television cannot only show such things, they can also show selective close-ups that will heighten our awareness and enjoyment of the events—speeding hooves, snorting nostrils, whirling wheels.

If the theatre tried to rival such scenes, it would have to offer compromises, as it did, for example, near the end of the nineteenth century when chariot races *were* shown onstage by putting the horses on treadmills. Common sense told the audience that the treadmills were there, or else the horses would have dashed off into the wings and there would have been no race to see. Yet audiences loved the scenes, even though they were seeing a rather obvious trick—and their enjoyment emphasizes a paradox in the theatre's problems with scenic space: the very restrictions on space and locale increase the audience's enjoyment *because they know the illusion is an illusion.* Put another way, this means that *the artificial nature of theatre gives everything put on the stage a paradoxically heightened reality.* It is a curious thing, but an audience will applaud a scene in which real food is really cooked on a real stove, exactly as if they had never seen food cooking on stoves, much less been able to see such things in their own kitchens.

Thus, the spatial and scenic limitations off the theatre are a seeming disadvantage that can most potently be turned to a remarkable advantage. It is the essence of theatre that compromises, often in the form of symbolic representations, must be made—the "Wooden O" must be made to hold both France and England; six men must be made to represent an army; a platform must be made to represent a throne.

The real art of the theatre lies, then, not in presenting life, but in presenting heightened visions of life within the special conditions of immediacy, intensity, and symbolic representation.

CHAPTER 2

Theatre and the Performing Audience

It was said earlier that a healthy society prizes artistic diversity. The statement suggests that there is a close connection between an art and its society, that the art is either an expression of that society or that it is a response to it. Both things, in fact, are true of the theatre; it directly expresses social structures and ideas, and it responds to social pressures to cause changes in itself. The expression and the response happen because of two groups: theatre artists and theatre audiences. Theatre artists—actors, playwrights, directors, designers—are themselves social beings and bring their social attitudes into their theatre work. Theatre audiences are members of the same society. There is often a difference between the groups, however, in that in Europe and America, theatre artists have often been either outcasts or exotics. There have been laws that made them "vagabonds" (as in Elizabethan England) and attitudes that saw them as unsuitable as wives or husbands for "proper" men and women, while at the same time they were viewed as exciting, romantic, and sexually attractive, so that the actress as "sex goddess" and the actor as "matinee idol" were common stereotypes. Theatre audiences, on the other hand, are often socially conservative—well-to-do, cautious, proper. The two groups meet at the curtain line, that interface of exoticism and conformity.

What Is an Audience?

An audience is people at an event, of course.

Isn't it?

Yes, but is it one person? Or ten? Ten thousand? Ten million?

One answer would be that the size of an audience depends on the artistic medium. Ten million people could easily make up the "audience" for a television production, and many more than that have watched certain hugely successful specials; however, to have an audience for even the most successful of stage plays or musicals and number it as high as ten million, we would have to imagine filling the largest of New York theatres every night for years. An "audience" of ten or twenty million people for a film is possible, if the film is shown often enough; ten or twenty million as the "audience" for an opera or ballet would require changing the way that most ballet and opera companies work, because they do not present the same things night after night after night for years and years.

To speak of an "audience" of millions for a play or an opera or a dance performance, however, is fruitless. The millions who watch a television show or who see a film over a period of months in many different movie houses are not an "audience" in the way that the people gathered to see a single

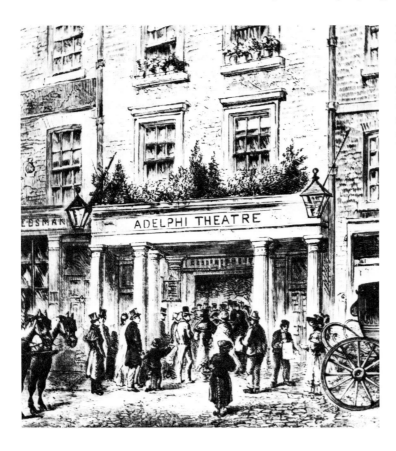

Figure 2–1. Audience. The theatre event itself is the force that makes an audience a unique, if temporary, society. Here, audience members gathering at the door of a nineteenth-century London theatre.

performance in a theatre are an audience. The television "audience," in fact, disintegrates into many smaller ones in living rooms and bedrooms and bars, just as the "audience" for a film disintegrates into many smaller groups who have seen it in many different places on many different occasions. In the sense that we use the word for the theatre, then, *an audience is a group drawn together by a theatrical event, at a certain time and place, that is aware of itself as a group.*

This group self-awareness is very important. The sense of belonging to the group and of contributing to its size is one of the remarkable aspects of theatre, the rich and exciting consciousness of a shared experience in which each individual's response is heightened by those sharing it with him and by the awareness that one's own response heightens that of others. Although television comedy often uses a "laugh track" or plays the laughter of a live audience to simulate the experience of the theatregoer, the experience simply is not the same for the individual sitting in his living room. In the theatre, the individual's laughter is buoyed up, expanded, made more joyous by the laughter around him, or the individual's solemn understanding of a serious play is made richer because other people are responding in the same way. Both kinds of response are tied into the idea of *permission,* the agreement common to the members of the social group—the audience— that it is all right to laugh at these events or to be solemnly moved by them. This *permission* is an extension of the very nature of theatre art: theatre as art tells its audience that what is being embodied is *not* life and that it is permissible to respond to it in sometimes unusual ways (laughing out loud, for example, at a character who is weeping in a comedy); the permission often needs reinforcement when audience members come from repressed or fragmented societies. (Interesting and sometimes frightening things happen when a part of an audience does not give its permission, as when, for example, an experimental theatre idea first appears in the mainstream theatre. An extreme instance of this would be the famous *Hernani* riot of 1830 [see p. 196], when the failure of two segments of the audience to agree over what was permissible on the stage of the Comédie Française—in this case, Romantic elements in verse, costuming, and behavior—was so extreme that physical violence broke out.) It needs to be said again that permission is a *social* phenomenon, carried over from the outer society into the temporary society of the audience itself.

The theatre is a social as well as an artistic experience, and *a theatre audience is a social entity, however temporary.* Its members are drawn together by the event and by the "appetite for art" that makes them want to enjoy the event. They enter into a relationship with the event and with each other.

To join a theatre audience is to enter willingly into two remarkable relationships, one with the artistic event on the stage and one with the other people in the audience.

A casual observer might say that the primary goal of an audience is to enjoy. Or it might be said that there could be several goals, such as to learn, to observe, to escape. At this point, however, the audience goal that we would emphasize is *to share.*

Figure 2–2. Audience Response—Riot. The audience at the first performances of Hugo's *Hernani* fought, shouted, and threw things to protest and to defend a new departure in theatre, 1836.

A theatre audience, then, is a group drawn together by an artistic event at a certain time and place, who are aware of themselves as a group and whose goal is to share—laughter, tears, solemnity, joy, wonder.

What Determines Audience Size?

It would be difficult, it seems, for one person to be an audience. Still, royalty used to have plays performed especially for them, and "theatres royal" had special boxes for the king or queen or duke. Anyone who has gone to a movie in the early afternoon has been a member of a very small audience, and frequently we sit alone to watch television. We have to admit, therefore, that the group is not essential to the idea of audience in every medium, but *where the group is lacking, the medium will make up for the difference by saturating the viewer or by providing an artificial group* (by using a laugh track, for example, or backing much dramatic action with appropriate music), or else *the medium, lacking a group audience, will be unsatisfying.*

But how large a group is an effective audience? Twenty? Two thousand?

Two forces are at work, and they often work against each other. One is the force of the group, partly unconscious but very strong. "Groupness" needs a number of people in a confined space, or at least a *defined* space; it is no accident that theatre interiors are designed, when possible, without enormous aisles or empty spaces along the sides, because people who sit there feel "cold"—they are left out. In the same way, large theatres that sometimes host events that draw small audiences frequently have movable walls or screens to enclose the small audience—to give it a defined space in which it feels enclosed and comfortable.

It is too strong to say that an audience wants to feel cuddled by its space, but it is certainly true that an audience wants to feel that it comfortably fills its space and is made into a unit by the walls or outlines of the space.

A group in too big a space or in an undefined space loses track of itself and stops behaving like an audience. It grows uneasy. It becomes self-conscious. Sometimes it becomes a mob. Schools that use their gymnasiums as theatres, for example, sometimes suffer because the huge, echoing gym space, with wide and empty gaps along the sides, encourages people to belong to a mob and not an audience.

The economics of the theatre is the force that is sometimes opposed to "groupness." It demands that the audience be big enough to pay the actors, the rent on the building, the author's royalties, the heat and light and mainte-

Figure 2–3. Little Theatre. "Coterie" theatres that do not depend upon box office income for their survival have existed in many periods, like this private performance in a drawing-room.

nance of the space, and so on. Thus, groupness may sense that three hundred people is the right audience size; economics may demand three thousand.

Some people would say that economics is a false force and should be ignored. "An audience is people," the argument would go, "and people are more important than money." However, actors are people, too, and so are authors and maintenance persons and those who sell heat and light. A theatre ignores economics at its peril; when it does, it will have to survive with actors who do not care about being paid, authors who do not collect royalties, and so on. Such theatres certainly exist and have existed off and on for a very long time. The tension between group sense and economics has been partly responsible for the waves of "group theatres" and "little theatres" that have appeared in every age since at least the democratic revolutions at the end of the eighteenth century.

From the varying points of view of different audience members and different theatre artists, there is no perfect audience size and no perfect audience space. Most theatres are compromises in this respect, and sometimes not very good compromises, especially when theatres have become physically huge in order simply to hold more people. In those cases particularly, the little theatres and the free theatres become the conscience of the time.

Again, variety and diversity must be allowed.

Who Goes to What?

Few people are so committed to a single performing art or even to a single activity that they pursue it to the exclusion of all others. Devoted theatregoers are also members of audiences for ballet, baseball, television, and opera, among other possibilities. Still, there are preferences among audience members, and there are tendencies toward alignments of audiences that are significant for theatre artists and theatre businessmen.

"Broadway" has come to symbolize commercial theatre in the United States. As so used, the word means the group of theatres in New York City that are governed by a certain group of union rules and that are a certain large size; as the word has come to represent loosely an idea of theatre in this country, it means the mainstream of middle-class and upper-middle-class, New York-oriented theatre and its audience. Despite an apparent loss of audiences in the 1960s and the early 1970s, Broadway continues to dominate the expectations of the mass of American theatregoers, both in New York and across the country, where Broadway plays and Broadway taste—in dinner theatres, community theatres and university theatres—are the most important single element. This Broadway audience is only a large slice in a very big pie, however, for by the mid-1970s, three performing arts (theatre, music, and dance) were spending almost $180 million on productions *outside the Broadway structure* for an audience numbering thirty-one million people each year.

Two surveys give an idea of who the people are who make up this huge audience and of what they go to see. It is fairly young, with the majority under forty; it has more women than men, although other figures suggest that the male–female imbalance is changing. There are very few blue-collar occupations among these audiences, but a large proportion of "professional and managerial" workers. Thus, for performing arts audiences at mainstream performances, the mainstream of the society is best represented: fairly young, affluent, mixed in gender.

Overlap from one performing art to another is significant. Recently, a very successful Midwestern repertory theatre had its highest overlap with audience members who attended symphony concerts, the lowest overlap with those who attended jazz concerts; the second highest overlap was with professional baseball, followed by opera, professional football, and ballet. Some of the diversity can probably be explained by the theatre's location in a city with strong professional sports teams and an excellent symphony orchestra, but the variety may be typical of the American situation, where breadth of taste typifies theatregoers. Shakespeare and baseball, Beethoven and Moliére—audiences are able to love them all.

The theatre audience is a social group, but it is a group only of the moment. Just as the performance is a will-o'-the-wisp, so, too, is its audience. For all their sharing and their common experience, there is no suggestion that by nature the people in a theatre audience will ever come together under other circumstances.

Figure 2–4. Audience. The society of a theatre audience disappears with the end of the performance, and its members disperse to other activities. Shown here is the ticket-box of the Comédie Française in the late nineteenth century.

Why Do They Come?

What brings an audience into a theatre in the first place? It is easy enough to say that people come to the theatre for entertainment. But *entertainment* has many meanings: some people are "entertained" by doing mathematical puzzles, others by patronizing massage parlors—and people are "entertained" at home by television, at baseball games, and at rock concerts.

Why is it that on a given night, people go to the *theatre* instead of staying home or going to a ball game or a movie or a rock concert?

What does the theatre offer its audience?

Three things can be cited.

The Stirring of the Imagination. All art stirs the imagination, sends it on inward journeys that, perhaps, only dreams and madness offer it otherwise. The theatre does this with enormous visual potency and tremendous immediacy; the theatre is *now*. Only contemporary film, with its intense color and its saturated, heightened sound, is a serious rival in the presentation of fictions, "stories." Certainly, the appeal of prose fiction—the novel, the

Figure 2–5. The Work of the Imagination. The theatre often fascinates its audience by demanding their imaginative participation, making one man into an army, two painted trees into a forest. Here, an eighteenth-century view of a London performance by Rowlandson.

short story—lacks immediacy and visual impact, although it substitutes other appeals. The opera and the dance, too, offer other qualities: superb, soaring vocal music in one, astonishing physical athleticism and gorgeous movement in the other.

The theatre, however, has traditionally stirred its audience's imagination by giving *less* rather than *more* stimulation—not by saturating it, but by tantalizing and catalyzing it with hints. It has often put a mask on the actor's face, taking away facial mobility; it has used symbolic or suggestive scenery, or even no scenery at all, to create a richer imaginative *idea* of reality than any imitation reality could give; it has taken its stories from dreams and myth and fantasy and thus touched levels of the mind and heart below the purely rational.

The Revelation of the Familiar. Perhaps because mirrors fascinate people, visions of themselves and of their own real world have fascinated audiences. "It's so real!" is a sometimes breathless compliment for a theatre piece. "Just like real life" describes a setting or an actor's performance. Are we entranced with our own image? Or is it that humankind is a very complex species worthy of its own deep examinings? It is certain that, especially in the modern world, we live with constant reminders of ourselves and our environment. "We have enlarged our sense of the contemporary," Daniel Boorstin has written. "We are overwhelmed by our sense of where we, and contemporaries around the world, are at this moment."

Reality surrounds us—look out the window, there is reality. Watch the man next door, the woman behind the desk, the child in the playground; they are reality. Do we build special structures to house them, pay money to watch them? Hardly.

Theatregoing is a paradox. People buy tickets, travel distances, go through great difficulty to see images of themselves and their surroundings "in play," in something that is "just like life." But it is *like* life, not life itself, and it is *like* life in a very special way: compressed, focused, made magical.

Part of the magic lies in the "safety" of what happens within the playing space. What happens there is insulated from causing anything to happen in the outer world; when the play is over, it is truly over, finished, completed, and it sends nothing out into the streets except its own memory. If an actor is shot onstage, he will not have to be taken to a real hospital; if a woman is widowed, she will not have to stand in a real welfare line or suffer real anguish tomorrow when she wakes up. The play is truly "play," as children's make-believe is play: "Let's play we're soldiers." Real soldiers die and suffer horrible mutilation; children at play suffer nothing and turn to another kind of play when tired of war. So, too, with the theatre: *as art, it is harmless.*

Now, some critics of the theatre would take it to task for being harmless; they would argue that even an art should affect events in the real world. George Bernard Shaw spoke of the play "doing its work in the world," but he was referring to the *ideas* that a play generates in the mind of its audience. The fact remains, however, that *as art* theatre is "harmless"—*and that is one of its attractions.* Many people speak of theatre (or film or television)

Figure 2–6. Recognition. An extreme example of the pleasure aroused in an audience by the presentation of the familiar—in this case, seeing a theatre audience and an actual London theatre as if from the stage. The audience seen here is actually made up of actors; the "theatre" is a setting, a replica of the Frivolity Music Hall. Audiences flocked to see this 1900 play and its imitation of a theatre interior they could have sat in as part of their own real lives.

as "escape," and, although the idea is a weak one to describe what really attracts an audience, "escaping the consequences" is an important element in the theatre's pull. We can watch horrifying or electrifying events; we can behave as we are not allowed to behave in life, guffawing at a human being's suffering or applauding murder—because those events are harmless.

A New York critic recently castigated the Broadway audience for finding a play "comfortable." Although the play was written from "great pain," the critic complained, the playwright had placed his own pain at "a distance" and "the audience escapes unscathed." But that is the point, especially in the mainstream, commercial theatre: the audience *wants* to escape unscathed, and it has every right to do so.

Alvin Toffler in *Future Shock* has suggested that as existence grows more complex, individuals will need areas of comfort and calm to return to. In one sense, the theatre is such a place. Being "a comfort" is not its only allure, to be sure, but it is one, and it must never be overlooked.

The Revelation of the Exotic. Here is another theatrical paradox: on the one hand, the theatre attracts people by dealing in the familiar and

Figure 2–7. The Exotic. The bizarre, the unique, and the foreign exert a strong appeal for theatre audiences, whether in the form of faraway places for settings and costumes or of unusual native things. Here, the American actor Edwin Forrest in the character of Matamora, the romanticized "savage"—the native American turned to exotic stage character. (c. 1850.) *(Courtesy of the New-York Historical Society, New York City.)*

the comfortable; but on the other hand, it also draws them with the new and the strange.

Thus, there is a three-way tension among three kinds of appeal to the audience: the stirring of the imagination, the satisfaction of the desire for the familiar, and the arousing of the appetite for the exotic.

The tension between the familiar and the exotic is greatly affected by the passage of time. To a considerable extent, those elements that stir the imagination persist, but *familiar* and *exotic* are rather relative terms, and it is sometimes difficult to understand which of these attractions was at work in a play from the past. What is familiar to one generation may be foreign to another; what is exotic to one may be familiar or even boring to a later generation. For example, Jules Verne's fantastic submarine in *Twenty Thousand Leagues Under the Sea* was exotic to his own time but is faintly amusing to ours, when the fantasy proves to be less wonderful than the reality. Science fiction, in fact, is one of the most obvious sufferers in this regard, for technology is always making yesterday's fantasies wrong or silly. Even the most poetic of such imaginings can be affected: Shakespeare's Caliban cannot be to our time what he was to Shakespeare's. We have lost the Elizabethan set of human–animal associations, and we have acquired too much knowledge about evolution and primates and psychology.

How Does an Audience Perceive?

If an audience goes to the theatre to be imaginatively stirred through a perception of the familiar or the exotic, how does it perceive what is going on? What eyeglasses does an audience wear?

Three general attributes of the theatre greatly affect the way that the audience perceives a performance.

Convention. Conventions could be called contracts. Conventions are shortcuts between what is meant and what is done. To the actor, a convention may be a gesture that, through continued repetition, has come to convey great meaning—the hand raised to the forehead, palm out, the eyes turned up, to indicate Romantic suffering. To a scene designer, a convention may be the placing of a scenic house so that only part of it is actually onstage, the rest of it seeming to lie outside the audience's vision at one or both sides of the stage. The onstage part that the audience sees may be a strict imitation of reality; *convention* allows the scenic designer to mean that the entire house is there although common sense says that it is not. In fact,

Figure 2–8. Convention. "Habits of presentation," "ways of seeing," "contracts"— the conventions of theatre are agreed upon by performers and audience. In this reader's theatre performance, the two actors facing the drape, right, have established a convention of being invisible so long as their backs are turned to the audience. *(Anstie's Limit at the University of South Carolina. Photo by William Storer.)*

the architecture of the theatre building may say that the scenery is impossible if the audience can see that the theatre building could not possibly extend far enough to include all of, for example, a palace of which one room is onstage. The very fact that both audience and actors accept the idea that there is *anywhere* offstage is a convention, instead of their insisting on the commonsense reality that *offstage* is simply a slightly dirty area in a theatre.

For the audience, a convention is an acceptable way of pretending to see what is not seen. A convention is a contract between the audience and the theatre artists, an agreement to do things this way for the good of all.

In the modern theatre, the acceptance of the idea that days or months or years pass between scenes or acts is a convention; the acceptance of taped music during dramatic action is a convention; the acceptance in many theatres of actors in partial undress is a convention for total nudity.

Innovation. Pulling against convention is innovation. It is the introduction of new ways of giving meaning. It is novelty, "originality."

Theatre artists and audiences both demand innovation—up to a point. That point, however, is not easy to define. Many outside factors affect people's willingness to accept a convention or to demand innovation in its place.

Usually, innovation comes from the artists' side of the theatre. Audiences do not "demand" a change, at least not in the way that we are accustomed to having people demand things. Audiences, after all, do not have a real voice. Their voice is in their hands and their pocketbooks. Their "demands" may best be seen in their enthusiastic welcoming of an innovation or a change in the way a convention is used. A good part of the nineteenth-century audience, for example, welcomed the innovation made by the "free theatres" of the last quarter of that century, which included such now-familiar things as actors turning their backs to the audience, asymmetrical settings whose proscenium line was the "fourth wall" of a room, and so on.

Technology is itself the parent of much innovation. The coming of movies at the end of the nineteenth century quickly drew a large audience; what it saw was much the same thematically as what it saw in the theatre of the day, and the acting conventions were identical, but the technology was innovative. This is not to say that the art form we now call film instantly drew an audience, for the art of film did not automatically spring into being with the invention of motion pictures any more than the art of oil painting sprang into being with the invention of oil-based pigments; use of the camera, the cutting of scenes, such effects as montage and stop frame all had to wait for artistic development. But what the technology of film did give its audience instantly was a one-to-one realism and a scenic breadth (outdoor scenes, trains, chases, explosions) that the technology of the stage could not equal, and in this sense, film was a technological innovation.

Other innovation may result from technology or may combine with technology. Ballet dancing on the toe—"en point"—was developed about 1825, perhaps in combination with the invention of the shoe needed to perform such a feat.

Figure 2–9. Innovation. Theatrical novelty sometimes grows out of new technology, as in this electrical waterfall whose introduction quickly followed the invention of electric lighting.

Still other innovation may come from the acquisition of new information. Historically accurate costumes were possible only when historical knowledge was broadened by people working outside the theatre, and period costuming was accepted as something other than an exotic rarity only when that knowledge was disseminated through the theatre audience by historically accurate books and pictures.

Style. Style is the result of interaction among convention, innovation, and the life of the times. The word *style* is one of the most useful, and yet one of the most confusing, that is applied in the performing arts. Clothes are said to be "stylish"; there is a "New Orleans style" of jazz as compared with a "Chicago style"; there are "kosher-style" dill pickles. Some performers are said to have a "personal style" that distinguishes them from other performers: Baryshnikov's athletic leaps are unlike anybody else's; Sir John Gielgud's timbrous voice and accent are unique.

Plays of the past are sometimes said to be produced in modern times in "period style," and sometimes productions are even labeled "style" productions. In the sense that we will mean it here, however, *style refers to the particular characteristics of a performance that the audience sees and hears that set it off from all other performances.*

Some characteristics that go to make up a production's style are:

1. *Historical period.* The way people talk and move, the kind of clothes they wear, and the way their living spaces are shaped and decorated are different from period to period. Because the performing artist usually works

from reality, his own speech and movements, his clothes and hairstyle, and his settings reflect his age.

2. *Level of abstraction.* Each group of performers in each age has its own artistic style—a mixture of inherited tradition, of meaningful convention and innovation, and of their own aesthetic sense of what is pleasing and beautiful. The style of a great mime is abstracted far from reality; the movements are themselves dancelike, beautiful, compressed. The movement and vocal attack of the traditional Comédie Francaise was spare and economical, with occasional outbursts of great verbal flourish; the movement and vocal attack of American actors of the 1950s was laconic and sinuous, very close to one idea of reality at one level of American society at one historical moment.

3. *Social class.* In class-conscious societies, mannerisms of speech, clothes, and body movement, as well as personal effects, furniture, decor, and almost every other aspect of life, reflect class and money or the lack of them. A French peasant of 1670 looked, acted, and spoke very differently from Louis XIV, his king. In the same way, a moneyed Easterner of our own day sounds

Figure 2–10. Style. Historical clothes, behavior, and living space are strong determinants of style. Note how the period can be recognized in costume and gesture, and even in the glimpses of the physical decor.

and dresses and moves differently from a Western ranch hand. Actors playing peasants and kings show the same degree of difference, although it must be remembered that *the style of the theatre is different from the style of life.*

4. *Given circumstances.* Sex, race, state of health, age, and profession create stylistic differences. A minister's sermon does not sound like a teacher's lecture; a black disco dancer does not move like a white golfer; a woman's room does not look like a man's. A sick man neither sounds nor moves like a healthy one; men and women have noticeably different styles of dress, speech, and movement *in certain ages.*

When theatre artists choose to produce a work from the past, they have a great range of styles to choose from. In doing a play from the 1670s, for example, such as a comedy of Molière's, they might choose to do it "authentically," that is, in as close a reconstruction as is possible of the original

Figures 2–11, 2–12. Styles. Plays from the past can be done in a wide variety of styles that suggest or reproduce or entirely ignore the period of the play's origin. Seen here are two plays by Molière performed as a double bill, *The Versailles Impromptu* (bottom) as historical reconstruction, abstracted through the elimination of scenery and the use of light that seemed to isolate the figures in space and time; and *The Doctor in Spite of Himself* (top) in costumes based on historical clothes but abstracted through use of large, bold areas of color and simple lines, against a background of a romanticized period setting. *(Directed by Kenneth M. Cameron at the University of Iowa.)*

scenery, costumes, acting, movement, and so on. Or they might decide that, the essence of the play being comic, it is most important to make stylistic decisions in terms of such comic values as brightness, color, and symmetry. Again, they might decide to work at a level of abstraction rather different from the original, so that the costumes might have large areas of pure color without detail and the setting might be very simple and even painted like a cartoon. On the other hand, the decision might be made to change the historical period entirely in order to make the play easier for a modern audience to grasp, and so it might be put squarely into contemporary clothes and settings, and there might even be contemporary references inserted into the script. In each case, consistency of style would be sought.

It should be pointed out that *historical accuracy* usually refers to social and not theatrical history. As a general rule, *revivals of past works seek to imitate the style of the life of the period and not the style of the theatre of the period.* An audience will accept a copy of the styles of a period if it is convinced that the copy is a reasonably good one of the life of the times; it generally will not accept a copy of the theatrical style of a past period because conventions and theatrical styles of the past, having been supplanted by successive waves of innovation, may well look foreign or even ridiculous. (Curiously, a modern audience seeing a meticulous copy of the acting style, settings, and theatre costumes of Molière might respond angrily that the style is "not accurate." They would mean that the acting, settings, and costumes were not like the modern idea of seventeenth-century life, forgetting that life and the theatre are sometimes far from identical.) When an audience does not understand a style, it will be annoyed, for the very good reason that it cannot go beyond the style to the real business of the theatre, the stirring of the imagination, and it will give up its own imaginative participation in order to try to cope with stylistic effects. When, however, an audience has a very strong concept of a style of the past (a theatrical style, not a lifestyle) and theatre artists choose to play on that concept, the result can be "camp"— using a past style for its own sake, most often to make fun of it. Nowhere is such a "camp" approach so common as in productions of what are loosely called nineteenth-century melodramas. The curious fact is that the dramatic style being made fun of never actually existed in precisely the way that either audience or most theatre people seem to think—but no matter, it has become a style of its own, and audiences are pleased by it, for all its howling inaccuracy.

Do Audiences Have Styles?

Insofar as an audience represents an age and a social class, it too will show a style, probably the same style that influences the theatre. But the question does not mean "Do they have distinctive ways of moving and dressing and speaking?" because these elements are unimportant *to their role as audience.* It means "Do different audiences react in different ways that will affect the performance?"

The answer, of course, is "yes." The social level of an audience greatly affects its response. The "gallery gods" of the nineteenth-century theatres or the audiences of the penny theatres of the same period were notorious for their raucous behavior when they were displeased, their applause when they were pleased. They were noisy, sometimes obstreperous; they interrupted plays, drowned out bad performances, and cheered their favorites to a standstill. Upper-class audiences, because of their supposed aesthetic sophistication, may put different, special demands on performers; much of the abstraction of the late eighteenth-century French neoclassical theatre came, for example, from its audience's insistence on a "propriety" that reflected an unreal concept of aristocratic behavior.

And the psychology of groups, as it varies from age to age, greatly affects the "style" of an audience. Our own is an age—in the theatre, opera, and dance—of restraint. Nobody throws ripe produce at the performers anymore; nobody has rioted in an American theatre in decades, although in the infamous Astor Place riot of 1849, when the fans of the English tragedian Macready and the American tragedian Forrest battled, twenty-two people were killed. Our audiences for athletic events and rock concerts, on the other hand, are far more boisterous than our theatre audiences. Rock audiences sometimes weep, laugh, get high, sing, dance; at Altamont in 1968, for example, people were killed. Athletic audiences at all levels, high school to professional, sometimes come near to breaking even the bounds of law: there

Figure 2–13. Audience Response. The Astor Place Riot, 1849. Fans of the rival actors Macready and Forrest fought bitterly. *(Courtesy of The New-York Historical Society, New York City.)*

have been fights; bottles and cans have been thrown on hockey ice and baseball turf; deafening noise has caused many officials to beg for quiet.

The determinants of audience style are so complex that they cannot be easily broken down for analysis. Most important, probably, is *group self-image*—the customs and manners of a certain kind of group. Of almost equal importance is *the sanctity of the place* and the way people respect it; that is, the behavior generally expected by society in a plush and gilt opera house is markedly different from that in a drive-in movie. And, finally, the *preparation for the event* greatly affects audience style: it is one thing to flop into a chair in pajamas and watch television, quite another to dress up in formal clothes and travel miles by car or taxi, to pay up to thirty dollars for a ticket, and, often, to eat a special meal before attending a play in a Broadway theatre or a dance concert at the Kennedy Center in Washington.

Audience style is more properly seen as a reaction and not as an action. It is, however, of greatest importance as an *interaction* between performers and audience, when it can become a determinant of the performance itself.

Does an Audience Work?

If audience and theatre workers interact, then it must follow that the audience itself has a responsibility in the system that we call theatre. A performance cannot be seen merely as the total product of all the work that is done on one side of a curtain line, as the whole that results from the efforts of actors, writers, directors, designers, technicians, and dozens of others who remain behind the scenes. Nor can it properly be seen as something "given" from one kind of person (the theatre artist) to another kind of person (the audience). It is, instead, something that exists in the very complex interaction between them; and it follows, therefore, that the audience has a task for which it must prepare and for which it can do certain things to prepare itself.

Ideas of "comfort" and "escape" have sometimes defined the audience role. The German theatre artist Bertolt Brecht, however, objected to audiences who viewed the performance as a "warm bath of comfort" into which they could passively sink, and long before Brecht—and after him—other theatre people have objected to audiences who wanted merely to behave passively. "They sit on their hands" is the theatre saying. But slumping into a seat and waiting to be entertained is not the proper posture of the theatre audience, because it is too limiting, both to the audience's own pleasure and to the potential of the theatre itself. "Entertain me" is like a child's "Tell me a story" in its passivity, and its end result in an audience is childish performance—the sort of mindless mush that sometimes turns up on television (where audiences are of necessity more passive) and that, regrettably, turns up in the theatre whenever the audience lets itself get complacent and lazy.

Performance is based on a *contract* between artists and audience. The

Figure 2–14. Shakespeare's Theatre of Imagination. In this interpretation of Shakespeare's Globe, two opposing "armies" are shown, along with set-pieces for different scenes that would have remained onstage throughout. An unwritten "contract" demanded that the audience work to exercise its "imaginative forces." *(Reprinted with permission of the Macmillan Company from* Shakespeare's Wooden O *by Leslie Hotson. First published in the United States in 1960. Courtesy also of Rupert Hart-Davis, London.)*

basic clause for the performers is "I will not hurt or offend you," but this clause gets broken either when the performers have disdain for their audience or when they believe that the audience seeks only its own passive comfort. The basic clause for the audience is "I will work to enjoy you," but this clause gets broken when the performers smash expectations or established practice or social codes without warning.

A good audience fulfills its part of the contract in two ways: first, by *making its imagination work* when that imagination is stirred by the performance; and second, by *remaining open* to new ways of being moved, entertained, and excited, by remaining open to having its imagination stirred in surprising ways. It does no good for Shakespeare's Chorus in *Henry V* to say,

> *Suppose within the girdle of these walls*
> *Are now confin'd two mighty monarchies. . . .*
> *Think when we talk of horses that you see them,*
> *Printing their proud hoofs i' the receiving earth;*
> *For 'tis your thoughts that now must deck our kings. . . .*

if the audience will refuse to do these things. The Chorus speaks of the audience's "imaginative forces." Forces *work.* The audience must "suppose" and "think." It is "your thoughts" that dress the actors. If the audience for such a play simply lay back in its easy chairs and said, "Ho-hum, I'm tired; entertain me," there would be no entertainment at all. Curiously, the more an audience causes its imagination to work, and the more open it forces itself to be to new imaginative stimulation, the more entertained it will be.

In addition to its imaginative responsibilities, the audience can also heighten its own pleasure through *preparation for the performance.* Its preparation falls into two categories: an *understanding of the theatre* and a *sympathy for the work.* Understanding of the theatre means a basic mastery of the "how's" and "why's" of what theatre people do, an appreciation of the arts of the performers that is distinct from the specific value of any performance. That is, it is not appropriate for an audience to say merely, "I didn't like it" or "I thought it was wonderful." Both statements say much about the speaker, little about the performance. Instead, it is the spectrum of appreciative statements that is revealing: one actor was excellent because of his understanding of his role, the way he used his body and his voice; the playwright created a stunning scene for two actors in Act I but didn't quite bring off a climactic speech in Act III; the set designer not only created a first-rate acting space but also created a visually beautiful treat for the audience; and so on. Through such understanding of the arts of the theatre will come greater audience pleasure; that, in turn, will contribute to an increased ability to let the imagination work.

Sympathy for the work is developed through an absorption of all of the material available about the performance before going to see it. This means familiarizing oneself with reviews and advertisements where they are available; it means reading the program once one is in the theatre. It seems a picayune point, but a theatre program does give essential information about where a scene is taking place and when it is happening, and it is mere laziness if an audience does not take that information in. Sympathy for the work means going to the theatre with a general idea of what sort of event one is going to see—so that, for example, somebody who has his heart set on a comedy does not leave the theatre because *Cat on a Hot Tin Roof* sounded like a funny title; or somebody who wants to introduce his children to the theatre does not become enraged because *Who's Afraid of Virginia Woolf?* is not a children's play. Titles have importance, but they are not always a good clue to plays; the whole area that we call *mediation* should be mastered by the audience member—advertisements, programs, reviews, public relations stories. It is fairly commonplace for someone to say, "I never read reviews or criticism; I don't want to be told how to think." But there is no reason at all why criticism should tell anybody how or what to think; it serves, instead, as a prod and a guide, leading the potential audience member away from works he may not want to see and toward those he will want to see.

An audience cannot afford to be lazy. Its own pleasure depends on its

Figure 2–15. Mediation. Advertising, like critical reviews and theatre programs, is part of the world of information that surrounds, and influences, the audience's awareness of the performance.

taking part; one can no more enjoy the theatre as a nonparticipant than one can enjoy playing tennis that way. Audience laziness leads to mindlessness, limitation of scope, and stagnation. As A. Nicholas Vardac wrote in *Stage to Screen,* "From the mid-nineteenth century to the Radio City Music Hall is a period of imaginative laziness—a laziness not on the part of the artists of the theatre, but rather on the part of their audiences. They had not come into the theatre to participate imaginatively. . . . They had come to be shown."

CHAPTER 3

The Audience in the Theatre

The Values of Performance

A city street, evening. Taxis arrive at the curb; men and women hurry out of them; others walk briskly to the same place, enter the same doors, stand in the same line by the ticket window. There is an air of excitement; the principal expressions on the faces are those of happiness, eagerness. As eight o'clock nears, they go in ever-increasing numbers from the lobby into the theatre building itself—across a red-carpeted foyer, through more doors, along passages that lead to orchestra seats or boxes, up stairs that lead to mezzanine, balcony. Ushers give out programs. The theatre itself muffles their vibrant buzz of talk, until the lights dim and an electric silence falls. The curtain rises. All the faces are turned toward the stage now. They break into smiles. Laughter comes from a thousand throats. Unconsciously, a woman squeezes her escort's arm, the gesture intimate, excited, eloquent: "Share this pleasure with me." The attention of the mass of people is remarkable.

How do we respond in the theatre? To what do we respond? Do we look on objectively—as if, that is, the imitation of human behavior were a scientific demonstration—or do we have other attitudes? Are we warm or cold? Passionate or indifferent? Intellectually interested or emotionally involved?

47

Figure 3–1. Preparation. The enjoyment of theatre often begins even before the theatre is entered, aroused by expectation and by experiences associated with the theatrical events and the "glamor" of theatre-going—as in this photograph, by the posters and even the ambience of a theatre district street.

Mediation has prepared us, we know that. The *conditions of the theatre* have defined both performance and audience, we know that. What is it, now that we are in the theatre, that rivets us to the performance? Is it the famous actor in the lead role? Is it the beauty of the setting? The story being acted out? The intellectual meanings suggested by the play?

It is all these things, and more. Performance acts on an audience from several directions simultaneously, so that each audience member is receiving a complicated blend of stimuli at each moment of the performance. For purposes of analysis and discussion, these stimuli can be separated into four main groupings. They are *sensory stimulation* (sight and sound); *human values* (story and character); *artistic excellence;* and *intellectual value.* All these stimuli can act on us *simultaneously* and *synergistically,* meaning that in the best performances, they not only harmonize with each other, but they also support and enrich each other.

An example may help. After World War II, Laurence Olivier played Oedipus in the Sophoclean tragedy. His performance is generally conceded to have been the greatest interpretation of that role in modern times. At the moment when Oedipus appeared, having just gouged out his eyes, the audience response was so intense that people gasped, and many of those who saw the performance still remember the moment as a high point in a lifetime of theatregoing. Because the bloody effects of the eye gouging were visual, we could say that the moment was an example of intense *sensory stimulation;* however, since the horror of the moment depended upon an understanding of story and character, the moment also sprang from an appreciation of the *human values* in the performance; yet again, it was Olivier's superb performance— his *artistic excellence*—that dazzled those in the audience who appreciated the art of acting. And finally, the symbolism and meanings of the eye gouging itself were the springboard for *intellectual value* in this classic tragedy of rich meanings. All four kinds of stimuli were at work, then, and it was the four, working *together,* that made the moment.

Contrarily, two or more of the kinds of stimuli may work against each other (although it happens far more commonly that one or two of them are not working than that they are actively in conflict). Perhaps the most familiar example of this situation is the sudden concentration in certain plays on intellectual value and the simultaneous suspension of other values. That is, serious playwrights sometimes place a meaning-laden speech at a crucial moment; in performance, however, the presentation of this speech

Figure 3–2. Preparation: Mediation. Through their designs, their graphic symbolism, their literal information, theatre posters prepare an audience by arousing expectations of key factors in the performance.

Figure 3–3. Spectacle. The visual appeal of color, motion, and mass can be remarkable, as in this equestrian theatre of the late nineteenth century, with its huge cast, real horses, gorgeous costumes, and exciting action.

may mean that the other values must "stand aside" while it goes on. Curiously, the effect may be the opposite of what is wanted: the moment, by concentrating on a single value, may be so theatrically weak that the meanings are ignored by the audience. In the same way, the audience members most interested in human values may feel that many of the sensory values of dance and song are weak points in a musical, while fans of music and dancing may feel the same thing about human values.

It is very difficult to make hard-and-fast rules. It seems clear that a great performance (as in the case of Olivier's *Oedipus Rex*) comes, ideally, from the simultaneous and synergistic action of all stimuli; however, it would not then be true to say that concentration on only three or two or even one of the stimuli would *necessarily* result in a poor performance. Each case must be taken on its own merits.

Of the four categories of stimuli, two are inherent in *production* (sensory values, artistic excellence) and two are inherent in the *text* (human values, intellectual values). This distinction lets us understand at least a few of the reasons that theatregoers see the same play many times over a lifetime without feeling bored. The text does not change (or changes very little), but other important facets change and, because of the synergistic effect of these factors, the total impact of the performance then changes. Thus, to say, "I've seen *King Lear;* why should I see it again?" is to ignore half of the value of performance. It is important to understand this point, for what it emphasizes is the enormous difference between *reading a play* and *participating as audience in a performance.* To read a play is to engage in appreciation of half its potential (and then only if the reader is trained in such reading); to see the play in performance is to approach its full potential.

It will be helpful to look at each of the categories in more detail.

Sensory Values

Theatre comes from the Greek word meaning "seeing place." The Latin *auditorium* means "hearing place." We often speak of a performance as a "show." Thus the vocabulary of the theatre acknowledges its remarkable visual and auditory power.

The audience relies on two senses: seeing and hearing. (Rarely, plays and movies have tried to appeal to other senses—Smell-o-vision, vibrating seats, physical contact with the performers—but the attempts are oddities.) Everything the audience understands about the performance comes through those two senses. The brain processes the information and uses it in several ways, but seeing and hearing remain the root senses of the theatre.

Spectacle. Of the two senses, it is vision that is the more powerful. We believe what we see. When an actor says one thing with words but

Figure 3–4. Spectacle: Sex. *Mazeppa,* with the actress Ada Isaacs Menken as the hero tied to the runaway horse, was a great nineteenth-century hit. It offered several kinds of appeal, not the least of which was this scene with the scantily-clad actress and the runaway horse (on a treadmill that is deleted in this artist's interpretation.) *(Courtesy of the Theatre and Music Collection of the Museum of the City of New York.)*

his gestures say another, we believe the gesture. Our language acknowledges this power: "I see," we say when we understand something; having met a friend we say, "I saw so-and-so." Doctors "see" us; people "see" ghosts (a much more frightening experience than hearing one). "Seeing is believing."

Our eyes believe. *Spectacle*—that which is seen—rules.

So potent was spectacle in the Greek theatre that a story is told of one of Aeschylus' plays in which the chorus appeared as the Furies (avenging beings): "When, at the performance of the *Eumenides*, Aeschylus introduced the chorus in wild disorder into the orchestra, he so terrified the crowd that children died and women suffered miscarriage." *Seeing* the Furies was the shock, supported by the sense of hearing and tremendously strengthened by the play itself. Until the moment when they entered "in wild disorder," the Furies had existed as creatures of the mind's eye; suddenly, they were visible to the physical eye: they existed.

A modern audience might laugh at these very same Furies, for response to the visual changes along with all other values. Most of us, no longer sharing or even understanding the ancient Greek religious system, might find such figures interesting or quaint or even comical, but we would not have the "mind's eye" vision to prepare us for the horror of the seen. Thus, spectacle does not mean merely "what is seen" in a purely objective sense;

Figure 3–5. Spectacle: The Impossible. Many circus and magic acts depend upon doing the seemingly impossible, as does this "Niagara Leap" in a nineteenth-century theatre. *(Courtesy of the New-York Historical Society, New York City.)*

it means "what is seen" in the context of the seer. The physical eye sees merely what is there; it is a physical system—lens, retina, optic nerve—for receiving physical stimuli. The mind, on the other hand, sees in the context of a rich and complicated mixture of symbolism, association, and meaning.

Spectacle is not merely the horrifying or the symbolic, however. It is also the beautiful and the impossible. Most of us, however sophisticated and however experienced, respond strongly to the sheer visual appeal of beauty—color, motion, mass. A parade is a "show"—often a great show—because of its visual beauty: the colors of flags and uniforms, the arranged mass of floats and drill teams, the pleasing movement of synchronization. Football halftime shows, circus performances, laser-light shows, and the visual element of rock concerts are all great appeals to our love of visual beauty. The visual impact of sensory values is enough of itself to explain the existence of some paratheatrical forms.

And perhaps of greatest importance to certain forms is the value of "seeing the impossible." Magic shows are spectacles of the impossible; so is circus trapeze work. So is much of dance, for example, the dazzling tap work of Broadway show dancing and the defiance of gravity that is classical ballet. We are greatly excited and moved by this "spectacle of the impossible"; through our vision, we come to understand that a certain artist is doing what we thought unlikely or undo-able. And we must *see* it "live." Notice how much weaker the value is, for example, of a magic show seen on television or a dance performance seen on film—not to mention one that is communicated to us by narration or that we merely read about.

No wonder that our expression for going to the theatre is going "to see a show."

Sound. Hearing is the other of the audience senses. It makes possible the beauty and excitement of the musical, emotional, rich timber of a great actor's voice. It takes in everything from the haunting flute music in Arthur Miller's *Death of a Salesman* to the score of *The Fantasticks.* Some of the audience's richest moments in theatre have come about because of sound, often because of quite subtle sound. For example, the actor Hume Cronyn tapped his foot quietly as he dealt the cards in *Gin Game,* the 1978 Pulitzer Prize-winner, and the sound *was* the theatrical impact of the scene.

Sound is not merely orchestral music or individual noises; it is the whole, rich world of the ear. Perhaps it is most important in the theatre because of the actor's voices and the words they say. That is, voices in production are "orchestrated," and directors cast actors so that their voices will blend and match. There is an analogy to opera here. Each actor develops his own voice to attain maximum range and flexibility. Moreover, the playwright supplies words, sentences, overlapping lines so that voices will "sing" together, and the words and sentences and voices themselves have beauty *distinct from the meaning of the words.* We are very much in the habit of listening to what actors say rather than listening to the aesthetic values of voice and language, but it is possible to do both; in opera, where the language is often not English, rather the reverse is true, and the meaning of the

Figure 3–6. Sensory and Human Values. When theatre works best, several values are usually operating together. In this mid-eighteenth century epilogue by the actress Peg Woffington, spectacle (beauty, sexuality), sound (her trained voice, rhyme) and human value (wit, humor) all worked together. *(Courtesy of the Astor, Lenox and Tilden Foundations, the New York Public Library.)*

language is ignored so that one may concentrate on the glory of the voice. Actors' voices can be effective in the same way, though audiences may not appreciate them with quite the same conscious understanding. Certain actors have voices whose unusual qualities are by themselves effective— the flexible contralto of the late Tallulah Bankhead; Joan Greenwood's husky, breaking voice. Other actors use their voices in surprising ways: Maggie Smith's vocal swoops in *Private Lives;* Sir John Gielgud's controlled tremolo and meticulous rhythm in his performances of Shakespeare, Pinter, and many other playwrights. The very sound of language, too, is part of the sensory value of the theatre, whether in obvious examples like rhyme (as in neoclassical French drama) or in the more subtle poetic language of T. S. Eliot, Tennessee Williams, or Samuel Beckett.

Human Values

Human beings are fascinated by other human beings. The fascination accounts in part for the popularity of gossip and of magazines like *People* and *US.* Invented lives are often even more fascinating, whether in the form of novels by great writers like Dickens, Stendahl, or Bellow, or in plays by Aeschylus, Molière, or Ibsen. The nature of imaginative art focuses attention so that these invented lives often seem more fascinating than most real ones. For many people, the memory of Anna Karenina or Hamlet is more powerful than the memory of many acquaintances.

The human values of such invented lives are many. They include *human understanding,* the increased awareness of what it is to be a human being; *emotional sympathy,* the participation through art in suffering and joy; *arousal* of pleasure, including a wide range of pleasures from the laughable to the erotic; and *psychic perception,* the observation of mythic patterns, as in dreams.

Audience response to human values comes from two principal factors: story and character.

Story. Stories are seemingly as old as human language. Some are complicated and long, like Homer's *Odyssey;* some are short and simple, like the Iroquois tales of the trickster Skunniwundi. Stories are made up of incidents, each of which has "coherence"; that is, each one is held together by a strong internal force. This force may be causality, but it is often something else, as in the case of the many tales and actual incidents where the binding force is chance or the oddity of the happening.

Stories serve the audience in two ways. First, they are compelling in themselves. Second, they serve as the framework for the other values of character, humor, and so on. In a sense, we understand the other values through our understanding of the story. As individuals, we tend to believe that people are understood by their behavior; behavior, focused by art, is story.

It is possible to watch a theatre performance for the value of story alone. The experience would be very rare in our time, although it was more common in the age of melodrama. (Even then it was usually coupled with the values of spectacle and artistic excellence.) Many of the action series on television—police shows, for example—offer story as their most important value.

Response to a story comes from suspense and surprise.

Suspense is the unfolding of events at the pace created by the theatre itself in an artfully crafted structure that will best ask and answer the question, "And then what happened?" We must note that a question is *both* asked and answered; that is, the art of suspense lies in manipulating events and time so that the audience will understand *what* story it is to anticipate and *how* that story is progressing through time. A critic said some years ago that art is the creation and satisfaction of appetite, and the definition is not at all inaccurate for suspense, because its two parts—creation and satisfaction—catch the necessary parts of both good suspense-making and good audience response to it. We cannot have story suspense without preparation for it (creation of appetite); that is, we cannot have a haphazard succession of events and call their sequence *suspense.* Who would care if we began a play by showing John, then shifted to Mary, then to Robert, then to Jack, and so on, all evening? This would be all preparation and no story; there could be no "And then what happened?" because *then* would be meaningless. Therefore, to have story suspense that will arouse pleasurable audience response, we must have preparation, connectedness, and resolution (the answer to the question, "And then what happened?").

Figure 3–7. Story and Suspense. Audiences of many periods have responded to stories with carefully prepared and worked-out suspense, twists and turns, and sudden changes. Shakespeare's *Macbeth* covers the spectrum of values from spectacle to idea, and suspense—even as performed in this rural theatre of 1790—is important. *(Courtesy of the Astor, Lenox and Tilden Foundations, the New York Public Library.)*

Changes of direction, reversal, dashing of expectations—these sound like the opposite of suspense, because they suggest that instead of having the question answered, we are being sent off in a different direction or being sent all the way back to the beginning. Not so, however; effective surprise is one of the principal pleasures of story, for it puts us through a pleasing imitation of real experience, which is so full of surprises and setbacks; yet the surprise of the theatre is "safe" and therefore pleasurable instead of painful, for it happens only within the contract between performers and audience. And surprise, like other story elements, must be prepared for. There can only rarely be surprise that is outside the world that the performance creates. That is, it would be "surprising" to have a flying saucer land onstage and carry off the leading character when he got into a terrible mess in Act III, but unless the play had prepared us for flying saucers, this surprise would not truly be a surprise at all; it would be a violation of the contract. As audience, it would give us not pleasure but considerable annoyance.

Figure 3–8. Surprise. Theatrical surprise works to the advantage of the performance only when it is prepared for and when it is part of the fictional event; when it is not—as in this sudden intrusion of a tiger into a fairground performance in 1810— it shatters the performance and destroys the audience's enjoyment. *(Courtesy of the Astor, Lenox and Tilden Foundations, the New York Public Library.)*

Surprise can take several forms. There can be the surprise of the unexpected. In the first act of *Arsenic and Old Lace,* for example, there is a moment when, without warning, a window curtain is whipped aside and a menacing figure abruptly appears. The moment is so surprising that audience members may well gasp or scream. There is also the surprise of reversal, of which George Bernard Shaw was a master. In *Man and Superman,* one character defies convention by announcing his staunch support of a young woman who is supposedly guilty of immoral behavior; she appears and surprises both the man and the audience by announcing that he can keep his staunch support to himself. In this case, it is our expectations (created by the playwright and the actor) that have been reversed. And there can be the surprise of the prepared-for but the unpredictable, when the event (often the high point of a play) astonishes us despite the fact that we know something of the sort must happen. In *Oedipus Rex,* for example, Oedipus' blinding of himself is effective because it is so horrible and shocking. We know that he will do something almost unthinkable to himself, but we do not know what. Related to this sort of surprise is the "least likely" of several choices, a necessity in murder mystery plays. Such plays—*The Mousetrap, Ten Little Indians*—rely heavily on story for their success, and the basic question that they pose ("Who did it?") makes surprise of choice essential in the last act. A related but more elegant example is a play like *Sleuth,* where we are pleasurably surprised to find that a seemingly new character in the second act is actually a character we already know from Act I, now in disguise. Like other sorts of surprise, this will work only if the surprise is carefully prepared for—if, in fact, we can say in retrospect, "Of course! That was inevitable!" (That is, it was set up for us.)

Character. Representations of human beings move through the patterns we have called stories. Their behavior in those stories reveals them to us. They are not mere stick figures, mere zeros. They are *characters.*

A *character* is the representation of a human being in a theatrical performance. A character is not a living human being, nor is it ever a completely rounded imitation of a living human being; it is a detailed representation of a human being *insofar as the audience needs to know that person in the work of art.* The aspects of character that the audience understands are often clearer than similar aspects of people in real life; we may come to know theatrical characters better than our closest relatives. Such is the focusing power of art. Willy Loman (of *Death of a Salesman*) and Blanche DuBois (of *A Streetcar Named Desire*) are not real people, but their artistic representation has put them in a place in our society that makes them part of the common image of "what it is to be a man and woman" in our time; they are quoted, discussed, made examples of as few real human beings ever are.

Character and story are interlocked. We understand each through the other. Nevertheless, they remain a little independent of each other, so that we may have different characters move through the same basic story. The same sequence of events can be used in several ways. "Boy meets girl, boy loses girl, boy gets girl," was a formula for stories of the 1920s and 1930s that could be dramatized around characters as different as classical divinities and factory workers. Incidents, then, allow us to understand character within a rough framework, but context and the place of the incident in the story let us perceive character more fully; when Fred hits John with a baseball bat, if we know that John was messing around with Fred's wife and that Fred has never recovered from his experiences in the Vietnam war, we can form a much better idea of character than we ever could from the event itself. (This is one reason that bare "plot summaries" are so often inaccurate. If we summarize Shakespeare's *Hamlet* as a play in which a young man murders his prospective father-in-law, his prospective brother-in-law, and his uncle while causing the suicide of his mother and his prospective wife, we will have a very strong story, it is true, but to respond pleasurably to it we need all the complex data that come from a topnotch performance.)

Responses to character may come from several impulses: identification, subconscious reference, and association.

"Like me" is a common positive response. "It's my story" or "He could be me" are sources of pleasure or suffering. We like to see the mirror held up so that we can watch ourselves. Connected with this idea is the idea of universality of character. The broader the identification, the wider the audience who will respond; the narrower the identification, the more most people will respond as if they are in a zoo.

CAMROSE LUTHERAN COLLEGE
LIBRARY

Figure 3–9. Historical Association. As in this performance of *Tom Payne*, associations with a historical name are an important appeal in some dramatic characters. *(Produced at Indiana University. Directed by R. Keith Michael, designs by F. Silberstein. Photo by Keith Hardisty.)*

Subconscious reference is another kind of identification, but so different that it needs to be talked about separately. This is a response to something that is like us, perhaps, but that we recognize as being like us at a level below the conscious—as in our dreams or our fantasies. We watch *Hamlet* because there are aspects of Hamlet that we can identify with, true, but we watch it also because the Prince of Denmark is the main character in an action that partakes of dreams and of myth, something we fantasize about living through—or fear living through. Frankenstein's monster is not at all "like me," but he may be terrifyingly like our nightmares. Such characters are also a mirror, but not one in which we see our superficial selves; we see the selves we carry, hidden.

Historical names and famous people have their own appeal. Shakespeare's histories were, in their own day, effective character plays for this reason (although that is far from being their only appeal). There was a "you are there" sense for the Elizabethan audience in seeing historical figures on the stage. The musical *1776* gained from the Bicentennial association with our own Revolution; two recent plays have had powerful character appeal because they were about Winston Churchill. In the nineteenth century, a semidocumentary treatment of such notorious events as real murders and trials created successful theatre. All such plays depend in part for their impact on convincing us that we are seeing "truth"—although the farther the real-life people on whom they are modeled are from us (in time and occasionally in culture) the less "truth" matters. To take advantage of the associative response, the play must choose people with whom the audience has strong ties, and it must present them in a convincing fashion (that is, by casting actors who look like the real people or by using effective makeup; by hewing closely to known events and not violating the "facts" of history).

Artistic Excellence

Beyond and behind the appeal of mimesis, of "embodied narrative," there is an element of artistry by which all other things are given value and are heightened: the performing skill of the actor, the talent of the designer and the director and the dramatist. Audience response to the actor is probably the easiest to understand and the one we most often sense, but the others are possible for knowledgeable theatregoers. It is an *understanding of the theatre art* that makes such a response possible, and that response greatly enriches all the others. A knowledgeable audience member does not applaud merely the *fact* that the actor created a brilliant character (which the indifferent audience member may confuse with the playwright's creation of character) but also applauds the artistry with which the actor did it. In the same way, the knowledgeable audience member is able to respond to the artistry of the director, because his knowledge allows an understanding of the contribution that the director made.

This kind of response is possible when the audience member is knowledgeable and when the audience member is somewhat objective about the performance. This is not to suggest that the audience member holds himself back and does not participate in the performance; rather, it suggests that the perceptive audience member is able both to participate and to watch with some objectivity. "Aesthetic distance"—the separation of audience from performance through art—is set up, as if the audience member were watching himself watch the play. Perceptions are divided between a subjective participation in the experience and an objective understanding of how the performance came about.

Above all, an appreciation of the artistic element of the theatre requires an understanding of how theatre artists work and of why they make the choices that become the performance. Why did the actor drop his voice to a whisper instead of raising it when the character was angry? Why did the costumer put him into blue instead of red? Why was only part of the house shown instead of the whole thing? The ability to perceive these choices and to understand how they were made comes from gathering knowledge about how theatre artists work, and such knowledge comes from going to the theatre, from working in the theatre, and from studying about the theatre (as in this book).

In part, an appreciation of the element of artistry comes from an awareness of potentials and possibilities. What are the limits of an actress's voice? What are the possibilities for variety, rhythm, and music in a single line of Shakespearean verse? What are the potentials of scene paint and canvas

MR. HOWARD HALL'S GREAT MELODRAMATIC SUCCESS

THE WAIFS' PARADISE

THE GREAT DREDGE SCENE. A DARING LEAP FROM THE BURNING BUILDING AND SENSATIONAL RESCUE

Figure 3–10. Artistry. Not all artistic excellence is devoted to elevated or classic works. This melodrama of 1904 demanded artistry from its designers and actors—spectacular effects, careful timing. Such productions can be theatrically good without being literarily good. *(Courtesy of the New-York Historical Society, New York City.)*

in reproducing a sky or a forest? Then, when these potentials and possibilities are understood, they can be used as a gauge of what happens in any given theatre. Memorable evenings come about when the potentials are fulfilled. At its best, the theatre should make us gasp, and one of the elements at which we will gasp is the ability of the artist to transcend what we think are his limits.

Intellectual Values

Generally, *idea* is given least thought while we sit in the theatre but is the thing that we talk about most after we have left. There is a good reason for this seeming contradiction: the theatre is "the place of the now." Performance is transitory. When it is behind us, preserved only in our memories, the vividness of the sensory and artistic pleasure fades and we are left with the intellectual content, which remains sharp and fresh because of the sharpness of our minds. *Idea*, in fact, becomes more acute with time, if we allow ourselves to be interested in it. As well, idea is frequently the element of theatre that reviewers and critics talk about because, being intellectual and capable of verbalization, it is far easier to put into words than the brilliance of an actor's gesture or the beauty of a lighting effect.

There is an idea behind or embodied in every play, to be sure, but some ideas are more interesting and more important than others. (As well, some ideas are more interesting and important to certain people, less so to others. One of the important ideas of Black theatre, "Blackness is good," for example, has a far different level of interest and importance for white than for black audiences, although we should note carefully that the difference does not necessarily mean that white audiences will not attend Black theatre. On the contrary, a somewhat different appeal may bring white audiences in and satisfy them—an appeal to their curiosity, to their sense of liberal guilt, to their racism. In a sense, when this happens, the "idea of the play" has changed for them.)

Questions of importance and relevance are highly debatable, as anyone who has sat in on a late-night bull session knows, and, more often than not, a debate about relevance and importance is really a debate about "what I like" or "what I believe." In the area of theatrical idea, however, the audience member makes an error if he tries to put himself into the position of judge for all. It is far better for him to ask, at least, why the idea was important to the theatre people who created the performances than to say unthinkingly, "That idea is not important (to me)" or "That idea is irrelevant (to me)."

The artistry of performance is best comprehended not by the intellect but by the body and the heart and the receptive self. Pure idea, which is dealt with directly by the intellect, belongs not in the theatre but in the lecture hall. Theatrical idea, which deals with the intellect through the medium of performance, belongs importantly in the theatre when it is entirely integrated into the other elements and neither manipulates them nor obscures them but speaks to the mind through them. (See "How to Read a Play," pp. 428–432.)

Too, idea is not the element that the performer cares most about. There is an old theatre adage: "If you have a message, send a telegram." Directors only rarely talk to actors about the "idea of the play"; designers do not try to express idea but try, instead, to provide good acting spaces and aesthetically pleasing spaces. A playwright may talk about "what my play means," but only rarely will director, designer, and actors work with him to enhance his ideas; rather, they will work on the other values—for they know that *in performance it is those values that must succeed.*

This is not to say that ideas do not belong in the theatre. Nor does it mean that performers have contempt for ideas or that ideas are themselves an intellectual, after-the-fact invention. What it does mean is that idea is not a be-all and end-all in the theatre. In a sense, it is the most important element in making a serious judgment about the importance of a play, but it is made only if the play succeeds brilliantly with the other values. *Hamlet* is a great play both because it is a stunning experience to see *and* because it is rich in complex ideas. Critics consider a play like Peter Shaffer's *Equus* a less important play because, effective as it may be in performance, its

Figure 3–11. Theatrical Idea. Even in the most effective of plays, ideas are expressed through performance rather than being imposed upon them. *The Trojan Women,* the University of Nevada, Las Vegas. *(Directed by Jerry Crawford, designs by Frederick L. Olson and Ellis M. Pryce-Jones.)*

ideas are less complex, less central to the culture, less tantalizing on the largest scale of human concerns. (But *Equus* also lacks Shakespeare's brilliance of language, deals in less compelling character, and has many other points that only the most detailed and patient analysis would show. This is not said to denigrate *Equus,* which is a justly praised play of our time, but only to try and explain why the rare great plays are worthy of that designation.)

Responses of the Audience

To discuss now the internal responses of audience members to performance is to delve into an area as complex and mysterious as human psychology itself. No one can say for certain how an audience will respond; no one can say for certain how an individual in an audience is responding at any moment. Performances differ from each other; audiences differ from each other; individuals in an audience differ from each other.

Individual postures toward a performance vary from extreme involvement (identification) to extreme objectivity. At any point along this spectrum, individuals bring such vastly different psyches to the experience that two people, sitting side by side at the same performance, may have entirely different experiences and may behave outwardly in entirely different ways. Thus any observations made about audience response are generalizations to which there must always be many exceptions.

The exterior behaviors that indicate audience response are covered in the following sections.

Laughter. Laughter is the actor's reward in comedy, the actor's torment in serious drama. In general, audiences seem to laugh for two widely different reasons: because they are truly amused and because they are uneasy. The laughter of amusement is largely a response to human values—that is, to an understanding of story and character—although there is considerable intellectual involvement in our laughter at satire, for example. The laughter of amusement may range from enormous belly laughs at wit or pratfalls ("We had them rolling in the aisles!") to low chuckles of appreciation that reflect warmth and approval.

The laughter of unease can be shattering for the actor. He may find

Figure 3–12. Laughter. To the comic actor, laughter is the most welcome of sounds. *(Courtesy of the Astor, Lenox and Tilden Foundations, the New York Public Library.)*

the audience laughing uproariously at completely improper moments. Such laughter springs not from amusement but from stress; it is not the laughter of an understanding of human values but the laughter of rejection of the experience represented by the performance. "Nervous laughter" is familiar in life; it has its counterpart in the theatre. Inevitably, it means that the performance has failed (but the failure may be the fault of the audience and not of the performers).

Silence. "You could hear a pin drop!" The silence of rapt attention is familiar. While we associate applause with the theatre, it is silence that is often the surest key to the effective response of an audience. Silence means attentiveness, for the body is being held still. The body at rest is not necessarily still; it shifts position, coughs, taps its fingers. A thousand people who do not make a single sound are remarkable, then. The performance has them in a very tight grip.

Such silence cannot be preserved for an entire evening. Like the pauses between movements of a symphony, when voices hum, coughs resound, and programs rattle, performances of even the most compelling sort must provide occasional release. Normally, such release points are built into the text of the play.

Applause. "Ours be your patience then, and yours our parts;/Your gentle hands lend us, and take our hearts" (Shakespeare's *All's Well That Ends Well*). The performers' request for applause—"plaudite"—dates to classical times. Clapping is still the way of signaling approval of performances of many kinds, from athletics to music to political speeches. It signals gratitude, approval, sometimes a request for more, an encore. In some instances, an audience will rise to applaud—the "standing ovation" that signals special favor.

Actors take their bows so long as applause lasts. "Milking" applause for more bows is considered bad form; contrarily, repeated bows at the curtain are the result of extended applause.

It is, perhaps, an oddity of theatrical convention that there is no audience behavior to signal positive response to serious or even tragic performance. In comedy, laughter follows comic events; in tragedy, profound silence is often the most significant response. Even at the end of many serious performances, silence will be the audience's behavior, as if even applause were too frivolous for the moment. (We do not, for example, applaud sermons or church music, for all that they are, in a real sense, performances.) Applause, then, is the usual sign of approval, but silence may be a sign of the deepest effect.

Tears. People do still weep in the theatre, although the copious waterworks of the nineteenth century are no longer seen. Such shedding of tears today may be—in fact usually is—silent; it may be only the tear in the eye, the lump in the throat. In either case, it is an outward sign of "empathy," the "believing with" an emotional moment. It is human value that stirs empathy, often at a far less than tragic level. Fictional deaths of animals

Figure 3–13. Tears. Rowlandson's 1789 "Tragedy Spectators" shows a response common in some ages and not seen in others because of changes in both audiences and performers. As a rule, tragedy in the Aristotelian sense is not necessarily associated with tears. *(Courtesy of the Astor, Lenox and Tilden Foundations, the New York Public Library.)*

and children, the parting of lovers, and similar human events can provoke tears.

We live in an age when public weeping is discouraged. Public laughter is approved; public tears are not. We still have such expressions as "having a good cry," and a certain kind of dated, highly empathetic movie is still called a "four-handkerchief picture." By and large, however, the taboo against public crying is almost too strong even for the "allowed behavior" of the darkened theatre. When we are moved, we try to hide our tears and keep our sniffles silent, and publicly, we at least pretend to agree with Oscar Wilde's caustic remark about one of Dickens's empathetic heroines, "Only one with a heart of stone could fail to be moved to laughter by the death of Little Nell."

Unease. Audiences have several negative behaviors (most of them unconscious) that reflect negative responses to performances. The most obvious of these is *noise:* coughing, shuffling of feet, whispering, shifting positions. When a thousand or more people begin to do these things at once, the noise level can get quite high, and the actor will believe that he is being deafened. All the sounds that are suppressed when an audience is attentive

Figure 3–14. Negative Response. When the performance does not work for its audience, behaviors can run from simple indifference to violence; this nineteenth-century illustration from Mrs. Trollope's *Domestic Manners of the Americans* shows several displays of boredom. *(Courtesy of the New-York Historical Society, New York City.)*

become noticeable the moment that the attention wanes. Coughs resound like gunshots; programs rattle like so many sails in the wind; feet scrape on the floor like coffins being dragged over a pavement. Bodies, tensed to watch and listen, are working off nervous energy. Each individual believes that he is being quiet, but the cumulative effect is loud—and horribly revealing.

More conscious negative behaviors include comments about the performance and getting up and walking out of the theatre. Rarely, nowadays, do they include catcalls, boos, remarks to the actors, or thrown objects.

Negative behaviors reflect negative responses; negative responses reflect a failure of communication between performance and audience. *Either* the performance or the audience—or *both* of them—may be responsible. Bad performances can cause negative responses, but bad audiences can have negative responses to a good performance.

What is a bad audience? It is an audience that is unable or unwilling to respond to the performance before it under the conditions of the theatre. Thus bad audiences are of two kinds: (1) the *unprepared audience,* which does not understand the nature of theatre art and so responds to performance as it does to life; and (2) the *unwilling audience,* which refuses to accept the nature of the performance before it.

The unprepared audience is usually new, or fairly new, to the theatre. It confuses art and life. It shows inappropriate responses because the intensity of theatre acutely embarrasses it; it may laugh at scenes of suffering, love, or nobility; it may, in extreme cases, try to interrupt the performance to prevent what, in life, would be offensive behavior.

The unwilling audience can be any audience alienated from the performance by poor mediation or by personal stubbornness. Some people simply dislike musicals; others hate the circus, and so on. They should stay away from the forms they dislike; if trapped into them by accident or mistake, they show an extreme of unease. Less obvious, but far more common, are audiences who are shocked or dismayed by elements of performance—usually intellectual value, sometimes human value or sensory value—that they are unaccustomed to. These elements run a wide spectrum from nudity to religion and include such varied matters as the verse form of French drama (which caused the *Hernani* riot of 1830), the appearance of a nude body (the musical *Hair,* 1968), or the story, dialogue, and characters of *Waiting for Godot* (whose first Broadway audience in 1956 was stunned and even angry). Again, as with the unprepared audience, there is an ignorance of the nature of art and the "harmlessness" of the theatre; in the case of the unwilling audience, however, the ignorance exists despite considerable theatre experience. The unwilling audience should know better but refuses to.

We all begin as the unprepared audience. We all have a potential for being the unwilling audience. We grow away from the first with experience and knowledge; we avoid the second with alertness to the theatre's essential nature and to the role of the audience in performance.

Figure 3–15. Negative Response. This "row" at a theatre was an audience's way of showing that the performance was "bad"—but was it the fault of the performance or of the audience itself? *(Courtesy of the Astor, Lenox and Tilden Foundations, the New York Public Library.)*

The Present and the Past

The same values have always existed for audiences in the theatre, although they have sometimes been defined in different ways. Audiences have always gone to the theatre out of love, expecting to be moved and delighted. The same forces have always worked in society and in the theatre, reordering the values, shifting the relationship between audience and performance, moving now toward experiment and now toward conservativism. The theatre exists as a constant in human culture, but it undergoes necessary shifts that seem to change its superficial appearance.

Because the theatre of the present is not merely a theatre of today's plays and today's techniques but is also a theatre of plays and techniques from many periods, the alert and responsive audience member will be knowledgeable about the theatre's past and its present. The prepared audience studies the past to enrich the present. It studies, too, to understand what the forces of change are and how they work and to see that audiences and artists of every age have been much like us, subject to the same pressures, glad of the same pleasures.

It is tempting, perhaps, to think of a theatre of the past as filled with people who were somehow different from us—more polite or stuffier or older or stupider or less sophisticated—but as a study of the theatre's history will show, they were not all that different. They laughed and wept, applauded and hissed, got bored by bad performances and gave standing ovations to great ones. To understand this fact—that the theatre is a great force and that its audience is a great, vital constant—is to understand why the theatre is an art that stands at the center of human concerns. Now and always, it offers human beings spectacle and music, artistry and idea, visions of themselves in the form of lifelike stories and lifelike characters. It does not compromise. It is human life elevated to humanistic art.

Part Two

The Theatre of Today and Yesterday

CHAPTER 4

The Contemporary Theatre: The Decades of the 1960s and 1970s

The Period

The decades of the 1960s and 1970s were puzzling. Filled with contradictions, at times they seemed alive with hope, but at other times overcome by despair. The political shifts, as reflected by the presidents in office, were indicative of the decades' changing values.

Politics

The period opened with the election of the young, handsome, and wealthy John F. Kennedy, an event that held the promise of an era of idealism moderated by sophistication. Indeed, the press referred to Washington under the Kennedys as "Camelot," an allusion to both the medieval land of chivalry and grace and to the Broadway musical *Camelot* (1960), which enjoyed enormous success during the Kennedy years. The assassination of Kennedy in 1963 stunned the country, and Lyndon Johnson, who succeeded to the presidency, failed to survive the political shock waves. Although many people recognized in Johnson a consummate politician and applauded his skills in working with the Congress, others considered him a vulgar, unschooled, and raw man—especially when compared with Kennedy. Johnson's personal style was gruff, his politics pragmatic. Never so popular as his predecessor, Johnson watched his appeal continue to erode, and he declined to seek reelection in 1968, making way for Richard Nixon's ascent to the White house. Nixon's election was heralded by many as the nation's return to sanity and stability, but it was feared by others as a rejection of various progressive social programs. Reelected by an impressive margin, Nixon was driven from office in disgrace in 1974 by a public enraged over his alleged abuses of power, culminating in the notorious Watergate affair. Again shocked, the country emerged under the leadership of Gerald Ford, a man not elected to any executive post but rather appointed by Nixon when his own Vice-President resigned because of alleged criminal acts. From an optimistic beginning, the decades of the 1960s and 1970s had reeled under a series of blows to the confidence of the American people and ended somewhat tentatively under the administration of a quiet born-again Christian from Georgia, Jimmy Carter, whose presidential style was often the apparent opposite of Camelot.

Unrest

John Kennedy's assassination marked the beginning of the end of Camelot. But American society underwent other social and political convulsions during the twenty-year period that followed his election. A wave of assassi-

Figure 4–1. War in the Sixties. Political assassinations and the Vietnam war in the nineteen-sixties created remarkable social tensions that surfaced, as well, in the theatre. *Oh, What a Lovely War* at the University of Missouri, Columbia. *(Directed by Larry D. Clark, design by Richardson Prouty.)*

nations, beginning with President Kennedy's, moving through Robert Kennedy's and Martin Luther King's, and ending with those of several members of the Black Panther Party, exposed the violence and tensions that society harbored. The once-peaceful moves toward civil and human rights turned impatient, strident, ugly, and finally lethal, with school buses being overturned and burned in cities like Boston and Louisville and with students being killed by police at places like Kent State University and South Carolina State College. The war in Vietnam began optimistically enough when a speedy victory seemed certain, but, dragging on, it sapped the will and strength of the country, caused many to question our role as international policeman, and led scores of citizens into acts of civil disobedience. The country's youth attacked the presumed hypocrisy of the "over-thirty" generation and rejected many traditional wisdoms on such subjects as loyalty, patriotism, marriage, motherhood, and the family. Adopting "odd" modes of dress and hair style, many youths openly advocated increased sexual freedom, legalization of other drugs (alcohol being already legal in most states), and an end to the military draft. The senseless murders committed in California by Charles Manson and his followers were held by some to be the tragic but predictable consequence of a society that had lost its moral values.

The International Scene

International as well as national problems grew increasingly complex. America appeared to grow weaker and more vulnerable as China emerged to join Russia as a major Communist power and as Africa and the Middle East jockeyed for the wealth and influence that the world had denied them earlier. Space travel moved from the realm of science fiction into the world of politics when Russia placed men in space and the United States put Americans on the moon. World tensions prevented concerted attacks on common problems that were only beginning to be identified. Nations realized that the earth's population was growing at a rate that threatened to deplete its resources and that was already polluting its air, water, and soil at a dangerous rate. The problems of energy, ecology, and population joined the fear of nuclear holocaust to produce a sense of pessimism, even hopelessness, about the future.

Society

Improved transportation and communications, certainly happy changes in many ways, had the less happy effect of speeding the pace of living. Planes got bigger and faster and required more fuel even as fuel grew ever shorter in supply. Computers permitted problems to be solved in minutes that before had required years. Television allowed vast numbers of people to be addressed and influenced as never before. People began to complain of having too many facts, too much information; the new problem was to sort out essential from inessential data, to avoid sinking in a sea of paper and fact, and to make reasonable choices when confronted with seemingly endless alternatives. Adopting a phrase from computer technology, some spoke of suffering from "information overload," which, combined with the accelerating speed of change, produced a new sort of anxiety among modern citizens, something called *future shock*. According to author Alvin Toffler, at least, society's leaders during the coming decades would be those people able to withstand rapid change, to live with high levels of ambiguity and uncertainty, and to escape the debilitating symptoms of future shock, the disease of tomorrow.

The Arts

The arts during the 1960s and 1970s reflected some of society's fads, problems, and solutions. In popular music, interest in simple folk ballads accompanied the early days of Camelot with its idealism and peaceful moves

Figure 4–2. Youth in the Sixties. *Kennedy's Children* at the Behrend College of Pennsylvania State University. *(Directed by Arno Selco, design by Jeff Palotas.)*

toward civil liberties. But as Haight-Ashbury decayed and the flower children disappeared, hard "acid" rock excited thousands of young people at music festivals like those at Woodstock and Altamont (at which several died). Its insistent rhythms and electric tones were a fitting accompaniment to the seemingly growing cynicism of the young, the rootless, and the members of the so-called counterculture. In the visual arts, Andy Warhol seized upon images of popular culture and enshrined tomato soup cans in museums, while abstract painters confused audiences and critics alike: a chimpanzee at the St. Louis zoo was applauded for his abstract paintings. The whole question of what was not a suitable art for contemporary society occupied the attention of poets and dramatists as well as musicians and painters. Many agreed that traditional works no longer satisfied the cultural appetites

Figure 4–3. Eclecticism. The use of elements and conventions from varying sources typified the theatre of the sixties. *Waiting for Godot* at the University of Rhode Island. *(Directed by James W. Flannery, design by Paul Masie, masks by Nicole Kozekiewicz.)*

of audiences, but few shared views on the directions that the new arts should take. And as always, many vigorously resisted any sort of change, seeing in it not progress but decline in values, in standards, and in morality.

Theatre and Drama

Theatre and drama, like the other arts, were involved in the controversies of the society at large. Writers and directors drew from a variety of practices from the past and present, selected those elements from each that were appealing, experimented with them singly and in new combinations, and spoke of alternative techniques for engaging the interest of audiences. Thus eclecticism—the gathering together of diverse characteristics—became a characteristic of theatre and drama of the 1960s and 1970s.

As in any age, the majority of artists continued to work in traditional ways, and so the commercial theatre remained the standard against which other practices were measured. But important alternative theatres also thrived.

The Theatre

While it is true that no classification can accurately capture and contain the richness of theatrical practices during this twenty-year period, categories can help clarify the many threads making up the contemporary theatre. For purposes of discussion, then, theatrical practices will be clustered about four major centers: commercial theatre, especially Broadway and Off-Broadway theatre; nontraditional theatres, including Off-Off Broadway and other experimental and political theatres; regional theatres; and educational theatres.

Commercial Theatre

Broadway

To duplicate, not to originate, is the aim and the method. Hence, if Broadway people take up a work that is different, they change it until it is the same.
Eric Bentley

Say the word *theatre* to an average American and he or she will probably think immediately of New York City's Broadway, for the word has become almost synonymous with theatre in America. The word in fact has several different meanings. *Broadway* is first of all the name of a street in New York that runs the length of Manhattan. But the word *Broadway* also designates the whole area around Times Square (Broadway and several streets adjacent to it), where most of the commercial theatres are located. The word is also

Figure 4–4. Broadway. A street name that has become an American theatrical symbol.

used in various union contracts, like those of the Actors Equity Association, to specify a certain kind of theatre in which only union members can work, and then only for a fee or salary that meets or exceeds the negotiated union minimums for that kind of theatre. And finally the word *Broadway* refers to a whole complex of qualities that people associate with the glamorous, glittering world of the legitimate theatre: elaborate settings, rich costumes, distinguished stars, polished performances, sophisticated plays and musicals.

New York's Broadway (once called the Great White Way) has been the heart of America's theatre for over one hundred years. Even during the 1950s and early 1960s, when the number of productions was declining steadily each year, when theatres were closing and those that survived were regularly playing at less than 50 per cent capacity, when some commentators were dourly predicting the end of Broadway, thousands of tourists from across the nation flocked to New York to see its plays. Indeed, at a time when New Yorkers appeared to despair and abandon Broadway, drama buffs from Louisville, Kentucky, and Columbus, Ohio, were organizing theatre trains and invading the Great White Way in large numbers.

The decade of the 1970s has shown that Broadway, despite the glum predictions of earlier years, has remained a vigorous and vital part of the American theatre. By the 1976–1977 season, for example, Broadway was again setting records in attendance, box office receipts, and weeks played. Nearly nine million people saw its plays that season (up 22.6 per cent from the preceding year); box office income was well over $93 million (up 31.9 per cent from the preceding season); and Broadway played over 1,300 weeks in all, a high mark in production that had not been reached since 1938. In the 1977–1978 season, Broadway theatres took in more money than ever before, and the number of patrons continued to rise.

Its Importance. The reasons for Broadway's resilience and its continuing appeal to theatre lovers is not mysterious. In the United States, the very best actors, directors, playwrights, and designers work there; indeed, most professional theatre artists believe that they have not established themselves until they have succeeded in New York's commercial houses. Consequently, the standards of American drama, acting, directing, and design are largely defined by the work that reaches and succeeds on Broadway. A further testament to its authority in matters theatrical is the effect of those who strive to imitate it. Many communities regularly import recent Broadway hits by booking the traveling theatrical companies that each year crisscross the country. Although such road shows seldom employ the original Broadway performers, they do use seasoned professionals, and since they travel with complete sets and costumes, they are usually able to offer polished performances seldom seen by audiences outside of New York. Broadway plays, too, form the staple of most dinner theatres and many community theatres. Such groups, because of restrictions on space and budget, tend to favor small-cast, one-set shows whose aim is to divert rather than instruct.

Its Plays. The richness and variety of its offerings may finally be Broadway's most exciting quality. A tourist coming into the city and wanting to see all of the productions playing on Broadway would have to attend the theatre six nights a week for over a month. In a recent week, for example, Broadway boasted thirty different shows. In such a typical week, about one third of the thirty were successes continued from recent seasons; somewhat fewer than one half were new plays that had either opened on Broadway or moved there after earning critical acclaim in London, in a regional theatre, or Off-Broadway; one or two were classics, either from the foreign theatre (Shakespeare, Molière, Shaw) or from earlier Broadway. Among the thirty productions, playgoers would almost certainly have found something suiting their tastes, for sprinkled among lavish musicals and sparkling comedies were an occasional mystery, biography, or serious drama.

The Musicals. Broadway is probably best known for its musicals, most of which appear intent on outdoing their predecessors in lavishness and expense. In 1956, the cost of producing *My Fair Lady* was $401,000, a figure that at the time seemed staggering. In 1964, the original production of *Fiddler on the Roof* cost $380,000; in 1976, its revival cost $700,000. The same year an ill-fated *Hellzapoppin'* was capitalized at $900,000, failed to survive until opening night, and lost over $1.2 million for its investors.

Despite the rising costs of production, musicals dominated the Broadway stage during the 1960s and 1970s. *Camelot* (1960) opened the period on a note of romanticism and idealism, which musicals like *Hello, Dolly* (1964), *Fiddler on the Roof* (1964), *Funny Girl* (1964), *The Man of La Mancha* (1965), and *Mame* (1966) echoed. The Broadway production of *Hair* (1967) marked a turning point of sorts, since it departed markedly from what was previously considered acceptable for a commercial musical. With the Broadway production of *A Chorus Line* (1975), it became clear that *Hair* was not a fluke and that "the typical Broadway musical" of old was no longer the only formula for a commercial success. To highlight the shifts in both the form and content of musicals, *The Man of La Mancha, Hair,* and *A Chorus Line* can be briefly compared.

The Man of La Mancha retells Cervantes' story of the gallant, charming, and slightly mad knight, Don Quixote. The play opens with Cervantes in prison, threatened by fellow inmates. To placate them and save his manuscript, Cervantes tells them the story of Don Quixote, transforming himself into the errant knight and shuttling back and forth between Cervantes and Don Quixote for the rest of the play. As Quixote, the character proudly rides his horse, defends the honor of his beloved Dulcinea, and recollects, in his age, the glories of his youth. From the lusty song "Man of La Mancha" to the stirring "The Impossible Dream," the gallant Quixote searches for honor and truth in the land of his imagination. The role of Cervantes/Don Quixote was an excellent vehicle for an actor/singer like Richard Kiley. The barroom brawl sparked by the strumpet Aldonza (whom Quixote sees as Dulcinea) provides the excuse for an intricately choreographed dance. In short, *The Man of La Mancha* presented the life story of a remarkable, affecting, heroic character, engaged in a series of quests and misadventures, by means of songs, dances, costumes, lighting, and scenery, integrated into a piece of popular musical theatre. Its focus on a major character, reliance

Figure 4–5. Broadway Musical. "Hair," 1967. *(Photo by Martha Swope.)*

on a strong story line, and use of rather elaborate spectacle made it fairly typical of the Broadway musicals of its day.

   Hair (1967) did not depend on star performers, glittering costumes, elaborate special effects, or even an interesting story. Produced first Off-Broadway by Joseph Papp, *Hair* portrayed a group of impoverished but affable hippies as they lived and loved together against a background of drug use, civil disobedience, war in Vietnam, and the military draft. Its liberal use of four-letter words, the gentle fun it poked at organized religion and government, and its unselfconscious display of nude bodies made it both controversial and provoking. For many, *Hair* came to symbolize all that was wrong with the society of the 1960s; for others, it epitomized the hope of the future, where hypocrisy and faulty values would fall before the power of love, trust, and cooperation. Certainly its success, in part based on scandal, marked a turning point in American theatre, for its acceptance hastened the end of many of the taboos of language, nudity, and sex in the commercial American theatre.

   As *Hair* was to the 1960s, *A Chorus Line* (1975) was to the 1970s. Moved to Broadway after achieving considerable acclaim in a production at Joseph Papp's Public Theatre, *A Chorus Line* also told the lives and hardships of a group, in this case dancers who found themselves together at an audition for a Broadway musical. Really little more than a loosely knit series of personally revealing monologues, *A Chorus Line* dazzled audiences through the energy of its dance and touched them with the intimacy of its revelations. Somewhere between a revue and a play, *A Chorus Line* accelerated Broadway's

Figure 4–6. Broadway Musical. "A Chorus Line," 1975. *(Photo by Martha Swope.)*

love affair with dance and spawned such imitations as *Ain't Misbehavin'*, *Dancin'*, and *The American Dance Machine*. Significantly, by the late 1970s, with the notable exception of Hal Prince, every major director of musicals on Broadway was also a choreographer.

Serious Plays. By contrast, the 1960s and 1970s were not noteworthy for their nonmusical offerings. Among the best of the period were those imported from the London stage, especially the works of the English director Peter Brook and the English playwright Harold Pinter. Two productions of Brook's in particular attracted attention: *The Persecution and Assassination of Marat As Performed by the Inmates of the Asylum of Charenton Under the Direction of the Marquis de Sade* (usually shortened to *Marat/Sade*, 1964) and Shakespeare's *A Midsummer Night's Dream* (1970). In both productions, Brook adopted staging techniques considered nontraditional and thus cemented his growing international reputation as a forward-looking, innovative artist. The plays of Harold Pinter perplexed and delighted American audiences, as they had Londoners. *The Birthday Party* (1961), *The Caretaker* (1961), *The Homecoming* (1967), *Old Times* (1971), and *No Man's Land* (1975) established Pinter's reputation as a major figure in contemporary dramatic literature.

The American playwright most often touted for greatness in the same period is Edward Albee. Certainly his early works were strong: *Who's Afraid of Virginia Woolf?* (1962), *Ballad of the Sad Cafe* (1963), *Tiny Alice* (1963), and *A Delicate Balance* (1966). But *Box and Quotations from Chairman Mao Tse Tung* (1968), *All Over* (1971), and *Seascape* (1974) failed to win similar acclaim.

Beginning in the 1970s, David Rabe attracted attention from critics with

Figure 4–7. Broadway Drama. Edward Albee's *Seascape* as staged at Wayne State University. *(Directed by Robert T. Hazzard, designs by Tony Eldis and Susan Lambeth.)*

works like *Sticks and Bones* (1971), *The Basic Training of Pavlo Hummel* (1973), and *Streamers* (1977). In all three plays, Rabe represented the military as dehumanizing, violent, and relentless. The first two plays, which were first performed at Joe Papp's Public Theatre, unfolded against the war in Vietnam. Pavlo, the lonely soldier from a broken home who is trained to kill so efficiently, is himself blown away by a hand grenade hurled into the brothel that he patronizes. Neither missed nor mourned, Pavlo dies, as he has lived, without roots and without purpose. David, in *Sticks and Bones,* has survived the war but is blinded. His wound forces him to see clearly, perhaps for the first time, the callousness of his own family. Their inane conversations reveal an indifference to suffering that the maimed veteran finds obscene; the family, for its part, is merely perplexed by David's incomprehensible anger and considers him maladjusted. Produced for public television after its stage debut, *Sticks and Bones* provoked controversy among the public and the press over its portrayal of the American way of life. In *Streamers,* Rabe returned to military training to display the violent tensions that threaten to flare whenever diverse lifestyles and values collide. Love and hate, cruelty and compassion surface as expressions of the hostilities caused when alcohol, homosexuality, and racism mix in the confined world of the army barracks. All three plays are powerful and indicate that Rabe may well earn a place among America's best dramatists.

With few exceptions, however, no new major American playwrights

	Nobel Prize	Pulitzer Prize	Drama Critics Circle	Tonys	Obies
1960	NA	Fiorello! (a musical)	Toys in the Attic	The Miracle Worker	The Connection
1961	NA	All the Way Home	All the Way Home	Becket*	The Blacks*
1962	NA	How to Succeed in Business Without Really Trying (a musical)	The Night of the Iguana	A Man for All Seasons*	NA
1963	NA	NA	Who's Afraid of Virginia Woolf?	Who's Afraid of Virginia Woolf?	NA
1964	Jean-Paul Sartre*	NA	Luther*	Luther*	Play†
1965	NA	The Subject Was Roses	The Subject Was Roses	The Subject Was Roses	The Old Glory
1966	NA	NA	Marat/Sade*	Marat/Sade*	The Journey of the Fifth Horse
1967	NA	A Delicate Balance	The Homecoming*	The Homecoming*	Futz, Eh?* and La Turista*
1968	NA	NA	Rosencrantz & Guildenstern Are Dead*	Rosencrantz & Guildenstern Are Dead*	The Memorandum*
1969	Samuel Beckett*	The Great White Hope	The Great White Hope	The Great White Hope	Used no categories

NA denotes no award made to a play or a playwright that year.
* Denotes a foreign play or playwright.
† Until 1964, three categories (American, foreign, and musical) were used; after 1964, the categories normally collapsed into two only, best play and best musical play.

emerged during the twenty-year period. Some earlier authors continued to produce (for example, Tennessee Williams and Lillian Hellman), and some new plays were cited for excellence. But it must be admitted that during the years 1960 to 1980, America produced few major plays or playwrights of consequence, as a brief summary of awards can attest. Achievement in drama and theatre has been recognized formally for some time by means of five major awards: (1) the Nobel Prize in Literature, a prestigious international award from the Swedish Academy of Literature, presented annually to a poet, novelist, or playwright; (2) the Pulitzer Prize in Letters, awarded annually by Columbia University for the original American play performed in New York that best represents the educational value and power of the stage; (3) the Drama Critics Circle Award, given each year to the best plays in New York as determined by the drama critics of selected newspapers and magazines; (4) the Antoinette Perry ("Tony") Awards, given annually to honor outstanding contributions to the current theatrical season (includes artists as well as plays); and (5) the Obie (Off-Broadway) Awards, presented annually since 1956 to recognize achievement in the Off-Broadway theatre (sponsored by the *Village Voice*).

Reproduced in the table is a summary of the annual awards given between 1960 and 1970. The relatively low status of serious American drama during the period is indicated by the number of groups declining to give awards in some years and by the relatively high percentage of awards going to plays of foreign origin. Awards for the decade of the 1970s followed the same general pattern.

Comedy. In comedy, the story was rather happier, primarily because of Neil Simon, a playwright who has been phenomenally successful with audiences if somewhat less so with the critics. Early plays like *Come Blow Your Horn* (1961) and *Barefoot in the Park* (1963) were soon joined by his most popular works, *The Odd Couple* (1965), *Star-Spangled Girl* (1966), *Plaza Suite* (1968), *Last of the Red Hot Lovers* (1970), and *The Gingerbread Lady* (1970). Simon's particular comic gift is an ability to display the daily problems of ordinary city dwellers in a sympathetic yet funny way, converting their frustration and woe into hilarious situations unfolding by means of wisecracks and urbane one-liners. Although Simon's later plays, like *The Prisoner of Second Avenue* (1976) and *Chapter Two* (1978), have a serious quality absent from his earlier works, the zany humor still pokes through, tickling audiences and earning box office dollars. In the 1976–1977 season, for example, Simon's *California Suite* returned a hefty 360 per cent, while its nearest competitor, Harold Pinter's *No Man's Land,* gave back 160 per cent. Simon's magic makes him a valuable commodity among theatrical producers.

Although no other comic writer produced a string of hits to equal Simon's, several scored successes. Jean Kerr (wife of critic/reviewer Walter Kerr) attracted a following with *Mary, Mary* (1961) *Poor Richard* (1964), and *Finishing Touches* (1973). Robert Anderson, whose earlier play *Tea and Sympathy* (1953) had established him as a promising writer, showed his comic skills with *You Know I Can't Hear You When the Water's Running* (1967). Comparing the popular comedies of the 1960s with comic works of the 1970s such as *And*

Miss Reardon Drinks a Little (Paul Zindel, 1971), *Six Rms Riv Vu* (Bob Randall, 1972), and *Same Time, Next Year* (Bernard Slade, 1975) suggests that the shift noted during Simon's career may have been repeated in other comedies: the lighthearted tone of the early 1960s was exchanged for more biting and more thoughtful dramatic comedies.

The Business of Broadway. Broadway theatre is big business, and money is at the root of many of its problems. The costs of producing there have long been awesome, and they continue to climb relentlessly. Several factors have contributed to the soaring costs. As real estate in Manhattan became more expensive, the cost of theatre space went up. Professionals in the theatre developed unions to look after their interests, and as their power increased, the salaries and fees of almost everyone associated with production rose dramatically. For example, during the ten years between 1966 and 1976, salaries and fees climbed 168 per cent. Moreover, the unions established protective regulations whereby they dictated the tasks and hours as well as the salaries of their members. For example, every Broadway production is required by the unions to employ a scenic designer and every Broadway theatre is contracted to hire a specified number of technicians (usually a minimum of five or six). Even if the producers envisioned a show needing no set and no technicians, the union regulations require that persons be hired for the designated positions. Such rules obviously contribute to higher costs. The price of materials for production (lumber for scenery, fabrics for costumes) rose with the rate of inflation and helped account for the accelerating expense of getting a show mounted on Broadway.

The complexity of opening a show and the expenses anticipated prior to opening can be better understood, perhaps, from an examination of the finances of a single play. The budget shown here was developed for one of the four least expensive shows to open on Broadway during 1976.

Fees and Advances	$ 11,500
Scenery design, costume design, lighting design, director, legal, auditing, author	
Salaries, cast and crew	11,600
Physical production	10,700
Theater expenses	12,800
Rehearsal expenses	2,600
Advertising and promotional expenses	6,500
General and administrative expenses	7,300
Equity, ATPAM, IATSE, box office union bonds	16,000
Total estimated production expenses	79,000
Reserve for possible preopening losses	21,000
Total capitalization	$100,000

Once open, the show needed approximately $28,000 additionally each week of its run. In a theatre seating 499 persons, the maximum projected income was only $51,000 each week (499 seats per performance × performances per week × $13.00 average price per ticket). Allowing an additional $5,000 for advertising costs after opening and assuming that the projected expenses and income are both sound, the show would require a minimum of six weeks to break even ($51,000 − (5,000 + 28,310) = $17,690 per week over expenses, which, multiplied by six weeks is slightly more than $100,-000).

The soaring costs of production account for a number of the practices now associated with Broadway. The long run, for example, became a necessity when shows required many performances to recoup their initial investment. One theatre businessman estimated that a play taking ten weeks to break even in 1956 would have required twenty weeks by 1976, and that a musical taking fifteen to twenty-five weeks in 1956 would have required a year or more by the mid-1970s. Even a very frugal show needed a minimum run of six weeks with the theatre playing to full capacity in order to break even. In fact, this show closed in less than six weeks and played to less than capacity, losing money for its investors. In this way, it was typical: few Broadway plays last even as long as six weeks, and of those that do, almost none plays to capacity audiences. Theatrical investment is a risky business indeed.

Broadway's Practices and Problems. The smash hit or the dismal flop has become a Broadway pattern. Each investor's dream, of course, is to sponsor a show like *Godspell* (1971), which returned over 20,000 per cent to its investors; but in fact most shows lose money. And as prices skyrocket, investors stand to gain (or more often to lose) vast sums of money, and so they try to minimize their risks. They avoid using people or practices with a record of failure, and they prefer to work with formulas and personnel shown to be successful in the past. Big-name playwrights and performers will usually draw people into the theatre, it is believed, thereby ensuring some early sales. It is for economic reasons, therefore, that the established playwright can get a hearing, while the unknown author cannot, and that a star will get a role that a talented newcomer might be able to play better. Since large casts cost money in costumes as well as salaries, plays that require only two or three or four characters can represent a considerable saving. And so Broadway has come to favor the small-cast, one-set show like *Gin Game* (1978) or *Cold Storage* (1978). Plays with a proven record as money-makers elsewhere are also appealing to investors, and as a result many recent hits from the London stage and the noncommercial American theatre join past hits from Broadway to make up most of a Broadway season. Since tourists and other groups can be sold tickets to a show even before it opens, scripts aimed to appeal to these often conservative, middle-class groups are frequently more favorably considered than are innovative or otherwise controversial works, and playwrights are encouraged to model their new works on lines acceptable to "middle America." In sum, the finances on Broadway affect every aspect of the production, from the plays selected, to the performers cast, to the decisions about scenery, costumes, and properties.

Rising costs of production have also had an effect on the cost of theatregoing. Ticket prices have increased repeatedly over the last two decades, until by the mid-1970s a musical that could have been seen for $12 in the 1960s cost between $20 and $25 by the late 1970s. Obviously, as ticket prices rise, some people can no longer afford to purchase them, and so the audience tends to become limited to the upper and upper-middle classes; the playwrights and producers more often devise productions to appeal to the tastes of this group. Eventually, rising prices for tickets may reach a point of diminishing return, where more people are prevented from buying tickets than new increases in price can offset. That point does not seem to have been reached yet, but when it is, other ways of meeting the mounting costs of production will have to be found.

Money is also at the base of a rather different sort of problem. Broadway has long suffered as others drained it of its best resources. For a long time, Broadway's best talents and its sure-fire hits have been transported to Hollywood, where the film industry has adapted them to its needs. Later, television joined film as an alternate outlet for performers, dramas, and dramatists. With their insatiable appetites for new artists and materials, film and television, but particularly television, have plundered the most successful products of the legitimate stage. Some artists, like Neil Simon, have been able to continue to work on the stage even while working in films and adding to television's fare. Simon wrote *The Goodbye Girl* (1978) and *The Cheap Detective* (1978) especially for film, and *The Odd Couple,* originally written for the stage, was later made into a film and then adapted and serialized for evening television.

Some actors, too, like Henry Fonda, George C. Scott, and Al Pacino, have moved easily from stage to screen and back again. However, the lure of bigger money in films and television has taken many away from the legitimate theatre permanently, and in these instances, the loss to the stage has become a problem of some magnitude.

Solutions and Alternatives. In the 1960s and 1970s, people who cared about theatre worried about its problems and worked for solutions. The Theatre Development Fund was established in 1967 to support commercial productions of particularly high artistic worth. TKTS and the Lower Manhattan Theatre Center were begun so that patrons could buy tickets at half price on the day of performance for shows not sold to capacity. Computerization of ticket sales was planned, at an estimated cost of $3–4 million, so that out-of-towners could compete equally with New Yorkers in obtaining good seats for any production. New York City offered incentives for constructing new theatre buildings. The success of these improvements, both contemplated and completed, cannot yet be gauged, but the early signs are encouraging.

A number of people believe, however, that no halfway alterations will ever change Broadway's basically commercial structure and that Broadway's reliance on the profit motive will always plague it. In the past, such persons have rejected Broadway and have moved to provide alternatives to it in the form of smaller, less commercial theatres. Although some alternative theatres were formed as early as the 1920s, the major impetus in that direction

Figure 4–8. Broadway Business: Problems and Solutions. The TKTS cutrate ticket booth in New York's Times Square was one solution to Broadway's financial problems of the sixties and early seventies.

has occurred since the 1950s, when Off-Broadway began to flourish and provide an escape from the economic pressures of Broadway, which, for some, threatened to smother innovation and creativity.

Off-Broadway

If the bete noir *of Broadway is its openness to commercialism, the specter that now threatens off-Broadway is its openness to sheer opportunism.*   Walter Kerr, 1961

The name *Off-Broadway* derived from the location of its theatres, which lay outside the borders of the regular Times Square theatre district. In addition to location, Off-Broadway houses were contractually defined by their limited seating capacity (no more than 299 seats) and by their lower salaries (substantially below Broadway minimums, through special arrangement with Actors Equity and other unions). But most importantly, the goals of the Off-Broadway houses differed from those of Broadway. Off-Broadway wished to serve as a showcase for new talents: untried actors could perform; new directors could work; established artists could experiment with new techniques; original plays could find production. Too, these theatres were determined to remain aloof from threats of censorship and enticements of large profits. Instead, they strove to be a theatre for artists and audiences who were serious about the art of theatre and anxious to develop and operate from consistent artistic policies so that some continuity of offerings and performers could develop.

Some faint stirrings of an Off-Broadway movement were detectable in the late 1940s, but the theatres were legitimized in 1952 when Tennessee Williams's *Summer and Smoke* (with actress Geraldine Page) gained critical acclaim in a production at the Circle in the Square. This was the first major hit in a theatre located below Forty-second Street in thirty years. By the mid-1960s, Off-Broadway boasted thirty theatres, a string of hits that it had contributed to the Broadway theatre, and the regular attention of the city's theatrical reviewers.

Among the best-known works presented Off-Broadway during the decade of the 1960s were the popular musicals *The Fantasticks* (1960), *Hair* (1967), *You're a Good Man Charlie Brown* (1967), and *Jaques Brel Is Alive and Well And Living in Paris* (1968). But Off-Broadway of the 1960s also provided a place where potentially controversial works could be aired; and so *MacBird*, a bitter (even scandalous) version of Kennedy's assassination, found production there in 1967, and *The Boys in the Band*, a comic, frank, and sympathetic

Figure 4–9. Off-Broadway. The longest-running musical of New York's theatre is "The Fantasticks," here in a production at the University of Northern Iowa. *(Directed by D. Terry Williams.)*

Figure 4–10. **Off-Broadway Plays.** Successful Off-Broadway productions sometimes moved to Broadway and became a regular part of the regional and university theatre repertories. *Vanities* at the University of South Carolina. *(Directed by James A. Patterson.)*

portrait of homosexual communities, opened in 1968. Other significant works and playwrights enjoying Off-Broadway production during the decade included: *The Day the Whores Came Out to Play Tennis* (Arthur Kopit, 1965), *The Old Glory* (Robert Lowell, 1964), *The Zoo Story* (Edward Albee, 1960), *The Tiger* and *The Typists* (Murray Schisgal, 1963), *America Hurrah* (Jean-Claude van Itallie, 1967) and *The Indian Wants the Bronx* and *It's Called the Sugar Plum* (Israel Horowitz, 1968).

By the mid-1960s, however, Off-Broadway was itself suffering from its successes. Although it continued to offer employment and opportunities to new actors, directors, and playwrights (producing on the average two shows for every one done on Broadway), its production costs began to spiral. Over its short lifetime, its preproduction expenses had risen from a modest $1,500 average to a significant $15,000; its weekly operating costs had more than tripled, moving from an average of $1,000 to $3,200. Furthermore, as one-shot producers came on the scene and experimentation ceased to be financially practical, Off-Broadway seemed less "a place to do your own thing," as George Cram Cook had early hoped, and more like a less expensive version of Broadway. By the mid-1970s, Off-Broadway successes were regularly moving to Broadway, and the early distinctions between the two blurred still further.

Nontraditional Theatres

Off-Off-Broadway

As Off-Broadway moved closer to Broadway—in practice if not in location—some artists felt the need again for an alternative theatre where authors, directors, and actors could work closely together to produce plays in a relatively uncomplicated environment. In the late 1950s, Joe Cino opened his coffeehouse to poetry readings and dramatic productions. Soon, other coffeehouses, lofts, cellars, and churches, tucked away in Greenwich Village and scattered into the East Village, were pressed into service as theatres. Here young writers were allowed to explore subjects, characters, and themes forbidden by the finances and traditions of Broadway and Off-Broadway. Off-Off-Broadway declared itself dedicated to the process of creating art as well as to the product and to exploring the possibilities afforded by the medium of theatre. Too, Off-Off-Broadway was not interested in becoming merely a tryout place for Broadway.

Ellen Stewart at Cafe La Mama, Al Carmines at the Judson Poet's Theatre, Michael Allen and Ralph Cook at Theatre Genesis, Richard Schechner at the Performance Garage, and Joseph Chaikin with the Open Theatre all promoted theatres where new playwrights could test materials and where other artists could examine the limits of their art. Although sometimes amateurish and often trivial, the offerings of Off-Off-Broadway provided an alternative to the commercialism of both the Broadway and the Off-Broadway houses throughout the 1960s and 1970s.

Many of the experimental groups and political theatres of the 1960s and 1970s whose impact on theatre has been greatest were products of the so-called Off-Off-Broadway movement. But the same impulses that gave rise to the movement in New York City were operating in other parts of this country and abroad, and so nontraditional theatres arose in England, France, Canada, and Poland as well as in the United States.

Experimental Theatres

In every age, a minority is dissatisfied and calls for change, and so in every age, some people exist outside the mainstream and experiment with new ways of seeing, understanding, and doing. The art of theatre is no exception to this general pattern.

Certainly experimental theatres have a past, but the decades of the 1960s and 1970s saw an unprecedented number of such groups organizing and producing plays. What they shared was an interest in changing the traditional, commercial theatre epitomized by New York's Broadway, London's West End, or Paris's Boulevard. What they did not share was a common solution to the problems they identified. For this reason, not only were the groups numerous, they were also diverse, adopting different working methods, selecting different kinds of plays, arranging themselves in various performing spaces, and formulating a welter of theoretical and critical positions.

The groups viewed the commercial theatre in all countries as merely a diversionary entertainment, devoted to lavish musicals, trite comedies, and sentimentalized portrayals of domestic unhappiness. The audience for this commercial theatre was believed to be drawn largely from the middle and upper-middle classes, who looked upon theatre as little more than an excuse to flee the problems of the real world by entering the sanitized universe of bland art. For these audiences, many subjects were taboo, and by general consent, profanity, nudity, obscenity, and sexuality were avoided or delivered gingerly and politely. Too, during the twenty years, worldwide inflation combined with increased salaries and ever-more-spectacular productions to drive ticket prices higher, virtually guaranteeing that the masses of people could not attend the theatre even if they wanted to. And it was a troublesome fact of life that live theatre was no longer the first choice of entertainment for scores of people. Athletic events, rock concerts, television, and film were competing successfully, probably too successfully, for the time and money of many persons seeking diversion. The conclusion reached by some thoughtful artists and scholars was that the commercial theatre was in trouble and that if theatre was to survive, serious attention had to be paid to correcting its shortcomings.

On these general points and on the need to correct them, almost everyone agreed. But on how to improve the situation, the experimenters held few views in common. Different groups formed to attack different problems and to explore alternative solutions to the same problems. Although the emphases varied, most groups addressed one or more of these four questions: (1) What is theatre? (2) Where should theatre be done and for whom? (3) How should theatre get produced? (4) What part should the script play in performance?

Defining theatre meant distinguishing it from other forms of art and establishing those characteristics that are essential (rather than accidental) to its practice. To answer the first major question—"What is theatre?"—

Figure 4–11. Nontraditional Theatre. *Jumpers* by Tom Stoppard, produced by the American Conservatory Theatre. *(Photo: Bill Ganslen, San Francisco.)*

then, required that a number of secondary questions be addressed. The major of these were: How does theatre differ from other performing arts? From the electronic media? From life? What are its limits? Its boundaries? What is at the core of the art? How much physical production can be eliminated and still leave good theatre? Any sort of theatre?

The second major question—"Where should theatre be done and for whom?"—implied that an audience is central to the theatrical event. To discover the audience's role in the event was a major goal of several groups. In attempting to answer this question, groups posed subsidiary questions, like: Is theatre an activity or a place? Should it be done indoors or outdoors, or does it matter? Should it be done in a special place or anywhere at all? Are some arrangements of actors and audience better than others? If so, which are better and under what circumstances? Is there a single ideal audience to which the performance should be geared, or are there several specific audiences? Are there limits on the size of an audience? If there are, upon what are these limits dependent? How are spectators different from performers? Must they be different?

Theatre, unlike musical composition or painting, is a group art, and some of its problems relate to its collaborative nature. Attempts to cope with the difficulties generated when a team of artists work together lie at the heart of the third major question—"How should theatre get produced?" The answer in turn requires the answers to questions like: Should theatre artists specialize in roles like actor, scenic designer, director, and playwright, or should they all contribute in each area? Should the traditional theatre hierarchy (of theatre specialists headed by a director) be replaced by a group effort in which all contribute equally? Should artists live together as well as work together?

The appropriate relationship between the written script and the performed event has been a theoretical issue dating from the ancients. To answer the fourth major question—"What is the part that the script should play in performance?"—groups posed related questions like: Is the script really a text, or is it a pretext? Is it necessary? What values, if any, should it promote? How heavily should its impact depend on language? How can it be unified? Which ways are most effective and in which situations? By what means does a play best affect spectators: should it address its appeals to the head, the heart, or the viscera?

In striving to answer such questions, experimental theatres developed techniques that served to characterize them and set them apart from the traditional commercial theatres. Experimental groups tended to scorn profit as a reason for doing theatre, preferring to make the theatrical event its own justification. Members of the group regarded theatre as a mission rather than a job, and so they often worked harder for less money than did traditional artists. The groups seldom used traditional scripts, either old or new, but when they did, they altered the texts in production until the originals were scarcely recognizable. The usual relationship between performers and spectators was modified, although the nature of the modifications varied widely.

During the 1960s and 1970s, many experimental groups were created,

Figure 4–12. Nontraditional Theatre. The Bread and Puppet Theatre, performing outdoors at the University of Kansas. *(Photo by Ronald A. Willis.)*

flourished, and—often—died. The life of an experiment is sometimes short, but the shortness does not negate its accomplishments. The major experimental groups of the period included the Bread and Puppet Theatre (Peter Schumann), the Byrd Hoffman School of Byrds (Robert Wilson), Cafe La Mama (Ellen Stewart), the International Center of Theatre Research (Peter Brook), the Performance Group (Richard Schechner), the Polish Laboratory Theatre (Jerzy Grotowski), the Ridiculous Theatrical Company (Charles Ludlam), and the Story Theatre (Paul Sills). To suggest the wide range of practices included within the class called experimental theatre, four of these groups will be considered in further detail: the Polish Laboratory Theatre, the Open Theatre, the Ontological-Hysteric Theatre, and the Ridiculous Theatrical Company. Not all of these four are still active, and probably none will prove to be permanent.

Certain other groups also employed some of these nontraditional approaches to production but did so in order to develop theatre as an effective instrument for bringing about social or political change. Since their aims were different, they will be discussed separately as political theatres. Only groups whose primary goals related to the investigation of the nature of theatrical art will be considered "experimental."

Jerzy Grotowski and the Polish Laboratory Theatre. Of the many experimental groups that sprang up during the 1960s and 1970s, Grotowski's Polish Laboratory Theatre was one of the most influential. Formed in 1959 in Wroclaw (Breslau), the group did not appear in an English-speaking country until 1968, and its American influence is normally dated from that performance. Grotowski's impact was immediate and profound. His book *Towards a Poor Theatre* became a major guide for experimentalists abroad and in the United States. Richard Schechner of the Performance Group was his principal American adherent, and since Schechner was also editor of *The Drama Review,* a leading journal in contemporary theatre, Grotowski theories and practices were widely disseminated.

Grotowski early showed an interest in probing the nature of traditional theatre. (After the early 1970s, his interest shifted elsewhere.) To the question "What is theatre?" Grotowski answered that only two elements were essential: the actor and the audience. He therefore advocated stripping away all external trappings (scenery, lighting, costumes) and producing instead a "poor theatre."

Obviously, in the absence of the customary music, makeup, and costumes, the actors would be called upon to create the world of the play and the truth of their characters using only themselves: their voices, bodies, and imaginations. Because of the great demands placed on his performers, Grotowski took personal responsibility for their training. He drew from such disparate sources as Hatha Yoga, Japanese No, Indian Kathakali, Peking opera, and Roman Catholicism to devise a regimen for preparing them physically and mentally to perform in his theatre. He encouraged them to strip away all protective devices, all masks that they might hide behind, all qualities that might obscure the truth about them from other people or themselves. He expected from his actors nothing less than "an exposure carried to outrageous excess." Called the *via negativa,* this removal of disguises and defenses supposedly opened the way for a genuine communion among the actors within the company and between the company and its audience. Because Grotowski's actors were to give themselves to the audience completely, "totally, in . . . deepest intimacy, with confidence, as when one gives oneself in love," it is not surprising that some in the company began to compare acting with sacrifice and martyrdom.

As the other essential element of a poor theatre, audiences were treated carefully and respectfully by Grotowski. He strictly limited the number of spectators at any performance, he arranged them differently for different plays and different spaces, and he encouraged them to become directly involved in the production. For example, on some occasions, the process of seating spectators became a formal part of the theatrical event, as when they were led by a member of the company to a specific place in the room and somewhat ceremoniously abandoned. Such seating, both solemn and repetitive, took on an aspect of ritual—a word with religious overtones that had increasing importance to theatre during the period.

After 1973, Grotowski became increasingly interested in breaking down the usual distinctions between performer and spectator. To this end, he experimented with a variety of "paratheatrical" (theatre-like or theatre-related) activities in which the traditional separation of actors and audiences was eliminated. This new direction was a logical extension of his past work. "Poor theatre" resulted from the elimination of all unnecessary physical accoutrements to the production. The *via negativa* urged actors to eliminate all blocks that separated them from the truth about themselves and from open communion with one another. With both the theatrical event and the performers purified, the only falsification remaining was the spectator, who continued to remain apart and play a role. It was this final distinction that Grotowski sought to eliminate. His company, therefore, divided into "cells" and began vigorous personal research into a new performing art, one freed from the supposedly undesirable split between performer and viewer. Obviously such a departure required a different vocabulary, and so Grotowski began to talk of "meetings" rather than performances, "challenges" rather than theatres, and "those who are prepared" rather than actors.

Even while Grotowski sought a theatre stripped of all inessential elements, he strove for one that was holy and sacred, one capable of portraying humanity's suffering and its ethical plights, its search for meaning and its moral imperatives. Its performances were to be spiritual, its assumptions existential. In practice, Grotowski's performances typically lasted fifty minutes and, at least early in his career, were based on traditional plays that he redefined and rewrote to examine their validity for contemporary society. For example, the group's most famous work was *The Constant Prince,* a romantic play written by a Polish author of the nineteenth century. In Grotowski's production, the original text was vastly altered, indeed almost obliterated, and in its place was a theatrical piece rich in allusions, images, and symbols designed to evoke an experience at once spiritual and communal, not unlike those sought currently in churches and formerly in tribal ceremonies.

Grotowski, then, believed that theatre was important in the life of people, that it should help them confront their own humanity. He looked upon it as akin to religion in that it dealt with people's quest for meaning in life, with their needs for both community and self-definition. Participation in such a theatre required a serious commitment on the part of both actors and audiences, and in his view, only those willing and able to make it should form a part of the new performing art.

Since Grotowski's call for simplification of theatre was widely disseminated through journals and workshops, his "poor theatre" made considerable impact during the 1960s and 1970s. The influence of his later work cannot yet be assessed. Certainly the Research University, which he organized in 1975, served to introduce many directors and teachers to the group's paratheatrical activities, but whether or not these techniques will find acceptance and to what degree will not become clear for several years.

Joseph Chaikin and the Open Theatre. Joseph Chaikin formed the "open" theatre in 1963 as an alternative to the "closed" theatre of Broadway. Like Grotowski, Chaikin thought traditional theatre was overburdened with inessential items, and he therefore worked for a performance in which primary focus was on the actor and his art. Although in theory all members of the group were to participate equally, in practice Chaikin's influence predominated from the outset and the theatre is seldom discussed apart from him.

Chaikin began in theatre as an actor trained in the "Method," itself a reinterpretation of Stanislavski's acting system (see pp. 148–150). After a period of studying, working Off-Broadway, and touring with the Living Theatre (see the section, "The Living Theatre"), Chaikin decided that traditional acting and actors' training were inadequate to the needs of the art, and that politicizing the theatre seemed to introduce more problems than it solved. Consequently he declined to accompany the Living Theatre on its foreign tour in 1964 and instead formed a new group that was to be open, susceptible to change, and devoted to the *process* (rather than the *product*) of theatre. It would also avoid what he believed to be the traps of political theatres.

From the beginning, the purpose of the group was to teach and learn about the nature of theatre rather than to perform plays for the general public. Specifically their workshops sought to experiment with the process of acting and the methods of teaching it and, at the same time, to explore the nature of theatre, its interfaces with life and with the other narrative and performing arts. When the group did appear in public, they used virtually no scenery, costumes, makeup, or special effects, relying instead upon the physical resources of their acting group to create the world of play.

The Open Theatre specifically addressed the question of how theatre should come about. Chaikin and his actors concluded that the plays and performances should evolve from the efforts of a group of artists working together. Thus ensemble became the cornerstone of the Open Theatre. To achieve ensemble, the actors needed to learn to work as a unit rather than as individuals competing for the audience's attention (in the manner of starring performers on Broadway), and so the Open Theatre used a variety of theatre games and improvisations designed to develop sensitivity to group rhythms and dynamics, to increase mutual trust, and to replace competition with cooperation.

The playwright, too, was regarded as a member of the ensemble and was encouraged to develop texts *for* the group out of the ideas *of* the group. Typically the writer would provide a scenario (an outline of the situation) and the actors would improvise actions and dialogue. These improvisations might be repeated several times, and the writer would select the best of them, add new materials as needed, rearrange sections, and finally develop "the text." Because the script emerged from the ideas of the group, it presumably reflected their current feelings and concerns, primary among which were various social injustices (racism, sexism, crime) and the war in Vietnam. Although the plays varied enormously, many shared some combination of these characteristics: (1.) a unity achieved through exploring a central idea or theme rather than through telling a story; (2.) a rather free and often disconnected treatment of time and place as different episodes were presented; (3.) the use of transformations, a technique in which actors play first one character and then another without corresponding changes in costumes or makeup and without clear transitions provided by the dialogue; and (4.) a reliance on the actors to provide their own environment by "becoming" the setting and sounds (for example, an actor plays a sheep in a field, another a snake on a tree, several become the sirens of ambulances), transforming into objects and characters as needed.

From the Open Theatre came two of America's more famous nontraditional playwrights of the 1960s: Megan Terry, whose *Viet Rock* (1966) and *Calm Down Mother* (1966) were developed for the Open Theatre, and Jean-Claude Van Itallie, whose *America Hurrah* (1966) and *The Serpent* (1969) were among the group's best-known works. Ironically, it was in part the successes

Figure 4–13. Nontraditional Theatre. Jean-Claude Van Italie's *Interview*, originally a product of the Open Theatre. Produced at Elmira College. *(Directed by Jack Jenkins, design, Peter Lach.)*

of the new plays of the Open Theatre that produced the tensions leading to the group's dissolution in 1974.

The success of *Viet Rock* and *America Hurrah* made the group reevaluate its commitment to process over product. The temptation was to capitalize on success and continue public performances. Although the immediate temptations were resisted, thanks to outside funding from private foundations and government agencies, the tensions between the need to perform and the need to explore became progressively more evident. Chaikin himself recognized and addressed the problem: "It becomes a kind of responsibility: you undertake the responsibility of being a successful person. For us there was no impetus left to do anything else, to do any research: there was not the time or the space. We had been processed as a 'success.' " Rather than accepting the responsibility of success, rather than redefining the group, thereby fixing it and making it static, Chaikin decided to disband the group while its original goals were still more or less intact.

The purity of the group's commitment made it vulnerable, and its demise was perhaps inevitable. Nevertheless, in its ten years, the Open Theatre made several significant contributions to the American theatre. It introduced important new plays and playwrights to the public. It focused attention on the centrality of the actor in performance and on the willingness of audiences to substitute their imaginations for the usual physical accoutrements of production. It popularized theatre games and improvisations as techniques of actor training and as sources of group-inspired plays. Finally, it suggested that the traditional hierarchy (a director leading a team of theatrical specialists) was not the only way to organize for theatrical production.

Richard Foreman and the Ontological–Hysteric Theatre. *Ontology:* "the branch of knowledge that investigates being, its nature and essential properties." *Hysteria:* "a psychiatric condition variously marked by excessive anxiety with sensory and motor disturbances or by repressed emotion and dissociation." Considering the name of the theatre, it is not surprising that words like *interior, subjective,* and *mental* were often used in discussing the productions of this experimental group. The final lines of *Sophie* (1973), one of the theatre's best-known works, suggest both the goals of the company and its unusual style of production: coming from an invisible speaker, a taped voice intoned flatly, "The play is over. The play is over. Go home. Go home. Go home. Think about the play if you like. But go home."

Foreman, like Grotowski and Chaikin, was interested in reconsidering the nature of theatrical art and in exploring its boundaries. Unlike them, however, Foreman rejected the idea of collective or cooperative art and believed that the actor was simply one part of the total, an element to be manipulated along with words, scenery, lighting, and so forth. Foreman's was a theatre for a master artist, a writer/director, and Foreman himself was the primary creator. In describing his work, he concluded, "I'm basically interested in stating what's going on in my head while I'm writing the play." His working method allowed him to make the attempt. He conceived a work, wrote the text, designed and supervised the building of the sets, recorded the sound track, and directed the actors with meticulous care. Rehearsals were long and tedious as Foreman moved his actors like so many stage props, trying "every conceivable alternative to make the text say what I think it secretly wants to say." Actors were assigned stage positions and postures not on the basis of psychological relationships or internal motivations but according to the requirements of visual patterns, spatial configurations, form, and the like.

Foreman retained his control even during performances, since he personally manipulated the tape and slide presentations that structured most of his scripts, dictating the pace of both action and dialogue: cues depended on them, scenes changed by them; actors were impotent without them. Indeed, Foreman once remarked of performance, "Finally, the audience comes, and I am in front of my text, and they are watching me watch my text. . . . the performance is a CONTINUATION of my writing process." Understandably, perhaps, Foreman preferred to use untrained actors since they could be more easily molded to his desires, and he would accept almost anyone who volunteered to rehearse and perform with the group.

Whereas Grotowski and Chaikin rejected electronic sounds, illusionistic scenery, and elaborate stage lighting, Foreman embraces such elements to an uncommon degree. In seeking the boundaries of theatrical art, Foreman experimented with techniques normally associated with painting and film, exploring how they might be adapted for stage use. For example, traditional theatre relied on narratives (stories) to capture the interest of audiences

Figure 4–14. Off-Broadway. Richard Foreman's *Rhoda in Potatoland. (Photograph copyright © Babette Mangolt, 1975.)*

and move their attention forward, but Foreman preferred to create a series of stage moments that were static but richly detailed, filled with pictures and sounds. He used filmic techniques like off-screen narration and titles for scenes; he often disconnected sound and picture and usually controlled his actors by electronic means. For example, the plays' dialogue, such as there was, reached the audience through loudspeakers. Actors might echo occasional words or phrases, but the mechanically reproduced language, intruding seemingly from nowhere and reporting without inflection, clearly dominated. The actors moved from one tableau to another, often in a single plane; they frequently faced the audience in the manner of a photograph. Actors gazed at the audience or beyond it, suggesting some sort of mysterious hypnotic attachment to the assembled spectators. The effect resembled a slow-motion or stop-action film, a series of two-dimensional individual pictures unrolling slowly before the eyes of theatregoers.

Clearly, filmic techniques used in a theatre produced rather different effects. When successful, they made the stage seem distant and unfamiliar, thereby rendering it an object demanding contemplation. Indeed, contemplation, meditation, and reflection appear to be the responses that Foreman sought from his audiences. He said that in his productions, he strove to "show the mind at work, moment by moment, . . . evoke ever-subtler resources of perceptual discrimination, and give the theatre-goer a chance to notice, to visit, to reconnoiter . . . , to wake up and explore the world before him." He strove to create an art that compelled by the accumulation of details rather than by their rigid selection. He wanted every viewer to create some personal meaning from the multiple images and concurrent sounds that the stage offered so that each would be engaged in *an act of creation rather than reception.* The text for Foreman, then, was a stimulus, an encouragement to each individual audience member to create an independent and meaningful work of art.

Founded in 1968, the Ontological–Hysteric Theatre has more than a dozen works to its credit, among them *Total Recall* (1971), *HcOhTiEnLa,* or *Hotel China: Part I and II* (1971–1972), *Evidence* (1972), *Sophie-(Wisdom) Part 3: The Cliffs* (1972–1973), *Pain(t) (T)* (1974), *Vertical Mobility: Sophia (Wisdom) Part 4* (1974), *Pandering to the Masses* (1975), *Rhoda in Potatoland (Her Fall Starts)* (1975–1976). In each, Foreman demonstrated his interest in this new kind of theatre, one that layered sounds and images in order to lead the audience not to experience but to *understanding,* to that which undergirds (or *stands under*) human experience.

In addressing the four theoretical questions, then, Foreman arrived at answers very different from those given by Grotowski and Chaikin, and so the Ontological–Hysteric Theatre (like Robert Wilson's Byrd Hoffman's School of Byrds, which it resembled) provided a clear alternative to "poor theatre" and collective art, to specially trained actors and unusual performance spaces. Although its ultimate contribution to the American theatre cannot yet be assessed, the Ontological–Hysteric Theatre pointed a different direction that tomorrow's theatres might take and suggested another whole range of possibilities for continued exploration.

Charles Ludlam and the Ridiculous Theatrical Company. *"I really wanted to work in the theatre. . . . God, if I hadn't discovered theatre I would almost certainly have become a juvenile delinquent,"* explained Charles Ludlam, founder and mainstay of the Ridiculous Theatrical Company.

Most experimental groups are serious about their investigations into the nature of the art and about their search for new forms and styles of production, but Ludlam formed a company dedicated to the notion that neither art nor life should be taken too solemnly. He boasted, "I wanted to commit an outrage. For me, nothing was too far out." Indeed, *outrageous* is a word often applied to their productions, for the Ridiculous Theatrical Company is bizarre even when measured against Off-Off-Broadway standards.

The source of the outrage is often the concept of the play, as when Ludlam envisioned a "ridiculous opera" based loosely on Richard Wagner's Ring cycle. In Ludlam's production, the original Valkyries were transformed into lesbian motorcyclists and the German's Valhalla into New York's Lincoln Center, famed complex for the performing arts. But unconventional sex also contributes a share in titillating unwary audiences. For example, in Ludlam's production of *Conquest of the Universe, or When Queens Collide,* a friend recalled that "Every transvestite in New York . . . made an appearance. . . . Each one would show up backstage in elaborate costume, join the dance long enough for some friend out front to take a picture, and then disappear." Unexpected and shocking titles *(Turds in Hell)* combine with outlandish jokes

Figure 4–15. Off-Broadway. Black-Eyed Susan and Charles Ludlam in his own *Stage Blood*. *(Robert Beers photo.)*

("I don't think of myself as castrated. I think of myself as extremely well circumcised") to add to the ambiguous sexuality so firmly associated with the company's work. Breakneck pacing, visual slapstick, and verbal non sequiturs (qualities that characterize the company's productions) unite to produce the mad world of Ludlam's stage, a picture of reality that verges on the anarchic.

As a playwright, Ludlam strives for verbal richness and allusiveness by means of a technique that he has dubbed "cultural recyclings," a phrase that apparently describes nothing more than Ludlam's tendency to appropriate snippets of dialogue, characters, and events from a startling and disparate array of sources. For *Camille* (1973), in which Ludlam portrayed the consumptive heroine Marguerite Gautier, the major sources were Dumas's play, *Our Lady of the Camelias,* Verdi's opera *La Traviata,* and Greta Garbo's filmed version. But for an earlier work, *Big Hotel* (1967), Ludlam plundered from several films (among them *Salome, Sunset Boulevard, Niagara,* and *The Red Shoes*), several plays (including *Macbeth, The Taming of the Shrew, The Merchant of Venice*), a newspaper advertisement, a television commercial, two foreign-language comic books, and Bela Bartok's opera *The Miraculous Mandarin.* Such random borrowings result in scripts that are chaotic and sprawling, qualities intensified by Ludlam's preference for rewriting, even writing, throughout the rehearsal process. His commitment to continuing revision during rehearsals reflects his desire to capitalize on "all the happy accidents which come up in rehearsal." Still, the outcome is occasionally unnerving, as when the final act of a play is not set down until the night before its first public performance. With more than a dozen plays and a decade of work to his credit, Ludlam summarized his accomplishments this way: "Compared with the great ages of the theatre, my plays are mediocre, but they're better than anything my contemporaries are doing."

Not everyone would agree with Ludlam's assessment. Since its formation in 1967, the Ridiculous Theatrical Company (and its leader Charles Ludlam) has been the subject of comment and controversy. Critics have been divided in their opinions of the group's worth. On the one hand, the company received an Obie in 1969–1970 for its distinguished achievement in the Off-Broadway theatre; on the other hand, the eminent reviewer Walter Kerr was greatly offended by "the spectacle of bald, full breasted hermaphrodites camping as before." Certainly the Ridiculous Theatrical Company is not for a typical patron of Broadway musicals and light comedies based on domestic complications. Both its scripts and its production style, replete with nudity, profanity, and bisexual jokes, are guaranteed to shock and offend conservative viewers. Yet during its lifetime, the company has built a core of devoted followers; its audience is small and loyal. Its regular patrons come to the theatre expecting extravagant theatricality and high camp, and they are seldom disappointed.

What lasting contributions, if any, this experimental group will make to the American theatre is unknown, but the Ridiculous Theatrical Company stands as a reminder to all that even experimental theatre can be fun, can have a sense of humor, and can exist to entertain. In sharp contrast to the spiritual intentions of Grotowski, the social concerns of Chaikin, and the contemplative strategies of Foreman, Ludlam's goal for theatre appears unpretentious. To the question "What is theatre?" Ludlam has provided no theoretical answer but has showed clearly by his works that he considers theatre a form of art based on a long tradition, rich in conventions; he does not view it as a political tool, a social corrective, or a spiritual palliative. Theatre exists, for Ludlam, to excite, to delight, to titillate, entertain, give joy. "Where can theatre be done and for whom?" Ludlam has answered by playing in small but traditional thetre spaces, in front of audiences knowledgeable about its conventions and the conventions of the other arts. He has sought out no unusual spaces for his productions and has experimented with no bizarre audience/actor relationships. As a producer, too, Ludlam is traditional, depending on a director leading a team of artists to bring forth the dramatic performance. He appears to believe that theatre gets produced best by amateurs and professionals willing to work hard for little money under the direction of someone like himself who loves the theatre and who understands its traditions. And in answer to the final question— "What is the relationship between written text and living performance?"— Ludlam takes the position that the performance, although based on texts from the past and the present, should be casual enough to incorporate the responses of a literate audience and the spontaneous contributions of devoted actors.

In sum, this experimental theatre, despite its declared determination to be outrageous, remains both the most conventional in its theoretical assumptions and the most loyal to the traditional conventions of the theatre. Its major importance may finally be the clues that it provides to aestheticians (like Susan Sontag) who seek a better understanding of the peculiar delights of camp.

Political Theatres

Of all the arts, theatre is most apt to become embroiled in society's controversies and conflicts. Its ability to display, rather than talk about, complex issues renders it peculiarly suited for dealing with broad social problems where simple answers are impossible and many contradictions exist side by side within a single political position. Too, living actors in close physical and psychological proximity to audiences make the impact of theatre more immediate and compelling than either film's or television's.

With the unpopular war in Vietnam, the civil rights struggles in the United States, and the social convulsions produced by both, the decade of the 1960s saw a quickened interest in theatre as a weapon for various political battles. Not only did playwrights treat current issues, but some groups also formed and pledged themselves to work tirelessly for one or another radical cause. The goal was to shake people from their complacency, to persuade them to more enlightened attitudes, and to convert them from passive observers into active participants for a social revolution.

Obviously, for such writers and groups, the audience was crucial. How could it be moved? converted? activated? Experimentation in new relationships between the actor and the audience flourished. Sometimes intimate, even conspiratorial, relationships were sought as actors invited audiences to join them on stage—or as actors left the stage to move about the auditorium and into the streets. At other times, the passivity of audiences was assaulted by actors who verbally abused and insulted their viewers, hoping to goad them into a denunciation of the status quo. Theatre was conceived of by many groups as an activity quite apart from any formal space, and so they moved out of buildings and into the streets, the fields, and even the elevators of office buildings. The terms *street theatre* and *guerrilla theatre* were coined to describe those productions that were brought directly to people wherever they congregated, for those labels stressed the supposed similarity of such groups to guerrilla fighters, with all that the term implied about a small cadre of well-trained, mobile, elite soldiers for the revolution.

Since many people fear change, attacks on the status quo are often threatening to large numbers of people, a fact that may explain why members of the Living Theatre were jailed on occasion and why the Cafe La Mama was harassed and closed down from time to time. Indeed, many citizens concluded that some of the guerrilla and street theatres stirred passions to levels that they considered dangerous. As the turmoil of the 1960s swirled and engulfed society, the notoriety of the political theatres grew and so did calls for their censorship.

Interestingly, however, it was not the censors but the changing times that dissipated the strength of political theatres. As social concerns abated, issues changed, the war wound down, and the country settled back into a

Figure 4–16. Political Theatre. Theatre's ability to show issues rather than to lecture on them has made it an often valuable didactic force. (*The Funniest Joke in the World* performed by Anstie's Limit.)

Figure 4–17. Street Theatre. The ability to perform short, issue-centered plays in any setting makes street theatres effective persuaders. This is an anti-nuclear power play performed on a street in Columbia, South Carolina.

more comfortable acceptance of itself, the outrageous antics of the 1960s were replaced by less flamboyant techniques and less public protests. As the revolutionary fervor of the 1960s cooled, political theatres either disappeared, withdrew and changed tactics, or moved toward the mainstream of the commercial playhouses.

Although many political theatres existed during the twenty years under consideration, only a few need to be studied in order to grasp their major traits. Two groups and two movements have been chosen: the Living Theatre and El Teatro Campesino; and the black theatre movement and the feminist theatre movement.

The Living Theatre. "Our intentions are to further the revolution, meaning the beautiful, non-violent, anarchistic revolution," said Judith Malina and Julian Beck, founders and developers of the Living Theatre, probably the most famous and certainly the most controversial of the several political groups of the 1960s.

After a somewhat tentative beginning in 1947, the group achieved recognition by the late 1950s as one of the most important experimental Off-Broadway theatres. During this early period, the group performed rather traditional, if often somewhat angry and bitter, works, including Jack Gelber's *The Connection* (1959) and Kenneth Brown's *The Brig* (1963) as well as works by Luigi Pirandello, Bertolt Brecht, and William Carlos Williams.

Problems with tax collectors and local police, however, encouraged the troupe to tour Europe in 1964. By the time they returned in 1968, they had a different identity, a changed working method, and new stature: the Living Theatre of the late 1960s was a theatrical commune devoted to the production of revolutionary drama. Their international reputation rested primarily on three works: *Frankenstein* (1965), *Antigone* (1967), and *Paradise Now* (1968), each a strong call for revolution and benevolent anarchy.

The text for *Frankenstein* was written by Beck and Malina only after months of discussion and improvisations with their group. Incorporating sections of Mary Shelley's novel *Frankenstein,* Goethe's play *Faust,* assorted scenes from several of Ibsen's dramas, and a section from Greek tragedy, they used characters as diverse as Sigmund Freud and Paracelsus to transform the famous legend into a strong political statement about oppression. Since the techniques used in this production were typical of much of the group's work during this phase, their description may be useful.

When the audience arrived, fifteen actors were sitting cross-legged on stage, staring fixedly at the spectators, who groped for seats without benefit of houselights. Behind the actors, a setting consisting of a series of platforms and bars laced into compartments resembled a modified jungle gym. For nearly thirty minutes, the audience sat while a loudspeaker explained in several languages that the actors were meditating in order to levitate the one seated center. When, at the appointed time, no levitation occurred, the actors chased and caught their subject and began a funeral. During this ceremony, ever-increasing numbers of those attending the funeral defected and fled, only to be hunted down and executed by posses of actors ranging freely through the auditorium. When the stage was at last cluttered

Figure 4–18. A Play from the Living Theatre. Kenneth Brown's *The Brig*, as performed by Indiana University. *(Directed by E. Stern, design by F. Silberstein, photo by Terry Weaver.)*

with bodies, Dr. Frankenstein and his assistants entered and began the creation of the monster, using spare body parts from the onstage corpses. During the remaining two acts, the monster came to life (accompanied by lighting effects), began destroying lives around him, threatened to kill his creator, and finally reconciled with Dr. Frankenstein. During the embrace and kiss between the monster and his creator, a loud cry of "NO!" erupted from the acting company and led to a reenactment of the final scene from the tragedy *The Eumenides*.

Antigone, like *Frankenstein*, used a well-known story and a reasonably traditional text (translated by Malina from the script of Bertolt Brecht). *Antigone*, too, however, was transformed in production: the company eliminated all light cues, scenery, and properties, focusing instead on the living presence of the actors. Throughout the play, the body of Antigone's brother remained on stage in view of the audience and war raged throughout the auditorium, with actors becoming soldiers, war machines, and air sirens. In retelling the familiar story of the young heroine who died because she chose to deny the ruler's order rather than leave her brother unburied, the Living Theatre shifted blame away from Antigone and Creon (the ruler) and placed it firmly on the citizenry as a whole: when Antigone was convicted of the crime, the actor citizens lost their human form. The result, according to one critic, was a "drama of pacifism and humor."

Paradise Now began wth actors milling about the audience, denouncing controls of one sort and another. Throughout the four or more hours that the play lasted, actors verbally abused any spectators who seemed apathetic or hostile, shouting slogans and obscenities at them. On one occasion, a spectator challenged Malina to disrobe; she accepted on the condition that the spectator join her. He did; she did; and they discussed political and social issues while nude. Such confrontations were common in performances of this thinly veiled political tract. Generally, at its conclusion, the group urged the spectators to join in taking the revolution out of the theatre and into the streets. When they did so during a performance at Yale University in 1968, several were arrested and charged with indecent exposure, breach of the peace, and interfering with a police officer.

As the group toured the States with these plays, critical responses were predictably varied. One critic dubbed Paradise Now "a full scale disaster"; another dismissed it as "a fraud." The group itself was characterized as "a platform for anarchy and nothing more." But even Eric Bentley, a critic respected by most traditional theatregoers, admitted that the troupe had to be reckoned with: "The Living Theatre represents the most resolute attempt during the past twenty years to create a theatre which would be a radical alternative to Broadway and Off-Broadway."

For many theatregoers, the Living Theatre came to epitomize what was wrong with the noncommercial American theatre of the 1960s: their productions were viewed as ugly, obscene, abrasive, and dull, filled with nudity and punctuated with foul language. For other audiences, however, the Living Theatre pointed the way for transforming theatre into an effective weapon for political change. Certainly Beck and Malina believed that any theatre worth doing had to affect the lives of the audience members in very basic ways and that any good theatre would hurry the inevitable social revolution:

One thing we have learned: that we cannot solve our particular problem, say, the artistic problem, outside the general context of the revolution. And it is clear by now [1967] that a revolution that starts in a theatre must go out of the theatre and involve the whole economic situation. . . . We feel that the revolution could take place if everything were to become a theatrical event.

Having infuriated conventional audiences and occasioned riots following performances, the group left the country again in 1969. With radicalism on the decline (as the Vietnam war wound down and civil rights agitation slowed), the Living Theatre entered yet another phase. In a formal declaration, the group announced its division into four cells, each to be centered in a different city and each focusing on a distinct revolutionary concern: political, environmental, cultural, and spiritual. Although the collective remained active and deeply committed to promoting the revolution, by the mid-1970s its impact on the American theatre was clearly waning. Beck and Malina, acknowledging the end of the politics of confrontation, turned to more subtle ways to attack the establishment and promote the revolution.

Despite their continued efforts and the development of two new pieces, *The Legacy of Cain* (begun 1970) and *The Money Tree* (begun 1973), the Living Theatre faded from prominence, its goals for revolution and peaceful anarchy unrealized. Leadership in political theatre passed to other theatres espousing more fashionable and current concerns.

El Teatro Campesino. "We don't think in terms of art, but of our political purpose in putting across certain points. . . . We know when we're not turning on the crowd. From a show business point of view that's bad enough, but when you're trying to excite crowds to go out on strike . . . it gains an added significance." As the quotation suggests, El Teatro Campesino was dedicated to the very specific goal of organizing farmworkers, particularly the Mexican-Americans (Chicanos) of the California grape fields. To achieve the goal, the group's founder, Luis Valdez, took his worker/actors into the fields and there performed comic sketches aimed at improving the morale of the workers and convincing them that collective action could improve their lot. Founded in 1965 at the height of labor disputes between the farm owners, the powerful Teamsters Union, and a rival union of Chicanos headed by Cesar Chavez, El Teatro successfully promoted the bid of Chavez by actually entering the labor camps, organizing workers, and satirizing the competing Teamsters Union along with the wealthy arbor owners.

The primary weapon was the *actos,* short, slapstick skits, about fifteen minutes long, punctuated with songs and cries for action. Since both actors and audiences often spoke only Spanish or English, the *actos* used few words and much action. Signs and masks helped workers follow the story, regardless of their native language. For example, in a favorite *acto,* a grower entered, wearing a sign reading "Smiling Jack." As he began to spew platitudes about his love of the Mexican-American worker, other signs began to appear near him: "Liar," "Gringo," "Jackass," and finally "Striker." In this way, the *acto* not only illustrated the problem the worker faced with hypocritical growers but also suggested a solution to the problem: organize a strike. The strikebreaker was often a target of the *actos.* One began, "After God had finished the rattlesnake, the toad and the vampire, he had some awful substance left over with which he made the Strikebreaker."

Within a few years, El Teatro Campesino had extended its political activity to other areas of Chicano life. *Actos* began to treat the Vietnam war, cultural identity, drugs, and Chicano history as well as farm labor problems. In 1970, however, an event occurred that caused a major change in the direction of the group. During a demonstration in Los Angeles, riots and violence led to death, and Luis Valdez, stunned, took stock and changed the direction of El Teatro.

Of the new El Teatro Campesino, he said, "We'll be getting deeper and deeper into ourselves, because the sixties was a time of outward explosion while the seventies is a time of inward explosion. . . . the Teatro has shed its skin, because it was *time* for *change.*" By the mid-1970s, El Teatro Campesino had become El Centro Compesino, a religious commune situated on forty acres of land and devoted to revitalizing Chicano culture with the help of God. The group's solicitation of divine aid was sufficiently outspoken so that some political revolutionaries began to dismiss the group as "Jesus freaks." Certainly the commune's performances were considerably more benign than before, but the language remained the interesting amalgam of Spanish and English that its adherents called "Mex-Tex" or Spanglish. As spiritualism replaced stridency, El Centro Campesino seemed an outpost of tranquillity in the midst of a movement fraught with controversy. It appeared determined to remain as much apart from its own agitation of the 1960s as from the hurly-burly mainstream of America in the 1970s.

Black Theatre

The plays of a real Negro theatre must be: 1. About us. That is, they must have plots that reveal Negro life as it is. 2. By us, they must be written by Negro authors who understand from birth and continued association just what it means to be a Negro today. 3. For us, that is, the Negro theatre must cater primarily to Negro audiences and be supported by their entertainment and approval. 4. Near us. The theatre must be in a neighborhood near the mass of Negro people.

(William E. B. DuBois, 1926).

Except for the use of the word *Negro,* this appeal could have been written today. In fact, it appeared in 1926. But not until the late 1960s did the goals set forth seem to be within reach.

As the racial turmoil of the 1960s and the early 1970s was winding down and the sit-ins, burnings, bombings, and assassinations were ending, blacks turned in large numbers to the arts as a way of repairing their ruptured society. When they did so, it was with a new sense of racial pride and cultural worth. The substitution of the word *black* for the word *Negro* was only one indication of their growing solidarity and self-esteem. Larry Neal (in "The Black Arts Movement," *The Black Aesthetic*) captured the new mood well, and so his remarks provide an interesting comparison with those written forty years before. Neal declared:

Black Art is the aesthetic and spiritual sister of the Black Power concept. As such it envisions an art that speaks directly to the needs and aspirations of Black America. . . . Theatre exists in direct relationship to the audience it claims to serve. The decadence and inanity of the contemporary American Theatre is an accurate reflection of the state of American society.

And so the call was out again for black artists to serve the needs of their own communities, and this time several responded. Black dramatists began to write plays about blacks and to present a vision of contemporary society from the vantage point of the black people. Or, as Ed Bullins wrote, "A Playwright writes to be understood by his community. My community is the Black Community."

Developing a theatre about blacks meant both writing plays that dealt honestly with black experience in a white society and evolving critical standards that seemed relevant to the needs of the black community. Prior to the 1960s, most commercial plays featuring black characters had been written by whites, who often shamelessly stereotyped blacks and usually placed them in inferior social positions, where they were humored and patronized by wealthier, wittier, and more powerful white characters. A cursory reading of Paul Green's *In Abraham's Bosom* (1926) and *Johnny Johnson* (1936), Carson McCullers's *The Member of the Wedding* (1950), and Marc Connelly's *Green Pastures* (1930) will illustrate quickly both the persistence and the range of the common stereotypes.

Public images died hard, but they did die. In 1959, Jean Genet in his play *The Blacks* reversed the traditions of the minstrel shows, where white actors played in blackface, by using black actors in whiteface to display the uses and abuses of power. Although many blacks rejected the play's thesis—that blacks will come to power only by adopting the tactics of their white oppressors—few failed to realize that the play represented a turning point in the portrayal of black people. In 1959, too, Lorraine Hansberry, a black woman, wrote *A Raisin in the Sun,* an early portrait of black family life in which the peculiar tensions between women and men were sympathetically and sensitively sketched. Some militant blacks do not include Hansberry in the contemporary black theatre movement, but her work—which won the Pulitzer Prize—was an important awakening for both black and white audiences, and in the history of black drama, it may prove of more lasting importance than many others.

By the mid-1960s, many black artists were producing theatre about, by,

Figure 4–19. Before Black Theatre. Jean Genet's *The Blacks* was a play by a white dramatist that rejected the usual ways in which blacks had been portrayed in the white theatre. This production was by the Department of Theatre and Drama of Indiana University. *(Directed by D. Wiley. Photo by John Cackler.)*

for, and near blacks. The false image of benign and happy Negroes living in harmony within a benevolent white society was assaulted successfully by LeRoi Jones in his first two plays, *The Toilet* (1964) and *Dutchman* (1964). Each play presented a chilling picture of racial barriers, human hatred, and the senseless suffering that results from racism. After 1964, the stereotyped stage Negro of earlier days was increasingly attacked and replaced with more honest, if often less agreeable, black characters. Perhaps for this reason, as much as for any other, the new Black Theatre Movement is said to have begun in 1964.

Just as dramas written by whites seemed to distort and cheapen the black experience, so too did the aesthetic sensibilities of whites violate the perceived needs of blacks. Black critics took the position that their audiences saw and understood art in ways different from whites. Traditional aesthetics, then, were at best irrelevant and at worst corrupting. Black artists and critics sought an aesthetic that was moral and corrective, one that applauded plays that would affect in a direct and immediate way the lives of black theatre-goers. Addison Gay described such an aesthetic: "The question for the black critic today is not how beautiful a melody, a play, a poem, or a novel is, but how much more beautiful has the poem, melody, or play made the life of a single black man."

In response to the pleas for plays that could unify the black commuity and improve the lot of blacks within a white culture, some playwrights were strident and inflammatory. The late plays of LeRoi Jones (known now by his Muslim name, Imamu Amiri Baraka), for example, were both moral and militant: In his play *Slave Ship* (1967), Baraka chose the brutalizing experience of African slaves bound for America both as a metaphor for a separate society bound together by its painful past and as an argument for the continued rejection of white society by the emerging black culture.

But as more and more plays by black writers appeared and as some of the rage of the 1960s subsided black drama became ever more diverse. Alongside antiwhite and separatist works were plays depicting the politics and economics of life within the black community and treating the particular problems of growing up black and of maintaining a traditional family inside the black community. Indeed, many sensitive and compelling plays by blacks ignored interracial conflicts altogether in favor of exploring the often fragile relationships within their own communities. For example, Ron Milner's *Who's Got his Own* (1966) presented the story of a strong black woman struggling to teach her son to love and respect his father and to understand the older man's hostilities and defeats; Alice Childress in *Mojo* (1970) suggested that black men and women could work out their differences and exist happily as equals if they loved and respected one another. In other plays, stridency was replaced by humor, as in Douglas Turner Ward's *Day of Absence* (1967), which poked fun at whites who were outwitted again and again by shrewder, cleverer blacks. And when the blacks disappeared for a day, the white society was shown to be utterly incapable of sustaining itself. With rather broad strokes, Ward painted the helpless collapse of the white social structure when it was deprived of the support of blacks.

It is doubtless a sign of maturity that black authors by the late 1970s

Figure 4–20. Black Theatre on Broadway. *For Colored Girls Who Have Considered Suicide/ When the Rainbow Is Enuf* had elements of both black and Feminist theatre. *(Photo by Martha Swope.)*

felt free to criticize other blacks and to portray them in villainous roles. Even the tyranizing of blacks by other blacks was treated. One of the most exciting theatrical events of the mid-1970s, for example, was the production of *For Colored Girls Who Have Considered Suicide/When the Rainbow Is Enuf* (1976). The play is a series of poems that explore the double oppression of being both black and female. The portrait of black males is unflattering, since some are portrayed as brutalizing black women as they themselves have previously been brutalized. The stark setting and simple costumes joined with an inventive use of light and music to focus attention firmly on the actresses, whose words and dancelike movements made vivid the issues raised in the poetry. Originally staged in a black theatre, this powerful yet compassionate "choreopoem" later moved to Broadway, where it captivated audiences and earned the coveted Tony Award. With the success of *Colored Girls,* it became clear that plays once considered suitable only for black audiences were now being assimilated into the mainstream of the American commercial theatre.

Even now, new plays by black writers are continuing to expand the options available for reaching their growing audiences. Predictably, perhaps, some recent works by black artists are indistinguishable from the typical commercial fare so roundly criticized by Neal just a few years earlier. *The Wiz,* a musical based on *The Wizard of Oz,* and *Bubbling Brown Sugar,* except for black casts, were standard commercial fare. But they were attracting large audiences of blacks and receiving acclaim from established reviewers.

The great number of black playwrights and plays of the 1960s and 1970s precludes a complete listing, but perhaps a few of the major authors and their best-known works can serve to indicate the healthy, even robust state of this relatively new theatrical tradition: Ed Bullins, *The Electronic Nigger* (1968), *The Pig Pen* (1970), and *The Taking of Miss Jamie* (1975); Lonne Elder III, *Ceremonies in Dark Old Men* (1968); Charles Gordone, *No Place to Be Somebody* (1969); Joseph Walker, *The River Niger* (1972); Adrienne Kennedy, *The Owl Answers* (1969) and *Funny House of a Negro* (1963); and Ntozake Shange, *For Colored Girls Who Have Considered Suicide/When the Rainbow Is Enuf.*

For black drama to reach its audiences, its theatres had to be in the neighborhoods. Accordingly, most of the major producing organizations were located in large urban centers that boasted high concentrations of blacks.

Figure 4–21. Black Theatre.
Lonne Elder's *Ceremonies in Dark Old Men,* Ohio University School of Theatre Production. *(Directed by Tony Coleman, design Wayne Idecker. Photo by Alan Fuchs © 1979.)*

Figure 4–22. Black Theatre
Beyond Broadway. Ernest
Ferlita's *Black Medea*, produced
by Loyola University and per-
formed there and at the Spo-
leto Festival, Charleston,
South Carolina. *(Directed by
Alexis Gonzales.)*

Although the precise number of such groups is unknown, by the mid-1970s
more than forty were active. Of the twenty-five or so in the New York
area, the most famous were the Negro Ensemble Company, the New Lafa-
yette Theatre, and Spirit House. Of the approximately twenty existing in
the Los Angeles and San Francisco areas, Watts Writers Workshop, the
Performing Arts Society of Los Angeles, and the Inner City Cultural Center
were among the best known.

Black theatres, like black plays, serve their audiences in very different
ways, some favoring intense political statements, others avoiding polemical
works altogether. In Los Angeles, for example, while one theatre specialized
in revolutionary plays, across town another produced a "black version" of
Death of a Salesman. Both believed they were serving the particular needs of
their specific audiences. Clearly, like the black experience, black theatre
and drama defy easy categorization. Although many urge a continuing separation of black arts from the rest of (white) society, others ask that black
plays serve not only as a reflection of their lives and dreams for the betterment of the black community but also that the dramas should offer whites
the means of improved understanding and appreciation of the black experience in all its contradictions and complexities.

Feminist Theatres. "This theatre has changed my life," said an unidentified woman after attending a feminist theatre project.

If black theatre and drama were products of the social upheavals of
the 1950s and 1960s, feminist theatres were clearly a phenomenon of the
1970s. From the formation of the first groups in 1969, increasing numbers

of people, mostly female, banded together into theatrical units that aimed to promote the goals of feminism, the careers of women artists, or both. By the mid-1970s, more than forty such groups flourished. Unlike black theatres, which were usually found in urban settings and amid high concentrations of blacks, feminist theatres sprang up in places as diverse as New York City and Greenville, South Carolina, Los Angeles and Richmond, Vermont.

Feminist theatres ranged in size from those depending on one or two unpaid and inexperienced volunteers to organizations of professionals numbering into the hundreds. Budgets, too, varied widely, with some groups existing on a shoestring and the good wishes of friends and others boasting a financial statement in the hundreds of thousands of dollars. Organization, repertory, working methods, and artistic excellence were highly diversified, but the groups all shared the conviction that women have been subjected to unfair discrimination based on their gender and that theatre can serve in some way to correct the resulting inequities.

Like the black theatres, feminist theatres attempted to serve different audiences and to serve them in different ways. Some groups, like Interart in New York City and the Los Angeles Feminist Theatre, existed primarily to provide employment for women artists. Such groups, seeing that women had inadequate opportunities to display their crafts, served as a showcase for the works of women playwrights, designers, and directors. Since their goal was to display women's art in the most favorable light possible, artistic excellence was a primary goal of each production. Critical acceptance by the theatrical mainstream was the ultimate measure of success. But other groups, like the now-defunct It's All Right to Be Woman Theatre (also in New York) believed the problems of women to be so deeply rooted in the society that only a major social upheaval could bring about their correction. Such groups were revolutionary and tended to adopt tactics designed to taunt, shock, or shame a lethargic society into corrective action. These groups cared not at all for the approval of established critics because they believed that traditional theatre was a male-dominated, and hence oppressive, institution.

Many feminist theatres resembled guerrilla and street theatres more than black theatres in the approaches they took to production and performance. Two techniques in particular came to be associated with women's theatres: a preference for collective or communal organization and the use of improvised performance material, much of it uncommonly personal. Like guerrilla theatres, many feminist groups replaced the traditional theatrical hierarchy (a director leading a team of actors, designer, technicians) with a leaderless group working together and with the audience to create a theatrical experience. The It's All Right to Be Woman Theatre explained; "Whereas theatre has been, to date, a combining of specialists, the essence of our theatre is to convey the collective experience. . . . a theatre without separation of roles, a theatre without a stage to separate audience and players." The idea seemed to be that hierarchy suggests competition, and competitiveness is a masculine trait; collectivity, on the other hand, involves cooperation, a quality to be prized in the new social order.

Figure 4–23. Feminist Theatre. Elinor Jones' *A Voice of My Own*, produced by The Acting Company. *(Directed by Amy Saltz. Photo by Nathaniel Tileston.)*

Perhaps this view accounts as well for the groups' frequent preference for scripts that were cooperatively developed through improvisations. The actors, occasionally aided by audiences, were encouraged to dip into their own experiences of being women in today's society and, from these shared personal experiences, to improvise dramatic presentations. One group described it:

We make theatre out of our lives, our dreams, our feelings, our fantasies. We make theatre by letting out the different parts of us that we have pushed inside all our lives. . . . Making theatres out of these private parts of ourselves is one way we are trying to take our experiences seriously, to accept our feelings as valid and real. . . . to believe what happens to us or what we feel or dream is important enough to share with each other and with other women.

Aparently such efforts, while naive, were capable of provoking audiences to awareness and action, for in several instances, women reported changed lives as a result of encounters with a feminist production.

Although most feminist theatres relied on guerrilla events and improvised presentations, others actively solicited new plays by women. Probably the most famous writers of feminist plays of the 1960s and 1970s are Myrna Lamb and Megan Terry. Lamb's play *The Mod Donna* (1970) was first produced by Joseph Papp at the New York Shakespeare Festival. Its bizarre style—episodes reminiscent of soap opera, interrupted by commercials and alternated with choral poetry—puzzled audiences, while the attacks on traditional roles for women and on the family polarized many of the viewers. Conservatives saw it as an attack on American values; feminists, on the other hand, considered it a major theatrical event and applauded its final lines: "LIBERATION, LIBERATION, LIBERATION." Other well-known works by Lamb include *Scyklon Z* (1969) and *Crab Quadrille* (1976).

Megan Terry first came to nationl prominence as a member of the Open Theatre (see pp. 99–102). In addition to a strong antiwar stance, best seen in her play *Viet Rock,* Terry took the position that stereotyping by gender, although pervasive, was wrong. Out of this conviction grew four of her best-known works: *Calm Down Mother* (1966), written specifically for women of the Open Theatre; *Keep Tightly Closed in a Cool Dry Place* (1967); *In the Gloaming, Oh My Darling* (1966); and *Approaching Simone* (1970).

While Lamb and Terry are the best known of the feminist writers, several others were active. The major of these, together with their best-known works are Rosalyn Drexler with Al Carmines, *Home Movies* (1964); Adrienne Kennedy, *The Owl Answers* (1969) and *Funny House of a Negro* (1963); Rochelle Owen, *Futz* (1968); Renee Taylor with J. Bologna, *Lovers and Other Strangers* (1968); Gretchen Cryer, *I'm Getting My Act Together and Taking It on the Road* (1978), as well as Ntozake Shange, *Colored Girls.*

If the feminist theatres follow the patterns observed in the earlier, but similar, black theatre movement, the stridency will abate as the initial hostilities are ventilated. As the number of moderate voices increases, more feminist theatres will move toward America's theatrical mainstream, and within the decade of the 1980s many of the themes and techniques will be comfortably absorbed there.

Regional Professional Theatres

The vitality of regional professional theatres was one of the most heartening developments of the 1960s and 1970s. In major cities throughout the United States and Canada exist vigorous professional theatres devoted to bringing art of the highest quality to their audiences. Unlike the commercial Broadway theatre, these groups are generally organized as not-for-profit enterprises and so can be more adventurous with play selection, production style, and personnel decisions. After a slow beginning in the late 1940s, the movement accelerated markedly during the 1960s, and by 1975 more than sixty such companies existed in fifty cities across this country. Their contributions to American theatre are substantial, because they serve to diversify and enrich the repertory of the art, to develop new audiences for the theatre, to train and revitalize theatrical artists, and to provide new opportunities for the employment of theatre people.

Regional resident companies have been thought of as the conscience of the American theatre. Certainly this conscience manifests itself in the plays selected by such theatres for their public performances. While the commercial theatre continues to produce mostly musicals and situation comedies, the regional companies range freely among the classics from the past and the developing scripts of the present. Some of the larger groups, like Minneapolis's Tyrone Guthrie Theatre (the Minnesota Theatre Company), operate two distinct seasons. In 1974–1975, for example, they did *King Lear* and *Love's Labour's Lost* (Shakespeare), *Tartuffe* (Molière), *The School for Scandal* (Sheridan), and *Everyman* (a medieval morality play). With such a season, a theatre becomes a showcase for the classics, a living museum for our theatrical heritage. Meanwhile, in Guthrie 2, their alternative theatre, new plays by living playwrights are constantly being sought and produced. Smaller regional companies fuse both functions into a single season of plays. Happily, since regional theatres seldom succeed or fail on the basis of a single production, they are usually more willing to take a chance on a new play by an unknown playwright, a luxury rarely afforded New York theatres with their tradition of the long run and the "hit or flop."

The regional houses have been increasingly successful in developing new plays that have later moved to other regional theatres and to Los Angeles and New York City. Among the most successful in this regard have been the Hartford Stage Company, the Long Wharf Theatre (New Haven, Connecticut), the Arena Stage (Washington), and the Dallas Theatre Center. Apparently the tradition of theatre's beginning in New York and then trickling down slowly to the rest of the country is being reversed. Drama is now bubbling up around the country, where it is nurtured and tested outside the financial demands of the large commercial houses in New York. The best of it, once refined, moves beyond its local area and throughout the country. In this way, regional theatre now offers a forum where the new play and the classic coexist and provide an alternative to the commercial comedies and lavish musicals that have long been the mainstays of Broadway.

But plays of any kind require audiences, and here, too, the regional theatres have performed a vital service. In the early days of America, every major city had its own professional theatre company, whose actors often were favored guests at social functions of the town. People in Philadelphia and Boston and Charleston could enjoy the delights of the theatre and share the life of their community. For a number of complex reasons, this early pattern broke down, and by 1900 little theatre existed except that originating in New York City. People in Texas, then, either had to travel to New York to see a professional production or wait for a national road company to tour Texas with a play sent out from Broadway. Obviously such a highly centralized theatre inhibited the growth and development of new audiences.

Fortunately, attacks on the problem began in the late 1940s and the early 1950s when Margo Jones established her professional theatre in Dallas, Texas, and Zelda Fichandler began the Arena Stage in Washington, D.C. By the late 1950s, several other important groups had formed: the Actors

Figure 4–24. Regional Theatre. Shaw's *Saint Joan* at the Long Wharf Theatre, New Haven, Connecticut—one of many high-quality professional theatres across the United States. *(Photo by William L. Smith.)*

Workshop (San Francisco), the Alley Theatre (Houston), and the Front Street Theatre (Memphis). The growth of the regional professional companies attracted attention: the Ford Foundation awarded major grants to those whose local audiences appeared supportive; and the Theatre Commuications Group (TCG) organized to facilitate exchange, encourage cooperation, and ease communications among the growing numbers of groups.

Still, in 1961, a New York producer felt confident in saying that "there is no American theatre outside New York City." Two events in the 1960s, however, invested the movement with new dynamism.

In 1963, Tyrone Guthrie established a first-rate professional repertory company in Minneapolis. Patterned on the highly successful Stratford Festival in Stratford, Ontario, Canada, in whose formation in 1953 Guthrie had been instrumental, the Minnesota Theatre Company burst on the scene amidst a flurry of highly favorable publicity. Bringing leading actors from Canada and New York and attracting audiences from throughout middle America, the Guthrie Theatre soon established a reputation for fine productions. Using a combination of box-office receipts, grants, and private contributions, the theatre survived and even flourished to testify that an audience existed outside of New York and that this audience would support both classical and original plays. Soon other cities in America aspired to the cultural status of Minneapolis and, using the Guthrie theatre as a guide, sought resident professional theatres of their own. Although many failed, many succeeded, and the interest generated in regional theatres mushroomed by the mid-1960s, spurred on by a second felicitous event.

In 1965, the federal government established the National Endowment for the Arts, whose purpose was to encourage the development of the arts throughout the country by means of state arts councils and to subsidize existing performing groups whose records seemed promising. By the late 1960s, there were thirty or so professional theatres of high quality operating throughout the United States. By the mid-1970s, the number of companies had more than doubled, and conservative estimates are that several millions of patrons for several thousands of productions of several hundreds of plays performed outside of New York City by these resident professional companies now exist. In cities with such groups, theatre is again a source of civic pride, and new audiences have discovered again the joy of live theatrical performance.

At the same time that resident theatres develop new audiences, they also serve as a training ground and an energizing center for theatrical artists. Prior to the twentieth century, any young person wishing to enter the theatre did so by something resembling an apprentice system. He or she would join a resident stock company, perhaps one near home, and understudy or play a series of small roles while observing and receiving instruction from the other company members. When these stock companies disappeared and the theatre centralized in New York, an important training ground was lost. Although to some extent colleges and universities have filled this vacuum, not all are able to provide enough opportunities in diverse plays before sophisticated audiences, and so the needs of a serious young performer cannot always be filled by collegiate programs. For this reason, the reemergence of resident professional companies was hailed as a new opportunity for developing artists. These professional companies provided a suitable stepping-stone for young artists needing intense work with practicing professionals before plunging into the commercial world of New York, and many of today's best talents in acting, directing, and designing got their start at one or more of these regional companies.

The companies perform an important service for the seasoned professionals, as well. Commercial threatre can sap creativity and vitality from theatre artists because its repertory tends to be restricted and because its productions, when successful, tend to run for extended periods. In New York, for example, an actor may well play a single role for several years. While lucrative, this

Figure 4–25. Regional Theatre. *The Mystery Circle,* performed by the American Conservatory Theatre, San Francisco. With R. Aaron Brown and Deborah May. *(Photo by Hank Kranzler.)*

practice may dull the sensibilities and blunt the skills of the actor. Moreover, in the commercial world, roles from the classical repertory that stretch the actor's craft and expand his vision are seldom available. Even the best New York actors, therefore, are often anxious to spend a season or two with a resident theatre where they can play a wide variety of roles from many of history's best plays within a period of a few weeks. And so, for both the inexperienced beginner and the practicing artist, the regional theatres provide opportunities unavailable in the commercial houses of New York. Most critics agree that as a result of the exchanges now taking place between the regional and the New York theatres, the standards of the whole profession are rising. With rising standards comes a generally improved quality of production, an increasingly sophisticated audience, and greater enjoyment for performers and viewers alike.

Finally, regional theaters perform a service to the profession as a whole by providing jobs. Year after year, thousands of young people succumb to the lure of theater and decide that they want to become professionals. In New York City, the opportunities are dismal. Persons trying to find work exceed, by at least five times, the number of jobs available. Fewer than one half of Equity's actors are employed at any one time; sometimes as few as 15 per cent are working, even including those Equity members working outside of New York. Employment statistics for directors and designers are scarcely better. The practice of the long run, the inbreeding of the theatrical unions, the enormous financial risks involved in production, and the sheer number of aspirants arriving daily in the city virtually guarantee that the bleak employment picture will continue in New York.

Outside the city, on the other hand, the growth of theatres, and thus opportunities for employment, continues. For several years now, more professional actors have been working outside than inside New York. Designers, few of whom land more than one show per season in New York, are now shuttling back and forth across the country providing scenery, lighting, and costumes for professional productions coast to coast. In purely practical terms, the increased number of jobs made available by the addition of about seventy theaters nationwide represents a healthy expansion of the job market in the profession.

In sum, the network of regional professional companies is large and growing. Both in quantity and quality, they are a major force in the future of the American theatre. They may, in fact, when taken together, be what so many critics and scholars have long sought: America's National Theatre.

Educational Theatre

Although differing in principal emphases, the functions of educational theatres closely parallel those of the regional professional companies: training future artists, developing new audiences, expanding the theatrical repertory, and providing jobs.

Obviously, the major goal of academic programs is the education and training of students. With the demise of the resident stock companies, training in acting, directing, playwriting, design, and technical production has been largely assumed by the academic institutions. While many persons complain of the limitations placed on such training because of the basically conservative, even stultifying atmosphere of many academic organizations, the fact remains that most training for the profession now takes place in this world. Although each program is unique, the general pattern of instruction involves some combination of formal classroom work and public performances of selected plays.

The number of educational theatre programs alone is sufficient to render their influence strong. Whereas America now boasts over sixty professional regional companies, it supports more than two thousand theatre programs in colleges and universities. In small cities without resident professional companies, theatre productions at the college are the best for miles around, and in smaller towns, such productions may be the citizen's only opportunity to view live performances. Through introductory classes and small touring companies, college and university theatres introduce thousands of students at all levels of education to a variety of plays. For many students, these are the first brush with live theatre. Thus, the role of educational theatre in building new audiences can scarcely be overestimated.

Happily, since education is a primary goal, such theatres usually display a strong commitment to a wide range of plays and production styles. Alongside standard musicals, comedies, and domestic dramas, collegiate seasons are likely to include significant works from the past and experimental works for the future. Consequently audiences for university theatre productions often enjoy far richer fare than would normally be possible in community or dinner theatres.

Figure 4–26. Educational Theatre. More than two thousand college and university theatre programs offer theatre productions across the United States and Canada. Here, Carlisle Floyd's opera *Susannah* at the University of Iowa. *(Directed by Cosmo Catalano, designed by Kate Keleher.)*

Too, the number of people required to maintain theatre in an academic setting has given the employment potential of the profession a healthy boost. At the college and university level alone, more than ten thousand productions are mounted each year and more than four thousand teachers are employed. When the growing number of high school drama classes, elementary programs in creative drama, and producing groups devoted to children's theatre are considered, it becomes clear that the academic complex is a major source of jobs. Indeed, educational theatre considered at all levels is probably the largest employer of theatre artists and scholars in the United States at the present time.

CHAPTER 5

The Modern Theatre:
The Rise and Decline of
Realism, 1850–1960

Although much of contemporary theatre in New York, London, and Europe has moved away from realism, and many artists and critics find the greatest theatrical excitement in turning their backs on it, most community and educational companies, and even many professional repertory companies and commerical theatres, continue to view realistic drama and production as the mainstay of their art. Ask typical college students or occasional playgoers from Georgia, Maine, or Nebraska what plays they most want to see and which playwrights they prefer; chances are they will name plays like *Cat on a Hot Tin Roof, A Streetcar Named Desire, The Glass Menagerie* (all by Tennessee Williams), *Death of a Salesman* (Arthur Miller), *The Little Foxes* (Lillian Hellman), and *Picnic* (William Inge). The continuing popularity of such plays and playwrights is explained not only by their enduring and appealing qualities but also by the way that changes occur in those arts that depend on mass audiences for their support.

Even with today's rapid systems of transportation and communication, change is both modest and slow. While small groups of people press to explore the limits of any art, most are content with familiar subjects and traditional forms. Some radical experiments prove exciting, but even these are seldom embraced without considerable dilution. Rather, their most compelling features are incorporated into more traditional forms. The result is twofold: the experiment becomes less radical (its effects being muted by

Figure 5–1. Modern Realism. Despite continuing changes in the theatre, many audiences insist upon realism as "real theatre." This is William Inge's *Picnic* at Florida State University. *(Directed by Amnon Kabatchnik.)*

its absorption into the mainstream) and the mainstream becomes more adventuresome (its traditional practices being expanded to accommodate the innovation). By such a process, the mainstream slowly alters, coopting first one and then another aspect of the experimental theatres competing with it and diluting the most extreme practices of each innovation.

By examining the beginning, the development, and the permutations of modern realism, we can discover the outlines of the historical process that has produced changes in theatre and drama throughout their history. To view the process as simple action and reaction or birth and death is far too simple and quite misleading. It is better to look upon the process as one in which an experiment begins and swells toward general acceptance. Of the many experiments that go on almost all the time, some captivate the interest of substantial numbers of people. The mainstream pulls in the direction of the new practices at the same time that the experiments move toward the traditional center. An artistic compromise results. In this way, the mainstream shifts often but modestly as it accommodates first one and then another experiment. It never moves far nor fast from what audiences are known to accept. Periodically an experimental form seizes the imagination of large numbers of people and eventually itself becomes the mainstream, although rarely in its original, radical form. Once its acceptance is general and its practices widespread, the problems inherent in *it* become increasingly obvious. In the search for solutions to these problems, a variety of alternatives are offered in the form of new plays, innovative staging practices, and so on. The pattern repeats.

Realism began as an experiment whose aim was to make theatre more useful to society. As with any new theatrical style, it did not begin from nothing or out of nowhere. Between 1850 and 1900, it surfaced in a variety of places and guises, peeping through a tradition that was bound up in spectacular melodramas set in exotic locales and farcical plays performed before elaborately painted scenic units. By World War I, realism was the theatrical mainstream in America and Western Europe. By the 1890s, however, it had already come under serious attack from artists who wished to explore other alternatives. Yet realism persisted as the clearly dominant style throughout the 1950s and, although no longer dominant perhaps, does remain central to many theatres today, its nature perceptibly changed since its heyday in the 1880s.

Since its major plays and history are still familiar, modern realism provides an excellent example of a developing and changing historical process and can function usefully as a case study of similar but earlier shifts in public taste.

The Commercial Mainstream, 1850–1900

Commercial houses in France, England, and America in the late nineteenth century featured works variously called *melodramas, spectacle plays, vaudevilles, burlesques, comic operas,* and *operettas.* The most popular of them ran for dozens, even hundreds of nights and played to audiences of all social classes and artistic tastes. The most popular playwright of the period was probably the Frenchman Victorien Sardou (1831–1908), who is best remembered for well-made comedies like *A Scrap of Paper* (1860). Although less well-known today, Sardou's historical spectacles *Fatherland!* (1869) and *Theodora* (1884), set in exotic locales like medieval Siena and Byzantium, were applauded by contemporaries for the lavishness of their costumes and scenery and the correctness of their many details. For the famous actress Sarah Bernhardt (1884–1923), virtually a cult figure of the age, Sardou wrote plays like *La Tosca* (1887), from which Giacomo Puccini's opera was derived. Although seldom produced today, Sardou's plays swept the stages of America and England as well as France in the last half of the nineteenth century. So consuming was the public's interest in them that the outspoken English critic George Bernard Shaw angrily denounced the theatre of his day as mere "Sardoodledom." Two of Sardou's countrymen were particularly successful authors of farce. Eugène Labiche (1815–1888) with *The Italian Straw Hat* (1851) and George Feydeau (1862–1921) with *A Flea in Her Ear* (1907) set the style for plays based on a highly complicated set of adventures unfolding at rapid-fire pace amidst rooms with many doors, through which

Figure 5–2. Popular Spectacle, c. 1880. An "aquatic theatre" of the late nineteenth century.

a variety of odd characters bustled on their way to and from ever-greater misadventures.

Among the most important popular writers of serious drama must be numbered Dion Boucicault (1822–1890), who added many now-forgotten plays to the stages of France, England, and America. Specializing in melodramas, Boucicault fused sentimentally with sensationalism, let the stories unfold against a background rich in local color, and captured large audiences on two continents with works like *The Corsican Brothers* (1852), *The Sidewalks of New York* (1857), and *The Octoroon* (1859). The popularity of his plays gave Boucicault a degree of financial security virtually unknown at the time; for example, he demanded and received a percentage of receipts for each performance of his plays, thus instituting the practice of *paying royalties* to playwrights. By 1886, an International Copyright Agreement had been instituted, in part because of his influence. Although none was so well known as Boucicault, a number of other dramatists of the time thrilled audiences with plays that featured heroes tied to railroad tracks, heroines trapped in burning buildings, authentic telegraph offices, onstage eruptions of volcanoes, chariot races, and other spectacular effects.

Although operettas like those of Jacques Offenbach (1819–1889) were popular, burlesque–extravaganzas and comic operas commanded even larger audiences. During the 1870s and 1880s in particular, the work of two Englishmen, William Schwenck Gilbert (1836–1911) and Arthur Sullivan (1842–

Figure 5–3. Melodrama. The exaggerated gesture shown here may be inaccurate as an attempt to recapture the enormously popular style of nineteenth-century melodrama, but this is a modern musical based on an older play. *The Streets of New York,* produced by the University of Minnesota Theatre Centennial Showboat. *(Directed by Robert Moulton, design by Cathy Susan Pyles.)*

1900) created musical works that still command devoted audiences. Among the most popular works of Gilbert and Sullivan are *HMS Pinafore* (1878), *The Pirates of Penzance* (1879), *The Mikado* (1885), and *The Gondoliers* (1889).

Probably the most popular play in the world during this period was an American melodrama called *Uncle Tom's Cabin.* A highly romanticized view of slavery in the Old South, the play included scenes of slaves escaping across the ice-clogged Ohio River (hotly pursued by dogs and slave traders), little Eva being carried to heaven by angels amidst the weeping of her family and friends, and Uncle Tom being cruelly beaten by that villain of villains, Simon Legree. Performed in England and France as well as America, the play's popularity remained strong through World War I, when over a dozen companies still traveled about performing only this one play.

American burlesque, too, was popular. Originally a topical review with songs and dances, burlesque (and its cousin vaudeville) changed markedly after a group of stranded dancers were added to a production of *The Black Crook* (1856), and Lydia Thompson's "British Blondes" (1896) took America by storm. Both events showed that scantily clad women had greater appeal than either parody or satire. Increasingly thereafter, the popularity of burlesque depended on a combination of spectacle, song, dance, and female legs, and increasingly the form burlesque appealed to male audiences. Soon after World War I, "striptease" was added, and burlesque moved still further to the outskirts of respectability, no longer fit for family entertainment.

In addition to new plays, revivals of all sorts captivated audiences be-

Figure 5–4. Melodrama. Perhaps the most popular play of its time, *Uncle Tom's Cabin,* is shown here in a French production at the very end of the nineteenth century.

tween 1850 and 1900. Shakespearean plays were produced often and were given elaborate settings designed to reproduce faithfully the illusion of specific locales mentioned in the text. "Illustrating" Shakespeare became popular, and so *The Merchant of Venice* used real water for onstage canals and *Romeo and Juliet* reproduced in detail a tomb for Juliet. Countless plays from the first half of the nineteenth century and a few from the eighteenth were also revived; most popular were spectacular melodramas that thrilled audiences by their special effects and elaborate costumes.

The pleasure of theatregoers, however, was not entirely bound up with the plays themselves, for the period was one of theatrical stars of the highest rank. Many leading actors traveled from city to city to play starring roles with resident stock companies; others traveled with their entire productions (cast, costumes, scenery) across continents to satisfy audiences who thronged to the theatres to see the latest star. France, in addition to Sarah Bernhardt, produced Benoît Constant Coquelin (1841–1909), the first Cyrano de Bergerac. England's most famous actor was Henry Irving (1838–1905), whose performances as Mathias in a now-forgotten melodrama named *The Bells* (1871) spanned thirty-four years and eight hundred performances. That, together with his Shakespearean successes, led to his being knighted, the first English actor to be so honored. In America, the leading actors were Joseph Jefferson (1829–1905), whose fame rested primarily on his portrayal of the title role

Figure 5–5. Melodrama. The great English actor Henry Irving in the role that made him most famous—Mathias in *The Bells.*

in *Rip Van Winkle;* Edwin Booth (1833–1893), regarded by his contemporaries as Shakespeare's finest interpreter but probably remembered today by more people as the brother of President Lincoln's assassin; and James O'Neill (1847–1920), who made an acting career in *The Count of Monte Cristo* (1883) and fathered America's highly regarded native dramatist, Eugene O'Neill.

In sum, the theatrical mainstream from 1850 to 1900 consisted mostly of lavish visual productions of romantic and sentimental plays, well-made comedies, farces, and various kinds of variety entertainments with music. Settings and costumes were applauded for their historic detail and attention to local color. Stars performed in plays that best exploited their talents. In short, the popular theatre was a continuation of what had preceded it, altered only occasionally in the direction of greater accuracy of visual details and the more frequent inclusion of three-dimensional details.

Figure 5–6. **Spectacle.** Equestrian theatre in Paris, c. 1900.

The Emergence of Realism

By the 1850s, certain problems that grew out of society's shifting bases of wealth and its developing industrialization were becoming clear. The products of industry were being distributed unevenly, and the gap between those who did the work and those who reaped the profits was widening, a development that led Karl Marx (1818–1883) to propose an alternative method of social and economic organization for society. Urban poverty was on the rise and with it, urban crime. Political instability gave way to political repression, which in turn fanned latent dissatisfactions that demanded immediate correction. Realism and realistic art arose, in part, as responses to these new social conditions.

Realists maintained that truth resided in material objects whose properties could be apprehended by means of the five senses and verified through the methods of science. Realists believed that any problem could be solved if only it was carefully defined and analyzed and alternative hypotheses were tested. In short, problems could be solved by application of the scientific method. Coupled with the realists' almost naive confidence in the ability of science to solve all problems was their conviction that the highest forms of science were those that dealt most directly with the problems of people and societies. In sum, realists were *materialists:* they believed that truth resided in the material objects observable in the physical, external world; realists were also *objectivists:* they believed that truth could be discovered through application of scientific observation and could be replicated by a series of objective observers.

According to the realists, the function of art, like that of science, was the betterment of humankind, and so the method of the artist should be akin to that of the scientist. Because truth resided in material objects, art, to be true, had to depict the material, tangible world. Because problems could be solved only through application of the scientific method, dramatists should emulate scientists and strive to become objective observers of the social milieu. Plays should be set in contemporary times and places, for only they could be observed firsthand by the playwright. As the highest purpose of art was the betterment of humanity, the subject of plays should be contemporary life and its problems. Scientists obviously operated in a world of things rather than instincts or feelings, and so playwrights should firmly ground their works in objective reality—not spiritual mysticism, subjective pining, or introspective reverie.

As in the case of any new and experimental approach, the acceptance of realism was neither immediate nor universal. One of the earliest manifestations of a new way of looking at the world occurred not in the drama at all but in the theatre, in staging and costuming practices. As early as the 1750s, a very few theatre practitioners had been attempting to make historical plays archaeologically and historically accurate, but almost all details of

Figure 5–7. Realism. Recognizable setting and contemporary characters marked *The Christian*, 1899.

Figure 5–8. Commercialised Romanticism. Contemporary settings, including what seemed to be a "real" working canal lock with water, were shown in *Les Deux Grosses,* 1900—a mainstream takeover of an earlier Romantic element.

the setting were two-dimensional and painted rather than real and three-dimensional. By 1800, some plays (most often melodramas) had required a number of three-dimensional details: bridges that could be walked on, doors that could be opened. But not until 1850 or later were most details of theatrical settings and costumes more or less historically correct and many (if not most) three-dimensional "real" details included in place of their painted representations.

One of the first important contributors to the realistic staging of prerealistic drama was Georg II, Duke of Saxe-Meiningen (fl. 1870s–1880s). In some ways, the duke was merely perfecting ideals of staging promulgated much earlier, but he succeeded where those before him had failed, and he popularized a kind of staging that was to influence producers who wished to undertake realistic dramas in England, France, and Russia.

Georg II, Duke of Saxe-Meiningen

Georg II (1826–1914) objected to many practices of the theatrical mainstream because they resulted in productions that lacked unity (internal consistency) and that seemed artificial and unreal. For the duke, the art of theatre was the art of providing the illusion of reality; he therefore sought methods of production that would lead to "an intensified reality and [would] give remote events . . . the quality of actuality, of being lived for the first time." As a means to this end, the duke stressed lifelike acting and accurate

scenery, costumes, and properties and required that all elements of his productions contribute to the excellence of the whole, a decision that helped
establish the director as the major artistic force in his theatre.

He moved early to break with the then-popular star system, a system
marked by the leading performers' beliefs that they had the right to deliver
their lines, move about the stage, and engage the audience without regard
to the effect on the whole production. In Saxe-Meiningen's group there
were no stars. Each member of the company was eligible to play any role;
and each member, if not cast as a major character, was required to play in
crowd scenes, something a star of the old sort would never do. Moreover,
each actor in a crowd scene was given lines and actions that were carefully
rehearsed and orchestrated for maximum effect. In order to make the crowds
seem real, the duke divided his actors into several small groups, appointed
an experienced actor as the leader of each group, and made that person
responsible for the group's effectiveness. Among the strategies adopted to
increase a sense of realism in crowd scenes were for the actors to avoid
parallel lines on stage, to make crosses on stage diagonally rather than parallel
with the curtain line, to keep one foot off the ground whenever possible
(by placing it on a step or kneeling on one knee), and to be aware of his
neighbor's stance so that it would not be repeated. The duke told his actors
repeatedly that *variety* within a crowd led to its seeming reality. Finally, all
actors were enjoined to look at one another rather than at the audience,
to react to what was said and done onstage, and to behave naturally (even
if it meant delivering a line while not facing the audience). As all of these

Figure 5–9. Realism: Groupings. One of the influences of Saxe-Meiningen's work
was on the creation of realistic crowds, even in historical plays, as in this 1898
production of Shakespeare's *Julius Caesar.*

procedures departed markedly from standard practices of the time, the effects of ensemble achieved, particularly in the crowd scenes, were considered unusually lifelike and uncommonly realistic. The duke's success in these matters did much to speed the end of the nineteenth-century star system.

In the physical aspects of the production, too, the duke strove for a unified, ensemble effect. He believed that all elements of a production required coordination. Otherwise a star actor or a particularly sensational scene would gain undue emphasis and block the emergence of a total picture of reality. He believed, as well, that the setting must be an integral part of the play, and so he encouraged his actors to move within the setting rather than merely playing in front of it (as was currently fashionable). Obviously, if actors were to move within (rather than in front of) an environment, the scenic details had to be three-dimensional rather than painted, and so the duke came to rely heavily on the use of actual objects in his settings. Simultaneously he strove to provide several levels (in the form of rocks, steps, platforms, and the like) so that the scenic design would not stop abruptly at the stage floor. In these ways, the duke did much to popularize the use of real, three-dimensional details on stage where in the past the larger part of the details were simply painted on canvas surfaces.

Historical accuracy, in both scenery and costumes, was important to the duke. Although others before him had experimented with period costumes and furniture, none had been so meticulous in their selection, reproduction, and consistent use throughout the production. Georg II designed and supervised every aspect of the physical production personally. To increase accuracy in the selection of details, the duke divided each century into thirds and even differentiated among various national groups within each period. To increase accuracy of construction, he required that authentic fabrics be used rather than the cheaper substitutes often resorted to in the commercial houses of the day and that the construction of many items be undertaken in his own shops. Moreover, he required all actors, from the most to the least important, to wear the costumes that were designed for them, regardless of the current fashions, and to acquaint themselves with the postures and stances peculiar to the period. Even the makeup was designed according to existing portraits of the time. In short, the duke achieved what others had sought only sporadically and irregularly: historical accuracy within the whole of the production.

Interestingly, the duke's success and influence were in many ways a historical accident. As a government official of a small, out-of-the-way duchy in part of today's Germany, he was able to impose his will on members of his theatre to an uncommon degree. Because it was his theatre, he could schedule its playing dates; he simply did not open a production until he believed it ready. Rehearsals were long: once, for example, eleven lines were rehearsed for over two hours. Discipline was strict, and the duke assumed almost complete control over all artistic decisions.

The success of the group, however, would not have attracted international attention had it not been for the decision to perform outside the small town of Meiningen. Beginning in 1874 (eight years after the duke took over the theatre), the Meiningen plays began touring Western Europe and

Russia. From then until its last tour in 1890, the troupe gave over 2,800 performances in thirty-six cities. From these performances came the group's international reputation and the theatre's influence on people like André Antoine, Henry Irving, and Konstantin Stanislavski.

As an experimental theatre, a theatre trying to provide alternatives to contemporary practices, the Meiningen focused primarily on the questions "What is theatre?" and "How should theatre get produced?" In answer to the former, the duke seemed to believe that theatre was an illusion of real life, and so ensemble acting, unity of production, and historical accuracy were necessary ingredients of successful productions. To the latter question, he apparently answered that the director is the supreme artist in the theatre. Although actors and designers are important, their contributions must be shaped and governed by the director so that the production as a whole achieves unity. Perhaps it is for this reason that the Duke of Saxe-Meiningen is called by many the father of modern directing.

At almost the same time, another theatre artist, also German, was advocating a single controlling force behind each theatrical production and was also perfecting scenic illusionism (although for purposes rather different from those of the duke).

Richard Wagner and the Bayreuth Theatre

Although Richard Wagner (1813–1883) is most often associated with the fields of music and opera, he was an important theorist and practitioner of the theatre as well. His major theories can be found in three essays: "The Art Work of the Future" (1849), "Opera and Drama" (1852), and "The Purpose of Opera" (1871). Two contributions in particular assured Wagner his place in the history of theatre: (1) his call for a unified work of art and (2) his development of a classless theatre.

At the same time that many experimental theatres were trying to establish and perfect realism as a style of production, Wagner was opposing the notion that theatre should present a faithful reproduction of everyday life. Instead he argued that the artist should be a myth maker, one who encapsulates and presents an ideal world to the spectators, providing them with a communal experience that highlights for them their shared culture. The best drama, according to Wagner, is one that combined music and poetry, for in that combination resides the potential for a complete, total art, one that fuses the emotional with the intellectual, human feelings with human understanding. Rather than recording the mundane details of everyday existence, the artists of the theatre should present an ideal world, one based on the culture's history and myths. In the idealizations of love found in *Tannhäuser* and *Lohengrin* and the myths of the German culture in the *Ring* cycle, Wagner provided examples of how his theories might be understood.

For Wagner, the experience of the audience was the critical factor in planning and shaping a work of art. He sought a stage production so compelling that spectators would be drawn in, would believe and empathize with the world behind the proscenium arch. Indeed, for Wagner, the success of

Figure 5–10. Wagner as Myth-Maker. Rejecting literal realism, Wagner combined music and poetry to create a mythic world, as in *Siegfried,* shown here at the Paris Opera, 1902, as seen from backstage. The effects—the drum and the bullhorn—are for the "orchestrated" voice of the dragon.

a production was measured primarily by its ability to capture the emotions of the audience and transport them to a new sense of shared purpose. He said, for example, "[T]he Folk will no longer be a separated and distinct class; for in his Art-work we shall all be one—heralds and supporters of Necessity, Knowers of the unconscious . . . blissful men."

To achieve the ideal production, one capable of entrancing an audience, Wagner proclaimed the need for a *Gesamtkunstwerk,* "master artwork," or "united artwork," by which he meant a work in which all elements of the drama and of the theatrical production were carefully synthesized into a unified whole. He said, "Not a single rich contribution of the separate arts will remain unused in the United Artwork of the Future; in *it* will each attain its first complete expression." Such unity could be achieved only, according to Wagner, when a single person, a supreme artist, controlled every aspect of the production. Indeed, it was Wagner's concept of the master artist, the single controlling force behind a work of art, that did much to establish the role of the director as the central artist in the theatre, a view dominating many practices of the modern theatre.

Wagner was able to build a theatre that would allow him to put some of his theories into practice. Opened in 1876, the Bayreuth Festspielhaus included features that helped Wagner establish his ideal world of the stage. Rather than the usual one proscenium arch, the theatre at Bayreuth has more than one; and the orchestra pit, customarily in full view of the audience, at Bayreuth extends partway under the stage and is entirely hidden from the sight of the audience. Too, Wagner had steam jets installed at the front of the stage to permit special effects like fog and mist, not only to help establish the mood of the production but also to help mask the changes in scenery. Such unusual architectural features were joined by certain new practices—like darkening the auditorium during the drama and forbidding the musicians to tune their instruments in the pit—to separate the real world of the audience (in the auditorium) from the ideal world of the drama (on the stage). This separation of the two worlds Wagner referred to as the "mystic chasm."

Unusual as some of these features were, they were less innovative and influential than changes that Wagner introduced into the auditorium at Bayreuth. For over three hundred years, the auditoriums of major theatres in Europe and (later) America had been arranged into three different seating areas: box, pit, and gallery. For some time, these locations in the theatre had implications about the social class of the patrons as well as the price of the tickets. Wagner, whether because of a desire to democratize the theatre or because of the increasing importance of seeing (rather than hearing) a play, eliminated the former seating distinctions in favor of a new "classless" theatre in which every seat had an equally good view of the stage and each ticket cost the same amount of money. The seats at Bayreuth were arranged in the shape of a fan, with the shorter rows closer to the stage and with entrances at the end of each row. This kind of arrangement came to be called *continental seating,* and some version of it was widely adopted as new theatres were constructed during the twentieth century.

"What is theatre?" For Wagner it was a means of bringing society back into contact with its shared past and of providing meaning for its common present. In that sense, theatre served a spiritual function not unlike that served by some religious celebrations. "Where should theatre be done and

Figure 5–11. **Wagner's Theatre.** The Bayreuth Festspielhaus, with its innovative seating arrangement and stage.

for whom?" Theatres were best when they emphasized, on the one hand, the separateness of the stage world and the audience world and, on the other hand, the community that existed among the spectators. "How should theatre get produced?" A single master artist should exercise absolute control over every element of the drama and the theatrical production. "What part should the script play in performance?" The music drama was the center about which all other elements of the production were united. They should be mythic rather than realistic, for myth was more truthful. Like the other elements of the production, the script should be under the control of the master artist. (The need for control was one of the reasons Wagner advocated music dramas rather than word dramas: music permitted the master artist rather than the actors to control the pitch, tempo, and emphasis of the words being performed).

Although, in fact, Wagner's productions seldom strayed far from the sort of illusionism common during the last years of the nineteenth century, his theories and architectural innovations placed him outside the mainstream of his day and made him a precursor of later experimenters like Adolphe Appia, Gordon Craig, and even Antonin Artaud.

Realistic Drama

As in staging practices, realism in the drama began tentatively and cautiously. It struggled for decades before it was first tolerated and later embraced by audiences. Although Frenchmen like Alexandre Dumas *fils* (1824–1895), Émile Augier (1820–1889), and even Eugène Scribe (1791–1861) presaged realism, it was the Norwegian, Henrik Ibsen (1828–1906) who brought

Figure 5–12. Realism: Ibsen. A scene from Ibsen's *Rosmersholm* with the great actress Eleonora Duse in a 1906 production.

the several philosophic and artistic strands into successful dramatic shape and launched realism as the major artistic movement of the next century. With plays like *Pillars of Society* (1877), *A Doll's House* (1879), *Ghosts* (1881), *An Enemy of the People* (1882), and *Hedda Gabler* (1890), Ibsen made a break with the sentimentalized problem plays of earlier days and assumed his controversial role as the attacker of society's values. Structurally his plays were fairly traditional: they told a story and moved logically from event to event just as well-made plays had done for years. But their content was shocking: when individuals came into conflict with society, they were no longer assumed to be guilty and society blameless. Indeed, social customs and traditional morality were exposed by Ibsen as a tangle of inconsistencies and irrelevancies. The problems addressed were customarily those of the middle and managerial classes. Questions like the proper role of women, the ethics of euthanasia, the morality of business and war, and the economics of religion formed the basis of serious probings into civilized behavior. Theatrical producers throughout the world who believed that drama should be involved in the social issues of the day applauded the Norwegian dramatist, and soon other artists began to translate, produce, and, later, emulate his plays.

Figure 5–13. Realism: Shaw. A scene from Shaw's *Pygmalion,* in a production by the Long Wharf Theatre, New Haven.

In England, George Bernard Shaw (1856–1950) became one of Ibsen's most vocal and influential supporters. A prolific writer himself, Shaw delighted in puncturing time-honored assumptions about human behavior and exposing various forms of social posturing. In an early play, *Arms and the Man* (1894), he spoofed romantic notions of love and war and satirized the then-popular comic form, the well-made play. Later, he turned to consider contemporary social situations in plays like *Major Barbara* (1905), *The Doctor's Dilemma* (1906), *Getting Married* (1908), and *Heartbreak House* (1914–1919). Sentimentalized history was among his targets in plays like *Caesar and Cleopatra* (1899) and *Saint Joan* (1923). Unlike many realists, Shaw always retained his sense of humor; he almost always wrote comedies, and their popularity did much to assure the final acceptance of realistic drama in England before the close of World War I.

In Russia, realism took a still different turn. Anton Chekhov (1860–1904) had written for the theatre in the 1880s but scored his first success in 1898 when *The Seagull* was produced at the Moscow Art Theatre. Within seven years, he had contributed *The Three Sisters* (1900), *Uncle Vanya* (1889, as *The Wood Demon*), and *The Cherry Orchard* (1902) to the growing literature in a realistic style. Chekhov's plays differed from those of Ibsen and Shaw in their tendency toward poetic expression and symbolic meanings. Chekhov's manipulation of language, with the careful rhythms, measured pauses, deliberate banalities, and artful repetitions, produced a sense of reality based

Figure 5–14. Realism: Chekhov. A scene from Chekhov's *Three Sisters* at the Trinity Square Repertory Company, Providence, Rhode Island. *(Directed by Adrian Hall. Mark III photo.)*

on compelling psychological truths as well as a degree of music and allusion uncommon in prose dramas. His incorporation of symbols within the texts (often the plays' titles bear clues) served to extend the plays' significance beyond the drab daily lives of the central characters. Chekhov took for his study the daily lives of people trapped in social situations. In some ways, he foretold the Russian Revolution by depicting the isolation of the aristocracy and their inevitable extinction. In another sense, he portrayed the loneliness and comic desperation of all peole who continue to hope while living in a hopeless situation, who persist in believing that help will come when none, in fact, is to be had.

For a realist, Chekhov was uncommonly allusive; for this reason, some critics prefer to label him a symbolist or an impressionist rather than a realist. But then some critics insist that Chekhov wrote tragedies, when Chekhov himself maintained that he wrote comedies. These critical controversies continue to the present day and serve as a reminder that genius is not easily reduced to titles and categories.

Naturalism

Soon realism, with its emphasis on the problems of the middle class, seemed too tame and too removed from the world's most pressing problems. In response, a more extreme style, *naturalism,* developed. While sharing with realists a belief in the efficacy of science as a solver of problems and in the role of drama in the improvement of society, the naturalists differed in their definition of what problems most needed attention and their hope for the future. Simply stated, naturalists were pessimistic. According to them, people were victims, not actors in life. Their destiny was *controlled* by factors like heredity and environment, factors over which they had little, if any,

Figure 5–15. Naturalism: Gorky. A scene from Gorky's *The Lower Depths* in Paris, 1905.

control. Because naturalists attempted to give the impression that their plays were an actual record of life, the dramas often appeared formless and unstructured, traits that gave rise to the phrase "a slice of life" to describe some naturalists' plays. Among the most successful playwrights in the style were August Strindberg (1849–1912), Gerhart Hauptmann (1862–1946), Émile Zola (1849–1902), and Maksim Gorki (1868–1936).

The new realistic and naturalistic plays required a new kind of acting. To portray ordinary people speaking in conversational prose about their daily lives demanded a different sort of training and an unusual commitment to small details. The need to play with fellow actors rather than to perform for an audience placed a premium on an actor's ability to concentrate and relate to onstage stimuli. Moreover, the audience was exceedingly familiar with the many details of everyday life that the actors sought to present on stage. How, then, could the actor make his impersonation believable? How could he be convincing about situations so well known to every member of the audience? It was in Russia that the most systematic attack on the problem of training actors for realistic and naturalistic theatre was made. But as always, the experiment in actors' training was bound up with other innovations in production.

Konstantin Stanislavski and the Moscow Art Theatre

Theatre in Russia has a tradition of strong involvement by the government. Even late in the nineteenth century, state theatres were still run by appointed officials and all theatres were subject to strict censorship. Too, starring performers still used plays primarily as a means of displaying their individual talents, and Russia's conventionalized scenic practices resembled those largely abandoned elsewhere almost a hundred years earlier. Thus, when the Meiningen company toured Russia in 1885 and again in 1890, their impact was strong indeed, for the German troupe was presenting a kind of ensemble acting and quality of visual detail not previously witnessed in Russia.

Two men, Konstantin Stanislavski (1863–1938) and Vladimir Nemirovich-Danchenko (1858–1943) saw the Meiningen company and were impressed. At an eighteen-hour meeting, they decided to establish a new kind of theatre in Moscow, an experimental theatre whose goals were (1) to remain free of the demands of commercialism; (2) to avoid overemphasis on the scenic elements of production; and (3) to reflect the inner truth of the play. For this theatre, Nemirovich-Danchenko was to select plays and handle the administration, while Stanislavski was to serve as the production director.

From its opening in 1898, the Moscow Art Theatre was known for its careful realistic/naturalistic productions. During its early years, the greatest attention was given to the accuracy of historical detail in all areas of the physical production, but within ten years, Stanislavski's interest moved from a largely external realism toward a psychological realism, toward finding an inner truth for actors. He strove, as he said, "to open all the potentialities of the actor and arouse his individual initiative. . . . to excite and kindle his imagination." External realism from this time on became, for Stanislavski, merely a key to opening the inner reality of the plays, and he strove to develop techniques that would help the actors achieve an inner truth.

In opposing the status quo, Stanislavki intended "to chase the theatre from the theatre." He wanted his actors to be naive, to believe in what they said and did on stage. He expected them to discover the motivations, or reasons, for what they said and did, relying for truth on the careful observations of people in real life in similar circumstances. And he urged his actors to imagine themselves in the character's situation. None of this was easy, Stanislavski knew, and as it presented a departure from current practices, he set about to discover ways of training actors to master this new approach. He believed that they had to learn to relax, to exert control over both their voices and their bodies, and to analyze a script with great care and with great attention to detail. To this end, he provided a series of exercises designed to increase concentration, promote relaxation, evoke remembered emotions, imagine the self as the character in the play, and so on.

By 1917, he had developed, from personal experience and observation of others, his major ideas for training actors, ideas that he codified in a series of books that have since been translated into more than twenty languages: *My Life in Art* (1924), *An Actor Prepares* (1936), *Building a Character* (1949), and *Creating a Role* (1961). Together they represent what has come to be called the Stanislavski "system" of actor training, although Stanislavski himself neither insisted that his was the only way to train actors nor that his methods should be studied and mastered by everyone.

Although today Stanislavksi's reputation rests largely on his contributions to actors' training, he was in his own time considered quite an innovative director. During the early years of the Moscow Art Theatre, while the influence of the Meiningen troupe remained strong, Stanislavski worked in a rather autocratic fashion, planning each detail of his actors' vocal inflections, gestures, movements, and so on. But as his interest in the problems of the actor grew (he was himself a fine and versatile actor), and as his actors became more skillful, he abandoned his dogmatic approach and became more of an instructor, interpreter, and helpmate to the actors. His ideal became for the director and the actors to grow together in their understanding of the play; therefore he no longer appeared at rehearsals with a detailed production book containing minute directions for the actors. Instead, after an initial reading of the play by Stanislavski for his actors, during which he tried to engage their interest and whet their enthusiasm for the script, the company began a lengthy period of analysis and discussion of the text. Only after the group had grasped the psychology of the roles and the complex interrelationships (often a three-month process) did the actors begin to work on the stage, moving about and developing "business." Beginning with very small units in the play and moving gradually to complete acts of the play and finally to the whole play, the actors and the director built a performance, a process often requiring six months or longer.

It was probably this careful attention to psychological detail that permitted Stanislavski's company to succeed with the plays of Anton Chekhov where others before had failed. On the other hand, it should be clear that such procedures are seldom possible in commercial ventures and rarely feasible outside an "experimental" situation.

"What is theatre?" For Stanislavski, it was the presentation onstage of something closely resembling real life, not only in the details of physical environment but also, and more importantly, in the truth of the inner lives of the characters. "How should theatre get produced?" By the actors and the director working together to discover an inner reality for each play and then to create the life of that play on the stage before an audience. "What part should the script play in performance?" The most important part of all, for the text was what bound together the efforts of the acting ensemble, the director, and the physical environment. Its production should expose the central social, ideological, and philosophical questions inherent in the script.

What began in 1898 as an experiment in external realism and was by 1906 an experiment in psychological realism had become an established tradition in Russia by the time of the revolution (1917). Because a number of Russians trained in "the system" left their country after the revolution, the teachings of Stanislavski came to the attention of the outside world. For example, Mikhail Chekhov (1891–1955) and Vera Kommissarzhevsky (1864–1910) fled Russia, worked in Europe and the United States, and brought their own versions of "the system" with them. But perhaps more important still, Richard Boleslavsky (1889–1937) and Maria Ouspenskaya (1881–1949) left Russia, came to the United States, and led the American Laboratory Theatre, where they had as students Harold Clurman, Lee Strasberg, and Stella Adler, founders of the Group Theatre, America's major propagators of Stanislavski's system of actor training (although by their time somewhat altered and renamed the "Method").

Realism and Naturalism in the Theatre

When staged, realistic and naturalistic plays shared similarities simply because they shared many assumptions and dealt with a fairly restricted range of subjects. Because realism dealt with the problems of the contemporary middle class, plays tended to be set in living rooms. Because realists believed that truth resided in objects, their settings tended to include actual items rather than their painted representations, and so the living rooms were filled with three-dimensional objects: furniture, pictures, ashtrays, vases, and so on. Because environment was believed to be an important contributor to a person's character, many objects were needed in order to define the environment carefully and precisely so that the character's traits could be better understood and his actions better motivated: in one sense, the more numerous the objects the better because the portrayal would thereby be made truer. Thus objects were often included for their own sake, to give a sense of greater reality, even when they did not contribute directly to the play's dramatic action. The *box set,* a stage "room" built of flats but with one wall missing so that the audience could look through it, was the standard scenic arrangement. The actors, dressed in the everyday clothes of middle-class men and women, moved amid the furniture and properties talking in the conversational prose of daily life. It was increasingly a convention of realistic staging that the characters were confined to their rooms and that they did not venture in front of the proscenium arch onto the apron or forestage, nor did they address the audience directly.

Naturalistic settings tended to emphasize squalor. They featured lower-class houses and sordid details. They unfolded less often in living rooms and more often in baths, kitchens, hovels, factories, bars, slums, and so on. The characters were poorly dressed and ill spoken. With these predictable exceptions, naturalism conformed to the major scenic conventions of realism.

Theatres that were built for realistic plays or those remodeled to improve their spaces for realistic productions tended to be intimate proscenium houses without apron or proscenium doors. Because the scenic requirements were relatively simple, few provided elaborate machinery for shifting scenery. The prized seats were in the orchestra. Auditoriums often abandoned the

Figure 5–16. Realism and Naturalism: Detail. Attention to the details of environment, with much use of specific properties and set "dressing" were typical, as in this scene from *La Bonne Esperance* at the Theatre Antoine, Paris, in 1903.

box, pit, and gallery arrangements in favor of some modification of Wagner's seating plan. Audiences consisted primarily of the middle classes, perhaps because it was most often their problems that were being addressed.

The intimacy of theatres intended for the production of realistic drama required an unusually careful attention to detail. Perhaps no one did more to set the standards for staging realistic and naturalistic plays than André Antoine in his early years at the Théâtre-Libre.

André Antoine and the Théâtre-Libre

André Antoine (1853–1943) abhorred the commercial theatres of Paris, disapproved of the way actors were trained at the Paris Conservatoire (France's leading school for actors), objected to the scenic practices of the major theatres, and decried the flimsiness of contemporary popular drama. What was needed, Antoine concluded, was an alternative theatre, one where new and controversial plays could gain productions that were both carefully mounted and realistically acted. Thus, when an amateur group to which he belonged balked at producing a daring new play, Antoine undertook the production himself and, spurred by early success, quit his job at the Paris gas company in 1887 to become the full-time director of his own new theatre. He named it the Théâtre-Libre (Free Theatre) and described

Figure 5–17. André Antoine. A caricature of 1902, some years after his pioneering work at the Théâtre Libre. Antoine continued to work in the theatre long after his experimental ideas had become part of the mainstream.

it as nothing less than "a machine of war, poised for the conquest of Paris."

Antoine believed with the naturalists that environment determined, or at least heavily influenced, human behavior, that environment molded character (rather than the other way round). Obviously, then, stage setting was very important indeed as it was the environment that determined how the characters/actors behaved and that provided the explanation of why they behaved as they did. For this reason, Antoine took great care to make his stage settings as believable and as much like real life as possible. For example, he adopted the practice of designing a room, placing the furniture and accessories in it, and only then deciding which "wall" of the room was to be removed so that the audience could see in. To emphasize the real-life quality of his stage settings further, Antoine depended heavily on the use of actual, three-dimensional objects rather than their painted substitutes. For one play, he brought real sides of beef onto his stage, for another real trees and birds' nests, for another a real student's actual room furnishings. The attention that he paid to realistic detail and his reliance on actual objects led to his being called by many the father of naturalistic staging.

Antoine believed that theatre should resemble real life in other ways. Actors should appear to be real people, not actors in a play. Unfortunately actors trained at the Paris Conservatoire (to which Antoine had earlier been denied admission) could not portray real life on stage because they had been trained to use their voices in special theatrical ways, to align their bodies in unlifelike poses, and to play to their audiences directly. Antoine wanted his actors to say their lines naturally, just as one might engage in a conversation with friends and, at the same time, to move about the furniture and accessories just as in real life. Sincerity and conviction were the qualities he sought, and so he advised his actors to ignore the audience and to speak to one another in conversational tones—in short, to try to *be,* rather than to *act,* the characters in the play. Perhaps for these reasons, Antoine often used amateur actors in his theatre, actors who had not received conventional training for the commercial theatre and who were therefore more receptive to the experimental, new style of naturalistic acting. Jean Julien, a contemporary of Antoine's, seemed to sum up the goal of Antoine: "The front of the stage must be a fourth wall, transparent for the public, opaque for the player."

Just as Antoine advocated new kinds of scenic and acting practices, he was also committed to new kinds of plays. Although he produced a wide range of plays while at the Théâtre-Libre, he seemed most comfortable with plays in the realistic and naturalistic styles. Although many such plays had been written before Antoine opened his theatre, few had escaped the censors and found their way into public performances. Because Antoine organized his theatre as a subscription house, he was able to escape the threats of censorship (much as private clubs today can avoid laws prohibiting liquor sales). Consequently he was able to introduce to Parisians a wide range of French and foreign authors whose works were considered too scandalous for production in major theatres of the day. Plays by Émile Zola, Leo Tolstoy, August Strindberg, Henrik Ibsen, and Gerhart Hauptmann were produced by Antoine even while they were forbidden productions elsewhere.

Figure 5–18. Realism: Detail. A scene from Zola's *L'Assomoir,* 1900.

From his practices and his writings, Antoine's answers to several theoretical questions can be inferred. To the question "What is theatre?" Antoine seemed to respond that it was a literal representation of real life, that scenery and acting should resemble episodes and behavior observable in the everyday world, that audiences should forget they were in a theatre and imagine rather that they were overseeing a small bit of real life. Plays were worthwhile for Antoine when they depicted episodes common to everday people, no matter that the events were seamy or even immoral by contemporary standards. Similarly the questions "Where should theatre get done, for whom, and by what means?" were answered implicitly in the choices Antoine made in establishing his theatre. Always working in small-sized (300-seat) or medium-sized (800-seat) spaces, during this stage of his career Antoine used fourth-wall staging, a style that clearly required a proscenium arch. He solicited audiences that were open to new plays and to new, often bold, ideas; he asked that they make a financial commitment to a series of performances by buying membership in a theatre, not just a ticket to a play. Finally, Antoine apparently viewed the text as central to the performance, if his devotion to new plays and playwrights of several nationalities and several stylistic preferences can be used as evidence.

The major contributions of Antoine and the Théâtre-Libre (1887–1896) were (1) to popularize acting techniques leading toward naturalness on stage; (2) to gain acceptance for scenic practices now known as "fourth-wall realism," with all that implies about scenic detail and literal objects; (3) to introduce a new generation of playwrights (both French and foreign) to the theatregoing public of Paris; and (4) to establish a model for a censor-free theatre.

The most significant experimental theatre of its day, the Théâtre-Libre

Figure 5–19. The Triumph of Antoine. Within a decade of his work at the Théâtre Libre, Antoine's ideas were accepted by many major theatre artists, as can be seen in this 1900 production of *L'Assomoir.*

gave rise to a number of similar theatres throughout the world. Although differing in several details from their parent, the independent theatres that sprang up in general shared the goals and working methods of Antoine's free theatre. The best known of these theatres were, in Germany, the Freie Bühne (headed by Otto Brahm) and the Freie Volksbühne and, in England, the Independent Theatre (headed by J. T. Grein) and the Incorporated Stage Society. Called the *independent theatre movement,* this blossoming of small, independent theatres in several countries almost simultaneously gave impetus to the ultimate acceptance of realism as the mainstream of the commercial theatre, an acceptance completed by early in the twentieth century.

The Commercial Mainstream: 1900–1960

Perhaps by 1900, but certainly by the end of World War I (1918), realism in the drama and in theatrical production had been widely accepted in the commercial houses of France, England, and America. By the 1920s, Parisian boulevard theatres regularly played serious pieces dealing with social problems, and audiences no longer found them controversial. Commercial theatres in London found both Ibsen and Shaw palatable and played realistic dramas as well as sophisticated domestic comedies by authors like Noel Coward (1899–1973) and Somerset Maugham (1874–1965).

Broadway was booming. Between 200 and 275 new productions a year were not unusual during the decade of the 1920s. The cost of a production

Figure 5–20. Comedy after 1900. Noel Coward was the epitome of the witty, sophisticated dramatist of the period between the wars. Here, his *Tonight at 8:30* as produced by the University of Minnesota. *(Directed by John Kerr, setting by Pete Davis, costumes by Katharine Maple Fletcher, lighting by Ed Krehl.)*

was as low as $2,000 for some of the simple pieces and seldom more than $10,000, even for elaborate realistic plays. New theatres were being built to keep up with the demand as audiences flocked to attend. For an average price of three dollars, a patron could buy the best seat in the house. The long run was an established theatrical fact: *Abie's Irish Rose,* a romantic comedy by Anne Nichols involving a marriage between a Catholic and a Jew, set a record with 2,327 performances after it opened in 1922, and *Tobacco Road,* a naturalistic play by Jack Kirkland filled with low-life characters, opened a seven-year run in 1933 and closed after over 3,100 performances. Inevitably, with the enormous vitality and the great number of original plays, many were trivial and some were downright awful (such plays were called *turkeys,* because weak shows were customarily scheduled to open on Thanksgiving Day in the hopes of improving their ticket sales). But many of the plays were memorable; some are still staged today.

George S. Kaufman (1889–1961), a master of the wisecrack, wrote (both alone and with a variety of collaborators, the most constant of which was Moss Hart) a series of zany comedies like *Beggar on Horseback, Once in a Lifetime, You Can't Take It with You,* and *The Man Who Came to Dinner.* Several sentimentalized versions of urban life and gangsterland formed the basis of popular melodramas of the decade like *The Front Page* and *Broadway.* The Ziegfeld

Follies was still enormously popular with audiences; this entertainment featured songs, dances, and variety acts and enjoyed the services of the nation's favorite composer, Irving Berlin. But musical comedy took on a new shape after Jerome Kern and Oscar Hammerstein produced *Showboat* (1927) and demonstrated that musicals in which music was well integrated with the characters and the story were even more appealing than old-fashioned variety acts.

The Theatre Guild (founded 1919) was the most dynamic and creative producing organization of the decade. Early in its career, it attacked the provinciality of American theatre by importing a series of foreign works by important and controversial new authors: Tolstoy's *The Power of Darkness* (1920), Strindberg's *The Dance of Death* (1920), Ibsen's *Peer Gynt* (1923), and a large number of plays by G. B. Shaw. By the mid 1920s, American playwrights were competing with the foreigners as authors of serious realistic drama, and so the Guild produced new plays by Elmer Rice, Sidney Howard, S. N. Behrman, and most of all Eugene O'Neill (1888–1953). Between March 1924 and January 1925, five of his plays were appearing in New York: *Welded, All God's Chillun Got Wings, Desire Under the Elms, The Fountain,* and *The Great God Brown.* By the end of the decade, his plays were producing profits in excess of those awarded to many pieces of commercial fluff. In the short period between 1926 and 1928, the Guild produced fourteen different plays, thereby leading Broadway into one of its most exultant periods and once and for all establishing serious realistic drama as an accepted staple of the Broadway theatre. As Brooks Atkinson, an important critic, said, the Ameri-

Figure 5–21. American Realism: O'Neill. A scene from O'Neill's comedy, *Ah, Wilderness,* as produced by the University of Missouri, Columbia. *(Directed by Mary Arbenz.)*

can theatre was suddenly transported from "adolescence into maturity and from provinciality into a cosmopolitan point of view."

After 1930, the Guild's influence waned as its financial picture became more precarious, and in an attempt to improve its balance sheet, it moved closer to the practices of other commercial producers, finally becoming scarcely distinguishable from them. Its mantle passed to the Group Theatre, which, after its founding in 1931, became a militant spokesman for anticommercial theatres in New York. The Group focused attention on various social causes, particularly those relevant to poor and downtrodden classes, and flirted with government displeasure for their presumably leftist leanings. More importantly, the Group popularized an American version of Stanislavski's acting techniques (called, in the United States, the "Method") and established a visual style for American plays that came to be called *selective* (or *simplified*) *realism*. When they produced Clifford Odets's play *Waiting for Lefty* (1935), the Group stunned audiences, launched the career of Odets, and heralded the arrival of "relevant" social drama in New York.

Other serious dramatists were at work as well. Elmer Rice received a Pulitzer Prize for his naturalistic portrayal of urban life in *Street Scene* (1929). Maxwell Anderson contributed a variety of succesful plays: one dealt with the evils of politics, *Both Your Houses* (1933); another with the futility of war, *What Price Glory?* (with Laurence Stallings, 1924); some, like *Elizabeth the Queen* and *Anne of the Thousand Days*, were experiments with verse drama in a pseudo-Shakespearean style; and in *Winterset* (1936), Anderson even tried to write a modern verse tragedy about young people caught up in urban gangs and street crime. Challenging Anderson as leading authors of the period were Robert Sherwood (1896–1955) and Lillian Hellman (b. 1905). Sherwood's early success, *The Petrified Forest* (1935), was followed closely by *Idiot's Delight,* which won a Pulitzer prize in 1936. Lillian Hellman burst on the scene in 1934 with *The Children's Hour,* a play with allusions to lesbianism in a girl's school, and then cemented her initial success with *The Little Foxes* (1939), a play that made Tallulah Bankhead's ascent to stardom more certain, and *Watch on the Rhine* (1941), a warning to the unheeding American public of the impending holocaust in Nazi Germany.

Musicals were in their heyday, with composers like Cole Porter (1891–1964) and George Gershwin (1898–1937) leading the way. Porter's long career peaked with his score for *Kiss Me, Kate* (1948), a musical based loosely on Shakespeare's *The Taming of the Shrew,* but as early as 1920, he had been contributing tunes to America's musical theater, tunes like "Let's Do It," "What Is This Thing Called Love?" "Night and Day," "Begin the Beguine," and "My Heart Belongs to Daddy." His biggest hit during the 1930s was the score for *Anything Goes* (1934), which featured the magnificent talents of Ethel Merman. With a very different but equally substantial talent, Gershwin wrote tunes for a variety of musicals before he finally hit his stride with *Of Thee I Sing* (1931), a stinging satire of American politics for which his music captured the lethal and jeering quality of the book by George S. Kaufman and Morrie Ryskind. Probably now, however, Gershwin is best remembered for his *Porgy and Bess* (1935). This American classic has been played in the theatres and opera houses of the world since its first production,

Figure 5–22. American Commercial Theatre. In the first half of the twentieth century, the American musical found its form; American drama matured; and the commercial mainstream became "Broadway." Today, a statue of the actor-playwright George M. Cohan stands in New York's Times Square to celebrate these events.

and people still hum its haunting "Summertime," "I Got Plenty o' Nuttin'," and "It Ain't Necessarily So." Gershwin's fame, of course, is not limited to his Broadway credits. His pioneering work in modern music with pieces like "Rhapsody in Blue" and "An Amercian in Paris" speeded the acceptance of American jazz as a legitimate musical form.

But perhaps the most exciting development in the American theatre of the 1930s was also the least characteristic. In 1935, the federal government launched the Federal Theatre Project, a program designed to assist the vast number of theatre artists who had been thrown out of work by the worsening Depression. Part of the program's excitement was its national character, for the Federal Theatre established units in many states—California as well as New York, North Carolina as well as Michigan—and revitalized a sagging industry by introducing both new forms and new artists to the American scene. In New York, for example, Elmer Rice instituted the first "living newspaper," a kind of staged documentary dealing with society's most pressing problems. In a series of living newspapers, the problems of housing, farm prices, and war were examined. Not surprisingly, when anti-Communism became the cry of government, living newspapers were denounced as Communist plots. Once they fell, the Federal Theatre Project was not far behind. In 1939, by failing to provide appropriations, the government closed its first far-reaching experiment in the support of the arts. But before its demise, the Federal Theatre had spawned a number of new artists and theatres, most notably Orson Welles (b.1915), John Houseman (b.1902), and the Mercury Theatre.

Quite different from the strident Federal Theatre was the benign voice of a new playwright who devised a simple drama of life in small-town USA. With *Our Town,* Thornton Wilder (1897–1975) affirmed human greatness at a time when America was recovering from a depression and listening to the sounds from Europe of an impending second world war. Requiring no scenery and few properties, the play quickly became a mainstay of high school, community, and college theatres across the land. Also in 1938, Wilder wrote *The Merchant of Yonkers,* which failed in its original production but enjoyed a successful revival as *The Matchmaker,* (1954) and then, set to music, as *Hello, Dolly!* (1964), one of America's most popular and enduring musicals. By 1942, Wilder was less exuberant, and his odd work *The Skin of our Teeth* failed to capture the public's esteem in spite of a sterling cast that included Tallulah Bankhead, Fredric March, and E. G. Marshall.

Despite the many excellent playwrights of the 1930s, the American commercial theatre was in trouble by the end of the decade. The Depression had made money scarce at the same time that other forms of entertainment began to compete for the public's entertainment dollar. Spectator sports and movies (particularly after Al Jolson talked in *The Jazz Singer* in 1927) demanded an increasing share of the shrinking dollar at the same time that theatrical unions were exercising new muscle and demanding better wages from a theatre less able than before to provide them. And the nation was moving toward involvement in a second disastrous world war.

During the war (1941–1945), Broadway artists supported the war effort, revived earlier successes, and occasionally produced a successful new show like Mary Chase's *Harvey,* a charming look at an aging man and his (imagined) six-foot-tall rabbit, and Garson Kanin's *Born Yesterday,* with Judy Holliday as the dumb blond girlfriend of a war profiteer. The decade's most exciting event, however, was the first performance of the musical *Oklahoma!* (1943), which lifted audiences from the ugly realities of a foreign war and returned them to a happier time in rural America. The musical by Richard Rodgers and Oscar Hammerstein II was brilliantly choreographed by Agnes de Mille, with the result that ballet and dance became an integral part of the musicals for the next several decades: never before had music and dance and character and story been knit into such a tightly constructed unit, and Broadway audiences loved it. *Oklahoma!* ran for 2,212 consecutive performances and turned a solid profit of $5 million in its first ten years. Rodgers and Hammerstein, encouraged by this success, followed with, among others, *Carousel* (1945) and *South Pacific* (1947), musical plays that still form part of our repertory.

The war years also launched the careers of two major American writers,

Figure 5–23. Away from Realism: Wilder. Few properties and a bare stage marked Thornton Wilder's *Our Town,* shown here in a production by the University of New Orleans. *(Directed by James M. Ragland, designs by Lane Halteman, Barbara R. Alkofer, and Robert Hardison. W. A. Hunt, III photo.)*

playwrights whose works were to dominate the stage for the next decade and firmly establish American realism and simplified staging as the styles of the 1940s and 1950s. Tennessee Williams (b.1914) won the Drama Critics Circle Award for his first major Broadway production, *The Glass Menagerie* (1945), a wistful memory play vaguely reminiscent of the impressionists and Chekhov. In 1947, *A Streetcar Named Desire* took Broadway by storm. Williams was hailed as a writer of the first rank, and Marlon Brando was propelled to stardom for his portrayal of the inarticulate and slovenly Stanley Kowalski, a success that popularized the "Method" as America's contribution to the acting of realistic and naturalistic plays. Elia Kazan's reputation as a director of great subtlety and sensitivity was assured, and "selective realism" was established as the model of designers for years to come. For this play, Williams received both the Pulitzer Prize and the Drama Critics Circle Award. Although some critics consider his subsequent plays inferior to his earlier efforts, many are memorable pieces that continue to find production around the country, among them *Cat on a Hot Tin Roof* (1954), *Sweet Bird of Youth* (1959), and *The Night of the Iguana* (1961).

Just as Williams's realism was different from that first introduced in Europe in the late nineteenth century, so too was Arthur Miller's, but in a somewhat different direction. *All My Sons* (1947) told of an American businessman who knowingly sold inferior products for America's war effort in order to turn a profit. Despite the Drama Critics Circle Award, the play was banned in occupied Europe after the war and denounced by some as a smear on the American business community. Miller was under suspicion, therefore, when he wrote *Death of a Salesman* (1947), an acknowledged American masterpiece. In this play, realistic scenes are interspersed with remembered scenes as seen through the eyes and ears of the disordered protagonist, Willy Loman. A moody piece with overtones of expressionism, *Death of a Salesman,* as directed by Elia Kazan and designed by Jo Mielziner, won both a Pulitzer Prize and the Drama Critics Circle Award and further promoted the conventions of American realism. Although Miller continued to write important American plays, some critics feel that he never again attained his early accomplishments with plays like *The Crucible* (1953), *A View from the Bridge* (1955), *After the Fall* (1964), and *The Price* (1968).

Although the successes of Williams and Miller tended to obscure the works of other promising writers, plays like *Picnic* and *Come Back, Little Sheba,* and *Bus Stop* (all by William Inge) and *The Member of the Wedding* (by Carson McCullers) and musicals like *Finian's Rainbow* and *Brigadoon* were also popular.

But during the 1940s and 1950s, despite the advent of Williams and Miller, the Broadway theatre appeared to be in serious trouble. Its death was often predicted—and not without justification. Whereas, in 1930–1931, there had been 187 new productions, by 1940–1941 there were only 72. Theatres were being abandoned, torn down, or converted into movie houses; some were even being used for girlie shows. The block around Times Square degenerated into an atmosphere more reminiscent of a carnival or a sex bazaar than the center of the American theatre. Opening nights more often heralded openings of Hollywood films than stage plays, and many once-glorious legitimate theatres were permanently dark. Theatre real estate had been made unprofitable by the soaring costs of land on Manhattan and by the strict fire codes that had been imposed. Just when it appeared that things could not get worse, television for the first time covered a presidential

Figure 5–24. Regional Theatre Movement. The Stratford, Ontario Festival Theatre, shown here in the 1950s, spurred the construction of other regional theatres in the United States and Canada after the mid-fifties. *(Courtesy of the Stratford Shakespearean Festival, Canada. Peter Smith photo.)*

convention and clearly established itself as an important national entertainment industry (1948).

Clearly the theatrical mainstream was in trouble. A variety of alternatives was advocated and tried. Some critics of Broadway blamed the blandness of commercial houses and sought remedies in small, less expensive theatres off Broadway where experimental plays and production styles could be undertaken. Others blamed the centralization of the American theatre in New York and suggested that, to be truly national, the theatre should have outlets throughout the forty-eight states; and so regional theatres proliferated, many modeled on Dallas's successful arena theatre begun by Margo Jones in 1947. Many believed that revitalization of the modern theatre required a strong dose of classical plays performed by well-trained actors; the success of the Stratford, Ontario, Shakespeare Festival (founded in 1953) gave impetus to the development of other festival theatres around the United States—and ultimately to other resident professional companies devoted to a classical repertory.

Apparently the death of the American theatre was greatly exaggerated, for by the mid-1960s, Broadway's vitality and strength were clearly on the upsurge. The threats of movies, television, and spectator sports had been successfully met. New playwrights like Neil Simon and Jean Kerr were attracting audiences longing for entertainment, as were revivals of plays from old pros like Clifford Odets, Eugene O'Neill, and George S. Kaufman. *Paint Your Wagon, My Fair Lady, The Music Man,* and *West Side Story* were successful enough to convince even pessimists that good musicals could still attract large audiences.

But during the 1960s, too, American realism, as popularized by Williams and Miller, was being attacked and its dominance eroded. Experimental plays and theatres sought antidotes to the lethargy that had attacked Broadway in the 1950s, and an unusually large number of artists were seeking the antidote in directions that led away from the American realism so popular since World War I.

Problems with Realism

Even before realism had become the mainstream of theatrical life in Europe and America, some writers and theorists had begun to chafe under its limitations. Four questions in particular were the focus of discussion and concern: How can realistic drama be kept interesting? How can it be made significant? What is the role of the audience in a realistic theatre? How can the theatrical event be kept probable (or believable)? Although playwrights of all periods and styles have grappled with these questions, writers of realistic drama were denied access to many devices traditionally used to solve the problems implied by them.

In the past, for example, authors had depicted characters who were considerably removed from everyday experience. They were often princes, kings, military heroes, elegant aristocrats, and even demigods. Whatever they were, they participated in events that were out of the ordinary and often exotic: a war, a national crisis, a cosmic struggle. The plays were set in faraway times and places, environments that were, in themselves, often mysterious and compelling. When confronting a crisis, these exalted characters burst into passages of extreme lyricism in which the full resources of the language (rhythm, rhyme, metaphor, and so on) were marshaled to produce heights of emotional intensity. Such plays were performed before sets and in costumes that were also removed from the details of ordinary middle-class life.

But realistic drama, by definition, portrays ordinary people involved in mundane situations. Their language necessarily resembles everyday conversation and their clothing reflects their middle- or lower-class status. What, then, makes them interesting? Why should an audience wish to come to the theatre? Neither the sets nor the costumes offered any particular pleasures; the conversational prose was neither so allusive nor so interesting as poetry; and actors who dressed and sounded like the neighbors lacked glamor and excitement. Audience pleasure seemed largely dependent on the factor of *recognition* alone. Although the factor is a very potent one indeed, it was being asked to carry the entire weight of provoking and maintaining interest, a burden that proved too heavy for many dramas denied the customary resources of scenery, costume, and language.

Related to the problem of interest was that of significance. Traditionally, in serious drama, playwrights depicted serious actions that were of consequence to a large range of people—a nation or even a world. The killing of Julius Caesar, for example, changed the paths of heavenly bodies and the future course of the Roman Empire; all citizens were affected, and so the action of the play by Shakespeare had inherent significance. But realistic dramas typically dealt with working-class men and women as they lived out rather humdrum lives. If no more was at stake than the happiness of a single individual or a small family, who beyond their immediate friends would find it significant?

Some realistic dramatists increased the significance of their plays' actions by having the hero represent something beyond himself, something more general. Willy Loman in *Death of a Salesman,* for example, was made to stand for all salesmen, or even all working men. Such a solution, however, was often not successful. In many ways, it pulled against the very philosophical assumptions on which realism was based. For a realist, truth resided in material objects, in things verifiable through scientific inquiry. Abstractions, allegories, and symbols, with their insistence on a truth beyond the tangible, flew in the face of realistic tenets. Perhaps more seriously, however, abstractions are often undramatic. Poetry and the novel, where the reader can return time and again to study and consider the text, are usually better media for abstractions and symbolizations than are plays, where the living presence of the actors urges toward specificity and where the basis of the form is action rather than idea or word.

The differences between nonrealistic and realistic drama with respect to interest and significance can perhaps be illustrated by a brief consideration

Figure 5–25. Beyond Realism: Musicals. By their very nature, American musicals were not as limited in language and setting as dramas were. In a musical like *Carousel*, the nonrealistic inclusion of scenes in Heaven and of supernatural characters was possible. Produced at Centenary College. *(Directed by Robert R. Buseick; designs by David Pellman and Patric McWilliams.)*

of the heroines in a pair of plays, one popular in the seventeenth century and one popular in the 1950s.

A character describes Cleopatra in a scene that we never see. But obviously, when the heroine appears on stage, her stature must be the equal of such a description:

> The barge she sat in, like a burnish'd throne,
> Burn'd on the water. The poop was beaten gold;
> Purple the sails, and so perfumed that
> The winds were love-sick with them; the oars were silver,
> Which to the tune of flutes kept stroke, and made
> The water which they beat to follow faster,
> As amorous of their strokes. For her own person,
> It beggar'd all description: she did lie
> In her pavilion—cloth-of-gold of tissue—
> O'er-picturing that Venus where we see
> The fancy outwork nature. On each side her
> Stood pretty dimpled boys, like smiling Cupids
> With divers-colour'd fans, whose wind did seem
> To glow the delicate cheeks which they did cool,
> And what they undid did.
>
> *Antony and Cleopatra, II, iii*

The extensive stage directions of the modern play describe the first appearance of our realistic heroine:

The house is extremely cluttered and even dirty. The living room somehow manages to convey the atmosphere of the twenties, decorated with cheap pretense at niceness and respectability. The general effect is one of fussy awkwardness. . . . The davenport is littered and there are lace antimascassers on all of the chairs.

. . . .

Lola comes downstairs. . . . Over a nightdress she wears a lumpy kimono. Her eyes are dim with a morning expression of disillusionment, as though she had had a beautiful dream during the night and found on waking none of it was true. On her feet are worn dirty comfies.

Come Back, Little Sheba, I, i

Obviously Shakespeare's description of Cleopatra is interesting in both its language and its content, while Inge's description of Lola seems determined to confine the spectator's imagination to the details of everyday, even sordid, living.

Even though the stage in realistic drama was a close reproduction of the real world and the actors a duplication of everyday people, the separation of the audience from the dramatic action in "fourth-wall realism" (as signified by the presence of a proscenium arch) was greater than ever before. The

Figure 5–26. American Realism. Carson McCullers' *Member of the Wedding,* staged at Centenary College. *(Directed by Robert R. Buseick, designs by Debra Hicks and Barbara Acker.)*

conventions of the style required the audience to sit in a darkened auditorium and to watch silently as a separate world unfolded behind the proscenium arch. Actors, for their part, behaved as if the audience were not there, turning their backs and mumbling lines in an attempt to reproduce the inarticulateness of everyday conversations. Actors played with one another rather than with the audience (as had been customary in earlier days). The result was a world on the stage quite separate from the real world where the audience sat. It is ironic that realistic drama and staging, that had seemed to bring the world of the stage closer to that of the audience, ended by separating them to a degree unparalleled in the history of the theatre.

Finally, writers of realistic drama set themselves an unusually difficult task. All playwrights, of course, must construct plays that are probable, or believable, if they are to capture the interest and commitment of an audience. But only the realist additionally required that the world in the play resemble on a one-to-one basis the world outside. The realist's ideal was to establish on stage a literal reproduction of the everyday world; the theatrical scenery was to be a photographic likeness of the outside world and the actors the embodiment of everyday people. To produce the familiar and to make it believable proved too demanding a chore for many realistic playwrights.

Because of these problems, a variety of alternatives to realistic plays and staging began to be proposed and tested.

Alternatives to Realism

The years between 1890 and 1960 saw a proliferation of *isms:* neoromanticism, formalism, symbolism, impressionism, expressionism, constructivism, futurism, adsurdism, and so on. Each strove to address and solve one or more of the problems inherent in realism. As each developed, grew, and declined, the mainstream of realism shifted slightly to accommodate various attributes of the competing styles. As a result, realism remained the mainstream of theatre from about 1900 through 1960 but shifted perceptibly throughout that period as it incorporated first one and then another new approach to playwriting or staging. Toward the end of the 1950s the works of Bertolt Brecht and Antonin Artaud seized the imagination of theorists and laid the foundations for many practices of the contemporary theater.

Among the more interesting *isms* to emerge at the end of the nineteenth century was *impressionism* (fl. 1890s), a style that sought to capture and reproduce the fleeting moments of awareness that were believed to constitute the essence of human existence. By reproducing faithfully these fleeting glimpses, art could provide insights into the truth that lay underneath the external world. Probably the playwright that wrote most successfully in the style was Maurice Maeterlinck (1862–1949). In short plays like *The Intruder* (1890), *The Interior* (1894) and in longer plays like *Pelléas and Mélisande* (1892) and *The Blue Bird* (1908), Maeterlinck presented a world far removed from that of mundane reality. Introspection and subjectivity permeate the plays,

Figure 5–27. Impressionism. Lack of detail and indeterminate location marked the style of Impressionism, as in this 1902 production of Materlinck's *Pelleas and Melisande.*

which are typically moody and mysterious works hinting at a life controlled by unseen and inexplicable forces manipulating passive and often perplexed characters. The actions seem hazy, distant, out of focus; indeed, in the theatre, the plays were often played behind gauzes (scrims) or clouds of fog and moved between patches of light, dark, and shadow.

Maeterlinck believed that the manipulation of language was crucial in achieving the muted and languid mood he so often sought:

Side by side with the necessary dialogue you will almost always find another dialogue that seems superfluous; but examine it carefully, and it will be borne home to you that this is the only one that the soul can listen to profoundly, for here alone it is the soul that is being addressed.

For impressionists like Maeterlinck, then, a play aimed to convey intuitions about a truth more profound than the tangible, objective, external world of the realists. Through symbols, it alluded to a significance beyond the immediate, and through its language and stories it aspired to arouse interest by its exoticism.

Impressionists were closely allied with the symbolists, of whom the most famous were the theatrical practitioners Adolphe Appia (1862–1928) and Gordon Craig (1872–1966). Appia believed that artistic unity was the fundamental goal of theatrical production and that lighting was the element best able to fuse all other elements into an artistic whole. Like music, its auditory counterpart, light was capable of continual change to reflect shifting moods and emotions within the play. Like music, too, light could be orchestrated by variations in its direction, intensity, color, and so on, to produce a rhythm designed to underscore the dramatic action. Because he found an aesthetic contradiction between the three-dimensional actor and the two-dimensional floor set at right angles to the two-dimensional painted scenes so popular in his day, Appia sought ways to provide the stage floor and scenery with mass so that the actor could better blend with them. He solved the problem in part by devising three-dimensional settings composed of series of steps, ramps, and platforms, among which the living actor could comfortably move.

Like Appia, Craig opposed scenic illusions and favored instead a simple visual statement that eliminated inessential details and avoided photographic reproductions of specific places. His emphasis was on the manipulation of line and mass to achieve first a unity of design and ultimately a unity for the total production. Although Craig placed less emphasis on the importance of the actor and the text than Appia, they agreed on the importance of the visual elements of the production. Perhaps it would not be an injustice to designate Appia as the formulator of the theories that Craig later popularized.

Impressionism in the drama was not of lasting importance, perhaps because its emphasis on internal states and spiritual glimpses was better suited to the page than to the stage. Some of its techniques, however, were appealing and so were adopted by realists like Ibsen (in his later plays), Chekhov, and more recently Tennessee Williams. The theories of Appia and Craig exerted a greater influence in the theatre and gained a secure foothold in theatrical practice following World War I.

Whereas impressionism sought to present echoes of a transitory and mysterious truth, *expressionism* (fl. 1910s–1930s) usually focused on political and social questions. If impressionism produced a dreamlike vision, expressionism created a stage world closer to the nightmare. The plays were often didactic and cautioned the world against impending cataclysms caused by uncontrolled industrialization, rampant impersonalization, and a host of other threats posed by the modern industrial state. Seldom did the plays tell a simple story; more often they developed as examinations or demonstrations of a central thesis. They customarily unfolded in a world of bizarre and garish colors, jagged angles, and oddly proportioned objects (perhaps because they were often told through the mind of the protagonist, whose mental vision was distorted). Actors, often dressed identically, moved in mechanical or puppetlike ways and often spoke in disconnected or telegraphic conversations. They bore names of types rather than people; for example, a cast might include characters named simply The Mother, The Son, The Cipher, and so on. Conventional ideas of time and space collapsed; in their place were elastic units where years could fly by as seconds crept and adjacent objects appeared as if seen through the opposite ends of a telescope.

Expressionism as a movement was most popular in Germany. Its two leading playwrights were Georg Kaiser (1878–1945), whose best-known plays are *From Morn to Midnight* (1916) and the *Gas* trilogy (*Coral*, 1917; *Gas I*, 1918; and *Gas II*, 1918) and Ernst Toller (1893–1939) whose best-known

Figure 5–28. Expressionism. A nightmare world of harsh angles and depersonalized figures marked Expressionism, as seen here in the 1923 production of Rice's *The Adding Machine. (Courtesy of the Billy Rose Theatre Company, the New York Public Library at Lincoln Center, Astor, Lenox and Tilden Foundations.)*

works are *Transfiguration* (1918), *Man and the Masses* (1921), and *Hurrah, We Live* (1927).

In Russia, the practices of Vsevolod Meyerhold (1874–1940) paralleled many of those associated with the German expressionists. Although early in his career Meyerhold directed experimental works for Stanislavski, during the 1920s he devoted himself to developing a theatrical art suitable for the machine age. He formulated two major theoretical positions: *biomechanics* and *constructivism*. Biomechanics referred to a training system and performance style for actors: they were to be well-trained "machines" for carrying out the assignments given them, and so they needed rigorous physical training in ballet, gymnastics, circus techniques, and so on. *Constructivism* referred to Meyerhold's conclusions that scenery should not attempt to represent any particular place but that it should provide a "machine" on which actors could perform. In practice, Meyerhold's sets were often elaborate combinations of platforms, steps, ramps, wheels, and trapezes. The goal of both biomechanics and constructivism was to undercut the realist's emphasis on internal motivation for actors and literal representation in scenery and costumes and to re-theatricalize the theatre.

Expressionistic plays are seldom produced today outside of university theatres, but their influence has been substantial for three reasons. First, many of the techniques were adapted and used by the growing film industry. Second, some expressionistic techniques were adapted to the needs of important playwrights in the realistic mainstream, notably Arthur Miller, Eugene O'Neill, and Edward Albee. Third, German expressionism was an early influence on Erwin Piscator and Brecht, whose "epic theatre" became a major force in European and American theatres during the 1940s, 1950s, and 1960s. Staging devices popularized by expressionism and constructivism, although softened, continue to influence designers in contemporary theatre and film down to the present day.

Just after World War II, another movement surfaced and caused a temporary flurry of excitement. *Absurdism* (fl. 1940s and 1950s) was itself a blend of earlier abortive experiments of the French avant-garde. With *dadaism* (fl. 1920s), it shared an emphasis on life's meaninglessness and art's irrelevancy and a commitment to irrationality and nihilism as appropriate responses to life and living. With *surrealism* (fl. 1920s), it viewed the source of insight as a person's subconscious mind, a place best tapped during a dreamlike state when reason, morality, and aesthetics are not exercising control over a person's responses. But most importantly, with *existentialism* (fl. 1930s and 1940s), it sought an answer to the plaguing question: What does it mean to exist and to be? Jean-Paul Sartre (b. 1905), a philosopher turned playwright and the major spokesman for existentialism, sought to establish a code of life based on a consistent atheism, where the absence of absolute moral laws left mankind adrift in a world without order or purpose. He declared, in his treatises as well as in his plays, that each person must define his or her own value system and then act accordingly. It was this position on which much that was absurdist was based.

Absurdism stressed that the world was unreasonable, illogical, incongruous, and out or harmony. The word *absurd,* then, meant not *ridiculous* but *without meaning.* According to absurdists, the only order in life was what a person constructed; the only moral systems were those that the individual defined. To incorporate these views into dramatic form, the absurdists abandoned telling a story in favor of communicating an experience; they left behind a dramatic unity based on causality and replaced it with one whose source, and indeed whose very presence, was not always clear to the uninitiated. The plays were often constructed as a circle, ending just where they began, after displaying a series of unrelated incidents; they were often built as the intensification of a single event, ending just where they had begun but in the midst of more people or more objects. Usually the puzzling quality of the plays was attributable to the playwright's decision to devalue language as a carrier of meaning: in the plays, *what happens* on stage often transcends and contradicts *what is said* there. Although words are important in the plays, their tonal and rhythmic dimensions are often more important to the play than is their literal sense. Absurdists, unlike their most important predeces-

Figure 5–29. Absurdism. Beckett's *Endgame* at the American Conservatory Theatre. *(Photo: Bill Ganslen, San Francisco.)*

sors, the existentialists, did not discuss and argue about the meaninglessness of life; they simply presented it concretely onstage, using actors to participate in apparently senseless non sequiturs amidst what seemed, on the surface, inarticulate and incomprehensible exchanges of dialogue.

Although absurdists like Samuel Beckett (b. 1906), Eugène Ionesco (b. 1912), and Edward Albee were exceedingly popular for a time, few of their plays find contemporary production outside the educational theatre—Beckett's *Waiting for Godot* (1953) is an obvious exception. Still, many of the techniques popularized by absurdists appear in the works of such currently successful playwrights as Harold Pinter (b. 1930), Tom Stoppard (b. 1937), and Arthur Kopit (b. 1938).

Although all of the styles described here have had an impact on today's theatre, the theories and practices of Bertolt Brecht and Antonin Artaud have probably been more influential than any others. These two theorists

operated from quite different sets of assumptions about the
and the purpose of art, but they shared a disdain for real
its trappings. Although it may be a falsification, at least in p
useful to consider Brecht as developing from the expression
traditions and Artaud from the impressionistic and surrealist.
of the French theatre. Together their theories can help account
of the experimentation during the decades of the 1960s and 1970

Bertolt Brecht and Epic Theatre

"What is theatre?" For Bertolt Brecht (1898–1956), it was a means of
educating and communicating with *citizens* (participants in a political system),
a way of making a controversial topic easier to consider. Traditional theatres,
whether those of Wagner or Saxe-Meiningen, attempted to create an illusion
on the stage so that members of the audience could believe and identify
with the actions there. In such theatres, Brecht observed, audiences reached

Figure 5–30. Epic Theatre. Great attention to detail in those things actually used
by the actors—properties and costumes—were part of the epic style. Unlike realism,
however, the epic left out large areas of detail in setting and background, striving
to give a didactic authenticity to action and not to environment. *Mother Courage* by
Berthold Brecht at Florida State University. *(Directed by Lynn M. Thomson.)*

ate of self-oblivion: "Looking around, one discovers more or less motion-less bodies in a curious state . . . they have their eyes open, but they don't look, they stare . . . they stare at the stage as if spellbound." As Brecht was a Marxist and viewed theatre as an instrument for change, he objected to a theatre that mesmerized its audiences and made them passive. He sought rather to jolt them into thinking about contemporary social and political issues and into acting on the most critical of them. Brecht, then, strove to redefine the relationship between the theatre, its audience, and the society at large.

Brecht knew that to accomplish his goals, he must engage the interest and attention of the audience, but he believed that he had to go beyond this. He felt that if he jarred them periodically out of their identification with the action, he would succeed in shaking their complacency and in forcing them to think about what they saw onstage. He sought, therefore, alternately to engage and estrange his audiences, a technique he called *Verfremdungseffekt* (usually translated as the *alienation effect* or, simply, the A-effect).

To achieve alienation, or distancing, required the various artists of the theatre to work in ways not customary in traditional theatres. Actors, for example, were encouraged to hold themselves distant from the roles they portrayed; some of the techniques that he suggested for accomplishing this alienation were for the actors to speak the stage directions out loud during the rehearsal process, to think of their characters in the third person rather than in the first person, and to use the past tense rather than the present tense when talking of their work. Thus an actor in talking of his role might say: "and then he moved to the right and he said . . ." Such procedures were used as a means of enhancing the position of the actor as commentator rather than impersonator and of helping the actor maintain the role of evaluator of the action as well as demonstrator of it.

Designers, too, were asked to abandon former assumptions about their function in the production and about the nature of their art. Brecht urged, for example, that lighting designers expose their instruments so that the spectators were constantly reminded that they were in a theatre and that the illumination was coming from a high-wattage lamp rather than from the sun. He argued that if a set was to represent a town, it should look like a town that had been built for the theatre; it should not be built with the goal of "fooling" the audience into accepting it as a real town. Furthermore Brecht proposed that the various theatrical elements be juxtaposed in unexpected ways so that each could make an independent contribution and comment on the ideas of the play. He said, "Their intercourse with each other consists of reciprocal alienation." Thus, if the set was to make one point, the costumes should make a different one. For example, a grisly story of war and atrocity might be set to a lively tune with a lilting melody; the seeming incongruity would force the audience to consider the apparent conflict of elements and to draw conclusions about the absurdity of war. In short, Brecht proposed that each artist make an independent contribution to the production and to the didactic purpose of the script and that each element be used not to create an atmosphere that encouraged the audience to identify with the action (as in traditional theatre) but to reinforce the didactic purpose of the drama. Obviously, in this regard, Brecht differed markedly from Wagner and others who advocated a unified work of art, one in which each element contributed to the mood or effect of the whole: Brecht considered such duplication merely redundant and wasteful.

Because Brecht was a playwright as well as a theorist and director, he presumably illustrated his theories by composing plays that exploited the A-effect and resulted in the thoughtful participation of audiences. His plays typically consisted of a series of short episodes connected by songs, narratives, placards, or similar devices. The purpose was to engage the interest and belief of the audience (within each episode) and then to break the spell by forcing the spectator to think about and evaluate the meaning and implications of the episodes (by manipulating various materials between them). He once described the way a play should work in this way: "Individual events must be tied together in such a way that the knots are strikingly noticeable; the events must not follow upon one another imperceptibly, but rather one must be able to pass judgment in the midst of them." Among his most successful and best-known plays are *The Threepenny Opera* (1928), *The Rise and Fall of the City of Mahagonny* (1930), *Mother Courage and Her Children* (1938), *Galileo* (1938–1939), *The Good Woman of Setzuan* (1938–1939), and *The Caucasian Chalk Circle* (1944–1945).

The whole complex of techniques of staging and playwriting used by Brecht came to be called *epic theatre,* a term he adopted to distinguish his theater from traditional drama of the sort described by Aristotle in his *Poetics* and from unified theatre of the kind advocated by Wagner in his several books. The name *epic,* too, captured many of the qualities that Brecht prized: the mixing of narative and dramatic episodes, the telescoping of time and place, the spanning of years and countries on a consequent grand scale (similar to that achieved in epic poetry.).

Although Brecht was not the first to use either these techniques or the term *epic* (Erwin Piscator, 1893–1966, had been active in the same kind of experimentation several years earlier), Brecht popularized the term and the practices through his own plays, his theoretical writings (particularly the "Little Organon for the Theater," 1948), and his productions at the Berliner Ensemble, after 1954 East Germany's most prestigious theatre.

In sum, Brecht called for a theatre that would educate citizens about their responsibilities in a social and political system. He believed that by "alienating" them from the stage, he could show them ways of participating in their own governance and destiny; that by shattering dramatic illusion, he could shake them from passivity and complacency. To achieve the A-effect, he advocated new relationships among the elements of the theatre and therefore among the various artists on the production team; and the text, like other elements of the theatre, was to serve the didactic, social, and political purpose of the production and therefore served rather than led the overall idea. Ironically, although Brecht envisioned theatre as a forum for clarifying ideas for all people, his own works tended to appeal to an intellectual elite and to confuse, bore, or annoy the so-called working classes whom he particularly longed to woo into the theater.

Brecht was not alone in searching for a way to make theatre central once again to society and to people's lives. Although very different from Brecht in many ways, Antonin Artaud likewise sought to reestablish theatre as a vital force in modern life.

Antonin Artaud and the Theatre of Cruelty

Antonin Artaud (1895–1948) fit well the nineteenth-century stereotype of the misunderstood and tormented artist. As a child, he suffered a bout with meningitis that may have contributed to his lifelong problems with ill health, both physical and mental. Perhaps in search of relief from his agonies, he sought truth and solace in various forms of religious mysticism, ranging freely from Roman Catholicism to paganism and back again. A visionary rather than a practical man, Artaud was an influential theorist by the time of the period immediately following World War II; by the 1960s, he was virtually a cult hero among the theatrical avant-garde in Europe and the United States; in the 1970s, his theories were touted by many fashionable experimental groups on both sides of the ocean.

Although Artaud was an actor, a director, a playwright, a poet, and a screenwriter, it was as a theorist that he made his greatest impact. *The Theater and Its Double,* published in France in 1938, was a compilation of Artaud's major essays; when it was translated into English and published in the late 1950s it was heralded by many as the needed antidote to the bland commercial theatres of Broadway and the Paris boulevards and to the didactic political theatres espoused by many German expressionists and Bertolt Brecht. Because Artaud believed that important ideas came not from cognitive activity alone (logical reasoning or rational thinking) but rather from intuition, experience, and feelings, he developed his major ideas and positions by poetic rather than prosaic techniques: he made his points by means of images and metaphors rather than through traditional argument or discursive prose. For this reason, many people have found the book difficult to read and understand. Although it is true that the nuances of his position are often obscure, Artaud's major points seem clear enough, particularly if the reader attends to major metaphors that appear: the *theater* as *plague,* as *double,* and as *cruelty.*

First, Artaud held that theatre should occupy a vital place in the lives of people. He called for theatre to return to its rightful place as a great force in humanity, a force for putting people back in touch with the intensity of living. In an extended metaphor that compared theatre to a plague, Artaud attributed to both the power to release conflicts, disengage powers, and liberate possibilities: "It appears that by means of the plague, a gigantic abscess, as much moral as social, has been collectively drained; and that like the plague, the theatre has been created to drain abscesses collectively." He declared that theatre caused people to confront themselves honestly, letting fall their individual masks and confessing their social hypocrisies.

The Eastern theatre realized this, Artaud believed, and had retained its reliance on symbol, myth, and gesture; thus the Eastern theatre remained more vital and central to its culture. Western theatre, on the other hand, had lost its magic and its vibrance and had become merely a pale imitation, a *double,* of the true theatre. In order to regain its power, the Western theatre must reject logical demonstrations and causal actions and instead seize and impel its spectators toward truth, forcing them to apprehend meaning through the whole of their bodies. To this end, he proposed "a theatre in which violent physical images crush and hypnotize the sensibility . . . as by a whirlwind of higher forces."

Another major problem with Western theatre, according to Artaud, was its heavy reliance on a written text that sought to tell a story based on logic and to present characters whose psychology was a major interest. Artaud wanted to remove the script from the center of his theatre, for he believed that words, grammatical structure, and syntactical patterns were insufficient carriers of meaning. Truth came instead from spiritual signs whose meaning emerged intuitively and "with enough violence to make useless any translation into logical discursive language." Artaud wished to substitute gestures, signs, symbols, rhythms, and sounds for ordinary language; he advocated "a superabundance of impression, each richer than the next." He was convinced that theatre was neither logical, nor paraphrasable, nor rational; it was intuitive, primitive, magical, and potentially powerful.

The audience, for Artaud, was a central and critical part of the theatre. He dismissed notions of art as a kind of personal therapy for the artist. Theatre was good only when it profoundly moved its audiences, when it returned them to the subconscious energies that lay under the veneer of civilization and civilized behavior. Stripping away the civilizing layers could be achieved by violating the social norms or artistic expectations of the spectators in order to force them into a deeper awareness. In many ways his aim to jar the spectator from complacency resembled Brecht's A-effect, but its reason for being was far different and its point of attack dissimilar. Whereas Brecht wished to cause an audience to think about a social or political issue, Artaud wanted to move an audience to feel or experience a spiritual awakening, to participate in something that might be called *a communion* in its real sense of *a coming together.*

He called for a *theater of cruelty,* a theater that showed the "terrible and necessary cruelty which things can exercise against us. We are not free. And the sky can still fall on our heads. And the theatre has been created to teach us that first of all." Cruelty, then, was primarily psychic rather than physical.

To achieve his theatre of cruelty, Artaud developed a number of techniques seldom used in commercial productions. Because he wanted to bombard the senses with various stimuli in order to cause the whole organism (not merely the mind) to be moved, he experimented with ways of manipulating light and sound: in both he adopted the abrupt, the discordant, the sudden, the shrill, the garish. Lights changed colors quickly, alternated intensity violently; sound was loud, sudden, often amplified. Scenery was subservient to the other elements of production, with the audiences placed in an environment created by actors, lights, sound, and the space for the production (Artaud preferred barns, factories, and the like to conventional theatres).

Actors were encouraged to use their bodies and their voices to provide scenery, sounds, and visual effects and not to be bound by notions of psychological realism and character analysis. Actors were to address the senses of the spectators, not merely their minds.

"What is theatre?" For Artaud, it was a way of stripping away the numbing layers of habit and propriety and logical process that most of us call civilization. It was the discovery and the regaining of elemental forces that make us human and bind us together in our humanity. It was a means of spiritual salvation for people deadened by social restraints and fragmented existences. "Where should theatre be done and for whom?" Because theatre was not a building but an event, it should be done in large, unencumbered spaces where people congregated; it should not be confined in a building set aside for use by an elite, like some sort of museum. Theatre was for all people because all people needed to get back in touch with their basic needs and feelings: theatre could stimulate them to renew their sense of wholeness and their sense of relationship with other people. "What is the role of a text in performance?" Words were insufficient to the needs of contemporary communication; therefore in their place should be sounds, gestures, lights, and other kinds of stimuli aimed at the whole body of the spectator. The theatrical event was to be experienced, not merely seen, heard, and understood.

Artaud's theories, in many forms and with many distortions, were appropriated and applied after 1950 by theatre artists like Grotowski and Schechner, by makers of movies, and by modern rock music stars. Whatever one may think of his pronouncements, it is clear that although long in coming, their acceptance has been widespread.

Artaud and Brecht, the impressionists, and the expressionists all influenced the realistic mainstream even as several of their innovative practices were engulfed inside it. Just as early realists incorporated many traits from the sentimental and romantic traditions that preceded their own, twentieth-century realists exploited possibilities unexplored by Ibsen and Strindberg.

As we examine the theatres of the past, we should remember the complexities of the contemporary and modern theatre—the competing ideologies, contradictory trends, rival practitioners. The passage of time tends to dull the myriad artistic alternatives of an age and to transmit instead a bland fusion, a "unified style," as if all artists were roughly agreed on the nature and form their art should assume. In fact, most theatrical periods were just as rich and diverse as our own. Each had its mainstream, and each had artists tugging at those practices in hopes of shaping a different art. The sluggishness with which the mainstream customarily responds to calls for change should be clear from the discussion of realism. By reminding ourselves that communication and transportation are more sophisticated and efficient than ever before, we can perhaps appreciate better why change occurred even more slowly as we move back through time.

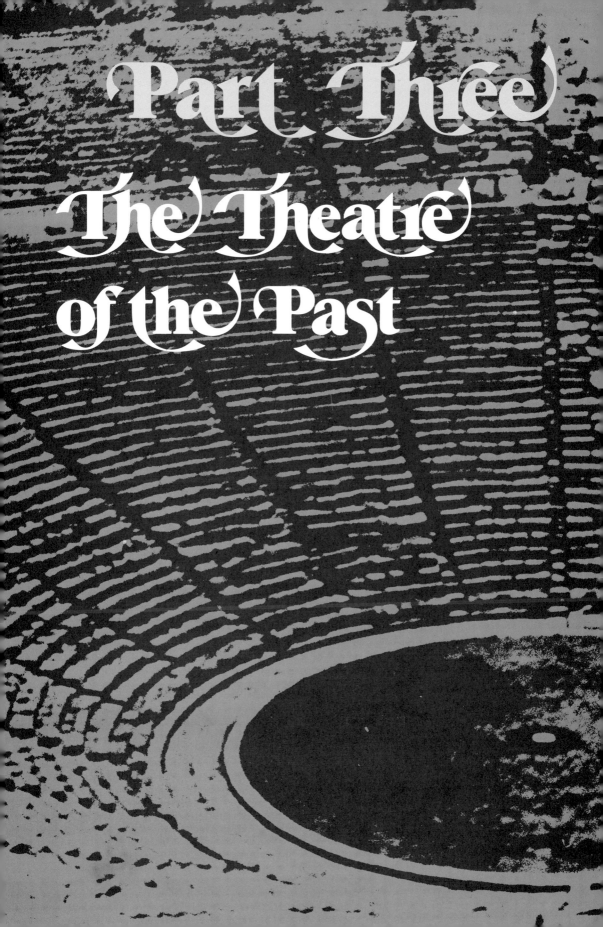

Part Three

The Theatre of the Past

CHAPTER 6

The Marvelous Theatre: The Rise and Decline of Romanticism, 1750–1850

Background

Anyone early in the eighteenth century who was closely watching the social customs, daily behavior, and reading habits of Europeans probably saw the stirrings of a new world view and sensed that profound changes were on the way. One prelude to the new way of thinking was the emergence of a doctrine called *sentimentalism,* which asserted the basic goodness of humanity and the innate goodness of each individual person. This doctrine contrasted markedly with the previous view that saw human existence as a continuing struggle between good and evil, with evil all too often victorious. According to the sentimentalist, evil came about through corruption—it was not part of human nature at birth; it was foreign to the basic self. Sentimentalism implied that although man might not be perfect, he was perfectible. Literature should therefore show virtuous men acting virtuously in their daily lives. There was no need to restrict heroic behavior and ethical perfection to some idealized world of pastoral poetry or exotic tragedy; rather, such characters in action should be depicted in all kinds of literary expressions, including drama and theatre.

Not surprisingly, the rise of sentimentalism paralleled the rising influence of the middle classes throughout Western Europe, as first trading and then manufacturing gradually joined agriculture as major sources of wealth and as tickets into "high society." As both the numbers and importance of the middle, merchant, and managerial classes increased, so did their concentrations in towns and cities, where their views about the worth of individual effort and virtuous behavior, honest work, and common sense solidified. As the influence increased, their values became more accepted; and the so-called bourgeois mentality gradually prevailed.

A second harbinger of the great changes to come appeared in the gardening practices of Europe. Whereas throughout the sixteenth, seventeenth, and early eighteenth centuries, formal gardens were defined by their carefully pruned trees and an almost sculptured array of flowers, grasses, and bushes, a changed view of beauty brought forth gardens in the late eighteenth and early nineteenth centuries that featured "natural" growth—gnarled trees, jagged rocks, tangled greenery. Previously regarded as ugly and barbarous, now such unsullied and unimproved gardens became prized and highly fashionable among both aristocrats and wealthy merchants.

Gradually and inexplicably, these changes were joined by others that sought to reconceive the nature of truth, the sources of beauty, the character of man, the function of art, and so on. When the various strands of new ideas coalesced into something resembling a system of views, it was called *Romanticism*. Romanticism took many different forms at different times and

Figure 6–1. Romanticism. Nature was celebrated, both as theatrical setting and as the "natural" element in human character, as seen in this performance at the Comédie Francaise in the early nineteenth century.

in different places. The strength of its several doctrines ebbed and flowed, and their emphases rearranged and reemerged as somewhat altered beliefs and practices. Its extraordinary complexity and diversity caused one critic to suggest that we should always speak of Romanti*cisms* rather than Romanti*cism* in order to remind ourselves constantly of its plural nature, its several expressions, and its changing faces. Certainly, Romanticism, as practiced by the English poets like Keats and Shelley, was very different from the Romanticism of French playwrights like Dumas or German philosophers like Kant.

Yet, in spite of its complexity, Romanticism, as it peaked throughout Western Europe and America between 1789 and 1843, seemed to share some basic views that can be summarized.

Characteristics of Romanticism

First, Romanticism was marked by an abiding trust in the goodness of nature. In its unspoiled and unsullied state, nature, both human and external, was without flaw or blemish. As a consequence of this view came several corollaries. Natural feelings and instincts were accepted as more reliable guides to proper behavior than educated opinion and reason, for the latter were products of learning and civilization and therefore were corruptible. A person should follow his instincts rather than his intellect because his innate goodness would not betray him though his education might. The Romantics' *distrust of reason,* then, was based on the view that reason was the product of education and thus corruptible, while instinct was the product of nature and thus reliable.

The celebration of nature and natural instincts led to a *glorification of the natural man,* the primitive and untutored personality. Literature, drama, and the visual arts applauded the virtue of *the noble savage,* the man whom civilization left alone to grow and mature in his natural state. American Indians, African blacks, and South Sea Islanders were considered worthy objects of observation and study because they showed man as he existed in his more natural, and therefore truer, state. Within contemporary society, *the common man* (as opposed to the aristocrat) was most admired because he was least affected by the artificial aspects of civilization: behavior based on intricate rules of etiquette, dress determined by artificial standards of beauty, social class defined by birth and wealth rather than by individual achievement.

The celebration of nature, natural instincts, and natural man was closely related to *primitivism,* a belief in the superiority of a simple and unsophisticated way of life, a life close to nature and unspoiled by the artificial requirements of organized society. With the interest in primitivism came a desire to study old civilizations, particularly those of ancient Egypt, ancient Greece, and the Middle Ages. (The science of archaeology developed during the Romantic era.) During the Romantic age, the glorification of Greek civilization (to

Figure 6–2. Romanticism. Many plays and their settings celebrated the "wild" and the "picturesque," and the straight lines and formal compositions of a previous age gave way to curved lines and irregular masses; here, an English performance of the early nineteenth century.

the detriment of the Roman) took root, and nationalism flourished as medieval studies highlighted the basis of modern European nations. The best days were those of old, not those to come, because the past lay closer to Nature, the bringer of all good things. Obviously, for the Romantics, history was a long process of decline or decay, not one of progress and improvement.

Second, Romantics shared an intense belief in the equality of man. The belief was not unrelated to their views on nature and history, for primitive societies permitted each individual to develop as he could, without pressure or artificial regulations on his conduct; contemporary society, on the other hand, prevented such individual development by creating a whole range of artificial social structures into which each person was born and that thereby bound him into a particular mode of life. Social stratification implied, wrongly in the Romantic view, that some men were better than others, more worthwhile. But if, as the Romantics believed, men were indeed equal, then social stratification was wrong. Because identification with classes was so much a part of the fabric of society and government, elimination of social classes often required the overthrow of government; and therefore the Romantic age became *an era of revolutions:* the American Revolution (1776), the French Revolution (1791); the Napoleonic Wars (1798–1815); the Europe-wide revolutions of 1830 and 1848; the American Civil War (1865).

The establishment of democracies was neither simple nor bloodless. Although early on the middle classes were merely challenging the aristocrats for access to positions of power and prestige, later the working classes struggled for their own recognition and acceptance. Whereas the early revolutions in America and France aimed to replace monarchies with republics or democracies, for example, both countries were later thrown into more convulsions over social issues like slavery, suffrage, and women's rights. Most of the political turmoils in the period can be explained simply as a continuing struggle between those attempting to maintain the status quo (monarchy or slavery or white male suffrage) and those striving to change in the direction of individual freedom and more democratic processes.

Third, Romanticism placed a premium on detail, for in the particular example rested the pathway to truth. What was important was the *particular,* the *specific,* and the *unique,* not the general or the typical. The Romantics' glorification of detail was related to their view of its relationship to nature and thus to truth. All creation was considered unified, to exist as a great oneness,

Figure 6–3. Romanticism. A Romantic setting as seen from backstage, showing the construction of the exterior scene.

a whole. Because every created thing was a part of this whole, each detail was important, as its study could lead to a better apprehension of the totality, the one great whole. Every detail became, in fact, a potential pathway to truth. Increasing the number of details improved understanding of the nature of the whole and thus the nature of truth. The study of history and geography was revered because by identifying the components of remote times and places, people could discover the elements that made them unique, that separated them from other times and places and from the here and now. To establish their uniqueness was to affirm their identity, to make them important.

Fourth, Romantics taught that ultimate truth must always be sought but that its attainment in this lifetime was unlikely. To strive for perfection was an obligation, but to achieve it was an impossibility. Certain people, notably philosophers and artists, were most likely to possess insights about truth; therefore both had a special obligation to help others approach their perceptions. But such insights were at once a curse and a blessing because the majority of people were seldom either able or willing to apprehend the truth that the artist or the philosopher strove to share. To be an artist, then, was often to be out of step with the rest of society: thus the romantic view of the *artist as a misunderstood genius,* at once blest and curst by his art. Moreover the constant yearning for the unattainable lent a *melancholy cast* to life, a trait that marked much romantic art.

Fifth, art, for the Romantics, served a rather exalted purpose. In this world, tensions existed between the physical and the spiritual, the material and the ideal. The role of art was to lead people to perceive the underlying unity of all of existence and thus to eliminate the apparent conflict: the purpose of art was, as one theorist described it, "to make man whole again," to bridge the gap between the two worlds, to bring peace to man. Because the artist was one who saw the unity amid apparent disunity, he was charged with sharing his insights. But because his insights were not rational, because they were based on natural feelings and genius rather than on intellect and craft, his art could not be taught and was not subject to rules or external constraints. *Subjectivity* became the hallmark of Romantic art. If the Romantic artist searched for truth in the myriad details of external nature, he found it within himself: hence the strong *introspective* tone of much Romantic art.

Sixth, criticism, according to the Romantics, was necessarily subjective and personal. One could not determine the worth of a picture or a poem by examining its social utility or by measuring it against a set of external criteria. Rather, its merit lay in its ability to stimulate feeling and understanding in the spectator. In a revolutionary leap, Romantic criticism removed the basis of *judgment of a work of art from the work and to the perceiver of the work.* One obvious effect of such assumptions about criticism was to democratize art by making one person's perception of art as good as another's. In fact, because the

Figures 6–4, 6–5, 6–6. Exoticism. Spectacular effects were often needed for Romantic plays, including magical and supernatural scenes. Here, magical appearances, aerial descents, and flight.

natural man's instincts and feelings were preferred over the educated man's training and prejudices, the common man's perception of art, as the more untutored, was probably the more reliable.

The effect of Romanticism on theatre (and the other arts) was significant if erratic. In general, the subjects of art stressed the remote and exotic, either in the guise of past civilizations (particularly those of Greece and the Middle Ages) or in primitive societies (the American Indian and the African were favorites). Tales of children, common folk, rustics, and savages unfolded against backgrounds of forests, caves, dungeons, pastures, and jungles, and revivals of Shakespeare swept the stages of the world in new settings that stressed their exotic qualities. Great care was taken to describe precisely the myriad details that made up the whole. In old as well as new plays, appeals were more often to the spectators' emotions and feelings than to their ideas or intellects, and visually interesting episodes predominated over verbally satisfying ones. Special effects involving wild animals and natural disasters, shipwrecks and snowstorms prefigured the disaster movies of today and sought to satisfy the tastes of the popular audience. While aristocrats flocked to the opera and ballet (both art forms reached new heights of popularity and excellence during the early nineteenth century), the middle and lower classes virtually took over the theatre. Thus the Romantic popular theatre—the theatre of the marvelous—was a theatre unknown to audiences of today, whose "marvels" have found a home in film and television.

Plays in the Theatres, 1750–1850

The plays staged during the period were diverse indeed, for Romanticism led playwrights and audiences in many different directions. For a while after 1750, many people continued to attend plays of the sort popular in the late seventeenth and early eighteenth centuries. For some people, the past is always more comfortable. But for many, new kinds of drama were more exciting, and so playwrights began providing materials to satisfy the new tastes. For purposes of convenience, we will look first at the most popular forms and then at other comic and serious plays of the period.

The most popular form of drama during the Romantic age was *melodrama*. Although not new (such plays have probably existed in all ages), melodrama attained new stature and significance in the theatre of the late eighteenth century and the nineteenth century.

Melodrama meant literally "music drama," a name derived from the extensive use of music within the plays. Much like popular television and movies of today, nineteenth-century melodramas used *emotional music* to provide the proper mood and background for the action and to underscore moments of suspense and surprise. Music was also often used to identify characters for the audience. Such music, called *signature music,* was played when a character was about to enter or leave or to perform some astounding feat.

Typically melodrama presented a highly simplified moral universe in which good and evil were clearly defined and obviously embodied in easily recognizable stock characters. A physically attractive hero and heroine (often in love) possessed a kindness and virtue that was as unmistakable as it was unblemished. These characters, along with their friends and servants, represented the forces of good. Propelling the action of the play was a villain, whose physical appearance as well as his behavior captured the essential attributes of evil. The remainder of the characters were most often friends or sidekicks of the three defining characters and almost always included at least one comic (relief) character. The villain initiated the action of the melodrama by posing a threat to the hero or heroine; he or she escaped, and the villain posed another threat; he or she again escaped, and so on. The episodic play thus progressed by a series of threats and escapes, each reversal becoming more extreme than the last, until the final incident, when the hero or heroine might move from almost certain death to a happy marriage in a matter of minutes.

Melodramas (especially those originating in France) were generally three-act plays. Although they were less often written in one, two, or four acts, they were almost never written in five, a form reserved for the "serious" dramatists of the day. (Even during the Romantic age, melodrama was dismissed by some scholars and literary theorists as unworthy, just as the contemporary university tends to dismiss television plays and popular films as unsuitable for serious study.)

Finally, many melodramas depended heavily on an array of special effects—fires, explosions, drownings, earthquakes—both as threats to the sympathetic characters during the action of the play and as a means of obtaining the downfall of the villain in the final scenes. As well, in keeping with the Romantics' interest in the exotic and the unspoiled, many melodramas developed around the use of various animals. Those using horses were called *equestrian dramas* and were the forerunners of modern-day westerns. Some depended on dog stars and were called *canine melodramas,* the obvious precursors of today's Lassie and Rin-Tin-Tin. The interest of the Romantic writers in sea stories gave rise to *nautical melodramas,* whose modern equivalent are probably the stories of space travel, like the movie *Star Wars.*

Although many people were writing melodramas during the hundred years between 1750 and 1850, two names in particular stand out: Kotzebue and Pixérécourt. The German playwright August Friedrich von Kotzebue (1761–1819) wrote over two hundred plays, many of which were translated into English and French and were performed throughout the world during the nineteenth and early twentieth centuries. Kotzebue was particularly successful with his domestic melodramas, which featured errant but repentant wives and upright but forgiving husbands. His plays had the ability to titillate audiences without offending them and to introduce potentially controversial views without seeming to attack the audience's standards of propriety. Most of all, Kotzebue took the lives of common people and gave them dignity by treating them seriously. From about 1780 until his death, Kotzebue was acknowledged as the most popular playwright in the world, and this popularity made Germany's drama the most vigorous and generally applauded during the early nineteenth century.

Figures 6–7, 6–8. Special Effects. A scene of a fire as seen from the audience and from backstage (second half of the nineteenth century).

Réné Charles Guilbert de Pixérécourt (1773–1844) held a position in France comparable to that enjoyed in Germany by Kotzebue. The author of over one hundred plays, he set a fashion for canine melodramas with his *Dog of Montargis* (1814) and for disaster melodramas with plays like *The Exile's Daughter* (1819) (which required a flood to sweep through the stage, uprooting a tree and bearing the heroine away on a board) and *Death's Head* (1827) (which used a volcanic eruption to foil the villain). Because the physical requirements were often so demanding, Pixérécourt insisted on directing his own plays in order to assure their success. Pixérécourt, therefore, figured prominently in the history of French directors as well as of French playwrights.

Although it has been the custom of some critics to scoff at melodrama and to dismiss it as silly, its popularity and persistence argue that attention should be paid it. In the nineteenth century, it was revered by many, and unquestionably it attracted to the theatre a mass audience new to the art of the stage. This audience of middle- and lower-class patrons cheered and laughed and wept openly and enthusiastically at the exploits of the heroes and heroines, and their support made theatre the major form of entertainment for over one hundred years.

A brief sketch of just one popular melodrama of the day may suggest the very real power of the form. The popular American play *Uncle Tom's Cabin* became a veritable enterprise following its first production in 1852.

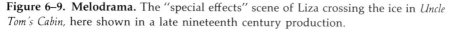

Figure 6–9. Melodrama. The "special effects" scene of Liza crossing the ice in *Uncle Tom's Cabin,* here shown in a late nineteenth century production.

As well as versions playing in Germany, France, and England, there were twelve different American versions in print in 1900. In 1879, there were twelve different "Tom" companies (theatre groups producing no plays except *Uncle Tom's Cabin*) crisscrossing America, but by 1899, there were between four and five hundred such companies. Some actors made a life's work of "Tomming," never acting in—or even seeing—another play. One itinerant "Tommer" described his experience in a letter mailed East in 1893:

Bessie and Lulu are doing splendid work in brass, and Mrs. Shea is becoming a good tuba player. Barny the donkey, is the big attraction on parade; his bucking, kicking, and chasing Marks make the crowd shout every day. We close [in Iowa] October 15, making just one year, four months, and nine days without closing the show, and having travelled eight thousand miles by wagon and boat without an accident.

Melodrama clearly provided what audiences wanted: good stories, clear-cut morality, spectacle, variety; and it dominated the stage during the very late eighteenth century and most of the nineteenth century, thereafter moving to television and films. Melodrama can be said, without exaggeration, to form the backbone of the theatre of the marvelous.

Figure 6–10. The Revival of Shakespeare. Shakespeare had never fallen completely out of favor in England, but Romantic taste brought a new popularity to his plays, which were now produced in more detailed settings that sought to capture the locales of the plays. Here, the wrestling scene from *As You Like It,* first half of the nineteenth century. *(From The Collection of the University of Rochester Libraries.)*

But other kinds of entertainments were also very popular with mass audiences. Specialty acts came into the theatres and featured jugglers, singers, tumblers, magicians, and others. Pantomimes, whose magical transformations called forth elaborate tricks in scenery and costume, began as short additions to the evening's entertainment but increased in length as their popularity grew, until they provided a whole evening's fare. Short musical revues or brief topical skits using music and verse (in France called *vaudevilles*) appealed to the politically minded. Comic operas, whose sentimental stories were set to original music, provided entertainment for those who liked music but found opera perplexing or dull. Parodies, burlesques, circus entertainments, and water shows all contributed to the theatrical offerings of the Romantic age.

Alongside such popular events existed those aiming to appeal to more erudite tastes and more sophisticated playgoers. Traditional plays, both comic and serious, flirted with several of Romanticism's faces and introduced innovations that enriched still further the dramatic and theatrical possibilities of the theatre's Romantic age. Revivals of Shakespeare were popular in all countries and were played in new theatrical settings designed to illustrate the locales mentioned in the dramatic texts.

At least three different sorts of comedies competed for public favor: sentimental comedy, "laughing" comedy, and the "well-made play."

Probably closest in tone to the early romantic ideas of man's innate goodness were the sentimental comedies, those written to appeal to the audience's sense of virtue rather than to its sense of humor. Although most contained some laughable situations and an occasionally funny character, the plays' primary appeal depended on their depiction of the successful struggles of virtuous characters whose laudable goals assured their ultimate success. One contemporary writer described them this way:

Almost all the characters are good, and exceedingly generous; . . . and though they want [lack] humour, have abundance of sentiment and feeling. If they happen to have faults or foibles, the spectator is taught not only to pardon, but to applaud them, in consideration of the goodness of their hearts; so that folly, instead of being ridiculed is commended, and the comedy aims at touching our passions.

Like melodrama, sentimental comedy has been scorned and its plays largely ignored in modern times. But in its own day, its popularity and importance to the theatrical life of the time was unquestionable. Among those importantly associated with sentimental comedy were the Frenchman Denis Diderot (1713–1784) and the German Gotthold Ephraim Lessing (1729–1781). Although some variety of sentimental comedies continued to be written throughout the nineteenth century (and indeed continue on television today), their popularity eroded after about 1800 as that of melodrama increased.

Even during the Romantic age, some argued strongly for abandoning the sentimental comedy in favor of another, "laughing" comedy. Three authors in particular were associated with its increasing reputation: Beaumarchais (Pierre Augustin Caron, 1732–1799); Oliver Goldsmith (c. 1730–1774); and Richard Brinsley Sheridan (1751–1816). Beaumarchais's reputation rests now principally on *The Barber of Seville* (1775) and *The Marriage of Figaro* (1783), both laughing comedies that develop by means of intrigue while poking fun at aspects of French society. Goldsmith's most popular comedy, *She Stoops to Conquer* (1773), depicts the laughable consequences of mistaken identity and benign trickery that temporarily keep two pairs of young lovers separated. Its popularity continues even today, and the play remains in the active repertory of many English and American companies. Sheridan's *The Rivals* (1775) and *The School for Scandal* (1777) were especially prized for their witty dialogue and colorful portraits of engaging characters. It is a testament to the strength of the doctrine of sentimentalism that both of Sheridan's plays employ its techniques even while objecting to its principles. In *The Rivals*, for example, the subplot is a rather conventional sentimental story; and in *The School for Scandal*, sentimentalism is at once satirized (in the characters of Joseph Surface and the school) and embraced (in the charac-

Figure 6–11. Laughing Comedy. A scene from Sheridan's 1776 comedy, *The School for Scandal*, performed at Wayne State University. *(Directed by Robert T. Hazzard, setting by Russell Paquette, costumes by Daniel Thomas Field.)*

ters of Charles Surface and Sir Peter and Lady Teazel). Certainly laughing comedy continued throughout the period, but its importance was eclipsed after 1830 by the growing popularity of the "well-made play."

The most popular comic writer of the hundred years between 1750 and 1850 was undoubtedly Eugène Scribe (1791–1861), a Frenchman who wrote over three hundred plays for the Parisian theatres. Their translation into German and English and their frequent production in those countries and in America throughout the nineteenth century caused French comedy to set the standard for the world by mid-century.

Scribe's techniques (like careful preparation and meticulous networks of relationships) were designed to give the appearance of an action tightly unified by cause and effect, when in fact the plays were built around multiple lines of action that unfolded by chance and coincidence. The phrase *well-made play* was used first as a compliment to describe the particular kind of play that Scribe perfected, but because later scholars deplored the superficiality of his works, the term became one of derision during the twentieth century. But Scribe and the well-made play exerted considerable influence on later writers, both among comic authors (most importantly Victorien Sardou, 1831–1908) and among the later realists like Alexandre Dumas *fils* (1824–1895) and Henrik Ibsen (1825–1906). In sum, Scribe's well-made plays and those of his emulators dominated the stages of Western Europe and America during the nineteenth century and, with melodrama, were probably the mainstay of that theatre.

Serious drama between 1750 and 1850 likewise took several forms, from sprawling, almost epic works laden with philosophical inquiry (and often not intended for stage presentation) to tales of domestic difficulties and middle-class intrigue.

Germany, in particular, produced philosophical dramas during this period. Following the publication of Lessing's *Nathan the Wise* (1779) and a surge of assorted dramatic experiments under the so-called Storm and Stress writers (fl. 1770–1790), two authors emerged as the significant spokesmen for the late eighteenth and early nineteenth centuries: Johann Wolfgang von Goethe (1749–1832) and Friedrich Schiller (1759–1805).

Goethe had early embraced many doctrines of the innovative, if chaotic, Storm and Stress movement, and under their influence had written *Goetz von Berlichingen* (1773), a piece that required over six hours to perform and more than fifty separate scenes to contain its sprawling action. Later Goethe renounced such excesses and sought to perfect an alternate style of production, one that would capture the patterns undergirding everyday life. His final work, *Faust,* was written in two parts (1808 and 1831) and told the story of man's search for truth and fulfillment. It came to epitomize for many the Romantic dilemma. Never intended for the stage, the work is an episodic presentation of a philosophical point of view and an acknowledged literary (as opposed to theatrical) masterpiece.

Schiller, like Goethe, began as one of the Storm and Stress writers but later joined Goethe in seeking a new style of production that would create a distance between the spectator and the stage and thereby present to him a glimpse of the ideal world. Of Schiller's many works, the best known now are his Wallenstein Trilogy (three plays based on the Thirty Years War 1798–1799); *The Robbers* (1782), whose immediate success created a vogue for other "Robin Hood" plays; and *William Tell* (1804), whose stirring celebration of individual worth and democratic government caused postrevolutionary France to award Schiller an honorary citizenship.

Less philosophical but considerably more stageworthy were the Romantic plays coming from France, the most famous of which was *Hernani* by Victor Hugo (1802–1885). Its first production in 1830 caused a riot in the theatre that continued for several performances. At issue was the question of whether or not to permit certain attitudes and practices of the Romantic authors (long accepted and popular in the commercial theatres of the boulevards) to invade and presumably sully the theatrical life of the national theatre of France, the Comédie Française. *Hernani* was written in elevated and poetic language; it portrayed rulers and noblemen involved in the affairs

Figure 6–12. Romantic Scenery. Such spectacular effects as the passage of an "army"—done here on a "practicable,"—became part of many plays, from those of Shakespeare to Schiller.

of state and was cast in a traditional five-act form. But the play incorporated some features of Romanticism to which traditionalists objected. Common people were shown in conflict with a ruler, scenes of violence and death were portrayed on the stage, and moments of humor were tucked into an otherwise turgid story. French literary conservatives resented such democratizing of their art. The passion of their opposition suggested, if nothing else, that theatre was a very important part of their lives and was something worth fighting about. The battle of *Hernani,* fought both in the pit of the Comédie Française and in the literary circles of Paris, was resolved in favor of the Romantics, and so 1830 is the date now given for the acceptance of Romanticism into the mainstream of France's theatrical life (several years after it had been accepted in England, Germany, and America). Between 1830 and 1843, several Romantic plays by Hugo joined those of the older Dumas (whose dramatization of *The Three Musketeers* is still popular today) to comprise the most important Romantic dramas of the age. The failure of another Romantic play by Hugo in 1843 marked the end of self-conscious French Romanticism, making it one of the shortest dramatic movements in history.

Of far less consequence were plays written by the English Romantic poets and novelists like Samuel Taylor Coleridge, William Wordsworth, John Keats, Percy Bysshe Shelley, Lord Byron, and Sir Walter Scott. Most were closet dramas (some intentionally, others by default), and none contributed significantly to the English or the American theatre.

Alongside philosophical pieces and Romantic tragedies on exalted subjects were some very appealing plays dealing with the everyday problems of the middle classes. Around 1750 in every country of Western Europe, playwrights and theorists began calling for plays that would have relevance for the growing merchant and industrial classes. In France, Diderot proposed recognition of a new kind of play that he termed the *drame,* and he provided a model for it with his play *The Illegitimate Son* (1757). In Germany, Lessing translated Diderot's works and added his own pleas for domestic dramas, providing Germany's first successful one when he wrote *Miss Sara Sampson* (1755). In England, after an early surge of interest in George Lillo's *The London Merchant* (1731), only sporadic and largely unsuccessful plays of the sort appeared. Although some domestic tragedies continued well into the nineteenth century, their uniqueness disappeared as melodramas began treating situations of domestic complication; and so the drama, *drame,* or middle-class tragedy was also absorbed into melodrama, whose appeal continued to soar and spread, overtaking and engulfing most other forms of serious drama by the middle of the nineteenth century.

Practices of the Theatres, 1750–1850

Because theatre was the form of entertainment preferred by vast numbers of people and because Romantic plays stressed spectacle, new theatres built and those remodeled between 1750 and 1850 featured ever-larger auditori-

Figure 6–13. Theatre Architecture. Expansion of the audience and scenic areas was typical of the Romantic period, as in this view of London's Drury Lane in 1801.

ums and ever-more-sophisticated stages and support areas. For example, in England, Covent Garden Theatre seated fewer than 1,500 people in the 1730s but could accommodate 3,000 by 1793. Drury Lane Theatre seated only 650 in 1700 but had a capacity of 2,300 and then 3,600 during the early years of the nineteenth century. In America, the original Chestnut Street Theatre of Philadelphia (opened 1794) was built to house 1,200 but was soon enlarged to accommodate over 2,000. In France, all major theatres were enlarged and modernized between 1750 and 1800, with particular attention given to improving sight lines, increasing seating capacity, and creating greater potential for staging spectacles. Between 1775 and 1800, more than thirty permanent theatres were built in Germany, most of which incorporated elaborate machinery to permit rapid and simultaneous changes of setting; by 1850, the number had grown to sixty-five.

During the one hundred years between 1750 and 1850, the standard configuration for the audience area was the *box, pit, and gallery,* with boxes originally the most prized and expensive seats. As *seeing* the spectacular effects gradually became more important than *hearing* the vocal displays of the actors, the advantage shifted to the pit (later called the *orchestra*); and so box seats gave way to orchestra seats as the most favored and expensive in the theatre. The cheapest seats were always those of the upper balconies (in large theatres there might be as many as five levels). Called the *gods,* the audience in the upper galleries were primarily working-class people who were noted for their ill manners at theatrical performances. "Jonathan Oldstyle" (Washington Irving) complained:

The noise in this part of the house is somewhat similar to that which prevailed in Noah's Ark; for we have an imitation of the whistles and yells of every kind of animal. . . . [When their displeasure was aroused] they commenced a discharge of apples, nuts, and ginger bread, on the heads of the honest folks in the pit, who had no possibility of retreating from this new kind of thunderbolts.

The misbehavior of audiences was not exclusively an American trait, as a German visitor to England made clear: "The most striking thing to a foreigner in English theatre is the unheard of coarseness and brutality of the audiences." In short, audiences of the time were both large and vocal; they came to see (rather than to hear) plays, and so they expected and got interesting scenery and dazzling special effects.

Scenery generally consisted of a combination of *flats* (wooden frames covered by fabric), *drops* (large pieces of fabric suspended from above the stage and extending to the floor), *borders* (fabric, either framed or unframed, that covered or masked the overhead spaces and theatrical rigging), and *ground rows* (cut-away flats adapted to stand free on the stage floor). All

Figure 6–14. Wings and Drops. Paired flats, or "wings," and a painted drop across the rear of the scene characterized even simple settings, as in this late eighteenth-century exterior. The New Theatre, Philadelphia. *(Courtesy of Cooper-Hewitt Museum, the Smithsonian Institution's National Museum of Design.)*

scenic pieces were carefully painted to achieve the illusion of reality, and some were cut away (in the shape of leaves at their edges, for example) or layered (in gauzes or other fabrics) to enhance still more the illusion of detailed reality. Because many plays of the Romantic period were set out of doors, borders often consisted of a combination of sky, clouds, and leaves, while flats and drops were forests, trees, grasses, rocks, and similar scenes in nature. For plays set in medieval castles, tombs, or dungeons, all flats, drops, and borders might be painted to resemble large stones.

All scenic pieces were aligned so as to be more or less parallel with the proscenium and placed at varying distances from it. Some of the flats were painted as pairs, and one of each pair was placed on each side of the stage. Called *wings,* these paired flats (customarily four to six on each side) and the drop across the back of the stage gave rise to the name for this standard scenic arrangement: *the wing and drop.* Whenever required by the play's action, three-dimensional details were included; for example, a bridge would be built if characters had to walk on it. But most of the scenery was two-dimensional, with all details painted on.

The scene was lit by candles or oil lamps (or, after 1830, in some theatres by gas) placed at the front of the stage as *footlights* and behind the several sets of wings. In no case was the illumination very high, and so both scenery and actors were only dimly visible. A German account from the middle of the nineteenth century identified the problems:

Worst of all was the illumination. Hundreds of oil lamps, even if they burned brightly (which they rarely did) threw over the stage just enough light to make the actors recognizable. It was not a rare occurrence for one or more lamp chimneys to break in the footlights . . . and for a dense black smoke to poison the atmosphere during the rest of the evening.

The basic settings were enlivened by an enormous variety of special equipment and effects. Characters and objects flew about by means of elaborate systems of ropes and pulleys; they disappeared and appeared magically through various traps in the floor and, less often, through rotating wall panels. Fountains and waterfalls gushed and flowed by means of specially installed water systems. Moving panoramas and dioramas permitted designers to achieve the illusion of travel onstage. By unwinding a large painted cloth from one giant spool onto another, the landscape behind an onstage boat or carriage could be made to unroll and the vehicle would seem to move. When late in the nineteenth century such panoramas were combined with treadmills, even horse races and chariot races could be staged. Volcanic eruptions, fires, thunder, lightning, rainstorms, explosions—all were a part of the theatre's spectacle, and all were popular with mass audiences.

The use of scenery and special effects appeared to be governed by three overriding and interrelated assumptions: (1) the stage picture should present the illusion of reality (thus the name *pictorial illusionism* was used to describe scenery during the period); (2) many details should be included in order to particularize the settings; and (3) because time and place were important, historical and geographical accuracy of detail was appropriate. Although

Figures 6–15, 6–16. Illusionism: Special Effects. Elaborate machinery was devised for such demanding scenes as this ship on a stormy sea; equally complex devices were needed for explosions and volcanic eruptions.

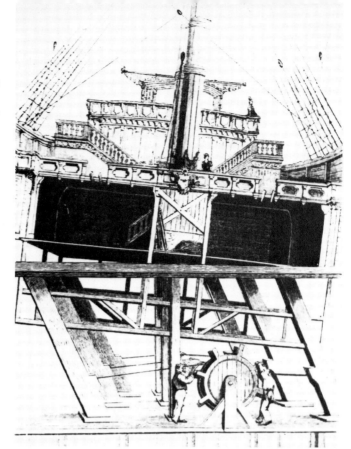

there was a considerable gap between the goals and their realization, designers moved steadily in the direction of their ideals from about 1750 to 1850.

Madamoiselle Clairon, a French actress, was one of the first to adopt the new trend toward accuracy in costuming. In 1752–1753, she confessed to an admirer, "In all my characters, the costume must now be observed; the truth of declamation required that of dress; all my rich stage-wardrobe is from this moment rejected; I lose twelve hundred guineas worth of dresses; but the sacrifice is made." And so saying she dressed herself as a sultana, omitting the customary hoop skirt and exposing her bare arms to portray the Oriental heroine. Diderot saw the performance and enthusiastically reported, "A courageous actress . . . has just discarded her hoops, and no one thinks it wrong." At about the same time, another French actress, Madame Favart, "dared to sacrifice her charming appearance to truth of character" when she abandoned the usual wide hoopskirt, elbow-length gloves, and diamond tiara in favor of a simple linen dress with bared arms and a plain hairdo to impersonate a country maid. We are told that the "novelty offended a few critics in the pit."

The next critical step was taken around 1760, when spectators were no longer permitted to sit on the stages in England and France, for onstage spectators clearly destroyed the illusion of reality and took up spaces now needed for scenery and acting areas. By the 1770s, with the spectators gone from the stage, designers were free to create a complete stage picture. In England, Phillippe Jacques de Loutherbourg (1740–1812), England's leading designer, began to reproduce familiar English locations on the stage and thus created a vogue for "local color" settings. In France, the scenery at boulevard theatres depicted examples of French local color as well as "authentic" reproductions of places in the Orient, the Americas, Russia, and so forth. By the 1830s in Germany, five different periods of theatrical costuming were believed necessary: classical, medieval, sixteenth-century, seventeenth-century, and mid-eighteenth-century; and by then an Englishman had staged a revival of Shakespeare's *King John* in which *all* characters dressed in historically accurate costumes—previously only the leading performers had done so.

Celebration of the remote and great attention to accurate details increasingly won public acclaim and so became increasingly practiced by theatrical managers during the nineteenth century. For example, William Charles Macready (1793–1873) managed London's two leading theatres during the 1830s and 1840s and was the first director who *consistently* sought historical accuracy in both scenery and costumes. By 1850, even in America, whose theatre was late in getting under way, antiquarianism had made its mark, and historical accuracy in theatrical settings and costumes was, if not achieved, at least approached.

In sum, for both costumes and scenery, pictorial illusionism and accuracy of detail were goals more nearly realized in 1850 than in 1750.

The same one hundred years saw rather great changes in the traditions of acting as well. Some state troupes, like the Comédie Française, and many provincial troupes operated as sharing companies throughout the period, with actors resembling shareholders in a modern corporation, but most per-

Figure 6–17. Historical Costume. By the first quarter of the nineteenth century, attention was being given to more or less accurate historical costume. Actors no longer appeared in more elaborate versions of the clothes of the time, but in a costume reminiscent of the play's period, as in this "ancient" gown worn by the English actress Adelaide Kemble as Norma.

formers worked for a fixed salary that was supplemented by the gate receipts of one or more "benefit" performances. For a time, the concept of the stock company dominated—that is, a group of actors who stayed together over a period of years, performing appropriate roles in a variety of plays and each contributing to the reputation of the company as a whole. After about 1830, however, perhaps as a consequence of the Romantics' growing attachment to the idea of "individual genius" and most certainly because of improved transportation networks (particularly the expanding system of railroads), the company system gradually gave way to the "starring system," which meant that leading performers moved from stock company to stock company, where they played the plum parts, supported by the resident players. The starring system, although exceedingly popular with audiences, caused numerous problems for the acting profession. One French actress, for example, demanded and received a salary equal to that of her country's prime minister, leaving little for her fellow artists. The American actor William Wood was rather bitter in his condemnation of the system:

[The star] system was now at its height; the regular actors no longer forming a joint stock company, but being reduced to the condition of mere ministers or servants

upon some principal performer, whose attractions it was now their sole and chief duty to increase, illustrate, or set off.

The inevitable outcome, he predicted, would be the fiscal and artistic bank-ruptcy of the theatre.

In time, there was a rage for child stars, who played not only Shakespear-ean roles like King Lear and Hamlet but also the heroes in various melodramas of the day where they single-handedly foiled the villains and saved the day. The public also relished "breeches roles," where women played men's roles in men's clothing—perhaps the attraction was that the breeches revealed the actress's body far more than current fashion permitted and therefore provided a bit of titillation quite separate from the play's dramatic offerings.

Acting style between 1750 and 1850 also underwent changes, the nature of which are not entirely clear. The ephemeral quality of the art of acting makes its description in any given period difficult, if not impossible. The problem is complicated by the tendency of each age to consider its own actors "natural" and those of preceding times "artificial." Because it is un-likely that every age brought the art of acting just one step closer to "the natural" or to "realistic performance," one must conclude that the sense of what is natural and real changes from age to age. With that understanding, the styles of acting between 1750 and 1850 might be viewed as presenting several alternate versions of "truth in acting." At one extreme was the formal (or "classical") and at the other pole the natural (or "romantic").

Formal acting predominated from the beginning of the period until about 1815, although its various expressions were quite diverse. The emphasis of most of these performers seemed to be on vocal power and prowess and dignified, restrained interpretations of character. Such performers typi-cally excelled in tragic roles, where poetic diction encouraged a declamatory or oratorical delivery. Perhaps the most extreme example of an accepted actor performing in this tradition was the Englishman James Quin (1693–1766), whose technique was described by a character of the novelist Smol-lett's:

His utterance is a continual sing-song, like the chanting of vespers; and his action resembles that of heaving ballast into the hold of a ship. In his outward deportment he seems to have confounded the idea of dignity and insolence of mien.

This was said about an actor who was recognized only a few short years before as the leading performer on the London stage.

But the public's sense of truth had moved away from Quin by the 1760s, and so he was considered "unnatural." Then David Garrick (1717–1779) was touted for his "easy and familiar, yet forcible style of speaking and acting." Acknowledged as the greatest English actor of the last half of the eighteenth century, Garrick was, however, far from our conception of natural; for example, he persisted in playing Shakespeare's Macbeth in the dress of a military officer of the eighteenth century, complete with a tail wig, and in drawing attention to himself (to the detriment of the acting company) by "the restless abundance of his action and his gestures."

Figures 6–18, 6–19. Breeches Roles. On the left in each illustration, a costume of the 1830s; on the right, one of the late 1880s, the characters Mother Goose and Aladdin. By 1880, these pantomime roles were being played by women, not by men as they had been in 1830; the costumes emphasized the sexuality implicit in the shift.

By the 1790s, the mantle of formal acting had passed from Garrick to a brother-and-sister team, John Phillip Kemble (1757–1823) and Sarah Kemble Siddons (1755–1831), who were applauded for the stateliness, grandeur, and dignity of their performances. Some found them near perfection, but others observed that Kemble's "want [lack] of variety and relief rendered [the performance] uninteresting and often indeed tedious." Every country had its classical actors: in America, Thomas A. Cooper (1776–1849); in France, Talma (1763–1826); in Germany, Emil Devrient (1803–1872). And in every country, the same general patterns of changing taste were observable.

A revolution in English acting appears to have occurred when Edmund Kean (1787–1833) made his London debut in 1814. Kean abandoned dignity and intellect in favor of flamboyance and passion. "The difference between Kean and Kemble," according to one contemporary, was that "Kemble knew there was a difference between tragedy and common life, but did not know in what it consisted, except in manner, which he consequently carried to excess, losing sight of the passion. Kean knows the real thing, which is

Figure 6–20. Romantic Acting: Booth. Edwin Booth as Iago in *Othello,* a role he played several times and which he alternated as Othello with Henry Irving. In such a role, Booth was an actor whom audiences came to see despite poor supporting casts. In Germany, audiences flocked to see him as Hamlet even though he played in English while the rest played in German. *(From The Collections of the University of Rochester Libraries)*

the height of the passion, manner following it as a matter of course"; according to another, to see Kean act "was to read Shakespeare by flashes of lightning." Apparently passionate outbursts and novel interpretations marked the actors labeled "natural" or "romantic" during the period. In addition to Kean, other important performers in this tradition were the English/American, Junius Brutus Booth (1796–1852) and the Frenchman Frédérick Lemaître (1800–1876).

Scarcely had Romantic acting seized the imagination of the public, however, when it too began to appear artificial. It was gradually replaced by yet another "natural" style after 1850, a style that came to be called *realistic* acting.

The profound changes that can be seen between 1750 and 1850 were the result of changes in the way audiences saw reality. In 1750, generalized scenery, costumes, and special effects formed a sparse background for the actors. Audiences, unperturbed by lack of detail or by its inaccuracy, thrilled to the verbal displays of excellently trained and elegantly attired actors. They sought and found their artistic truth in the formal, generalized portraits of the upper and middle classes that formed the basis of most new plays.

A theatre patron visiting Paris in 1760, for example, could attend any of three theatres and, during a few weeks, select from a number of operas or plays, the most recently fashionable being the sentimental comedies, the

Figure 6–21. Eighteenth-Century Production. A generalized "reference" to the time and place of the play is made in the costumes, but they are exotic and spectacular without being specific. (Note, especially, the eighteenth-century cut of the actress's dress.) A performance in 1776 of a play with an Oriental setting.

domestic dramas, and the exotic or chivalric tragedies. People who chose to attend Voltaire's *Tancred* (1760) were treated to a new wing-and-drop setting that was painted to suggest (if rather tentatively) a scene from medieval chivalry, complete with a few picturesque details of French local color. The actors wore an approximation of medieval costume and arranged themselves either in semicircles around the leading actors or in quasi-military formations that framed the hero. Although some real properties like lances, shields, and weapons were included, most of the details were painted onto the set pieces. An atmosphere of generalized French chivalry was evoked, and this background enhanced those vocal displays by the actors that were the primary pleasure of the audiences.

Could that same patron somehow have returned to Paris seventy years

Figure 6–22. Romantic Production. Complexity of staging, attention to scenic detail, and a new exoticism marked the early nineteenth century. The theatre had always used *traps* for appearances and disappearances, but, like other stage machines, they were greatly improved to meet the demands of the nineteenth century.

later, he or she could have chosen from plays being performed at more than a dozen theatres. At the commercial boulevard houses, historical melodramas set in exotic locales and featuring extravagant sets and costumes competed with equally spectacular equestrian shows, canine melodramas, comic operas, and pantomimes. At the state theatres, romantic tragedies, domestic dramas, and well-made plays competed for audiences with operas and ballets. Those attending a performance of the historical melodrama *Les Malcontents de 1579* (1834) on the boulevard were treated to a magnificent visual display. The designers had provided "a remarkable evocation of the court of Henry III and Marguerite de Navarre, of the Louvre as it existed at that time, of the quais and towers of sixteenth century Paris." Each setting was carefully detailed, down to the precise location and variety of the vegetation in the gardens and the diverse materials used in the several buildings. Lights, shadows, and sounds were manipulated to create mood and atmosphere that heightened the action. Although most of the scenic details were painted on the sets, many properties and costume pieces were "real" (three-dimensional). The care with which the actors pantomimed the smallest movements enriched the audience's experience of the play. In all, the visual display more than made up for the play's lack of poetic flight and the actors' reduced verbal pyrotechnics. The thrill was for the eye, not the ear, as *Les Malcontents* successfully offered the illusion of a particular time and place in France's past, complete with abundant details, both accurate and consistent. Gone was the *general* evocation of medieval times and in its place was the reproduction of a *particular* time and event. Part of the audience's joy, then, was that of discovery and recognition.

Comparing these two productions can serve as a reminder of the major trends in the theatre between 1750 and 1850:

1. The number and seating capacity of the theatres increased.

2. The middle and lower classes came into the theatres in increasing numbers.

3. The size and complexity of stages and support areas increased (although the size of the forestage decreased).

4. The number, accuracy, and consistency of visual details (scenery, properties, costume) increased as emphasis shifted from the aural to the visual aspects of production.

5. Interest in the natural and exotic encouraged new plays set in faraway places and times, while the rise of the middle class prompted a surge of domestic comedies and dramas.

Romanticism moved from the status of a tentative experiment in 1750 to an active and popular theatre style by 1800. Between 1800 and 1850, Romanticism ruled productions throughout the Western world: it was the theatrical mainstream. Its popularity remained strong in the commercial houses until the beginning of the twentieth century. But by 1850, new ways of viewing life and art were beginning to surface and coalesce into a challenge to the Romantic point of view. As always, the early signs were weak and uncertain, but for the careful observer, several elements of realism came into view around 1850.

The Golden Ages in Italy, England, and France: The Rise and Decline of Neoclassicism: 1550–1750

Background

Beginning around the year 1300, new ideas, social organizations, attitudes, and discoveries were peeking through the old order of Europe. For the next two hundred years, these new ideas gradually took hold and, in country after country, heralded the arrival of the *Renaissance* (literally "rebirth"). For reasons of politics, religion, geography, and even accident, the Renaissance did not reach all countries simultaneously, nor did it manifest itself identically in every place, but by the beginning of the sixteenth century, its power throughout Western Europe was evident, and it had revolutionized many former attitudes and practices of Europe.

For hundreds of years, the Church at Rome had defined the social and political realities of the Western world, working closely with secular princes to thwart all encroachments on their shared power and wealth. But when internal strife and external politics caused the removal of the papacy to Avignon, France, in 1305, both the legitimacy and the power of the Church as a world leader became increasingly suspect. In keeping with the doctrine of Apocalyptism, people of the early Middle Ages had supposed that within a few years, the present, temporal world would be destroyed in a holocaust, that the unrighteous would be purged, and that the righteous, now purified, would be transported to a world of bliss. But by 1300, a growing suspicion had surfaced that the Last Judgment was not so imminent as was first supposed. As the immediacy of the hereafter receded, an awareness of the joys of this life increased, and so new secular and temporal interests joined earlier divine and eternal concerns. A love of God and His ways, long the basis of human behavior, was joined by a newfound admiration for humankind, whose worth, intelligence, and beauty began to be celebrated.

Alongside this concern for people and their earthly lives (an attitude called *humanism*) emerged important new philosophical positions. The older theology, a complete system of thought presumably based on divine revelation, gave way to competing philosophical systems that stressed *secularism* (that is, they advocated ethical conduct as an end in itself rather than as a prerequisite to heaven, and they argued for logical systems of thought capable of existence independent of divine revelation).

Nor was science immune to the ferment produced by the reexamination of previously held assumptions. The church-supported cosmology of the Egyptian philosopher Ptolemy, which placed the Earth at the center of the universe, and man, God's favorite creation, at the center of the Earth, was assaulted and finally toppled by another view (supported in the Renaissance by Copernicus, fl. 1545) that pictured a sun-centered universe in which human beings were relegated to life on a relatively minor planet, clearly no longer at the center of things. Nor was the Church so united as before. As its wealth accumulated and its allegiance to the noble classes solidified, its worldly interests came into ever-greater conflict with its spiritual pronouncements. Unable to reform its practices from within and unwilling to remain a party to its abuses, some Christians (like Martin Luther, fl. 1546) protested against the Church at Rome and launched the so-called Reformation.

In sum, although God, His Church, and His theology remained the central fact of human life in the Renaissance, they were no longer absolute and unquestioned. Humanism and secularism were competing with them for acceptance. But the emergence of new ideas and attitudes were only part of the phenomenon. Vital, too, were factors that encouraged the widespread dissemination of the new spirit. Two elements in particular were critical: the growth of trade and the arrival of the printing press in Italy.

So long as the basis of wealth and social structures was agricultural activity on an essentially self-contained manor, exchange of goods and ideas was limited. But by 1300, shipping and trade were joining agriculture as important means of livelihood. Towns grew and overshadowed the manors, and commerce increasingly involved coinage as well as barter. Trade, both national and international, permitted and even encouraged a flow of ideas as well as of goods, an effortless exchange not possible as long as self-contained agricultural units dominated the economic life of Europe. At the center of most of the various trade routes of the fourteenth century were the several city–states of Italy, which soon became the focuses of a blossoming commerce of ideas, skills, and products. When Constantinople fell to the Turks in 1453, many scholars and artists came to Italy from the Middle and Far Eastern civilizations, bringing with them their knowledge and their books. Thus plays and treatises from ancient Greece and Rome, rescued from libraries endangered by the advancing Turkish troops, arrived in Italy, where their study and interpretation began almost at once.

The introduction of the Gutenberg printing press to Italy at about the same time (1467) allowed the rapid reproduction of documents arriving from the East as well as the interpretations and imitations of these documents. Certainly the printing press allowed a veritable explosion of accessible information, so much so that, by 1500, numerous academies in the city–states of Italy were devoted to the study and production of Roman plays. Shortly thereafter, Italians began writing their own plays in imitation of the Roman models.

Because patronage of the arts was a major and acknowledged source of prestige, and because Italian noblemen engaged in rivalries over which court was to become the cultural center of the peninsula, painters, musicians, sculptors, architects, and writers in Italy flourished early.

Theatre in Italy, 1550–1750

In drama and theatre, three contributions of the Italians were to have far-reaching effects: (1) the Neoclassical ideal in playwriting and criticism; (2) the Italianate system of staging and architecture; and (3) the popular theatre known as *commedia dell'arte.*

Neoclassicism

Neoclassicism literally means "new classicism," but in fact it was based far more heavily on Roman than on Greek practices and models. Central to Neoclassical doctrine was a complex concept called *verisimilitude*—literally, "truth seeming." But the meaning of *verisimilitude* is more involved than its facile definition might suggest, for serious artists of all ages have aimed to tell the "truth." Because the characteristics of art throughout the ages have changed, it is probably safe to conclude that arts differed from age to age because the truth that the artists saw and sought to depict had changed. Thus the critical problem for a student of Neoclassicism is to understand what "truth" meant to the Neoclassicist.

Truth for the Neoclassicist consisted of a set of norms and thus resided in the essential, the general, the typical, and the class rather than in the particular, the individual, or the unique (as in Romanticism). To get at truth a Neoclassical artist had to cut away all that was temporary, aberrational, or accidental in favor of those qualities that were fundamental and unchanging. To be true meant to be usually true, generally accurate, typically the case. The humanness of one person, for example, rested in those essential qualities that he shared with all other people, regardless of the historical accident of place, century, or nationality of birth. Individual differences

Figure 7–1. Neoclassicism. An ideal of purity in both staging and dramaturgy informed the Renaissance theatre. This is an illustration of a sixteenth-century edition of the works of Terence. *(Rare Book Division, The New York Public Library, Astor, Lenox and Tilden Foundation.)*

were of little moment because they were not of the essence of humanness. Obviously such a view of truth placed a premium on classification and categorization, and obviously *verisimilitude*, or *truth-seemingness*, had a meaning very different from that ascribed to it by those steeped in the Romantics' admiration for individuality and uniqueness.

But Neoclassical truth implied other matters as well. Verisimilitude in drama required the elimination of events that could not reasonably be expected to happen in real life. Although an exception was made when ancient stories or myths incorporating supernatural events were dramatized, even then the dramatist was expected to minimize the importance of such events, perhaps by relegating the action to offstage. Because in real life people generally talked to one another rather than to themselves, monologues and soliloquies were customarily abandoned in favor of dialogue between major characters and their trusted friends (or *confidants*). Too, the tendency of real-life people to behave in certain ways based on their age, social rank, occupation, gender, and so forth could be observed; therefore characters in drama were expected to display proper *decorum* (that is, they were to embody traits normally held by members of their class) or, if they did not, to suffer ridicule or punishment for their deviations.

Finally, because it was believed that God ruled the world in accord with a divine plan and that He was a good God, verisimilitude required that dramatic actions be organized in such a way that good was rewarded and evil punished, in keeping with eternal truth. Although in daily life good occasionally went unheralded and evil unpunished, such observable events were believed to be aberrational and, as such, unsuitable subjects for drama.

From the concept of verisimilitude came another bulwark of Neoclassicism, *purity of genres* (or purity of form). In the drama, this meant that the two major forms, tragedy and comedy, must not be mixed. The injunction against mixing did not mean merely that funny scenes were improper for tragedy or that unhappy endings were inappropriate for comedy. Both tragedy and comedy were far more rigidly defined than today, and the rule against mixing the forms meant that no element belonging to the one should appear in the other. For example, tragedy was to depict people of high station involved in affairs of state; its language was to be elevated and poetic, its endings unhappy. Comedy, on the other hand, was to display persons of the lower and middle classes embroiled in domestic difficulties and intrigues. Its language was always less elevated, and often prosaic, and its endings were happy. Purity of genres meant, then, that a prose tragedy or a domestic tragedy could not exist—both were a contradiction in terms. It also meant that kings and queens did not appear in comedies, nor were affairs of state suitable subjects for the comic author.

Finally, based on verisimilitude and on current interpretations of ancient commentators, the Neoclassical notion of "the three unities" (time, place, and action) developed. Although the ancient Greek theorist Aristotle (see p. 286) had argued cogently for plays with a unified action, Neoclassical theorists were more concerned that their plays unfold within a reasonable time and a limited place so that verisimilitude would not be strained. No audience would believe, the Neoclassical argument went, that months had passed or oceans been crossed while the audience sat in the same place for a few hours. Although theorists varied in the strictness of their requirements for unity (some argued for a single room, others allowed a single town; some required that the playing time of the drama equal the actual time elapsed, others permitted a twenty-four-hour time period), most Italian theorists accepted some version of the three unities after about 1570. By then as well, Neoclassicists had adopted *the five-act play form* as standard for drama, a norm probably derived from theories of the Roman theoretician Horace and practices of the Roman writer of tragedy Seneca.

Finally, Neoclassicists sought a justification for drama and theatre and found it in their ability to teach moral precepts while entertaining and delighting an audience. *To teach* and *to please* were touted as *the dual purposes of drama,* and playwrights desiring critical acclaim took care that their plays did both. The idea of a drama's existing only for its own sake or as an expression of an individual artist (as in Romantic theory) was not supported by major Renaissance theorists. In sum, then, Neoclassicism, as first developed by the Italians and later adopted throughout most of Western Europe, rested on six major points: (1) verisimilitude, with its offspring; (2) decorum; (3) purity of genres; (4) the "three unities"; (5) the five-act form; and (6) the twofold purpose, to teach and to please.

After about 1570, Neoclassical ideas became the standard for Italian dramas. Increasingly thereafter, educated playwrights in Italy sought to embrace its principles, and critics praised plays to the degree that they adhered to its points. By 1600, Neoclassical standards were being exported to other parts of Europe, where they remained dominant for the next two hundred years among educated and courtly audiences. Neoclassicism's propriety and concentration may account for its lack of appeal to many common people, who sought more spectacle than the three unities permitted. Thus, despite the acceptance of Neoclassicism as an ideal, its tenets were undercut in a variety of ways until its eventual replacement in the late eighteenth century by a new set of critical precepts, those of Romanticism.

Italianate Staging

Italianate staging, like Neoclassicism, developed as an amalgam of ideas and techniques received from classical Rome (and to a lesser extent from ancient Greece) with those cultivated in contemporary Italy. In 1486, Vitruvius's work on Roman architecture, *De Architectura* (16–13 B.C.), was printed. In this ten-volume work, Vitruvius devoted a lengthy section in Book V (on public buildings) to the proper construction and appearance of theatres and to the sorts of scenic displays appropriate to them, and in Book X (on machines), he wrote of the function of rulers in providing "shows" for their subjects. The dissemination of *De Architectura* was so rapid that by 1500 its major points had been accepted as authoritative and a number of contemporary Italian interpretations of it had been undertaken.

Although his books dealt with architecture and scenery, Vitruvius provided no illustrations of his ideal theatre, and so the Italians translated his words and ideas in light of contemporary practices in art and architecture, most notably the current fascination with linear perspective. Although known to the ancients, perspective, when it was rediscovered by the Italians around 1500, caused an artistic revolution. Artists struggled to master the intricacies of the "new" technique, while uninitiated spectators hailed its ability to trick the senses as if by magic. Soon the potential of perspective painting for scenic decoration was recognized, and in 1545, Sebastiano Serlio (1475–1554) published the second book of his seven-volume *Dell' Architettura,* which became the most authoritative interpretation of Vitruvius to date. Serlio's work established the guidelines for theatrical architects and designers for the next hundred years.

Serlio's interpretation of Vitruvius's Roman theatre, however erroneous, set a model for permanent theatres built in Rome during the Renaissance. Vitruvius was obviously describing the Roman theatre that he knew; it was erected out of doors and in a circular configuration. Wealthy Italians, on the other hand, were accustomed to plays produced in banqueting halls in the homes of the wealthy. When the first permanent theatres were envisioned, therefore, the task was to fit the classical theatre as described by Vitruvius into the rectangular spaces familiar to the Italians and, in some way, to accommodate the result to the current fashion for linear perspective. An early solution was the Teatro Olimpico in Vicenza, Italy (completed in 1585), whose five doors corresponded roughly to Vitruvius's description of five stage openings, except that in the Teatro Olimpico, each door boasted a vista in forced perspective. The later Teatro Farnese (at Parma, completed in 1618) exhibited a permanent proscenium arch that protected the illusion of perspective and featured a series of additional arches farther back on the stage, each increasing the sense of depth and heightening the illusion of reality.

In scenic display as well as theatrical architecture, Serlio's interpretation of Vitruvius set the standard. From Vitruvius's scant descriptions of tragic, comic, and satyric scenes, Serlio elaborated each into detailed directions, with illustrations drawn in perspective. A brief comparison of Vitruvius and Serlio as they described one setting will suggest the differences.

Figures 7–2, 7–3, 7–4. Serlian Scenery. These are Serlio's tragic, comic, and satyric scenes from an edition of 1569. The scenes were not changeable in the modern sense, but featured forced perspective and a sloping stage, built-up architectural detail, and a careful adherence to the classical forms of drama.
(Rare Book Division, The New York Public Library, Astor, Lenox and Tilden Foundation.)

Of the satyric scene, Vitruvius said, "Satyric scenes are decorated with trees, caverns, mountains, and other rustic objects delineated in landscaped style." Of the same scenes, Serlio (as translated into English in 1611) amplified, "The Satiricall Scenes are to Represent Satirs, wherein you must place all those things that be rude and rusticall." He then went on to quote Vitruvius as calling for "Trees, Rootes, Herbs, Hils, and Flowers, and with some countrey houses. . . . And for that in our dayes these things were made in Winter, where there were but fewe greene Trees, Herbs, and Flowres to be found; then you must make these things of Silke, which will be more commendable than the naturall things themselves."

In the remainder of the book, Serlio provided such tips on stagecraft as the proper use of colored lights, the production of fire effects, the building of fanciful costumes, and the use of pasteboard figures on a perspective stage. After its printing in 1545, Serlio's account, a blending of the classical descriptions of Vitruvius with current Italian scenic practices, swept Western Europe and became the basis of what was called "the Italianate system of staging."

With certain modest modifications related to the particular country and the specific date, Italianate settings shared these features throughout the sixteenth, seventeenth, and early eighteenth centuries:

1. The scenery was painted in single-point perspective, calculated from a seat toward the back of the orchestra (usually reserved for the most important nobleman associated with the theatre).

2. The scenery consisted of a series of wings positioned in pairs at each side of the stage, with each pair placed relatively closer to the center line of the stage than the one in front of it, so that the apparent distance increased. The setting culminated at the back of the stage in a single backdrop painted in perspective (or alternately, a shutter formed when a set of wings was shoved together and then painted in perspective).

3. The scenery was placed behind the proscenium arch and thus behind the actors, forming a background against which they played, rather than an environment for the action.

4. The stage was raked, or slanted, to increase the sense of depth by forcing the perspective. Sometimes the front part of the stage, where the actors performed, was flat and only the portion of the stage behind the proscenium arch was raked; at other times the rake began at the front of the platform and continued uninterrupted to the back wall.

5. Overhead machinery and theatrical rigging were hidden from view by a series of borders arranged to enhance perspective.

6. A proscenium arch (or several) framed the whole picture, thereby protecting the illusion created by the perspective painting.

Having developed this basic system for decorating the stage, Italian artists set about almost at once to perfect it. Specifically, they investigated ways of shifting scenery in order to permit a rapid change of place. Experimentation soon revealed that quick changes required the replacement of all three-dimensional details, such as those suggested by Serlio, with two-dimensional, painted settings, and the replacement of angle wings (flats consisting of two parts hinged together) by flat wings. By the 1640s, the methods of scenic change were well developed and were summarized in two influential works: Niccolo Sabattini's *Prattica de Fabricar Scene e Machine ne' Teatri* (1638) and Joseph Furttenbach's *Architectura Recreationis* (1640). But the real breakthrough came in 1645, when Giacomo Torelli (1608–1678) astonished the theatrical world with his invention of a new mechanism for changing scenery: the *chariot-and-pole system*. The name derived from the small wagons (or chariots) that ran on tracks beneath the stage and carried on them a long pole that extended from the chariots through slits in the stage floor up to a height sufficient to provide a sturdy support for scenic pieces, which were attached to the poles at stage level. The idea was a simple one: as the chariots moved on their tracks toward the center of the stage, a piece of scenery came into view; as the chariot moved off to the side, a piece of scenery disappeared. By devising an elaborate system of ropes and pulleys, Torelli succeeded in rigging everything together so that the turn of a single winch could produce a complete, simultaneous change of setting. By coordinating such changes with the machinery used to produce special effects, like flying, trapping, wave making, thunder, lightning, and explosions, a truly magical effect was possible. Such tricks earned Torelli the name of the Great Wizard and made him feared in some quarters.

A contradiction clearly existed between the ideals of drama, where Neoclassicism called for the unities of time, place, and action and an avoidance of supernatural events, and the ideals of scenic display, whose Italianate

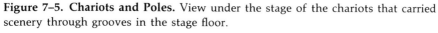

Figure 7–5. Chariots and Poles. View under the stage of the chariots that carried scenery through grooves in the stage floor.

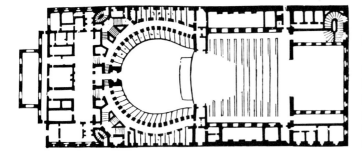

Figure 7–6. Italian Opera Theatre. A plan of the La Scala Opera House in Milan, Italy. Half of the building is devoted to the stage and its support areas; wings and multiple drops or back-scenes are shown.

artists stressed increasingly elaborate splendors involving multiple scenes, instant transformations, and a variety of spectacular effects. In Italy, as elsewhere, the tension was resolved by producing dramas simply and by expending imagination and money for the production of lavish operas, dances, and *intermezzi* (courtly entertainments typically given between the acts of a play). Italian opera became by the mid-seventeenth century the most popular form of dramatic entertainment in Italy, thereby attesting to the enormous attraction of spectacle. As Italian opera was exported to France, Germany, and the rest of Europe, so were many of Italy's latest scenic techniques.

Commedia dell'Arte

Neoclassical dramas and elaborately staged operas were primarily the entertainment of the noble, the wealthy, and the erudite. Among the common folk, another, very different kind of dramatic entertainment was flourishing: the *commedia dell'arte*. Although neither the origins nor the sources of *commedia* are well understood, its major characteristics were well established by 1550, and Italian troupes of *commedia* players were touring all of Western Europe by 1600.

Commedia players worked from a basic story outline *(scenario)* within which they improvised much of their dialogue and action. Each actor in the troupe played the same character in almost every scenario and therefore wore the same costume, reused the same bits of comic business *(lazzi)*, and even repeated some of the same dialogue from scenario to scenario. Most troupes had ten or twelve members, each of whom assumed the role of one of the stock characters. Each troupe boasted one or two sets of young lovers *(inamorata)* and a host of comic characters, the most common of which were Capitano (the captain), Pantalone (the merchant), Dottore (the doctor), and the several *zanni* (servants) like Arlecchino (Harlequin), Brighella, Scaramuccio, and Pulcinello.

Figures 7–7, 7–8, 7–9. Commedia Dell'arte Characters. Pulchinello, Scaramouche, the boastful Capitano, and such tricksters as Scapino and Fricasso were stock characters for generations of this partly improvised, popular form, seen here in the drawings of *commedia* characters by Jacques Callot (seventeenth century) whose own style may exaggerate the characteristics of the actors.

Pulliciniello.   Sig.ᵃ Lucretia.

Scapino.   Cap.ᵗ Zerbino.

Scaramucia.   Fricasso.

Organized as sharing companies, such troupes toured constantly as they tried to scratch out a living in the theatre, without the protection or the financial support of noble houses. Although the influence of *commedia* extended throughout Europe, its ephemeral nature militated against its leaving a lasting record (especially scripts), and so today this popular Italian comedy is viewed primarily as a phenomenon whose excitement and vigor cannot be recaptured.

Despite Italy's unquestioned leadership in dramatic theory and scenic display and in spite of its unique popular comedy, Italian theatre and drama did not attain lasting international prominence. By 1750, except for opera Italy was no longer a world leader in theatre. Both England and France outstripped their teacher and attained an international reputation by the end of the seventeenth century, and both achieved a lasting acclaim never given the Italians, from whom they drew.

Theatre in England, 1550–1750

Because England lay distant from Italy, the ideas and practices of the Renaissance were slow in reaching the island nation. Moreover, once there, Renaissance influence was both more tentative and less binding than elsewhere.

Conditions favored artistic growth when Shakespeare began to write in the 1590s. The reign of Elizabeth I (r. 1558–1603) had already brought greatness to the country. With her ascent to the throne, England achieved the political and religious stability that permitted its arts and literature to thrive. When, in an attempt to mute religious controversies, the queen outlawed all religious drama in 1558–1559, she opened the way for the rapid development of a secular tradition of plays and playgoing. When the queen finally agreed to the execution of Mary Stuart (1587), her chief rival for the throne and the core around which Catholic assaults upon the English church and throne swirled, Elizabeth's political situation was secured and the domination of Anglican Protestants within the Church of England affirmed. The English navy defeated the mighty Spanish Armada in 1588 and established itself as ruler of the seas and leader among the trading nations. England, for the first time in generations, was at peace at home and abroad and filled with a national confidence and lust for life seldom paralleled in history.

Added to the general well-being of the nation was the vigor of the court, the schools, and the universities where scholars were digesting and remaking Italian humanism and Classical documents with an eye to English needs and preferences. In particular, four university students (called the *University Wits*) were applying classical scholarship to the needs of the English public stage and laying foundations for the vigorous theatre to come. Robert Green (1558–1592), Thomas Kyd (1558–1594), John Lyly (c. 1554–1606), and Christopher Marlowe (1564–1593) all represented major improvements

Figure 7–10. Elizabethan English Theatre. The first London theatre buildings were round or polygonal with an open yard in the middle of the audience area, and they were located just outside the boundaries of the City of London for legal reasons.

on the native dramatists preceding them, particularly in the development of elegant prose and blank verse, romantic comedies, and complex protagonists. These University Wits brought the erudition of humanistic scholarship to the English stage and flirted very tentatively with some Neoclassical practices.

But before the Renaissance reached the consciousness of the average Englishman, London already boasted two different kinds of theatres: the outdoor, or "public," playhouse, and the indoor, or "private," playhouse. Owing to scant and occasionally contradictory evidence, the precise appearance of these theatres cannot be known, but some general features can be deduced from a careful reading of extant plays in the light of information gleaned from a contemporary building contract for the Fortune (public) Theatre, a contemporary sketch of the Swan (public) Theatre, a contemporary drawing of the Cockpit at Court (private) Theatre, and various accounts taken from contemporary diaries, letters, and financial records (particularly those of Philip Henslowe). From these sources, a general picture emerges.

The outdoor, public theatres (of which nine were built between 1576 and 1642) consisted of a round or polygonal, roofed, multileveled auditorium that surrounded an open yard, into which jutted a platform raised to a height of four to six feet. The entire yard (or pit) and part of the stage platform were unroofed. The audience, probably numbering as many as 2,500, surrounded the playing area on three sides, some standing in the *pit*

Figure 7–11. Elizabethan Theatre Interior. Although agreement is lacking on the details of the Elizabethan theatre, there is a consensus for the existence of a broad, raised stage in the midst of the audience, for a pillared roof over the playing area, and for doors at the rear of the playing area. A reconstruction by Richard Southern from his *Seven Ages of the Theatre. (Reproduced with the permission of Hill and Wang (now a division of Farrar, Straus and Giroux, Inc.) from THE SEVEN AGES OF THEATRE by Richard Southern. Copyright © 1961 by Richard Southern.)*

and others seated in the *galleries* or the still-more-exclusive *lords' rooms.* The actors worked on the raised stage and apparently awaited cues and changed costumes in the *tiring house* located at the rear of the platform. Covering part of the stage was a roof (called *the heavens*) that was supported by columns resting on the stage and apparently decorated on its underside with pictures of stars, planets, and signs of the zodiac. From the heavens flew in gods and properties as needed by the action. The stage floor was obviously pierced with *traps,* through which devils, spirits, and grave diggers could appear and disappear. Connecting the tiring house with the stage were *two doors,* which often represented widely divergent locations (as, for example, when one led to the fields of France and the other to the shores of England). Atop the tiring house, a flag flew on days of performance, and at a level just below, in an area called *the hut,* were probably housed the various pieces of equipment and machinery needed for special effects. A *musician's gallery* was apparently located just below the hut, at the third level above the stage.

At this point in the description, scholarly agreement ceases. Extant plays clearly required two playing levels, an upper and a lower, and some sort of *discovery space,* a place where objects and characters could be hidden from view and discovered at the appropriate time. The nature and appearance of the discovery space has been the subject of endless speculation. Most agree that it was located between the two doors, but some conceive of it as a permanent architectural part of the theatre, whereas others conceive of it as a portable unit to be added or deleted as required; some picture the discovery space as a recessed alcove (a kind of miniproscenium theatre), whereas others see it as a pavilion that jutted out into the stage. Obviously any decision about the conformation of the space at stage level had implications for the upper level as well. Obviously, too, the degree of permanence

Figure 7–12. Elizabethan Interior: The Swan Drawing. This famous contemporary drawing, re-drawn and with the labels translated here, is an important part of the evidence for details of the Elizabethan theatre.

of the discovery space would radically affect the general appearance of the theatre. The whole problem has been made thornier by the absence of such a space in the Swan sketch and by the appalling problems with sight lines that any sort of discovery space seemed likely to introduce. Because the available evidence will not permit the issues to be resolved, ideas about the appearance of Shakespeare's playhouse must remain tentative.

About the indoor, or private, playhouses, even less is known. They were roofed, smaller, and therefore more expensive to attend than the public playhouses. Despite their name, they were open to anyone caring to pay to attend. Initially the private theatres attracted the most fashionable audiences of London: they came to see erudite plays performed by troupes of boy actors. By 1610, however, as the popularity of children's troupes waned, adult troupes who performed in the public theatres in the summer took over the private houses for their winter performances. The fact is significant because it indicates that the arrangement of the stage spaces in the theatres was very similar.

By the time of Shakespeare, English actors had attained a satisfactory level of financial and social stability. It came in part because Queen Elizabeth gave to the Master of Revels, a member of the royal household, the responsibility for licensing acting troupes and guaranteeing those licensed the right to play unhampered by threats of arrest for vagabondage, and in part because most troupes were at least nominally attached to the house of a nobleman above the rank of baron. Although few actors became truly wealthy, most were well paid by the standards of the day, and some (like Shakespeare) were able to retire in style and live like gentlemen.

The troupes themselves were organized as democratic, self-governing units whose members shared expenses, profits, and responsibilities for production. A very few owned a part of the theatre building itself; these were called *householders.* The most valuable members of the company held a whole share in the costumes, properties, and other company possessions; lesser members owned only half or quarter shares, with their influence and income reduced accordingly. In addition, each company hired some actors and stagehands (*hirelings*), who worked for a salary rather than for a share of the profits. All members were male, the roles of women being taken by men or young boys, many of whom were apprenticed to leading actors in the troupe. Among the actors, most specialized in certain kinds of roles (clowns, women, heroes), and some were widely admired in Shakespeare's day: Richard Tarleton, William Kemp, and Robert Armin as clowns, and Richard Burbage and Edward Alleyn as tragedians.

The precise style of acting is unclear, but vocal power and flexibility were clearly prized. Plays of the period offered ample opportunity to display breath control and verbal dexterity in the monologues, soliloquies, complicated figures of speech, symmetrical and extended phrases, and so on. On the other hand, oratorical and rhetorical techniques did not seem to have overpowered the actors' search for naturalness. Contemporary accounts, including lines from Shakespeare's *Hamlet,* spoke of an acting style capable of moving actors and audiences alike. The goal was apparently a convincing

Figure 7–13. English Comedian. The actor Tarleton, a famous comic actor of Shakespeare's time.

representation of a character in action performed by an actor with a well-tuned vocal instrument.

By Shakespeare's day as well, the importance of drama and theatre had been argued and demonstrated by leading literary figures. In response to attacks on the theatre as an instrument of the devil, a temptation designed to lure people from useful work, both Thomas Lodge and Sir Phillip Sydney countered that drama was a most effective way of providing moral instruction and encouraging worthwhile actions in ordinary people. Drawing heavily from continental Neoclassicists, Lodge and Sydney succeeded in pacifying many of the theatre's critics, at least for a while.

By the time Shakespeare arrived in London to begin his career, then, England was a proud and growing nation whose power was only beginning to be recognized. Its seat of government, London, boasted permanent native theatres, a group of educated playwrights, a stable of trained and experienced actors, and a legitimacy derived from its supposedly exalted purpose.

William Shakespeare (1564–1616) was the greatest playwright of the English-speaking world and one of the greatest dramatists of Western civilization. Between 1590 and 1613, a period now acknowledged as the Golden Age of English Drama, Shakespeare wrote thirty-eight plays, which for convenience are customarily divided into three types: the history plays (those treating *English* history), like *Henry IV* (Parts 1 and 2), *Henry V, Henry VI* (Parts 1, 2, and 3), *Henry VIII, Richard II,* and *Richard III;* the tragedies, like *Romeo and Juliet, Julius Caesar, Hamlet, King Lear, Othello, Macbeth,* and *Anthony and Cleopatra;* and the comedies, ranging from popular romantic works like *Love's Labors Lost, As You Like It, Twelfth Night, Much Ado About Nothing,* and *A Midsummers Night's Dream,* to the darker tragicomedies like *All's Well That Ends Well* and *Measure for Measure.*

Although no short discussion can capture the genius of Shakespeare's works, some attempt must be made to describe features that tended to recur throughout his plays and that are typical of English plays from about 1590 to 1642:

1. Shakespeare generally adopted an early point of attack; that is, he began his plays near the beginning of the story, with the result that the audience sees the story develop onstage rather than learning about it second-hand, through messengers or reporters.

2. Shakespeare customarily developed several lines of action ("subplots"). Early in his plays, the various lines appear to be separate and independent, but as the play moves toward its resolution, the several lines gradually merge so that by the play's end, the unity of the various lines is evident.

3. Shakespeare filled his plays with a large number and variety of incidents. The mixing of tears and laughter is not uncommon, nor is the close juxtaposition of tender scenes of love with brawling scenes of confrontation.

4. Shakespeare ranged freely in time and place, allowing his actions to unfold across several months and in several locales.

5. Shakespeare employed an unusually large number and range of characters. Casts of thirty are common, and among the *dramatis personae* can be found kings and gravediggers, pedants and clowns, senility and youth, city dwellers and rustics, the very rich and the very poor.

6. The language in the plays is infinitely varied. Within the same play are found passages of exquisite lyricism, elegant figures of speech, ribald slang, witty aphorisms, and pedestrian prose, all carefully chosen to enhance the play's dramatic action.

In sum, the art of Shakespeare was an expansive one that filled a very large dramatic canvas with portraits of a wide cross-section of humanity engaged in acts ranging from the heroic to the mundane. The texture of the plays is rich, detailed, and allusive.

Staging such plays cried out for a flexible and fluid style of production. Elaborate scenery, frequently shifted, was impossible in the English theatres of the day; various small properties, carried off and on by the actors themselves, suggested the specific locations. Costuming was far more important than scenery to the visual excitement of the performance. Contemporary

Figure 7–14. Shakespearean Casts. Large and varied casts of characters were typical of the plays of Shakespeare and his contemporaries. Here, a production in nineteen hundred of his *King John*. It is useful to compare this staging with the Swan drawing (Figure 7–12) and Richard Southern's reconstruction (Figure 7–11) to see some of the differences between the detailed antiquarianism of 1900 and the open, very generalized, almost placeless staging of Shakespeare's own theatre.

accounts spoke of luscious fabrics in rich colors. Although fanciful characters like devils, angels, sprites, and allegorical figures appeared in garments designed and made especially for the theatre, most roles were played in Elizabethan garments, regardless of their historic reality. Occasionally different periods, countries, or races were signified by the addition of a drapery or a turban, but historical accuracy was never a goal of the costume. Most actors wore contemporary dress that differed from that of the audience only by being more elegant. The similarity of dress between actors and spectators doubtless served to heighten the sense of a shared theatrical experience, as did the relative proximity of the audience to the stage and the constancy of the lighting (stage and auditorium were equally visible).

With Shakespeare's death in 1616 came a decline in the quality, if not the quantity, of drama. Although many of the playwrights were esteemed in their own day (most notably Ben Jonson, 1572–1637; John Fletcher, 1579–1625; Francis Beaumont, c. 1584–1616; John Webster, c. 1580–c. 1630; and John Ford, 1586–c. 1639), none has achieved the modern admiration accorded Shakespeare. Thus the golden age of English theatre was already in decline after 1616.

Within thirty years, a civil war had broken out between the Monarchists (those wishing to keep Charles I on the throne and, implicitly, Roman Catholic influence strong within the Church of England) and the Puritans (those

Figure 7–15. **Modern Shakespeare.** *Love's Labours Lost* in a modern production at California State University, Dominguez Hills. *(Directed by Jack A. Vaughn and designed by Peter Lach.)*

who wished to purify the Church of England of all its Romish practices and, therefore, to remove Charles I from power). In 1642, the Puritans deposed Charles, seized power, formed a government—and closed the theatres. It took a second civil war, however, to place Oliver Cromwell (1599–1658) in power and bring stability to the war-torn island. Upon Cromwell's death, no agreeable successor could be found and so Parliament finally called Charles II, son of Charles I, from France, where he had lived in exile. For the period of the Interregnum (the period "between kings," 1642–1660), the English theatres were closed.

When the theatres reopened in 1660 with the restoration of the monarchy, both the drama and the staging traditions were very different indeed. Before turning to consider these changes, however, we must glance briefly at a courtly theatre that existed alongside Shakespeare's own for most of his career.

By invitation only, some individuals formed a courtly audience for plays and spectacles staged in royal and noble houses. Although both Henry VIII (Elizabeth's father) and Elizabeth had staged theatrical entertainments from time to time, it was the Stuart kings who followed them, James I (r. 1603–1625) and Charles I (r. 1625–1642), who perfected the splendid court *masques.* Stuart masques were allegorical stories designed to compliment a particular individual or occasion. Their texts were little more than pretexts for the elaborate scenic displays and lavish costumes that characterized the presentations. Although major roles and all comic or villainous characters were portrayed by professional actors, the courtiers themselves performed the heart of the masques, three spectacular dances. Great sums of money assured the splendor of the entertainments; a single masque, *The Triumph of Love,* for example, cost a staggering 21,000 pounds at a time when the average *annual* wage for a skilled worker was about 25 pounds.

Although many leading dramatists wrote masques, Ben Jonson and William Davenant (1606–1668) were the most significant. Jonson, perhaps the leading playwright of the period excluding Shakespeare, became annoyed that the text assumed such a clearly secondary position to the scenery, and so he stopped writing masques in 1631, leaving Davenant as the primary author of the courtly entertainment thereafter. The star of the masques, however, was neither Jonson nor Davenant but the scenic designer Inigo Jones (1573–1652). An Englishman by birth, Jones studied design at the court of Florence in Italy, where he learned the newest techniques of stage painting, rigging, and design. He introduced many of these into the English court when, in 1605, he staged his first masque for James I. *By the end of his career, Jones had introduced into the English courts all the major elements of Italiante staging then developed.*

Stuart masques, then, have a significance that exceeds the number of persons who saw them. First, they were employing Italianate systems of staging during the first half of the seventeenth century, at a time when the English public and private theatres still relied on scenic practices that were essentially medieval. Second, the close association of the masques with the monarchy, added to the Puritans' displeasure at their expense, were major factors in the Puritans' decision to outlaw English theatre in 1642 when they seized power. In this way, the overthrow and subsequent execution of Charles I brought an end to one of the most glorious and productive periods of English theatrical history.

The rise to power of the Puritan Oliver Cromwell put an end for a time to legitimate theatre in England, but as music was not interdicted, Davenant produced operas during the period, and in these productions, he introduced the Italianate system to the general public. Also, the bribery of petty officials apparently made it possible to produce plays occasionally, for contemporary records of arrests and repeated legal sanctions suggest continued, if reduced, theatrical activity between 1642 and 1660.

When the monarchy was restored in 1660, theatre was reinstated almost immediately. Until new permanent theatres could be built, companies used whatever spaces were available (spaces left over from pre-Commonwealth days or tennis courts remodeled for theatrical productions). Soon after English theatre recommenced, both its plays and its practices sought to move closer to the Italianate and French ideals. The increased French influence was predictable because the English courtiers went to France (many to the court of Louis XIV) to wait out the Interregnum.

When the theatres reopened, many plays written during the age of Shakespeare continued to be produced (usually in severely adapted versions), but the new plays, both comic and serious, were closer to continental Neoclassicism than to Shakespeare, and both became increasingly sentimental as the eighteenth century wore on.

Most famous today are the Restoration "comedies of manner," plays whose witty dialogue and sophisticated sexual behavior reflected the highly

Figure 7–16. Restoration Comedy. *Flora,* attributed to Thomas Doggett, as presented at Florida State University. Note the wings and borders and the split in the center of the back-scene. *(Directed by George Bogusch.)*

artificial, mannered, and aristocratic society of the day. The heroes and heroines were "virtuous" if they succeeded in capturing and satisfying a lover or in cuckolding a husband and avoiding detection. "Honor" depended not on integrity but on reputation, and "wit," the ability to express ideas in a clever and apt way, was prized above all. Admirable characters in the plays were those who could operate successfully within the intricate social sphere; the foolish and laughable were those whose lack of wit or upbringing denied them access to social elegance. In short, the comedies depicted the mores and conventions of a courtly society where elegance of phrase and the *appearance* of propriety were more highly prized than lofty morals and sincere feelings. Among the most famous authors of Restoration comedies were William Congreve (1670–1729); George Etherege (c. 1634–1691); and William Wycherley (1640–1715).

By the beginning of the eighteenth century, the amoral tone of these plays had become offensive to many, and the Neoclassical view that drama should teach morality prevailed, resulting in comedies that were more conservative, middle-class, moralistic, and, eventually, *sentimental.* Central to the sentimental literature was a strong conviction that man was naturally, innately good and that if he would simply follow his instincts (rather than the advice of friends or the example of books), he would behave ethically. The change at first was merely in the plays' endings: libertines philandered and cuckolded throughout four acts of the play but, in the fifth, repented and declared their intention to lead a moral and upright life henceforth. By the 1730s, heroes and heroines were becoming the virtuous embodiments of middle-class values, struggling cheerfully against adversity until, at the end, their courage and persistence were rewarded. Prized especially were characters able to express their insights about human goodness in pithy statements (which came to be called *sentiments*). Thus the label *sentimental hero* or *heroine* implied not only those who embodied virtues and who recognized such virtue in others but also those whose speech was rich in sentiments. The audiences of the day experienced "a pleasure too exquisite for laughter," and so the terms *tearful comedy* and *sentimental comedy* predominated in the comic literature by the middle of the eighteenth century.

Serious drama followed a similar pattern. Immediately after the Restoration, "heroic" tragedies presented the inevitable conflict between love and duty. In a world far removed from that of the Restoration comedies, tragic heroes were flawless and their heroines chaste. The dialogue was bombastic and replete with "heroic couplets," two-line units of rhymed iambic pentameter (probably an attempt to reproduce in English the verse form of French Neoclassicists, the twelve-syllabled Alexandrine). The idealization and formality of this kind of tragedy made it unusually susceptible to parody, and so burlesques of it soon appeared, with results that can be easily predicted by comparing a speech from a heroic tragedy with its parody. An original stanza read:

> So, two kind Turtles, when a storm is nigh,
> Look up; and see it gath'ring in the skie:
> Each calls his Mate to shelter in the Groves,
> Leaving in murmures, their unfinish'd Loves.
> Perch'd on some dropping Branch they sit alone,
> And Cooe, and harken to each others moan.
> > from *The Conquest of Granada* by John Dryden, II, I, ii.

In the hands of the burlesquer, the passage became:

> So Boar and Sow, when any storm is nigh,
> Sniff up, and smell it gath'ring in the sky;
> Boar beckons Sow to trot in Chestnut Groves,
> And there to consummate their unfinish'd Loves;
> Pensive in mud they wallow all alone,
> And snore and gruntle to each others moan.
> > from *The Rehearsal* by George Villiers, 2nd Duke of Buckingham. I, ii.

Succumbing both to the onslaught of burlesque and to the changing tastes of audiences, heroic tragedies declined in public favor, their place being filled by Neoclassical tragedies, like John Dryden's *All for Love* (1677), a rewriting of Shakespeare's *Anthony and Cleopatra* that brought it closer to the principles of Neoclassicism.

But as in comedy, conservatism, middle-class morality, and sentimentality developed early in the eighteenth century. George Lillo's *The London Merchant* (1731) was a major break with the Neoclassical ideal. In *The London Merchant,* a middle-class hero was led astray by love and was ultimately punished. Although teaching morality by showing the punishment of evil (the play was done in London for years to educate apprentices in proper working attitudes), the "tragedy" was nonetheless a far cry from strict Neoclassicism because it was written in prose, featured a middle-class hero, and dealt with affairs of the heart and the marketplace rather than affairs of state.

As in Italy, Neoclassical plays did not satisfy the Englishman's taste for scenic splendor and spectacular effects. Thus opera and a number of so-called minor forms developed to provide outlets for visual display. Native English opera was gradually replaced in public esteem by spectacular Italian operas, whose popularity soared in the eighteenth century. But also burlesques, ballad operas, and most of all *pantomimes* grew in public favor. English pantomimes typically combined elements of *commedia dell'arte,* farce, mythology, and contemporary satire with elaborate scenes of spectacle to produce a short afterpiece, that is, something to be performed after the evening's play. Often the dialogue was merely an excuse for major scenes of transformation, in which Harlequin, by a wave of his magic wand, changed all

Figure 7–17. Popular Comedy. The characters of the *commedia dell'arte* spread throughout Europe in the seventeenth century and were popular almost everywhere. Their individual attributes became exaggerated. Later, they were sentimentalized in English pantomime and French theatre.

places and people into new and dazzling locales and characters. Because new scenery was often commissioned for pantomimes, many innovations in design and execution of settings in England can be credited to pantomimic displays.

Just as English plays now owed much to Italian and French influence, so too did other of England's theatrical practices. When the English theatre reopened in 1660, it was organized as a monopoly in which only two troupes were licensed, originally those of William Davenant and Thomas Killigrew (1612–1683). Although these monopolies were often challenged and although they changed hands and specific regulations from time to time, they were continuously reaffirmed, most strongly in the *Licensing Act of 1737*, which allowed only two legitimate theatres in London, those at Drury Lane and at Covent Garden, and at the same time forbade the presentation of any play not previously licensed by the Lord Chamberlain. Throughout the period, therefore, only two "legitimate" theatres played.

In these theatres, the influence of France and Italy was clear (not surprisingly, as both Davenant and Killigrew knew the Stuart masques, knew English opera during the Commonwealth, and were close to the English court during its exile at Louis XIV's palace in France). The auditorium of the Restoration playhouse was divided into box, pit, and gallery. The stage, although still jutting out into the pit, now also boasted a proscenium arch and a raked stage behind it, where grooves were installed to facilitate scene changes. Most of the acting took place on the *forestage* (later the *apron*, that part of the stage in front of the proscenium arch). Most of the scenery, on the other hand, was located behind the proscenium. Initially the forestage was as large as the stage behind the proscenium, probably an attempt to synthesize earlier Elizabethan practice with currently fashionable Italian practice. As the period wore on, however, the size of the forestage decreased and the stage space behind the proscenium increased, so that by 1750, little difference existed between English and French or Italian stages. Between 1660 and 1750, both the stage and the auditorium increased in size as the composition of the audience and the repertory of the plays changed. The Restoration theatre seated perhaps 650, while Covent Garden by 1750 could accommodate about 1,500 patrons.

Scenic practices, too, were Italianate. Wings, drops, borders, and shutters were standard. A group of stock sets appropriate for each form of drama (comedy, tragedy, pastoral) allowed the theatres to provide scenery for most Neoclassical plays. When the theatres required new settings, which was seldom except for pantomimes, they simply commissioned them from painters of the day. Because lighting was still by candles, audience and actors were equally illuminated, although by the early eighteenth century some modest attempts were being made to dim and color lights. Costuming continued to be the major source of visual excitement, and most actors, with the exceptions noted earlier, wore an elaborate and sumptuous version of contemporary fashion.

Probably the most revolutionary change to occur at the Restoration had been the introduction of women onto the stage and into the acting companies. Their presence seems to have encouraged, fairly or not, the reputation of frivolity and even libertinism that early pervaded the Restoration playhouse. Actresses after about 1661 assumed all female roles except those of witches and comic old women (roles that continued to be played by men). The earlier tendency of actors to specialize in certain kinds of roles became gradually more rigid until clearly defined *lines of business* emerged. New actors or actresses were hired as utility players where they gained experience playing a great number of small and varied roles. They then declared a specialty in a specific kind of role: a walking lady or gentleman (third line), a specialist in low comedy or stage eccentric (second line), or a hero or heroine (first line). Once committed to a particular line of business, the actor did not stray far from it, regardless of age. (Shakespeare's Juliet, for example, was often played by women in their fifties because they were "first-line" players). Along with lines of business came a practice known as *possession of parts,* an agreement that an actor who played a role in the company possessed that role for so long as he remained in the company. Both practices obviously encouraged conservatism in acting and placed a premium on tradition rather than innovation. The tradition perpetuated was one heavily dependent on vocal power and versatility and on formality and elegance rather than "truth to life." For example, some actors apparently intoned or chanted the poetic and lyrical passages of tragedies, much as the recitative of opera is delivered today, and many actors played for points, expecting to receive applause for passages particularly well delivered (in which case the actor might repeat it).

Although some acting troupes continued to be organized as sharing ventures, some performers by the early eighteenth century preferred a fixed salary that they could augment by benefit performances. For "benefits," the actor or group of actors received all of the profits from the evening, a sum that occasionally equaled or exceeded a year's salary.

Although the actors and actresses of this period were too numerous to catalogue, the most famous can be cited: Thomas Betterton (c. 1635–1710), whose portrayal of Shakespearean heroes was unrivaled at the time; Nell Gwyn (1650–1777), whose success in "breeches roles" made her almost as famous as her position as an official mistress of the king; Colley Cibber (1671–1757), noted for his portrayal of fops; Anne Oldfield (1683–1730), the first actress to be buried at Westminster Abbey; James Quin (1693–1766), whose oratorical and formal style epitomized the "old school" of Neoclassical acting; and Charles Macklin (1699–1797), whose prosaic readings and "natural style" anticipated the end of the old and the beginning of the new English style of acting.

The mainstream of English theatrical activity, then, changed markedly between 1550 and 1750. During its peak, the 1590s through the 1610s, Shakespeare's plays swept grandly across time and continents, depicting an enormous range of incidents and people drawn from all walks of life, and depicting them in theatres that were uniquely English, with minimal scenery but lavish costumes. The audiences came from all social classes of the time. After the death of Shakespeare, the theatre slowly lost ground for a generation, until it was outlawed by the Puritans for about twenty years. When the monarchy was restored and the theatres reopened, their conventions

Figure 7–18. Durable Shakespeare. Despite changes in theatre practice, the plays of Shakespeare have survived and have been staged in a wide variety of styles. Here, *Twelfth Night* at Wayne State University. *(Directed by Robert Emmett McGill, designs by Steven Sarratore, Kathryn Mantone, and Susan Lambeth.)*

were much closer to those of the Continent. Although the Restoration playhouse fused the features of Elizabethan and Italianate theatres, the eighteenth-century English theatre was squarely inside continental traditions. Scenic practices, costuming conventions, and even English drama had moved significantly toward French and Italian practices by 1750. Almost immediately, however, alternative practices arose that violated the mainstream of English theatre and would soon produce major changes in its practices.

Theatre in France, 1550–1750

As France and Italy are geographically close, it should not be surprising that the ideas and practices of the Italian Renaissance reached and affected French courts and universities early. Indeed, by the end of the fifteenth century, French monarchs and scholars were familiar with the Neoclassical

Figure 7–19. French Farce. France had a popular, partly improvised theatre not unlike the *commedia dell'arte,* shown here at the Hotel de Bourgogne in Paris. Some of the leading farce actors joined Molière after about 1660.

principles of playwriting and the Italianate systems of staging. Unfortunately, however, France, unlike England, failed to achieve political and religious stability in the sixteenth century, and so the development of a vigorous public theatre was delayed.

Not until about 1600 did a popular playwright, Alexandre Hardy (c. 1572–1632), emerge to challenge the improvised French farces performed by itinerant actors as the mainstay of French popular theatre. And not until 1625 did the first acting troupe establish itself permanently in Paris at the Hôtel de Bourgogne, a theatre built almost seventy-five years earlier by a religious fraternity devoted to the production of religious plays in Paris (before they were outlawed in 1548). Thus, at a time when English theatre had already enjoyed the vigor and excellence of Shakespeare, the French public theatre was merely at the brink of its golden age.

As religious controversies were squelched by the firm control of Cardinal Richelieu (1585–1642) and political stability arrived in Paris following the ascent of Louis XIII to the throne (r. 1610–1643), the French public theatre began its climb to greatness. A number of educated men started to write for the theatre, among them Pierre Corneille (1606–1684), whose play *Le Cid* (produced in 1636) marked a turning point in French drama. Based on a Spanish play that depicted a welter of events strewn through several locations and many years, *Le Cid* was rewritten by Corneille to bring it into close accord with the Neoclassical ideal. Thus the six acts of the Spanish piece were reduced to five, the several years compressed into a single day, and the numerous locales squeezed into a single town. Still the play departed from Neoclassical tragedy; for example, it had a happy ending, and its numerous incidents strained verisimilitude. Richelieu, long a promoter of Italian culture, resolved to use the play as a test case in his efforts to bring France closer in line with Italian practices. He therefore submitted the play for evaluation to the recently formed French Academy, a prestigious literary society charged with maintaining the purity of French language and literature. The verdict of the Academy was clear. It praised *Le Cid* wherever it conformed to the Neoclassical precepts and condemned it wherever it strayed from them. French playwrights, including Corneille, were quick to conclude that critical acclaim rested on strict adherence to the principles of Neoclassicism. And so, after 1636, Neoclassicism dominated French drama for over one hundred years.

Cardinal Richelieu likewise was committed to Italianate scenic practices. In 1641, he opened the first Italianate theatre in France, the Palais-Cardinal, where he patronized productions of operas and Neoclassical plays. But Richelieu died before the splendor of recent Italianate advances could be introduced into France. That fell to his successor, Cardinal Mazarin, who shared Richelieu's taste for Italian opera and perspective decor and who set in motion a train of events that led to the arrival of Giacomo Torelli in Paris in 1645. Already famous in Italy for his elaborate special effects and magical scene shifts, Torelli brought his craft to France, installing his chariot-and-pole systems into the Palais-Royal (formerly the Palais-Cardinal, but renamed when Louis XIV appropriated it upon Richelieu's death) and also into the newly remodeled Petit Bourbon. Torelli's early productions marked the acceptance of all major Italianate scenic conventions into the French theatre. Henceforth the Neoclassical plays with their stark and simple settings competed with lavish operas, ballets, and machine plays (plays written particularly for the display of scenic marvels) for the attention of the Parisian audiences.

The stage was set for France's golden age when Louis XIV assumed power and moved his court to the magnificent palace at Versailles. Between 1660 and 1700, France attained a glory equal to that of Shakespeare's England. The period was characterized by four major traits: (1) the continuing strength of Neoclassicism as the dramatic ideal; (2) the continued acceptance of Italianate staging conventions; (3) the emergence and outpourings of three master playwrights: Pierre Corneille, Jean Racine (1639–1699), and Jean Baptiste Poquelin, or Molière (1622–1673); and (4) the presence of five permanent acting troupes in Paris. As the first two of these have already been discussed, only the remaining two need to be considered here.

Although Pierre Corneille wrote important plays until after 1675, his fame was eclipsed by that of Jean Racine. Born three years after the first production of *Le Cid,* Racine, orphaned at age four, was raised by Jansenists, a Catholic sect with an overriding preoccupation with sin and guilt, concerns that permeated Racine's major plays. Educated in the Greek and Roman classics, Racine based his only comedy, *The Litigants,* on Aristophanes' Greek

Figure 7–20. Italianate Staging in France. The lavish spectacle for a fete at Versailles in the late seventeenth century.

comedy *The Wasps,* and his most esteemed tragedy, *Phèdre,* on the play *Hippolytus* by the Greek Euripides.

Phèdre, one of the finest tragedies ever written, was a model of Neoclassicism. Phèdre, the queen, falls hopelessly in love with her stepson, Hippolytus. When a false rumor causes her to conclude that Theseus, her husband, is dead, Phèdre reveals her love. Scorned by Hippolytus and enraged to learn that he loves another, Phèdre falsely accuses him of lust and indirectly causes his death. Because the play's major conflicts occur within the character of Phèdre, Neoclassical requirements for unity were easily accommodated; and because Phèdre's passion leads to her downfall, Neoclassical commitment to the punishment of evil was amply satisfied. In short, *Phèdre,* unlike *Le Cid,* was Neoclassical through and through, and its achievement in plot, character, and diction placed it clearly among the masterpieces of dramatic literature. In short, France accomplished what England did not: lasting and popular drama based on Neoclassical theory.

At about the same time, French comedy found its genius in the actor–dramatist Molière. At about the time that theatres were closing in England, Molière was leaving home to form a traveling theatrical troupe in France. By 1660, he was head of the troupe, wrote most of its plays, and had firmly established it at court as a favorite of Louis XIV. Perhaps the greatest comic writer of all times, Molière used his own experiences as an actor as well as his knowledge of Roman comedies, Italian *commedia,* and indigenous French farces to develop comedies that ridiculed social and moral pretentiousness. Far less artificial, mannered, and witty than English Restoration comedy (its contemporary), Molière's comedy typically depicted characters made ludicrous by their deviations from decorum. Although his dialogue is often clever, verbal elegance and wit for their own sake do not form the core of his plays; instead the comedies depend heavily on farcical business (like *commedia*'s *lazzi*) and visual gags for their power. Of his more than twenty plays, the best known are probably *The Doctor in Spite of Himself* (1666), *The School for Wives* (1662), *Tartuffe* (1669), *The Miser* (1668), and *The Imaginary Invalid* (1673). While acting the leading role in *The Imaginary Invalid,* Molière was seized by convulsions and died a few hours later, denied last rites by the church because of his life as an actor and granted Christian burial only through the direct intervention of Louis XIV himself.

Obviously the life of French actors was not easy. Some troupes were granted royal subsidies, and Louis XIII had tried to improve their reputation and social acceptability by royal edict. Nonetheless French actors were denied civic and religious rights throughout most of the seventeenth and eighteenth centuries, a situation that led many actors to adopt pseudonyms in order to spare their families anguish and reproach. Forced to tour continuously

Figure 7–21. French and Italian Comedians. The combined troupes of Molière (far left), Tiberio Fiorilli, or Scaramouche (third from right) and the French farceurs (last row, center), all of whom shared a theatre at one time. The influence of both the French farce and the Italian *commedia* on Molière is often emphasized. Note the chandeliers for stage lighting and the perspective houses. *(Photo by Raymond Laniepce, courtesy of the Comédie Française.)*

until 1625, only the most talented actors were gradually able to settle in Paris as members of a permanent troupe. By 1660, there were five such troupes in Paris: the players at the Hôtel de Bourgogne; those at the Théâtre Marais (a tennis court converted into an Italianate threatre, as was a common continental practice); Molière's troupe at the Palais-Royal; and a *commedia* troupe from Italy, which alternated with Molière in using the Palais-Royal; and at court, the opera, music, and dance troupe headed by Jean-Baptiste Lully (1632–1687). All were sharing companies and all maintained a full complement of actresses. Unlike England, however, France had no house-holders, no actors who owned parts of the theatre building.

Molière's death set in motion a train of events that made French acting and acting companies among the most financially secure but artistically con-servative in the world. With Molière's death came the amalgamation of his troupe with those of the Bourgogne and the Marais to form the new Comédie Française, which became France's national theatre. Membership in this sharing company was fixed; therefore new members could not be elected until others had retired or died. Because of its financial rewards, including a substantial pension for retired members, the list of applicants was long. Many never made it, but those who did held a monopoly on the legal performance of tragedies and comedies for the Parisian public. Lully's troupe likewise held a monopoly on the production of musical enter-

Figure 7–22. Durable Mo-lière. Like Shakespeare in En-gland, Molière created plays that have survived many changes and that are still pro-duced. Here, a nineteenth-century performance of the fa-mous table scene in *Tartuffe*.

tainments and spectacles, and the *commedia* troupe (after a brief banishment for a political indiscretion) had exclusive performance rights to comic operas. Members of these three troupes were expected to continue the traditions already established, not to initiate new techniques. The result was a highly polished but quite tradition-bound style of production.

Around 1700, in France as in England, a new conservatism was noticeable in both theatre and drama. Louis XIV had grown old and pious. Dramatists, perhaps intimidated by the genius of Corneille, Racine, and Molière, strove by and large to copy their style. A modest shift toward morality and sentimentality occurred in France as in England. In tragedy, for example, Voltaire (1694–1778) sought to loosen the bonds of Neoclassicism by introducing some Shakespearean features to the French stage, particularly more spectacle and a greater range of permissible subjects, but his efforts before 1750 were largely frustrated. In comedy, Pierre Claude Nivelle de La Chausée (1692–1754) pitted virtuous heroes against numerous obstacles that they finally overcame in a burst of energy and good humor. The audience was moved to tears by the expressed sentiments of the sympathetic characters and by the rewards heaped on them for their virtuous behavior. Such sentimental and tearful comedies were a far cry from Molière's works, where the frailty and stubbornness of the characters provoked hearty laughter from spectators of all social classes.

Scenic displays in the opera and the ballet, although perhaps more sump-

Figure 7–23. Italianate Settings: Bibiena. Monumentality and angle perspective mark the work of the eighteenth-century Bibiena family of stage geniuses. *(Courtesy of The New York Public Library.)*

tuous than before, changed little in basic concept. Two innovations, however, did make their way to France from Italy by the first half of the eighteenth century. The first, *angle perspective,* meant that scenic artists relegated vistas to the sides, and actors could work closer to the scenery at center stage without violating the perspective. The second, a *changed scale,* meant that only the lower portions of the scenery were portrayed. With the tops no longer visible, the scenery seemed to disappear into the overhead spaces and out of sight, thereby multiplying the apparent size of the setting and producing a sense of vastness and monumentality that dwarfed individual actors playing before it.

Acting was still applauded to the degree that it was oratorically interesting and vocally sound. Costumes, in keeping with the Neoclassical view that time and place were relatively unimportant, consisted of the most splendid contemporary outfits that the actors could afford, the lavishness of the costume always a more accurate index to the wealth of the actor than to the character being impersonated.

In sum, the French theatre for the first half of the eighteenth century recalled its past glories when the genius of Corneille, Racine, Molière, and Torelli had established it as the leader of the civilized world. Changes from seventeenth-century practices were few and infrequent. When made, they were almost always in the direction of elaborating Neoclassical dramas and Italianate staging. Thus, by 1750, French theatre was tradition-bound, highly conventionalized, and perhaps out of touch with the lives of everyday Frenchmen. In a short one hundred years (1650–1750), the threatre had moved from a vigorous and forward-looking activity to a depressed and backward-gazing one.

Only outside of the mainstream could experimentation and innovation be found. With no outlet for the talents of the many actors and writers who were denied access to the Comédie Française, and with only limited satisfaction from the erudite plays of Neoclassicism, some French men and women worked in illegal theatres, that is, theatres other than the Comédie Française and the Opéra. Joining jugglers, dancers, and similar entertainers who had long appeared at French fairs, theatrical troupes began to form and play just outside the law, practicing all manner of stratagems to avoid open conflict with the monopolies held by the licensed troupes. From the experiments of these illegitimate theatres developed the forerunners of comic opera and melodrama, forms that flourished in the great Romantic theatre of the next century.

CHAPTER 8

The Civic and Religious Theatre: Greek, Roman, and Medieval, 534 B.C.–A.D. 1550

The final phase of theatrical and dramatic history to be considered began in the sixth century B.C. and ended around A.D. 1550, a period of more than two thousand years that saw vital traditions flourish in Greece, Rome, and the European Middle Ages. Despite their many differences, the drama and theatre of all three shared traits that were perhaps more significant than any differences, for their similarities set these theatres apart from all that were to follow.

In each of the cultures, theatre was intimately bound up with one or more aspects of religion. In all three, the plays were presented as a part of larger religious celebrations: in the Middle Ages on saints' days, holy days, and at great festivals like Corpus Christi; in Rome, at public games organized in honor of many of its numerous deities; and in Greece, at festivals dedicated to the god of wine and fertility, Dionysus. In all three cultures, as well, the presentations of drama were viewed as an integral part of the citizen's or the state's responsibility to its religious life: in medieval times, lay people, both individually and in organized groups, devoted time and money to see that the plays were properly mounted and acted; in Rome, the state paid for the productions and allowed all citizens to attend without charge; in Greece, the state and selected wealthy citizens shared the financial burdens of production. Although some theatre-for-profit could be identified in each culture, commercialism like that prevalent after the Renaissance was simply

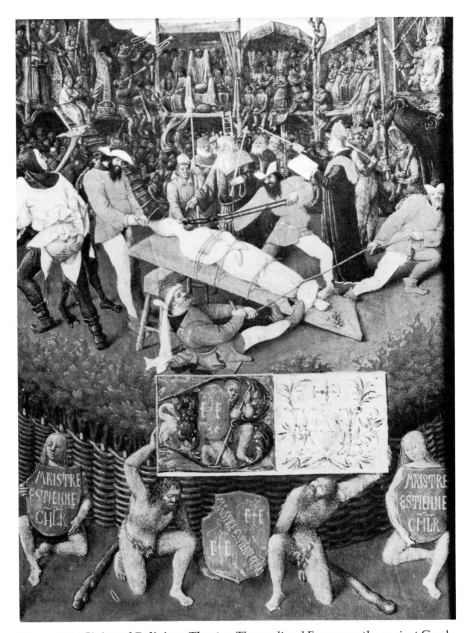

Figure 8–1. Civic and Religious Theatre. The medieval European, the ancient Greek, and much of the Roman theatre had powerful religious elements that were part of the very texture of the societies from which they sprang. This is a fifteenth-century painting of a religious play, *The Martyrdom of St. Apollonia,* which shows many of the outstanding characteristics of medieval theatre. Note particularly the semi-circle of scaffolds behind the central torturers, the musicians, angels and throned figure, and the contemporary costuming of the actors. *(Photographie Giraudon. Courtesy of the Musée Condé.)*

unknown. Finally, theatre in each of these three societies was an occasional event; that is, it was associated with important occasions. Some of the great medieval plays were done once a year, or once in five or ten years, or perhaps once in a lifetime; in Greece and Rome, drama appeared at annual festivals, but never often enough to be taken for granted.

We are accustomed to a theatre that justifies itself artistically and commercially—a concept of theatre we inherit from the Renaissance. What most sets the theatres of Greece, Rome, and the Middle Ages apart from our own is the lack of such justification or the need for it. These theatres were central to the spiritual lives of their societies, and, however artistically refined they became, it was their position in the culture that defined them.

The Middle Ages

Background

Although civilization in Eastern Europe was flourishing, that in the West was in a state of increasing confusion after the fourth century A.D. From then until the eighth century, Western Europe sank into political disarray, out of which emerged, after slow rebuilding, a different kind of Europe, one based on new nations and diverse languages and traditions.

With the collapse of Rome in the sixth century, various forces that had before served to unify Europe weakened or disintegrated. The Roman system of roads and waterways fell into disrepair, and transportation and communication became at first troubled and at last almost impossible. Laws were ignored and order broke down and was replaced by the rule of force: bands of pirates and brigands grew wealthy and influential enough to challenge kings. Without the support of a government, the monetary system failed, and barter, with all of its cumbersome trappings, was the basis of trade.

Into the power vacuum created by Rome's defeat came a variety of competitive interests, each sparring for political and economic clout. The Church exerted increasing influence, in part because its rigid hierarchy assured an orderly governance and in part because its enormous influence in the daily lives of all people gave it a substantial base. The other prevailing social organization was feudal, whose primary social unit was a manor. On the manor, each serf owed absolute allegiance to the lord, who in turn owed allegiance to lords more powerful than he, and so on. Similarly, in the Church, the priests ranked below the bishops, who ranked below the archbishops, and so on up the pyramid, at the top of which was the Bishop of Rome, the Pope, who spoke with authority on Church matters. Both power hierarchies were essentially pyramidal, with one person at the top, relatively few persons immediately under him, and so on until at the base of each pyramid were the peasants, that great mass of people who tilled the land and provided all those above them with the necessities and amenities of life. The two pyramids interlocked when Church leaders were drawn from the noble classes, and the peasants provided goods and services for both Church lords and secular lords.

The series of crusades after the twelfth century against the Muslims and other forces served to encourage trade and the opening of new sea routes. This in turn led to the development of towns, a movement well under way by the eleventh century. These towns and the merchants and tradesmen in them existed outside the feudal structure and gradually undermined it. As tradesmen organized themselves into guilds (similar to trade unions), they were able to confront the feudal lords and eventually were able to challenge them successfully. With the rise of towns and the consequent breaking up of feudalism, nations began to take shape and kings emerged to govern them. By the fourteenth century, the unquestioned domination of the Church was likewise under attack and its monopoly on matters of faith successfully eroded.

With the decline of feudalism and the authority of the Church and

Figure 8–2. Early Renaissance Theatre. The terms "Renaissance" and "medieval" describe movements that overlapped by more than a century. This illustration of a theatre (perhaps only imaginary) for the plays of Terence shows the Renaissance commitment to a revival of classicism; however, its audience arrangement and its stage should be compared with Figures 7–12 and 8–1.

with the emergence of towns and a sense of nationhood, the stage was set for the Renaissance, that flowering of arts and letters that marked a new direction for life in Europe.

Medieval Drama

For many years historians believed that no theatre or drama outlived the collapse of the Roman Empire in the sixth century, but it is now certain that, after the empire divided into two parts, plays continued to be performed in the Eastern Empire around Byzantium and that even in the West, remnants of the professional performers traveled like nomads about Italy, France, and Germany, plying their trade and eking out a living. Scattered references to *mimi, histriones,* and *ioculatores* (all words used to describe actors) surfaced periodically in medieval accounts, but the degree to which such performers engaged in actual plays, as distinct from variety entertainments like juggling,

Figure 8–3. Renaissance or Medieval? This fifteenth-century interpretation of how the plays of Terence were staged may reflect the artist's own experience or it may be purely imaginative. The idea that actors mimed the roles while a reader ("Calliopius," the figure in the curtained booth) read the play was an old one; however, the masks, the presence of the musician, and the audience-actor arrangement may show actual knowledge of medieval theatre. Compare with Figures 7–12 and 8–1 and 8–2.

tumbling, dancing, and rope tricks, is not known. Clearly, if traditional dramas were performed between the sixth and the tenth centuries, their scale was much reduced and they no longer enjoyed the support of those two most powerful social organizations of the time, the Church and the State.

Usually the revival of institutionalized drama is dated somewhere between 925 and 975 and credited to practices within the Church itself. Once reintroduced, theatre quickly established its place in the religious and civic life of the West and became once again a vital and vigorous expression of that society.

For purposes of convenience, theatre and drama during the Middle Ages can be divided into two traditions: that performed inside the Church and that performed outside. As drama in the Church was a part of the standard worship service, or liturgy, it was called *liturgical drama.*

Liturgical Theatre. Liturgical dramas were done in monastic and cathedral churches and were acted by clergy, choirboys, monks, and occasionally traveling scholars and schoolboys. All actors were men. As a part of the church service, liturgical plays were given in Latin (the language of the Church) and were sung or chanted rather than spoken. Their subject matter was almost always drawn from the Bible or the Apocrypha, a group of books and documents that treat Judeo-Christian history or myth but that are excluded from the Jewish and Protestant Bibles. The stories most often dramatized were those involving events surrounding Christmas and Easter. Initially the audiences for such works were probably monks and others living in monasteries, but once cathedral churches became common (during the thirteenth century), lay people were the principal audiences for the plays.

Plays. During the ninth and tenth centuries, the Church had become increasingly self-aware and had begun to decorate and elaborate various of its practices; the music, calendar, vestments, art, architecture, and liturgy all changed in the direction of greater embellishment. Although the reasons for the emergence of liturgical drama are not entirely clear, probably its development proceeded as a part of this general movement. Central to the drama was a particular sort of liturgical embellishment known as a *trope,* a name given to any interpolation into an existing text. An Easter trope dating from 925 was sung by the choir antiphonally and began "Quem quaeritis in sepulchro, o christocole." Translated into English, the piece reads, in its entirety:

> *Whom seek ye in the tomb, O Christians?*
> *Jesus of Nazareth, the crucified, O heavenly beings.*
> *He is not here, he is risen as he foretold;*
> *Go and announce that he is risen from the tomb.*

By 975, someone had taken this choir song and turned it into a small drama, complete with stage directions. The record of this new drama first appeared in the *Regularis Concordia,* a monastic guidebook written by Ethelwold, Bishop of Winchester. Leaving nothing to chance, Ethelwold described in detail how this part of the Easter service was to be performed:

While the third lesson is being read, four of the brethren shall vest, one of whom, wearing an alb as though for some different purpose, shall enter and go stealthily to the place of the "sepulchre" and sit there quietly, holding a palm in his hand. Then, while the third response is being sung, the other three brethren, vested in copes and holding thuribles in their hands, shall enter in their turn and go to the place of the "sepulchred," step by step, as though searching for something. Now these things are done in imitation of the angel seated on the tomb and of the women coming with perfumes to anoint the body of Jesus. When, therefore, he that is seated shall see these three draw nigh, wandering about as it were and seeking something, he shall begin to sing softly and sweetly, Quem quaeritis.

Translated by Thomas Symons

From this modest beginning, liturgical drama blossomed into many plays of varying lengths and varying degrees of complexity. The stories most often dramatized dealt with the visit of the three Marys to the tomb, the travel of the Magi, Herod's wrath, and the Slaughter of the Innocents, but other plays depicted such diverse stories as the life of the Virgin Mary, the raising of Lazarus, and Daniel in the lion's den. Almost all were serious, but on some rare occasions, drama in the church was anything but solemn. At the Feast of Fools and the Feast of the Boy Bishops, the usual dignity was abandoned and in its place substituted considerable tomfoolery, as this French account makes clear:

They danced in the choir, at entering, and sang obscene songs. The deacons and subdeacons took pleasure in eating puddings and sauces on the altar, before the nose of the celebrant priest; they played cards and dice; they placed in the thurible some pieces of old shoes to make a terrible odor. After the mass, each one ran, leaped and danced out of the church with so much impudence that some of them had no shame in clothing themselves in all sorts of indecencies or stripping themselves entirely naked. Then they processed through the streets in carts full of dung, which they took pleasure in throwing on the populace crowded around them. They stopped and struck indecent postures and made lascivious gestures.

Translated by George Bryan

Staging. The staging of liturgical drama was highly conventionalized and rested on two sorts of scenic space: the mansion and the platea. Mansions were small scenic structures that served to locate a particular place; the platea was a neutral, generalized acting area. It was a convention of this theatre that widely separated places could be presented simultaneously in full view of the audience. In complex plays, therefore, many mansions were arranged about the generalized space. Actors first established the specific location by reference to the appropriate mansion and were then free to move about the platea. For the mansions, existing church architecture was often used and supplemented wherever necessary. For example, the choir loft might represent heaven or other high places; the crypt, hell or other

Figure 8–4. Hell Mouth. This processional pageant (apparently a form of sled) is quite typical of the Hell set-piece used throughout the middle ages. This is a fairly late one from the Low Countries. Such special effects as fire and smoke were common.

low places; and the altar, the tomb of Christ. For more elaborate plays, special mansions were constructed, some small but others large enough for several persons to be hidden inside by means of curtains.

An important part of the scenic display in the church was machinery capable of flying objects and actors in and out of the playing area. In more than one play, angels and doves flew about, Christ rose to heaven, and the three kings followed a moving star that led them to the stable of the Christ child and there stopped to mark the spot.

Costumes for the liturgical plays were ordinarily church vestments to which signifying elements had been added: keys for Saint Peter, wings for angels, hoods for women, wallets and staffs for travelers. Occasionally clerics playing kings or prophets might be garbed in ornate, nonclerical costumes, but these were exceptions.

Plays continued to be performed in many churches into the sixteenth century, but by 1200, some religious plays were also being given out-of-doors. Records of such productions were scant until about 1350, when relatively abundant accounts describe a civic and religious theatre of magnificent proportions throughout most of Western Europe. Sometime between 1200 and 1350, a number of significant changes had occurred. The plays out-of-doors were spoken in the vernacular rather than chanted or sung in Latin. Priests and clerics were no longer the actors; interested laymen assumed the roles. Because the plays were no longer a part of the liturgy, their stories and themes were more far-ranging. Probably, too, the plays now tended

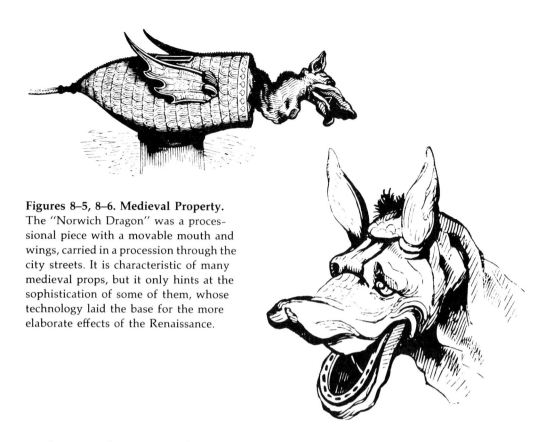

Figures 8–5, 8–6. Medieval Property. The "Norwich Dragon" was a processional piece with a movable mouth and wings, carried in a procession through the city streets. It is characteristic of many medieval props, but it only hints at the sophistication of some of them, whose technology laid the base for the more elaborate effects of the Renaissance.

to cluster in the spring and summer months, particularly around the new Feast of Corpus Christi, rather than, as before, scattered throughout the church year. Of these several changes, the most significant was doubtless the shift from a universal language (Latin) to the various national tongues (English, French, German, etc.), for with this shift came an end to an international drama and the beginning of the several national dramas, a trend made permanent in the Renaissance.

Why religious dramas moved from the churches has been endlessly debated. Some argue that abuses in the church buildings, like those at the Feast of Fools, caused the Church to force the drama out-of-doors. Certainly, some Church displeasure with the plays was evident as early as the eleventh century, but nowhere are there records of clerical bans on the plays. Moreover, even after the plays left its buildings, the Church continued to provide support in the form of costumes and properties and to review plays prior to their public production. It seems more likely, then, that the move out-of-doors merely reflected the changing needs of the plays and their audiences rather than any Church-directed banishment.

Drama Outside the Church. Once outside the Church, religious plays were supported in various ways. Sometimes entire towns oversaw productions; sometimes special committees were formed and charged with the task. Most often, however, labor and religious organizations (called *guilds* and *confraternities*) assumed the financial and artistic responsibility for finding and rewarding actors, providing scenery and properties, and establishing and enforcing regulations. If a guild was weak or poor, it might combine with others to meet its obligations. Plays were apparently assigned to guilds on the basis of their members' particular skills; for example, plays depicting the Last Supper were given to bakers' guilds, those of the Three Kings to goldsmiths', of Noah's Ark to shipbuilders' and fishermen's. Once assigned, plays usually remained with the same guild(s) year after year.

Roles in the plays were open to all male members of the community (in France, occasionally a woman might perform) and were generally performed without compensation. As with any primarily amateur operation, the quality of the performances varied considerably, and it was probably in an attempt to upgrade the general level of acting that many cities hired "property players" to take the leading roles and to instruct the less talented in improving their performances. Although these few actors were paid, they too were considered amateurs and so not looked down upon as socially undesirable, as were professional actors (see p. 241).

The enormous complexity of the cycles and cosmic dramas caused some people to be hired to oversee the production and serve as the medieval counterpart of the modern director. Although responsibilities differed with the particular circumstances, the tasks of one medieval director in France included (1) overseeing the building of a stage and the use of the scenery and machines; (2) overseeing the building and painting of scenery and the construction of seating for the audience; (3) ensuring the accuracy of all materials delivered; (4) disciplining the actors; (5) acting in the plays whenever necessary; and (6) addressing the audience at the beginning of the play and at each intermission, giving a summary of what had happened and promising greater marvels to come.

Because mechanical reproduction and printing were unavailable, a single copy of the script, with its various directions for production, was handwritten and retained from year to year. This master copy, called a *register,* was held by a designated party, often the producing organization or church. Obviously, if any political group could secure the register, they could prevent further production, as indeed was increasingly common by the late sixteenth century, when religious dramas were being censored and then banned.

Because special effects in the dramas were so extraordinary, some men, called *masters of secrets,* became specialists in their construction and workings. Flying figured prominently in many plays: angels flew about; Lucifer raised Christ; souls rose from limbo into heaven on Doomsday; devils and fire-spitting monsters sallied forth from hell and back again; cotton-covered platforms, resembling clouds (and called *glories*), bore choruses of heavenly beings aloft. Traps, too, became sophisticated enough to permit appearances, disappearances, and substitutions, as when Lot's wife was turned into a pillar of salt, and tigers were transformed into sheep. The artistic control of fire was also an essential part of the special-effects repertory, for hell belched smoke and flames regularly (in 1496 at Seurre, an actor playing Satan was severely burned when his costume caught fire) and buildings ignited on cue. The scale of these effects can perhaps be suggested by the following account of a French production:

The spectacle lasted twenty-five days, and on each day we saw strange and wonderful things. The machines of the Paradise and Hell were absolutely prodigious and could be taken by the populace for magic. For we saw Truth, the angels, and other characters descend from very high, sometimes visibly, sometimes invisibly, appearing suddenly. Lucifer was raised from Hell on a dragon without our being able to see how. The rod of Moses, dry and sterile, suddenly put forth flowers and fruits. Devils carried the souls of Herod and Judas through the air. Devils were exorcised, people with dropsy and other invalids were cured, all in an admirable way. Here Jesus Christ was carried up by the Devil who scaled a wall forty feet high. There He became invisible. Finally, He was transfigured on Mount Tabor. We saw water changed into wine so mysteriously that we could not believe it, and more than a hundred persons wanted to taste this wine. The five breads and the two fish seemed to be multiplied and were distributed to more than a thousand spectators, and yet there were more than twelve baskets left. The fig tree, cursed by Our Lord, appeared to dry up, its leaves withering in an instant. The eclipse, the earthquake, the splitting of the rocks and the other miracles at the death of Our Lord were shown with new marvels.

Chronicler of Valenciennes

Staging. The conventions of staging grew out of those used during the liturgical period: mansions and platea were the spatial elements and simultaneous display of several locations continued. But within this general pattern, two rather different traditions developed: *fixed staging,* mostly on the Continent (excepting Spain and parts of Italy), and *movable staging,* mostly in Spain and parts of England.

Fixed staging differed from liturgical practices primarily in the degree of elaborateness. Mansions were set up, usually out-of-doors, in whatever spaces were available: courtyards of noble houses, town squares, "Cornish rounds" (large circular spaces dating from much earlier times and possibly used originally as forts), Roman amphitheatres, and so on. Depending on the space, the mansions were arranged in straight lines, circles, or rectangles, and the platea and audience area established accordingly. Although the individual arrangements varied, heaven and hell (ordinarily the most ornate mansions) were customarily set at opposite poles.

Movable stages, or pageants (pageant wagons), allowed the audience to remain in one place while the plays were brought to them and performed in sequence, much like a homecoming parade with floats. Each play, then, was performed several times. A common pattern was for the first play (Creation) to be presented at dawn at the first station; when it moved to the second station to perform, the second play (the Fall of Man) was presented at the first station. For most of the day, several plays were performing at once. The word *pageant* is important in a discussion of movable staging because it was used to describe the play itself, the spectacle of the plays in performance, and also the vehicle on which the presentation was staged.

The appearance of pageant wagons has been much discussed, but as available evidence is scant, few firm conclusions are possible. Only one

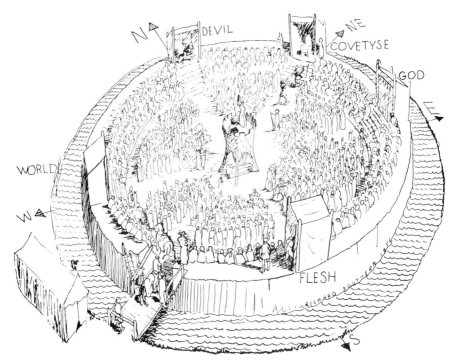

Figure 8–7. Medieval Simultaneous Staging. Outdoor theatres with "scaffolds" arranged in a circle (or other convenient shape) around a central playing area were common. The presence of the audience in the central playing area is debatable. (*From Richard Southern,* Medieval Theatre in the Round.)

English description, dating from slightly before 1600, has survived, and its reliability is suspect:

Every company had his pagiant, or parte, which pagiants weare a high scafolde with two rowmes, a higher and a lower, upon four wheeles. In the lower they apparelled themselves, and in the higher rowme they played, beinge all open on the tope, that all beholders mighte heare and see them. The places where they placed them was in every streete. Archdeacon Robert Rogers

An obvious problem with the description, and one of the reasons its accuracy has been questioned, is that the wagons as described would need to be more than twelve feet tall to allow for the wheels and the two levels yet narrow enough to be pulled by horses through the medieval streets. The resulting structure would be highly unstable and perhaps unable to turn corners as required in its trek from station to station.

Plays. Regardless of the conventions of staging adopted, the same sorts of plays were done in all countries. The plays remained decidedly religious,

Figure 8–8. Processional Car. Evidence for medieval pageant wagons is scanty, but later processional wagons like the Flemish "Car of Caloo," shown in this Rubens sketch, suggest how they may have looked. (*Courtesy of the Koninklijk Museum, Brussels.*)

if not always scriptural. In general they dealt with events in the life of Christ or told stories from the Old Testament (plays often called *mysteries*); the lives of saints, both historical and legendary (called *miracles*); and didactic allegories, frequently portraying the common man's struggle for salvation (the *moralities*).

Although the plays differed in subject matter and form, they shared several characteristics. First, they aimed to teach or to reinforce belief in Church doctrine. Second, they were formulated as melodramas or divine comedies; that is, the ethical system of the play was clear, and good was rewarded, evil punished. Third, the driving force for the action was God and His plan rather than the decisions or actions of the dramatic agents; thus, to a modern reader, the plays often appear episodic, with their actions unmotivated, their sequences of time and place inexplicable, and their mixture of the comic and serious unnerving.

In fact, their traits expressed well the medieval view that called for all people to repent, to confess, and to atone for their sins. The plays presented the lure and strength of sin, the power and compassion of God, and the punishment awaiting the unrepentant sinner. Because history was God's

Figure 8–9. Medieval Pageant. The "pageant" of Noah, shown here from the 1966 performance of the Lincoln ("N-Town") Cycle at Grantham, England, meant both the moving wagon and the play itself. Ships for the Noah plays were often quite elaborate and large. *(Courtesy of Margaret Birkett. Chris Windows photo.)*

great lesson to mankind, the most vivid drama that could contain His plan was nothing less than the entire history of man, from Creation to Doomsday. Characters were representations of that grand scheme. Any combination of events, any juxtaposition of characters, any elasticity of time or place that would illuminate God's plan and make it more accessible and compelling was a good thing.

Secular Theatre. At the same time that these great cosmic dramas and religious cycles were at their zenith, another, experimental, tradition moved tentatively toward maturity.

Secular plays surfaced about the time that religious dramas appeared outside of the churches, and by the fourteenth century, they were flourishing. In the schools and universities, Latin comedies and tragedies were being studied, copied, translated, and emulated. For less erudite tastes, medieval farces poked fun, with impish delight, at all manner of domestic tribulations, particularly infidelity and cuckoldry. Some morality plays developed within the secular tradition, their allegories based on classical gods and heroes rather than Christian virtues and vices. Too, moralities became involved in the battles of the Reformation: anti-Catholic moralities costumed devils as Catholic prelates and Christ figures as Protestant ministers; anti-Protestant moralities did just the reverse.

At court and in the homes of the very wealthy, plays were given at tournaments (perhaps in an attempt to make these war games less lethal) and on holidays, particularly Christmas and Mardi Gras, when entertainments called *mummings* and *disguisings* were popular. Almost any interruption within an activity—for example, between the courses of a formal banquet—was an excuse to perform a short dramatic entertainment, the *interlude.* But the most spectacular of the court entertainments was the *masque,* in which allegorical compliments to the guests of honor were framed by intricate dances involving the courtiers themselves.

Towns, too, staged street pageants and royal entries for a variety of special occasions. As a part of these events, plays were embedded within the elaborate processions designed to mark the event and were given for the entertainment and instruction of the dignitaries, often on the subject of wise governance.

Secular plays, unlike the religious dramas, were most often performed by professional actors, most of whom were attached to noble houses as servants by the fourteenth century. When they were not needed to entertain there, they could enrich themselves by performing throughout the surrounding countryside. Such actors were considered professionals and so were viewed as social undesirables. Because they performed most often in interludes and moralities, these forms came to be associated with the rise of the professional actor.

Decline and Fall. By the sixteenth century, then, medieval theatre was both vigorous and varied. But events throughout Europe, at mid-century, caused the deterioration of the religious branch of its development and the consequent flowering of the secular tradition.

The Catholic Church, already weakened by internal dissension, looked on while a series of rival factions splintered away from Roman domination. To complicate matters, the religious Reformation quickly became embroiled in various dynastic squabbles, a circumstance that more often inflamed than retarded nascent conflicts. Because each side of a controversy often cast its position and arguments in dramatic form, the religious theatre served as one focus for the religious and dynastic struggles of the period and added to the problems of rulers striving to maintain civic tranquillity. In country after country, therefore, religious plays were outlawed (in Paris in 1548, in England in 1558, and by the Council of Trent in 1545–1563).

The results were profound. The religious and occasional nature of theatre and drama was replaced by a worldly and professional outlook. Amateur actors who had participated in great civic pageants every few years were no longer needed, but professionals who were available on a continuing basis were in demand. No longer used to glorify God and teach Church dogma, drama and theatre had to justify their continuance on other grounds. Deprived of financial subsidy, theatre had to become a commercial venture. With religious plays forbidden, secular plays were needed if audiences long accustomed to dramatic entertainments were to be satisfied, and so potential playwrights turned to classical plays and stories for inspiration and sources. The Renaissance and the theatre had come together.

The Roman Period

Background

Rome was unparalleled among great Western civilizations simply because it remained intact so long. From a small prehistoric settlement, it grew to become the center of a far-flung empire that touched Asia and Africa as well as England and Western Europe.

The city, although founded in the eighth century B.C., did not control the Italian peninsula until the third century B.C. By that time, Rome had developed a republican form of government, the leaders of which were noted for their economy, discipline, loyalty, and rhetorical prowess. In technology and military matters, moreover, Rome had no contemporary equal. By the first century B.C., its territory was vast and included much of Western Europe as well as many of the lands once within the sphere of Greek influence. Whenever Romans made contact with another culture, they freely borrowed its arts, religion, technology—anything that seemed useful. Roman culture, then, in many ways was an amalgam of attitudes and practices drawn from other lands but always adapted to the particular needs and interests of Rome and Romans.

In 27 B.C., the Republican form of government was abandoned in favor of an imperial form; that is, power once vested in many representatives now resided in the person of the emperor. By that time, too, the energies of the government were becoming increasingly directed at maintaining control of the conquered territories, which were both numerous and distant. That the empire lasted until the sixth century A.D. is doubtless a tribute to the administrative and technological sophistication of the Romans, but eventually dissension within and attacks from without led to the dissolution of the once-great empire, so that by the middle of the sixth century A.D., Rome's influence was no longer a significant factor in the political life of Europe.

For convenience, the Roman theatrical era can be divided into two parts: the Republic (364 B.C.–27 B.C.) and the Empire (27 B.C.–c. A.D. 550). Because the first stone theatre in Rome was not constructed until 55 B.C., information about the physical theatres dates primarily from the Empire; extant dramas, on the other hand, come from the period of the Republic; therefore the period of the extant drama and the period of archaeological evidence do not correspond well, and so students of Roman theatre and drama are faced with a difficult task as they try to envision how the drama looked in its theatre, in production.

Sources for the Roman Theatre

The first record of a theatrical production in Rome dates from 364 B.C., when Tarquin the Great, an Etruscan, established the Ludi Romani (the Roman festival, or games) and imported dancers from Etruria to perform, presumably to appease the gods and bring an end to a plague. The first record of drama comes from 240 B.C., when Livius Andronicus, a Greek, was brought to Rome, where he produced a single play at the Ludi Romani. Although Greek influences on Roman theatre and drama were important, two other sources predated them and accounted for major differences between Greek and Roman practice.

Roman theatre, unlike the Greek, had from the outset a circus-like atmosphere in which a variety of entertainments competed for the attention of the audience. Chariot racing, boxing, wrestling, gladiatorial combats, and rope dancing occurred simultaneously with dramatic performances during the games, and each strove to lure audiences to its wonders. This carnival-like arrangement apparently came to Rome with the establishment of the first Ludi by Tarquin of Etruria. In addition to establishing the first games and introducing variety entertainments into them, Etruria also probably contributed the stadiumlike seating later used in Roman theatres and the extensive reliance on music within its plays.

During the fourth century B.C., as Etruscan influence waned, the Oscans (from an area slightly to the south of Rome) introduced a kind of short, improvised play that made use of a wide range of stock characters whose costumes and masks remained the same from play to play. Called the *Atellan Farce,* this Oscan importation probably influenced the direction that Roman comedy took and may even have served as the basis for the *commedia dell' arte,* a kind of comedy originating in Italy and sweeping Western Europe during the Renaissance.

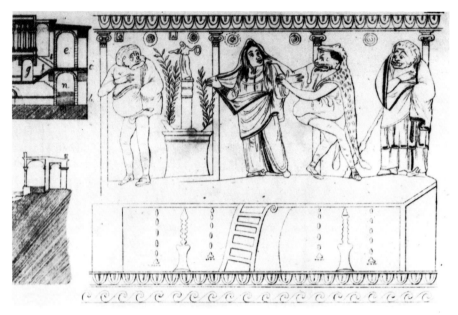

Figure 8–10. Ancient Popular Theatre. This tracing from a "phlyakes" vase shows a form of farce or comedy played several centuries before Christ. Note the raised stage and the ladder to it, the masks, and the grotesque costumes.

By the time Rome came into contact with Greece in the third century B.C., then, some of its theatrical traditions were already set. Moreover, by the time of contact, Greece was well into its Hellenistic period, a period whose drama and theatre are less understood than those of the earlier so-called classical period.

Production Arrangements

Theatre in Rome took place at *ludi,* or games, most of which were state religious celebrations devoted to the worship of any of Rome's several gods; occasionally *ludi* were staged in celebration of birthdays, funerals, military victories, and political rallies, and so from time to time, plays would be done on these occasions as well. *Ludi* were managed by a civic or religious magistrate who received a government grant to cover the expenses of the festivals, whose complexities he was expected to oversee. Typically, among his other duties, the magistrate contacted the heads of several acting troupes that he wanted to hire for the occasion and established fees for the performances. This fixed fee, paid by the state, might be augmented either by the magistrate himself (as the success of a festival reflected well on him) or by a bonus that the state awarded whenever public acclaim was unusually vocal. This bonus apparently resulted in some people's being paid to applaud wildly the work of certain troupes and in government officials' being bribed to notice such responses.

Drama in Rome was free and open to everyone. Apparently it was quite popular, for the number of performances steadily increased, from only one play in 240 B.C. to more than one hundred during the third century A.D. Typically, several troupes participated at each festival, and on the days set aside for performances, plays were presented continuously, without intermissions.

Plays

Although no tragedies survived from the Republic, titles and fragments indicate that they resembled Hellenistic Greek tragedy: sensational and melodramatic elements took precedence over philosophical inquiry, and the role of the chorus was peripheral rather than central to the development of the action. Depending on the subject matter and the costumes worn by the actors, Roman tragedy was divided into two types: (1) those written about Greeks, in which the actors dressed as noble Greeks, and (2) those written about Romans, in which actors were dressed as upper-class Roman citizens.

From the period of the Empire, ten tragedies are extant, nine by the playwright and rhetorician Seneca (c. 5 B.C.–A.D. 65) and none intended for production in a public theatre. The importance of Seneca's tragedies rests neither on their literary excellence nor on their position among contemporary Roman audiences but rather on their monumental effect on Renaissance writers, who discovered, translated, and copied them. To persons whose

Figure 8–11. Roman Tragic Mask. From a wall painting of the first century B.C. *(Courtesy of the Metropolitan Museum of Art, Rogers Fund, 1903.)*

primary contact with the theatre was the farces, comedies, and melodramas of the Middle Ages, Seneca's works provided an alternative way of viewing the world and formulating plays.

Seneca's plays (all tragedies of the first type) had a definite beginning and end and portrayed the emotions and attitudes of characters who participated meaningfully in the decisions and actions of the plot. Moreover they displayed a secular, even domestic, view of life and often ended unhappily, with evil remaining unpunished and good unrewarded. None of these characteristics was apparent in medieval plays, which often began at the Creation and ended at the Last Judgment and incorporated whatever scenes in between seemed useful in exalting God's handiwork or instructing His flock. In short, Seneca introduced Renaissance authors to ways of formulating tragedies (as opposed to melodramas or divine comedies) and of devising tragic characters capable of participating in the decisions and actions of the play (rather than agents who merely revealed God's divine plan).

Seneca also introduced Renaissance writers to a variety of dramatic techniques uncommon during the Middle Ages. First, Seneca's tragedies typically had five episodes separated by four choral odes. Renaissance writers, adapting Seneca, began to write plays in five acts. Second, because Seneca's chorus was a decoration that commented on rather than participated in the action, Renaissance authors who included the role assigned it to a single character named, simply, Chorus. Third, Seneca's plays often indulged in scenes of remarkable gore and violence and seemed to inspire similar scenes in many Renaissance works, or perhaps only to reinforce medieval practice, which also included scenes of violence onstage. Fourth, Seneca's emphasis on rhetorical and stylistic figures encouraged Renaissance writers to include in their plays similar extended descriptive and declamatory passages, pithy statements about the human condition (sententiae), and elaborately balanced exchanges of dialogue. Fifth, Seneca's frequent use of messengers, confidants, and ghosts led to such characters in many Renaissance tragedies. And sixth, Seneca's portrayal of characters driven by a single, dominant passion found expression in several Renaissance tragedies. Although it is now customary to scoff at the plays of Seneca, their influence on the subsequent development of tragedy in Italy, France, England, and even Germany has been incalculable.

Comedy, like tragedy, was divided into that written about the Greek middle class and that written about Romans. Although many titles, names, and fragments remain, only twenty-seven comedies survived, all from two authors: Plautus and Terence. Both wrote during the first century B.C., and both wrote about the Athenian middle class. Both drew heavily from Greek "new comedies" for their materials and stories, and neither used a chorus. Despite these obvious similarities, however, the plays of Plautus and Terence are very different from one another and suggest a considerable range within Roman comedy.

Plautus (254–184 B.C.) made a good deal of money as an actor/manager before turning to playwriting at about age forty. Once he became an author, he was both prolific and popular. Of the more than one hundred works credited to him, twenty-one have survived, doubtless a tribute to the esteem in which he was held. A further testament to his stature came from a contemporary who eulogized him: "Comedy goes into mourning, the theatre is deserted; then Laughter, Sport, Jest, and Immeasurable Measure have all burst into tears."

Plautus's sense of humor was always evident. The three names by which he was officially known (Titus Maccus Plautus) translate roughly as "big, splayfooted clown," perhaps a reference to his acting the role of the clown in Atellan farces. Probably his experiences as an actor working to entertain a fickle public accounted for the *theatrical* (as opposed to literary) qualities of his comedies. Plautine comedies are noted for their loosely linked episodes, which are filled with visual gags, verbal wordplay, and characters who are ludicrous in appearance as well as behavior. Never one to pass up an opportunity for a laugh, Plautus often broke the dramatic illusion, addressed his audience directly, and incorporated references to contemporary Rome in his comedies about the Athenian middle class. Among his many plays, *The Braggart Warrior, The Menaechmi, Pot of Gold,* and *Amphitryon* have provided material for authors like Shakespeare, Molière, Wycherley, and Giraudoux, to mention only the most obvious.

As a playwright, Terence (d. 159 B.C.) was less boisterous than Plautus. His use of language, for example, was so careful and elegant that his plays were used in schools throughout the Middle Ages as models of Latin eloquence. His plots, although based on those of the Greek Menander and his contemporaries, often combined two or more of the Greek comedies into a single, highly complicated dramatic action. He avoided the episodic quality of Plautus's plots in favor of more carefully contrived actions that proceeded by means of seeming cause and effect; his characters, too, appeared more normal and human, and thus more sympathetic. The result was, of course, comedies that were more elegant and refined but less robust and free, more thoughtful but less fun.

Finally, Terence's use of the prologue was unusual. Unlike Plautus, whose prologues contained exposition, preparation, and summary, Terence used his to argue matters of dramatic theory, to encourage audiences to behave politely, and to defend himself from the attacks of drama critics. In a prologue

Figure 8–12. Roman Characters. These late drawings of two figures may suggest what Roman comic actors looked like. The types represented— the parasite and the boastful soldier—appeared again in Renaissance comedies.

Figure 8–13. Renaissance Terence. An early Renaissance woodcut showing Terence characters and an interpretation of a stage.

that is as revealing of republican audiences as of Terence's prologues, the playwright explained, "*Hecyra* is the name of this play. When it was represented for the first time, an unusual disaster and calamity interrupted it, so that it could not be witnessed throughout or estimated; so much had the populace, carried away with admiration, devoted their attention to some rope dancing."

Although comedy had always been more popular than tragedy in Rome, even *its* popularity waned within fifty years of Terence's death, its favor usurped first by the Atellan farce and later by *mime* and *pantomime.*

About the time regular tragedy and comedy were disappearing from public theatres, Horace (65–8 B.C.) wrote his *Ars Poetica,* a work that exerted even more influence on the Renaissance than Aristotle's *Poetics* (on which it was loosely based). *Ars Poetica* was concerned with the standards and procedures to be followed in writing poetry, with special references to comedy and tragedy. Unlike Aristotle's work, which was a philosophical inquiry into the nature of the form *tragedy,* Horace's was a practical guidebook intended for people wanting to write. As such, it was considerably more prescriptive than Aristotle about such matters as the unities, the separation of the genres, and the appropriate arrangement of language. In many ways an "unmethodical miscellany" of rules, *Ars Poetica* seemed to capture views current among theorists of the day but far afield from contemporary practice in the popular theatre of Rome; therefore Horace's importance rests on his appeal to the erudite dramatists of the Renaissance and Neoclassical theatre, who used his work as a guide for constructing their orderly and decorous works.

Despite the theories of Horace and men like him, drama and theatre during the Empire became increasingly nonliterary. The two most popular forms, pantomime and mime, depended on spectacle and not language and thus can scarcely be appreciated at a distance of two thousand years.

Pantomime was a solo dance that told a story by means of movement alone. Accompanied by an orchestra and a chorus, the dancer generally enacted a serious story taken from history or mythology. Because the dancer never spoke, pantomime masks were built with closed mouths. Although pantomime for a time took the place of tragedy as a serious entertainment popular with the audience, soon it too was overwhelmed by the growing popularity of mime.

Paralleling the rise of Christianity, the rise of mime caused several changes in Roman theatre. First, from its earliest days, mime had numbered women among its performers, the only theatrical entertainment in Greece or Rome to do so. Second, performers in the mime did not generally wear masks, and so their personal appearance was both noticeable and important. Indeed, mime performers were often successful because of their looks: the very handsome or beautiful and the extraordinarily grotesque or ugly had the best chance of success, for they could more readily appeal to the audience as sympathetic or comic characters. Some mime actresses set fashion in clothes and behavior (one, Theodora, married the emperor Justinian of Rome), and many actors were the Roman equivalent of movie stars and matinee idols. Mimes could be either funny or serious, simple or spectacular, but whatever their form, they usually dealt with some aspect of daily living.

Mime was both Rome's most popular and its most notorious theatrical entertainment during the Empire. Because some mimes presented violence and sex *literally* as a part of the performance and because many of the works scoffed at Christian beliefs and Church practices, Christian writers and clerics called often and loudly, if unsuccessfully, for outlawing the theatre in Rome. Even though the artistic merit of mime was low and its performances often offensive to the growing Christian community, mime continued to thrive for as long as the Empire survived. Finally, like today's television, mime was, for the Empire, the entertainment of choice.

It is well to remember that Roman drama and theatre were forced to compete with other forms of entertainment for public support. Perhaps many of the excesses of the mime can be explained, if not excused, by the enormous popularity of imperial athletic activities like chariot racing, gladiatorial contests, wild animal fights, and staged sea battles, where violence and death were both accepted and applauded. Although such activities were generally performed in specially constructed buildings like amphitheatres (e.g., the Colosseum) and circuses (e.g., the Circus Maximus), occasionally a theatre would be temporarily converted and appropriated for such events, serving again to whet the appetites of those arguing for theatre's abolition.

Production Practices

The first permanent stone theatre was not built in Rome until 55 B.C., very near the end of the Republic. Almost immediately, construction began on other theatres, until, by the end of Roman influence, more than one hundred theatres existed around the Roman Empire. Because they bore similarities to each other, a brief survey of their typical features can be provided.

Unlike Greek theatres, Roman theatres were typically built on level ground and the seating was built up, stadium style; at the rear of the Roman auditorium was a wide, covered aisle, whose roof joined to that of the scene house to form a single architectural unit. The orchestra remained but, unlike in Greece, was a half circle, whose diameter was marked by the front of a stage raised to a height of about five feet and extended to a depth of up to forty feet. The stage was very long (100–300 feet) and was enclosed at each end by side wings jutting out from the scene house. At the back of the stage was the scene house, whose elaborate facade was decorated with numerous statues, porticoes, columns, and so on. Perhaps to protect this elaborate structure from the weather or perhaps to improve acoustics, a roof extended from the top of the scene house over part of the stage. The corridors between the scene house and the audience area were covered over and used as audience exits. Architectural evidence suggests that in the Roman theatre, a front curtain may have been used. Its introduction may well have been Rome's most significant contribution to theatre, as its use had implications for the kinds of plays written as well as the kinds of scenic displays possible.

Accounts suggest that Roman theatres could seat between 10,000 and 15,000 patrons and that considerable care was taken to ensure the comfort of the audience. Aisles were apparently wide and numerous, permitting easy comings and goings. An awning was used as protection against the sun, and in one theatre at least, a primitive air-conditioning system was contrived that used fans and ice brought down from nearby mountains. Important people could have reserved seats in the orchestra or in the special boxes atop the audience exits.

Most historians assume, perhaps incorrectly, that Roman theatres of the Republic were similar to those of the Empire, but as evidence is limited and often perplexing, the appearance of the earlier wooden theatres remains a mystery.

Roman masks, costumes, and scenic practices resembled those of Hellenistic Greece. Roman masks for tragedy and comedy were full and exaggerated, with high headdresses and large mouths; costumes resembled either Roman or Hellenistic fashions, depending on the kind of comedy or tragedy being done. As in Greece, all actors in the Roman theatre wore masks except for the mime performers. Clearly, as the popularity of mime increased, the use of masks on the Roman stage declined.

The basic setting in the Roman theatre was apparently the scene house itself. For comedies, its several doors represented entrances to separate homes; for tragedies, its doors were entrances to various parts of a palace or a temple. The stage itself represented either a street running in front of dwellings (in comedy) or a gathering place before a temple or a palace (in tragedy). *Periaktoi,* three flats attached to form a triangle whose visible face could be changed by means of a central pivot, were used to suggest changes of place. According to one ancient commentator, they were located near the ends of the stage and could be rotated to reveal one of three scenes: a tragic scene (with columns, statues, etc.), a comic scene (with balconies, windows, etc.) and a satyric scene (with trees, caves, and "other rustic objects"). Because

THEATRI ORTHOGRAPHIA.

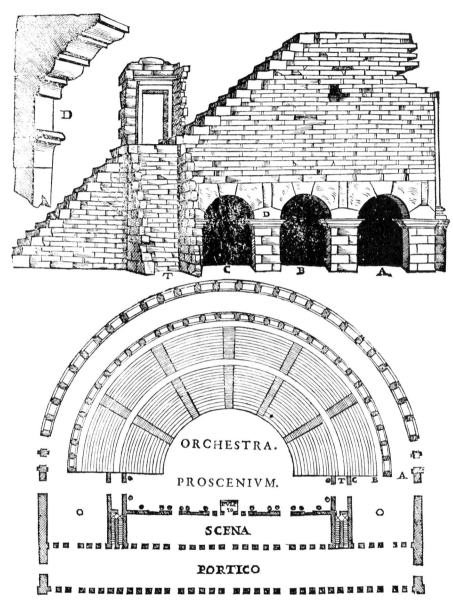

Figure 8–14. Roman Theatre. Serlio's sixteenth-century reconstruction of the ground-plan of a Roman theatre, after Vitruvius. The semicircular orchestra, the scene-house *(scena)* and the very wide stage (labeled *proscenium*) can be seen. *(Rare Book Division, The New York Public Library, Astor, Lenox and Tilden Foundation.)*

Figure 8–15. Masks. These nineteenth-century drawings of a variety of masks show both comic and tragic ones from both Greece and Rome.

the *periaktoi* could not possibly have hidden the facade of the scene house, they probably served simply to inform the audience of location, not to portray the place in a realistic way. Oddly, the mime used a back curtain that hung against the facade of the stage house; the size of this curtain increased during the Empire at about the same time that the elaborate stone theatres were being built. The seemingly contradictory trends are a mystery.

Also tantalizing are contemporary accounts of wondrous special effects. How they were achieved is unclear, but for one event there were reportedly "sliding cliffs and a miraculous moving wood" and for another a fountain of wine springing from a mountain top just prior to the mountain's sinking into a chasm and out of sight. In what certainly must be hyperbole, Pliny, an ancient commentator, recounted yet another marvel:

[*There were*] *two large wooden theatres built close together; each was nicely poised, turning on a pivot. Before noon, a spectacle of games was performed in each, with the theatres back to back so that the noise in each would not interefere with the other's performance. Then, suddenly, toward the latter part of the day, the two theatres would swing around to face each other with their corners interlocking, and, with their outer frames removed, they would form an amphitheatre in which gladiatorial combats were presented.*

As a series of barbarian invasions from the north first dissipated and finally destroyed the power of Rome, the theatre survived shortly because

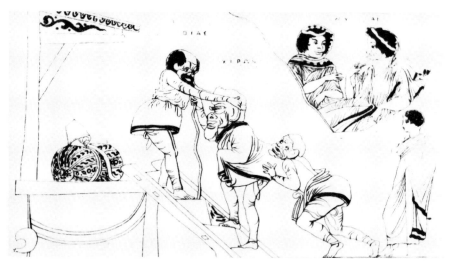

Figure 8–16. Ancient Popular Comedy. This "phlyakes" drawing shows the farcical action, grotesquely padded costumes and masks, and raised stage with ladder; deleted are the enormous *phalloi* worn by the actors. Scholars have suggested connections between this form and Greek Old Comedy, Roman farce, and even the *commedia dell' arte.*

of its popularity but finally succumbed. The "fall of Rome" managed to accomplish what the opposition of the Christian Church could not: the end of formal and organized theatrical activity in Roman lands, an event usually dated from about the middle of the sixth century A.D.

For many years, it was fashionable to dismiss Roman theatre as inartistic and unworthy of serious study, but clearly it was a vital theatre, one enormously popular with its audiences. With the collapse of Rome, its theatre disappeared, only to be reborn, not in the period immediately following but in the more distant Renaissance, whose scholars studied Roman theories and plays, emulated them, and thus assured a Roman legacy to the theatrical world.

The Greek Period

Background

Although civilizations had existed in Greek lands for thousands of years, the civilization that produced the first recorded theatre and drama dated from about the eighth century B.C. By the fifth century B.C. the society had developed a sophisticated system of government and culture. The basic governing unit was the city–state, or polis, which consisted of a town and its surrounding lands. Many were important (Corinth, Sparta, Thebes), but Athens emerged during the fifth century as the cultural and artistic leader of Greece. The Athenians established the world's first democracy (508 B.C.) and provided a model for the participation of citizens in the decisions and policies of government, achieving a level of participation unequaled except perhaps by the New England town meetings.

Under Pericles (c. 460–430 B.C.), Athens soared to new heights in art, architecture, and drama. During this time, Athens headed an empire in the eastern Mediterranean, providing protection and trade outlets for other city–states in exchange for payments and other forms of tribute. It developed a drama that still is acknowledged as superb; its buildings, like the Parthenon and the Theatre of Dionysus, raised architecture to new heights; and the arts in general achieved a status seldom rivaled since.

A defeat in the Peloponnesian War (404 B.C.) ended Athenian supremacy among the city–states, and an invasion of Greece by Alexander the Great (336 B.C.) changed the political and social configuration of the whole penin- sula. By the time the Roman Empire encroached on the area in the second and first centuries B.C., little of the former glory of Athens remained.

Greek theatre and drama lasted for over a thousand years. Records of organized theatrical activity date from the sixth century B.C. and continue well into the Christian era. Its unquestionable impact on the audiences of its day can be explained, at least in part, by four qualities that characterized this very vital theatre: (1) Greek theatre was closely associated with Greek religion; (2) Greek theatre was performed only on special occasions; (3) Greek theatre was a competitive venture; and (4) Greek drama was choral. Because these qualities are all foreign to modern theatrical experience, some time spent considering their impact will be useful.

Greek Theatre and Greek Religion. Although a number of theories have been advanced to explain the origin of theatre and drama in Greece, none has been universally accepted. Whatever its origin, however, Greek theatre was closely associated with Greek religion, which, unlike the Judeo- Christian tradition, depended on a pantheon of gods: Zeus, the king of the gods; Hera, his wife; Athena, goddess of wisdom; and so on. Private worship was interwoven into the daily lives of people, but public worship occurred at festivals dedicated to a particular god. The festivals might last several days, and each city–state (polis) had several festivals each year. In and around Athens, there were four festivals every year devoted to the worship of Dionysus, god of wine and fertility, alone. At three of these festivals (the Great, or City, Dionysia; the Rural Dionysia; and the Lenaia), dramas were regularly performed as a part of the festivities. For at least two hundred years after the first surviving records, all drama in Greece seems to have been performed only at Athens and only at religious festivals devoted to the god Dionysus.

The close association of Greek religion and Greek theatre is further shown by the invariable presence of an altar within the playing area and by the designations of places of honor in the theatres for the priests of Dionysus. Although the intimate connections between religion and theatre were loos- ened by the end of the fourth century B.C., their relationship persisted: when an actor's union was formed in the third century B.C., it took the name

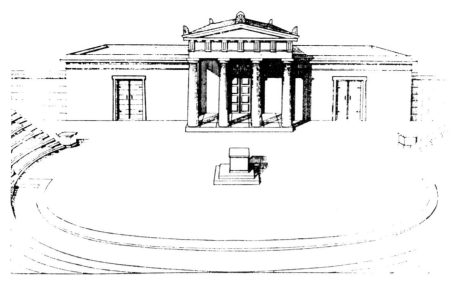

Figure 8–17. Greek Theatre. This interpretation of the classical Greek theatre shows no raised stage but includes the circular orchestra and the altar in the middle.

"Artists of Dionysus" and drew its officers from the ranks of Dionysian priests.

The Occasional Nature of the Theatre. The fact that a festival is religious does not make it solemn—Mardi Gras and Halloween are, after all, religious festivals. Indeed, the fact that drama was performed at religious festivals in Greece seems not to have inhibited its joy or power. Experience suggests that annual celebrations often result in a more festive atmosphere and a more exuberant audience than regular affairs, simply because the event is relatively rare and therefore special. Because Greek drama was performed at festivals, it was performed only occasionally, several times a year rather than several times a week. In trying to capture the effect of the festival arrangement, it might be well to compare it with celebrating a birthday or attending Mardi Gras rather than with attending a play or a movie.

The Competitive Side of Theatre. To add to the excitement of the event, dramatic works in the festivals were cast as competitions, with dramatists competing among themselves for awards in writing and actors competing for prizes in performing. The audience was interested not only in hearing the individual plays but also in learning who won the various contests. Greek theatre, then, probably had some of the elements of a long-standing football rivalry or of a basketball game as well as those elements normally associated with drama and theatre.

The Choral Drama of Greece. In addition to actors, Greek drama required a chorus, a group of men who dressed alike, who were masked alike, and who moved and spoke in concert most of the time. The chorus often figured prominently in the working out of the play's action, and its importance to the total theatrical experience can scarcely be overemphasized; indeed, it has been theorized that *choral* song was the beginning of Greek theatre.

Its presence in the performing area throughout the performance provided considerable spectacle. Much as a modern drill team or a marching band can provide pleasure by their synchronized movements and uniform dress, the Greek chorus, through costume, song, and dance, added to the visual experience of the production. Because the chorus danced as it spoke, chanted, and sang, it established and underscored important rhythms in the play and thus indicated changing moods and shifting fortunes. Moreover, by focusing attention on certain characters and events and avoiding others, by supporting some actions and denouncing others, the chorus provided a point of view and focused attention on the issues of the play and the implications of the action, serving often as an ideal spectator by responding as the playwright may have wished the audience to respond. Too, the chorus established the ethical system operating in the play and indicated the moral universe of the characters. Finally, and perhaps most importantly of all, the chorus participated often and directly in the action of the play, behaving just as any other actor, by providing information and making discoveries and decisions.

Whether in comedy or tragedy, the chorus was an invariable fact of the performance and, as such, influenced a number of practices in the theatre. Although estimates of its size are often based on questionable records and flawed assumptions, the traditional view is that in tragedy, the number of

Figure 8–18. Vase Painting. One of the principal sources of information about the Greek theatre is the detailed representation in vase paintings. Masks, costumes, and properties can be seen in this depiction of actors for a satyr play, showing the chorus and Hercules.

men in the chorus was first fifty, then twelve, and then with Sophocles, fifteen, where it remained throughout the Classical Age; in comedy, the chorus numbered twenty-four. Because the chorus usually came into the performing space soon after the play opened and remained there until the end, its presence had to be considered both in the physical layout of the theatre and by the authors of the drama: the chorus required a space large enough to move about in; and the presence of the chorus had to be justified and their loyalties made clear when secrets were shared. Because the vocal and visual power of the chorus was great (the contribution of each chorus member was, after all, multiplied by fifteen or twenty-four), the actors doubtless adjusted their style accordingly, lest they be overwhelmed by the impact of the chorus.

The Study of Greek Theatre and Drama

Beyond the facts that Greek drama and theatre were closely associated with religion, were performed on specific occasions, were competitive and choral, little else is certain. Evidence is scanty and often contradictory. Most of what is known comes from five kinds of sources: the extant plays; scattered dramatic records of the period; commentaries such as those of Aristotle (c. 335–323 B.C.) and others; the archaeological remains of theatre buildings; and certain pieces of visual art, most notably vase paintings. Ironically most of the extant plays date from the fifth century B.C., but most of the other evidence dates from the fourth century and later. The result is that for the period in which we know most about the theatre *buildings*, we know least about the plays; and for the years we have plays to study, we know very little about the buildings in which they were done or the techniques used to produce them. Unfortunately some writers and teachers have "solved" this problem by grouping all of the evidence together and speaking of the Greek theatre as though its practices remained invariable throughout its thousand-year history. But Greek theatre changed as markedly during its existence as the modern theatre has changed in a thousand years (since c. 980). And so it is necessary to identify which period of the Greek theatre is meant when one is considering production practices. To simplify matters, it is customary to divide the life of the Greek theatre into three major periods: the Classical (c. 534–c. 336 B.C.), the Hellenistic (c. 336–c. 100 B.C.), and the Graeco-Roman (c. 100 B.C.–c. A.D. 500). As most of the extant dramas date from the Classical Age, its practices will be described first and in greatest detail.

The Classical Period

The Theatre. The Theatre of Dionysus, where the first plays were done, was situated on a hillside, with a circular playing area at its base and the audience seated on the slope looking down. The first production that can be documented occurred there in 534 B.C., and the winner of the contest

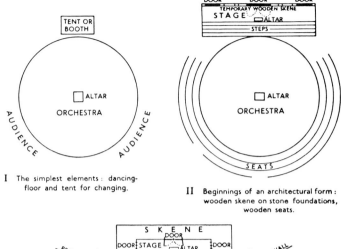

I The simplest elements: dancing-
   floor and tent for changing.

II Beginnings of an architectural form:
    wooden skene on stone foundations,
    wooden seats.

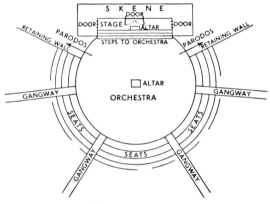

III The theatre in stone.

Figure 8–19. Classical Theatre. An interpretation of three stages in the evolution of the classical theatre. (*From Peter Arnott,* An Introduction to the Greek Theatre. *Courtesy of Macmillan, London and Basingstoke.*)

was Thespis, who both wrote and acted in the winning tragedy. For a time, the playing area *(orchestra),* the audience area, and the corridors separating the two may have been the only parts of the theatre.

By 458 B.C., however, a scene house had been erected adjacent to the orchestra. Although its exact appearance remains a matter of conjecture, it probably had two or three doors and was used first as a place for the actors to change costumes and masks, later becoming a background for the play's action, representing variously a palace, a temple, a home, or even a cave. *If* a raised stage was present (scholarly opinion is divided on this point), it probably ran the length of the scene house and was low enough to allow easy access from the orchestra, thus permitting the necessary mingling of the actors and the chorus members. So long as the scene house was built of wood, it was temporary and may well have been remodeled often; once built in stone, the scene house must be considered permanent, inflexible.

The Audience. That the theatre was out-of-doors meant, of course, that the audience, numbering perhaps as many as fourteen thousand, was subject to the caprice of the weather. Being outside also meant that the audience was as visible as the performers, an attribute shared by modern football games but not by modern theatres. As laws were passed in Greece that made violence in the theatre punishable by death, theatrical audiences of the time were probably sufficiently unruly to provoke the passage of such laws.

Production Practices. Of the production practices themselves, little is certain. The basic setting, at least after 458 B.C., was the scene house. Whether or not its basic appearance was altered in an attempt to suggest changes in locale is not known. Something resembling modern day flats existed, but their exact use is unclear. *Periaktoi* may have been available during the Classical Age, but their use can be documented only for a later period. Two machines were used for special effects: an *eccyclema* and a *mekane.* The *eccyclema* was a movable platform capable of being rolled or rotated out of a door in the scene house, typically to reveal the bodies of characters presumably slain indoors. The *mekane* was a cranelike machine that allowed objects and people to be "flown" into the acting area. So often did the playwright Euripides fly in gods to bring his plays to a suitable conclusion that the

Figure 8–20. Greek Stage Machinery. No details are known of the *ekkyklema* and the *mekane,* but conjectural reconstructions like these can be made.

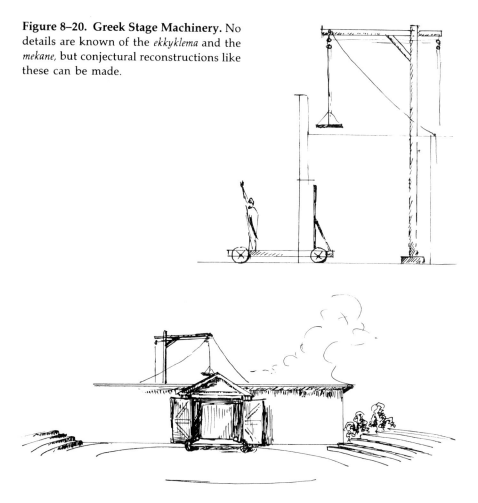

expression *deus ex machina* now refers to any obviously contrived ending in dramatic literature. Various properties were used in productions. Tragedies called for altars, tombs, biers, chariots, staffs, and so on; comedies often required domestic furniture.

Costumes and masks helped differentiate one character from another and often provided clues about the characters wearing them. For example, in some plays, references can be found to characters who are dressed in the manner of Greeks and others who are dressed as foreigners. Black is a color often worn by characters in mourning; and in a comedy, the god Dionysus is dressed in yellow to make a point about his effeminacy. Although some historians have argued for a standard tragic costume, it seems more likely that costumes were a variation on the garments worn by contemporary Athenians: in the case of tragedy probably like the elegant garments of the upper classes, and in the case of comedy more like the clothes of the lower and middle classes, but made laughable by having them ill-fitting, too tight, and too short. To the costume of many male characters in comedy was attached a very large phallus, intended probably as much for comic effect as for a reminder of the drama's associations with fertility and the god Dionysus.

Figure 8–21. Greek Actors. Masks were worn by most characters, except, in this illustration, the musician.

Masks were worn by all of the performers (except possibly the flute player). The masks were full and carried on them hairstyles and beards as well as appropriate facial expressions. During the Classical Age, the masks, headdresses, and footwear were not particularly exaggerated (the high boots and large-mouthed tragic masks often seen in books belong to a later period). Whereas the masks and costumes of the actors served primarily to distinguish one character from another, those of the chorus members stressed the *groupness* of the chorus by all looking alike.

Acting, like playwriting, was a competitive activity during the Classical Age and rules governed its practice. For example, apparently no more than three speaking actors were allowed in the tragedies and five in the comedies, although any number of extras might be used. Because the leading actor, or *protagonist*, was the only one competing for the prize, he was assigned to the playwright by lot, so that chance rather than politics decided who got the best roles. The second actor and the third actor were probably chosen by the playwright and the protagonist in consultation. With only three actors, doubling of roles was required, for the plays themselves often have eight or more characters. If the protagonist had an exceedingly demanding role, like the title role in *Oedipus Rex*, he might play only one character, but the second and third actors were expected to play two or more secondary or minor roles. Doubling, the use of masks, and the absence of actresses all suggest that the style of Greek acting was more formal then realistic; this means that although the acting was true and believable *in its own terms*, its resemblance to real life was of considerably less importance than its fidelity to the dramatic action. Given the size of the audience, the physical arrangement of the theatre, and the style of acting, it should be no surprise that vocal power and agility were the actor's most prized assets.

Plays. Of the thousands of plays written during the thousand years of Greek theatre, only forty-six survive. Most of these date from the Classical Age and can be attributed to four authors: Aeschylus (seven), Sophocles (seven), Euripides (eighteen), and Aristophanes (eleven).

Aeschylus (c. 525–456 B.C.) was credited with several innovations. His predecessor Thespis supposedly wrote tragedies using only one actor and a chorus. Although none of Thespis' works is extant, they probably were based on the intensification of a single event rather than the development of a story, because stories require changes to occur. With only one actor and a chorus, the opportunity to introduce new information into a scene (and thus *change* into a situation) was severely limited. The continual disappearance of either the actor or the chorus to fetch new information would obviously have been awkward and was thus necessarily curtailed.

Aeschylus presumably introduced a second actor, thereby permitting *change* to occur within the play. Although a second actor would also allow conflict between two characters, Aeschylus still tended to depict a solitary hero, one isolated and facing a cosmic horror brought about by forces beyond his control. With such a grand tragic conception, Aeschylus required three plays to encompass it, and so he often wrote *trilogies*, three plays on a single subject that were intended for performance on the same day. One of his trilogies, the *Oresteia* (comprised of the *Agamemnon,* the *Choëphoroe,* and the *Eumenides*) has survived intact along with the single plays *The Persians* (472 B.C.), *Seven Against Thebes* (467 B.C.), *The Suppliants,* and *Prometheus Bound* (probably after 468 B.C.). All display characteristics for which Aeschylus is admired: heroic and austere characters; simple but powerful plots; lofty yet sturdy diction. His general tone is well summarized by an ancient commentator: "While one finds many different types of artistic treatment in Aeschylus, one looks in vain for those sentiments that draw tears."

Sophocles (496–406 B.C.) was credited with adding the third actor (Aeschylus also used three actors in his late plays) and with changing practices in scenic painting and costuming. Less interested than Aeschylus in portraying solitary heroes confronting the universal order, Sophocles wrote plays that explored the place of humans within an established order. The tragedy of Sophocles' heroes typically erupts from decisions made and actions taken based on imperfect knowledge or conflicting claims. Various aspects of the hero's character combine with unusual circumstances to bring about his disaster, a disaster caused not by his wickedness or foolishness but merely by his humanness. For Sophocles, to be human was to be potentially a hero of tragedy.

The role of the chorus in Sophocles' plays remained important but not so central as in Aeschylus'. Conversely the individual characters in Sophocles tend to be more complex, to display more individual traits, to make more decisions: the result is that in Sophoclean tragedy, the actors, not the chorus, control the rhythm of the plays. Unlike Aeschylus, Sophocles did not need a trilogy to contain his tragedies; his plays stood alone. Of the more than one hundred attributed to him, seven have survived: *Ajax* (450 B.C.), *Antigone* (440 B.C.), *Oedipus Rex* (430 B.C.), *Philoctetes* (409 B.C.), *Electra, Trachiniae,* and *Oedipus at Colonnus* (dates unknown but probably late fifth century B.C.). Of these, *Oedipus Rex* is recognized by most critics as among the finest tragedies ever written.

Euripides (480–406 B.C.), the last of the Greek tragic writers, was never very popular during his lifetime but came to be highly regarded after his death. Growing up at a time when Athens was embarking on policies of imperialism and expansionism that many patriots found repugnant, Euripides became a pacifist and a political gadfly. Although the populace at large viewed him with considerable distrust and suspicion, the intellectual elite apparently admired him. It is reported, for example, that Socrates, one of the wisest men of the age, came to the theatre only to see the tragedies of Euripides and that Sophocles dressed his chorus in black upon learning of the death of Euripides.

Figures 8–22, 8–23, 8–24. Oedipus Rex. Sophocles' great tragedy has proven durable enough to outlive many theatrical styles. Shown here are the 1955 production at the Stratford Shakespearean Theatre, Canada; a performance by the French actor Mounet-Sully toward the end of the nineteenth century; and a performance by the actor Sheridan in London in 1774. The illustrations will bear close study for comparison of costume and gesture and for their attempts to evoke the Greek original. *(Figure 8–22 courtesy of the Stratford Shakespearean Festival, Canada.)*

In comparison with the plays of Aeschylus and Sophocles, those of Euripides are less exalted and more realistic. His characters seem less grand, more human; their problems are less cosmic, more mundane. Euripides tended to examine human relationships and to question the wisdom of social actions: the purpose of war, the status of women, the reasons for human cruelty. Explorations of abnormal, even pathological, characters were his major interest in plays like *Medea, Hippolytus,* and *Electra,* while antiwar sentiments can be most clearly seen in *Andromache, The Trojan Women,* and *The Suppliants.*

In keeping with his changed outlook came changes in dramatic technique. Replacing the philosophical probings common in the plays of Aeschylus and Sophocles, Euripides substituted rapid reversals, intrigues, chase scenes, and romantic and sentimental incidents of the sort later associated with the plays called *melodramas* (Euripides is said by some to be the father of melodrama). He further reduced the role of the chorus, until on occasion it was little more than an interruption for the play's action. As the role of the chorus declined and the subjects became more personal, the level of the language dropped, becoming less poetic and more conversational. Many of the changes that Euripides introduced into Greek tragedy, although denounced in his own time, became standard dramatic practice during the Hellenistic Age.

Comedy was introduced into the Great Dionysia in 486 B.C., some fifty years after tragedy. It seems never to have been comfortable there, perhaps because the festival was a showcase for Athenian culture and thus often visited by foreign dignitaries. The real home of comedy was the winter festival, the Lenaia, where a contest for comedy was established in 442 B.C. At both festivals, an entire day was set aside for competition among the comic playwrights, five of whom competed.

Of the twelve extant Greek comedies, all but one are by the playwright Aristophanes (c. 448–c. 380 B.C.); therefore information about comedy during the Classical Age is necessarily from these plays. It is possible, of course, that Aristophanes was atypical, and so the conclusions drawn from his works may be incorrect.

During the Classical Ages, comedy was highly political and filled with references to contemporary people and events. Although no two extant comedies are exactly alike, they bear similarities and suggest a highly formal structure that can be summarized briefly.

Greek "old comedy" was written in two parts divided by a section during which, typically, the chorus or the choral leader broke the dramatic illusion and addressed the audience directly in carefully prescribed metrical patterns.

The first portion of the play generally consisted of a prologue, during which the outrageous assumption on which the comedy was based was set forth: in *Lysistrata,* it was the notion that women could stop men from fighting by withholding sexual favors; in *The Frogs,* it was that literary excellence and prior glory could be reclaimed by retrieving Euripides from the land of the dead. Following the entrance of the chorus, there was a debate about whether or not the basic assumption, or "happy idea," should be adopted. The first part of the comedy ended with the decision to put the "happy idea" into practice.

Figure 8–25. The Trojan Women. Euripides' tragedy, as performed at the University of Nevada, Las Vegas. *(Directed by Jerry L. Crawford. Designs by Fredrick L. Olson and Ellis M. Pryce-Jones.)*

The second portion consisted simply of a number of episodes and choral songs showing the "happy idea" at work. The comedies ended happily on a note of feasting and merriment. Although all of Aristophanes' comedies follow this pattern more or less, no one of them corresponds in every detail.

Near the end of the Classical Age, when Sparta defeated Athens in war, some sort of censorship was apparently imposed and so comedy became less political. Aristophanes' later plays refrain from the numerous topical references and often vitriolic attacks that mark his earlier comedies. The change has been noted by a number of scholars, and so the early comedy is called *old comedy,* and the less political, later works, *middle comedy.*

Contest Rules. During the Classical Age, plays were produced in Athens by the city–state in cooperation with selected wealthy citizens. By the fifth century B.C., contests were held for the best tragic writers, the best comic writers, and the best actors in both sorts of plays. Rules were established at each festival, but little is known about the arrangements at the Rural Dionysia. At the Great Dionysia, three tragic writers competed each year for the prize. To compete, each submitted three tragedies and one satyr play (a short comic piece that followed the tragedies and occasionally burlesqued them). One day was set aside for the work of each tragic author;

Figure 8–26. The Birds. Aristophanes' comedy in an 1899 production at Cambridge University.

therefore, each year there were nine tragedies and three satyr plays presented at the Great Dionysia. At the Lenaia, four tragedies only competed each year, each by a different playwright. At both festivals, five comic playwrights competed for a prize, and a single day was set aside for this competition.

Anyone wishing to compete in either contest applied to the leading civic or religious official for a chorus. How the competitors were selected from among the applicants is unknown, but, once chosen, each author was matched with a wealthy citizen–sponsor, who was then responsible for meeting the costs incurred by the chorus. The city–state provided the theatre in which the plays were performed and the prizes that were awarded to the winners. A good sponsor apparently could do much to assure the success or failure of a play. *Oedipus Rex* failed to win the prize the year it entered, presumably because a stingy citizen failed to provide an acceptable visual production. Although most sponsors considered production expense a part of their civic and religious duty, a legal recourse was available in the event that one seemed inclined to slight or ignore his duty.

The Hellenistic Age

With the coming of Alexander the Great, the Hellenistic Age arrived and brought with it a number of changes. The system of city–states was replaced with a more centralized form of government, and the seat of power shifted away from Athens. Theatres began to be built outside of Athens and throughout the eastern Mediterranean lands. Productions came to be seen in many cities and on numerous occasions, military and social as well as religious. Indeed, in general, the civic and religious nature of the theatre eroded as its professional standing increased. Actors, for example, were no longer merely citizens; they became professionals who organized along with other performers into the Artists of Dionysus, an agency that oversaw contracts between the actors and the cities wishing to hire them. The citizen–sponsors turned over their financial responsibilities to the state.

Theatres were built of stone during this period, and so archaeological remains are available. The primary features of the Hellenistic theatre included a two-storied scene house, to which was attached a very long and narrow and high stage. Usually the stage could be reached by steps or ramps affixed to each end, but in some theatres the only access was apparently through the scene house. The orchestra circle remained essentially unchanged, but its use during this period is uncertain. Was the chorus there and the actors on stage? Or were they both one place or the other? Or did it depend on the play? Because answers to the questions are unavailable, speculation about staging practices continues.

Tragedy appeared to decline in popularity during the Hellenistic Age. Those tragedies written seemed to show the influence of Euripides' innovations, including the reduced importance of the chorus and the increased importance of sensational and melodramatic scenes. Satyr plays disappeared altogether.

Comedy, on the other hand, remained very popular indeed. Its strong political flavor now gone, *new comedy,* as it came to be called, portrayed the domestic situations of the Athenian middle classes, featured problems centering on love, finances, and family relationships, and often included intrigues involving long-lost children and recognition scenes. The highly formal structure of old comedy disappeared, leaving behind only a series of episodes and choral songs, with the chorus often quite incidental to the action of the play. Because Greek new comedy greatly influenced the development of Roman comedy, its qualities assume an importance beyond that accorded

Figure 8–27. Hellenistic Greek Theatre. Remains of the Theatre at Epidauros, Greece.

Hellenistic tragedy. Fortunately one example of new comedy, Menander's *The Grumbler* (c. 300 B.C.), survived and found its way to modern times.

During the Hellenistic Age, too, there emerged the world's first, and probably most influential, dramatic theorist: Aristotle. In his *Poetics,* Aristotle strove to provide a theoretical definition of the dramatic form *tragedy.* Along the way, he identified and discussed the parts of a play (plot, character, thought, diction, music, spectacle), the materials of plot (suffering, discovery, and reversal), and the form of plot (complication and denouement); he then considered the attributes of character, thought, diction, music, and spectacle in turn. Because the work is so cryptic and its translation so difficult, its meaning has been continuously debated. Certainly, the *Poetics* remains a base from which most discussions of dramatic theory must proceed, through either acceptance or rejection of its primary tenets. (See also pp. 432–435.)

The Graeco-Roman Age

By about 100 B.C., the expanding Roman Empire was exerting pressure on the Greek islands. Trends begun in the Hellenistic Age continued but were altered so that they were brought more in line with Roman ideals and practices. For example, Roman theatres were built in Greek lands, and Hellenistic theatres were remodeled to resemble Roman theatres more closely. Although some records of theatre in Greek lands persist throughout this period, the center of influence clearly shifted to Rome around the time of Christ, and so attention to Greek theatre declined and was replaced by interest in Roman practices.

The Uncertain Origins of Western Theatre and Drama

Why did drama and theatre flourish in Greece? Where did they come from? Why did they emerge? How can their several forms be explained? The issues surrounding the origins of Western theatre have been raised again and again and have never been satisfactorily resolved. As the evidence we have does not permit clear answers to such questions, a number of theories have been suggested.

Everyone agrees that theatrical and dramatic elements exist in life and therefore in all societies. The question is why, when, and by what means such elements were transformed into activities whose primary aim was artistic (as distinct from religious or instructional).

Some scholars have proposed that Western drama developed from storytelling. Telling and hearing stories, according to this theory, are pleasurable and natural; so too is the tendency of a narrator to elaborate parts of the telling by impersonating the various characters, using appropriate voice and movement. From here it seems merely a short step for several people to become involved in the telling of a story; and from this, it is thought, drama and theatre arose.

Other theorists suggest that movement rather than speech was at the core of the drama. By imitating the physical behavior of animals and humans, and by donning appropriate skins or garments, a dancer first impersonated them and later embroidered his performance with sounds and words. The single dancer was joined by others who likewise impersonated and garbed themselves, and a form of theatre was born, it is supposed.

A few scholars have sought the form of drama in the judicial system of Athens. Alluding to the many instances where debates and arguments occur in the plays and to the instances in which judgments are required, such theorists have sought the beginnings of Greek drama in the courtrooms of its early societies.

Probably the most fashionable, but not necessarily the most correct, view of the origin of theatre is the so-called ritual theory. A ritual is an activity that is repeated in order to gain a specific and predictable outcome. Religious rituals have developed in all primitive cultures as a means of affecting events, propitiating gods, transmitting information, educating the young, and so on. The ritual theory of drama proposes that from primitive religious rituals, in particular those connected with fertility and the spirits of the seasonal cycle, dramas evolved. Although few respectable scholars still accept the idea that drama "evolved" in some organic, necessary way from religious ceremonies, most acknowledge that ritual probably influenced the emerging theatrical forms.

Two statements by Aristotle, too, bear on the question of the drama's origin. He claimed, in Chapter Four of the *Poetics*, that "tragedy was produced

Figure 8–28. The Bacchae. Euripides' tragedy, as performed at the University of Northern Iowa. *(Directed by D. Terry Williams, designs by Harvey Sweet and Kathleen G. Runge.)*

by the authors of the dithyramb, and comedy from [the authors] of the phallic songs." Dithyrambs were choral odes sung to the god Dionysus; phallic songs were fertility rites whose precise nature is not known. Although tantalizing, Aristotle's account does little to clarify for what reasons or in what manner the authors shifted from dithyramb to tragedy or from phallic song to comedy. He also observed that "imitation is natural to men from childhood and in this they differ from the other animals . . . and then everybody takes pleasure in imitation." Because Aristotle was writing closer to the event than any of those advocating other theories, his account deserves consideration; still it should be remembered that Aristotle was himself writing over two hundred years after the event he was describing.

Finally, some scholars view the appearance of tragedy and comedy as a supreme creative act of an unidentified artist (perhaps Thespis, perhaps Aeschylus, perhaps another). Arguing that art neither evolves like a biological organism nor happens by chance, such scholars look for the birth of drama in a revolutionary discovery made by a human being, an artist: that the synthesis of many elements already established in the Athenian society (dance, music, storytelling) would produce a more sublime work of art—and thus drama was born.

In its essence, the argument over the origin of theatre is an argument over the most important element of theatre. To the anthropologist who looks at mimings or impersonations as different as the Mandan Buffalo Dance, the Iroquois False Face Society and the Egyptian "Passion Play," the essence of theatre is ritual, and the ritual theory will be favored. To the critic who finds the bedrock of drama in conflict, myth-making or legal battle will seem the most like dramatic action, and he will favor the storytelling or the judicial theory. To the artist who looks at world theatre and sees a form rich in human meaning and almost indescribable in complexity, only a nonrational leap will explain its beginnings.

In fact, we do not know how theatre began. And, finally, it is not so important for us to know its beginnings as to theorize and to argue about them, for in that thinking and that argument we preserve our sense of the extraordinary richness of a great art that will not allow itself to be reduced to simple explanations.

Part Four

Theatre Makers

CHAPTER 9

The Actor

Introduction

The actor stands at the center of the theatre. The actor is its linchpin, its keystone; without him or her, there is nothing—an empty building, a hollow space. Directors cannot direct nor designers design without actors; the playwright can create only works to be read like novels in their absence.

The actor alone can make theatre without the help of other artists. The plays that he invents may not be very good, it is true, and they may even be merely stories told well (as in oral cultures, when the storyteller is an actor-narrator.) The actor can costume himself, can build a theatre, can provide at least crude scenery for it. At a level of development that can be identified in several periods, we see just such an actor and just such a primitive theatre, the plays improvised or crudely crafted, the costumes emblematic of the craft of acting rather than of a character (as a circus clown's is, for example), the stage a platform with a curtain behind it instead of elaborate scenery. Out of such an actor-intensive theatre may occasionally grow an even more developed one, such as the *commedia dell'arte* of Renaissance Italy (see p. 220). More often, however, such an actors' theatre changes in the direction of the theatre that we know, adding playwright, designer, and director. No matter how far it develops, however, it remains the descendant of that primal theatre—actor-centered.

Figure 9–1. Actors' Theatre. The *commedia dell'arte* remained largely an actor's form, its scenery incidental, its plays inconsequential. Stock character and elaborate, marvelously performed *lazzi* were its strengths until its decline and decadence in the eighteenth century. *(Courtesy of the Fitzwilliam Museum, Cambridge.)*

We often identify the greatness of certain ages in the theatre with the names of plays and playwrights, when in fact what we are doing is identifying great ages not of theatre but of drama. Plays survive and are easier to recapture than that ephemeral now, the actor's performance. The existence of great plays from fifth-century B.C. Greece, Elizabethan England, or seventeenth-century France should not cause us to forget that these were also great ages of acting. It is no accident that Sophocles, Shakespeare, and Molière were actors as well as dramatists.

We cannot have great plays without actors, but we can have great acting without plays.

The Paradox of the Actor

The French theorist Denis Diderot (1713–1784) used the expression "the paradox of the actor" as the title for an essay on acting, in which he tried to capture what seems to be an essential contradiction in the art: in order to appear natural, the actor must be artificial.

This contradiction takes several forms, whose language and whose specifics change from age to age; nevertheless the paradox remains at the center of most thinking about the art.

Natural Versus Artificial. One of the things to be learned from a study of the history of acting is that almost every change in acting for the mainstream theatre has been seen as an improvement of the "natural" or the "real." Partly, changes in philosophy are at work, for the idea of "natural" and "real" human behavior is one of the root concerns of philosophy. When an age's idea of "what it is to be human" changes, the manner of depicting human beings on the stage changes as well, and what is typical of the older concept is viewed as outdated and "nonhuman"—that is, artificial.

However, there is a distinction to be made as well between the idea of

Figure 9–2. Natural or Artificial? The tension between the two extremes in acting is always present, and the emphasis on one or the other is partly a matter of the limitations on the actor's—and his audience's—own way of seeing humanity. *Hamlet* at the Long Wharf Theatre, New Haven. *(Directed by Arvin Brown; Stacy Keach as Hamlet, Stefan Gierasch as Claudius. William L. Smith, photo.)*

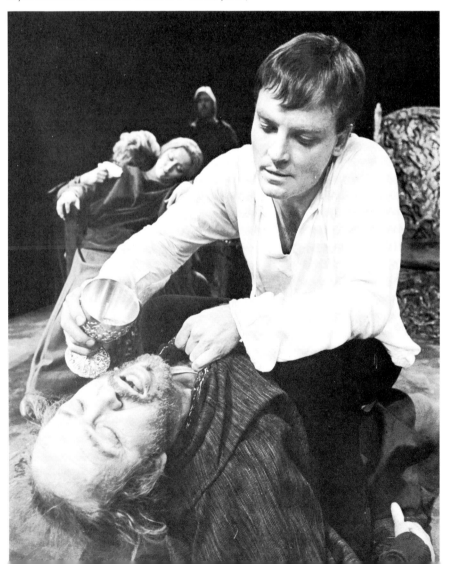

what humanity is and the idea of what humans might or should be. Certain ages and certain forms of theatre have prized an idea of humanity that was sometimes rigidly defined in its behaviors; such an idea of humanity sets up many "proprieties"—rules based on the ideal—that must be observed. On the stage, elegance of diction, grace of movement, and limitation of gesture may become almost moral issues, and we find such extremes of stage propriety as the "rule" that the left hand must never be used for important gesture. Such a strictly limited kind of acting will seem highly "artificial" to anybody who believes that the stage must imitate life explicitly, and what will seem "natural" will then be a kind of acting that does not stay within the proprieties. Much of the conflict between French and English acting in the eighteenth century and between Neoclassical and Romantic acting in the early nineteenth century arose from precisely this difference. The "artificial" actor in such a dispute would see his greatest allegiance to the rules of the theatre, based on an ideal and not on a literal concept of "what it is to be human"; the "natural" actor would see his greatest allegiance as being to life—or to his interpretation of life. Neither idea is better than the other, although bitter battles have been fought over their differences.

Technique Versus Inspiration. Our own age is one whose theatrical heritage is primarily a "natural" one, at least in the realistic theatre. (Opera and classical theatre are sometimes another matter. Opera, especially, is still largely a traditional and "artificial" form. As recently as the early years of this century, Enrico Caruso scandalized audiences by putting his hands in his pockets while singing the role of Rodolfo in *La Bohème*. His argument was that Rodolfo is a starving writer and it is winter, so his hands are cold; the audience's "artificial" argument was that a singer in grand opera did not put his hands in his pockets.) Modern American actors sometimes speak disparagingly of an actor who is "technical," meaning one who builds his character out of careful, conscious use of body and voice—meticulously rehearsed inflections, carefully chosen poses and gestures, and so on. Their belief is that the "technical" actor works mechanically and so fails to bring imagination and life to his work. They are likely to see the technical actor as "full of tricks." Again, there is a strong belief that "technique" is somehow an enemy of the convincing, the lifelike, the believable.

At the far extreme from the technical actor is the "inspirational" one. His work, although carefully rehearsed, is not assembled from external behaviors but is created through application of mental and emotional techniques that supposedly work to reach the actor's emotional and mental center and then somehow push outward into onstage movement and vocalization. In theory, the character created by the inspirational actor will be (in his own view) more "real," more "natural" because it does not rise from conscious intellectual work but from the inner sources that also give rise to music and poetry. To the inspirational actor, the approach is fresh and the creation original and not stereotyped. Of the "technical" actor, Diderot said, "When, by dint of hard work, she has got as near as she can to this idea, the thing is done; to preserve the same nearness is a mere matter of memory and practice." Of an "inspirational" actor, he said, "It is a different matter. . . . She comes on the stage without knowing what she is to say; half the time she does not know what she is saying; but she has one sublime moment."

Inner and Outer. Technical and inspirational acting have their direct counterparts in "outer" and "inner" acting. As one actress put it some years ago, "I like to build my house first—then I start to live in it." She meant that she liked to create the "outer" part of the role; then, comfortable with that—voice, posture, costume, gesture—she could move inward toward emotional intensity and conviction, believably "living in" the shell she had created.

Other actors work from the inside out. All of their early work will be devoted to mental, emotional, and spiritual exploration. Only when that is completed do they feel that an outer structure can be built. In the cases of both the "inner" and the "outer" actor, truth to the character is being sought, and the difference is really a difference of emphasis and of sequence. The "inner–outer" distinction is not quite the same as the "technical–inspirational" one; the "technical" actor's work begins and ends with externals, while the "outer" actor's work finally leads inward, and the "inner" actor's work leads toward externals in a way that the "inspirational" actor's does not. Inspiration supposedly gives rise to externals through a nonintellectual leap, and as Diderot suggested, those externals can vary from performance to performance and may supply only an occasional "sublime moment."

Being and Pretending. To reach emotional truth, it might be said, the actor must be the character he plays; on the contrary, another point of view insists, the actor must always stand aloof from the character and *pretend.* Here is precisely the paradox that Diderot observed. If an actor were really to be the character, how would he control onstage behavior? What would keep the actor from becoming inaudible at times? What would keep the actor, as Othello, from actually killing the actress who plays Desdemona? What would cause the actor to modulate his voice, control the tempo of a performance, listen to other actors? And, contrarily, if the actor always pretends, what will he be but a lifeless imitation of humanity, a puppet, a windup toy? How will the actor keep the speeches from sounding like empty nonsense? How will gestures be anything but graceful hand-waving?

Because the actor is at the center of the theatre, this paradox is the paradox of the theatre itself: in order to be convincing, one must lie. The actor both "is" *and* "pretends"; he must exploit both inner and outer, both technique and inspiration. It is never enough for the actor to be satisfied that a sigh or a smile is perfectly truthful *for himself;* the sigh or smile must also have the carrying power and the communicative value to be perfectly truthful *to the audience.*

The two halves of the paradox of the actor are always in tension. Their relative strengths vary from actor to actor and from age to age. It is only rarely that a really good actor will be found at either extreme.

Figure 9–3. Being or Pretending? In our own time, we are accustomed to the exaggerations of "pretending" mostly in comedy. *The Recruiting Officer* at the Long Wharf Theatre, New Haven. *(John Horton and Emery Battis as Plume and Brazen.)*

The Actor and the Role

It should now be clear that actors do not create real human beings, on the one hand, nor do they somehow transform themselves and erase their own personalities utterly. Instead they engage in a creative act whose end product is a *construct,* that is, an entity made by human agency for a particular purpose. Both the actor and the audience must be very careful to remember that the creation *is* a construct and not a full-fleshed, living human being; for all that actors and audiences may speak of the constructs by their names just as if they were real people named Hamlet or Stanley Kowalski or Hedda Gabler, they are not. The construct remains an invention, and one actor's construct may be quiet different from another's construct of the same name— Richard Burton's and John Barrymore's Hamlet, for example.

In order to maintain the distinction between the actor's construct and a live human being, we must make a distinction between two words, *person* and *character*. *Person* is a word that applies to life, to the world of real beings; it has no place in a discussion of theatre or of drama or of acting, unless we are talking about the *person who creates theatre.* Hamlet is not a person; Hedda Gabler is not a person. They are letters on a page, ideas in a mind, constructs bodied forth on many stages by many actors. Nobody should ever say that an actor "played a person named _____."

Character *is the word reserved for the purpose of naming the actor's construct.* There is the character of Hamlet, the character of Hedda Gabler. But the word itself is capable of misinterpretation, or at least of confusion, because we have at least two other senses in which we use it: first, we use it loosely

Figure 9–4. Actress and Character. In posture, in facial expression, in the wearing of the costume, the actress is able to create and express character even in repose. Here, Rachel as Mary Stuart.

to describe a potential for certain kinds of behavior ("He has character") or even more loosely to describe unusual behavior ("He is a character"). Second, we use it to describe the imitations of human beings (the constructs) that appear in stories—literary character. It is this second meaning, with its further limited theatrical application to acting, that concerns us here.

In the literary sense, character is a construct that represents human personality and that expresses itself through *action;* it is best understood as being made visible by and embodying itself through *decisions.* In the vital sense of the word used by Aristotle, *character is aesthetically good insofar as it contributes to plot,* by which we mean that the effectiveness of a character in a work is judged by how well it fits into the narrative whole and affects plot (or makes decisions to act directly on the main line of action). Such a critical judgment has a very important implication for the actor: we make the judgment on the basis of the function within the artistic whole and *not merely on the basis of how well it imitates a human being.* Therefore a dramatic construct may be a convincing imitation of a human being in its superficial attributes—it may talk like one, have preferences in clothes and food and entertainment like one—and yet it may be a "bad" character in that it makes no important contribution to the artistic whole and the action. The American novelist Ernest Hemingway spoke of "sideshows" in fiction, and he meant somewhat the same thing that we mean by "badness" of character. A "sideshow," no matter how entertaining, does not belong in the same work with the main events. An actor who concentrates on mannerisms of the character—sideshows—and fails to grasp the character's function as contributor to the action will fail; he will be guilty of what the Russian actor and theorist Stanislavski called "tendencies."

For the actor, *character* means something like "the imitation of a human being as it expresses itself through the words and the decisions created by the author, *in relation to the other characters in the play and their decisions and words.''* The actor's character exists on the stage (only) and has no life off the stage; the actor's character exists in an artificial time scheme that is quite different from the time scheme of real life. It is helpful for the actor to figure out where his character is coming from when he walks on the stage, what he has been doing, and so on, but such analysis has to be limited strictly to conclusions relevant to onstage action and onstage time or it will lead to sideshows and tendencies or even to the creation of a play that the author never wrote (and one that, regrettably for the audience, takes place offstage).

Interesting games can be played with actors' characters, but they are only games. Tom Stoppard's play *Rosencrantz and Guildenstern Are Dead* is about two minor characters in *Hamlet* and what "happens" to them when they are not onstage. It is an interesting exercise, but it has nothing to do with *Hamlet,* and no actor playing Rosencrantz or Guildenstern would profit from using it as a guide to the offstage life of either character in playing him in *Hamlet.*

The actor is a person; the character is a construct. In order for the character to *seem* to be a person during the two or three hours of performance, the actor must use parts of his own real self, observations of other people, and sheer invention and imagination.

The Actor's Creative Whole

In approaching the character, the actor brings three aspects of himself to the task. And the actor does *approach* the character; he does not make a grab at it or reach it with one enormous leap. In a sense, he uses the entire self in the act of creation; in another sense, parts of the real personality never take part. It is true that all of the actor's experience and all of the actor's mind may at one time or another prove useful, but it is also true that at any given moment large areas of the personality lie dormant.

We can identify the three parts of the actor's creative self as:

1. *The actor's consciousness.* Several components of successful acting are conscious. Primary among these are *concentration, selectivity,* and *analysis.* Without concentration, the actor might at times dissolve into neurotic collapse, haunted by personal problems that would destroy the work. What can be noted about successful actors is the astonishing degree of concentration that they bring to their task. "The show must go on" is a cliché, but it does describe the good actor's tenacious ability to continue when the physical or emotional self is hurt or threatened.

Selectivity is the ability to discriminate among possible solutions to an acting problem. (The process is more or less conscious in different actors.) Choices may be as simple as between two qualities of voice for a word or line or as complex as identification of a memory, among many memories,

Figure 9–5. Concentration. Even in a photograph that captures a fleeting moment, it is sometimes possible to identify actor concentration or the lack of it, as well as differences between acting and performing, between "natural" and "artificial" among different actors. *Rip Van Winkle* at the University of Minnesota. *(Directed by Cathy Dezseran, designs by Keith Setterholm.)*

from which an emotion springs. Often there is no one correct answer in such a selection; there is one that may work best for a particular actor in trying to illuminate a certain moment of a performance. It is because of this selectivity that actors so often experiment, trying, rejecting, and trying again with different voices, gestures, rhythms. To an outsider, an actor's process in creating a character often seems slow, repetitive, and aimless. Even in his conscious work, however, the actor does not proceed as, for example, a businessman or a scientist might proceed, and often he is still trying to frame a creative question while he is already searching for the answer, because the conscious process is so highly complex. The guidance of the director is of enormous importance here, of course, and the same outside observer who wondered why the actor seemed to work so slowly might also wonder why the director asked the actor so many questions; the answer is that the director is trying to help the actor to frame his own questions and to select the best answers to them.

Analysis is the element of the actor's consciousness that deals with his reading of the dramatic text on its first level—breaking it into units and understanding its complex inner relationships. The analytic element is exercised throughout the prerehearsal, rehearsal, and performance periods by the actor who is determined to perfect his understanding and interpretation of the script and of his character.

2. *The actor's instrument.* By the *instrument* we mean the entire physical self that the actor uses in playing a character; it is conveniently separated into body and voice. Whereas the audience does not see or hear the work of

Figure 9–6. Effective Use of the Instrument. Concentration, preparation, analysis—the actor's work is perceived by the audience through his effective use of the instrument. *A Flea in Her Ear* at the University of Nevada, Las Vegas. *(Directed by Jerry L. Crawford, designs by Fredrick L. Olson and Pat Crawford.)*

the consciousness or the imagination directly, it always sees and hears the instrument, for the instrument is the medium through which the others express themselves.

The "external" or "artificial" or "technical" actor might appear at first glance to be the one who makes the most conscious use of the instrument. However, this association of the instrument with the externals of acting is at least partly an appearance and not a reality. The properly trained actor of any method will make maximum use of body and voice, because without them his consciousness and his imagination are strangled. What the bad actor of any method will do, however, is use *learned* instrumentation— "tricks," clichés, personal mannerisms—rather than instrumentation that springs from creative understanding of the character and the play.

His instrument is given to the actor. What is given can be developed, and good teaching can do wonderful things to improve voices and the use of bodies; nonetheless the fact remains that the size and shape of bones, the delicate tuning of vocal mechanisms, and the size and shape of the body are in large part given at birth. "Talent" does not consist of having a beautiful face or a beautiful voice, or even of having a body and voice that are flexible and expressive without training. Insofar as "talent" applies to the instrument, it consists of making maximum use of what is given and of recognizing its strengths and its limitations.

3. *The actor's imagination.* Within the actor's mental and emotional self lies the wellspring of his creativity, the imagination. It is the force that impels all creativity, working often in images rather than in rational discourse, surfacing into the consciousness unpredictably, frequently working while the rest of the organism sleeps. In all fields, including science, great and original ideas and creations have come while the conscious mind rested or actually slept: "I woke up with the problem solved," or "It came to me in a dream," has been a common story for millennia. Sometimes the imagination works while the conscious mind is "at rest" because of a condition other than sleep; the disassociation used in marathon running, for example, has given rise to the solutions to problems, and other such irrational "leaps" have come through Yoga and other meditative disciplines.

Contemporary psychology and physiology now suggest that the "lateral hemispheric specialization" of the brain may play a large part in what we call the actor's imagination (see, for example, Carl Sagan's *Dragons of Eden*). Recent findings indicate that the right and left halves of the normal brain have separate but interconnected functions, the left dealing with logic and language, and the right with image, metaphor, pictures, and music. Early training "teaches" the brain to mute signals coming into the consciousness from the right half (probably because language and logic are vitally important to European and American culture); it may be this muting that causes us to see the imagination as irrational, mysterious, and hidden. The muted or "hidden" quality is also the reason for the many exercises used in actor training and rehearsal to penetrate through years of habit in order to help the actor to work directly with his imagination. It is as if, in early life, we learn to erect shields around the imagination—the work of the right half of the brain—and to lower those shields only in sleep and altered states of consciousness; then, as adults, we must learn new techniques to penetrate them or lower them for artistic, creative work.

Imagination is the key that opens the door to memory, itself a rich source of the actor's understanding and playing of character. Imagination is also the function that processes nonrational data (from such sources as the text, the creative work of other actors and the director, the setting and costumes) and that gives back new understanding of play and character. It is the function that gives the actor an understanding of stage space and his body's relation to it. It is the source of whatever is new, particular, and magical in his performance, for it is unique to the individual actor, and its nonrational "leaps" are like the working of magic. Yet, because it comes from a part of the brain that does not process data rationally, it is held suspect by purely rational people; in an age that considers itself rational, imagination in acting is suspect and is made to give way to the more understandable, visible process of analysis. Conversely, when a society permits extensive inner searching and is familiar with such searching through its own religion and thought, an acting that relies perhaps excessively on the imagination

Figure 9–7. Imagination. The audience perceives through the work of the instrument; the actor creates through exercise of the imagination, making theatrical those characters, events, words he may never have experienced. *Hamlet* at the Stratford Shakespearean Festival, Canada, 1957. *(Christopher Plummer as Hamlet, Mervyn Blake as Marcellus, Max Helpmann as the Ghost, Lloyd Bochner as Horatio.)*

may result, and such acting may, like the workings of the right half of the brain, lack the logical, communicable links to the external world that make most performances understandable to the audience. The result in such a case might be a performance that could be called "novel" or "original" but that is beyond comprehension (for example, some of the performances of Jerzy Grotowski's Polish Laboratory Theatre) or a performance whose appeal is limited to a small, communal audience.

The successful actor in the mainstream theatre, then, effectively uses his consciousness, his imagination, and his instrument in balance. His conscious mind analyzes the playscript and the "conditions of performance" and translates that information into a form usable by both the instrument and the imagination. Even as they work, however, the consciousness continues to analyze and to shape and change its findings; at the same time, the decisions and findings of the imagination are communicated directly, along with the decisions of the consciousness, to the instrument. The complexity of the process is virtually beyond description—and, in fact, it is not adequately understood by either scientists or artists. Perhaps it is enough for our purposes to suggest that if we seek to define the word *talent* in acting, we do so by looking at this three-way, continuing, constantly changing interconnection and interchange. Talent, we may be able to say, is the ability of the consciousness to inspire in the imagination a set of actions and sounds that the instrument can express to an audience as theatrical character, excitingly and brilliantly.

Acting and Performing

A full-fledged talent for acting cannot be thought of merely as an ability to entertain well in public, to clown at parties or tell jokes superbly. The latter are parts of a talent for *performing*—that is, for reaching and delighting an audience without regard to character or theatrical action. As we have already tried to suggest, there is more to acting than this. A good actor, of course, is also a good performer; a good performer, however, may not be a very good actor.

Some kinds of theatre or the related arts put a higher premium on performing than on acting; circus high-wire work, for example, requires great performers and has no use for actors. Musical comedy, on the other hand, requires both acting and performing, but the ability to "sell" a song in the belt-it-out manner of an Ethel Merman requires, above all, performing of a high level. Liza Minelli in *The Act* was a consummate performer—but she was also an actress, for all that she was playing herself. (And indeed, the character that the performer most often plays is himself. For this reason, strong performers who undertake the acting of theatrical roles sometimes have difficulty, or they so overpower the dramatic character that it is obscured. In the star-oriented theatres of Broadway and London's West End, productions are sometimes thrown out of balance by the casting of famous performers who are so habituated to playing themselves that they cannot or will not break out of a habitual pattern.)

Figure 9–8. Performing and Acting. When the creation of character and the external-ization of the character's part in an action is less important than reaching the audience with immediacy and skill, *performing* becomes paramount. Here, it appears likely that the farcical tone and the broad style may have required considerable playing to the audience. *Trial by Jury* at the University of Minnesota *Centennial Showboat. (Directed by Frank M. Whiting, designs by Ann Erb and Deborah Bartlett.)*

Performing must not be confused with external or artificial acting. It is true that in the realistic theatre internal acting *seems* to be the reverse of performing. We may note, for example, the description of the pioneering Théâtre-Libre as having "a fourth wall, transparent to the audience, opaque to the actors," which is to say that it emphasized internal acting and discouraged performing. By contrast with such inner-oriented realistic acting, external or artificial acting may seem like performing because of its planned and deliberate gesture, its sometimes exaggerated vocal effects. External acting is still focused on communicating an idea of character in theatrical action; performing is not.

The performer plays *to* the audience; the actor plays the character *for* the audience.

Actor Training

Although there are supposedly actors who are "born," and although there have been young children who were talented actors, it is a fact of theatrical life that every actor must train long and hard and must refresh that training throughout his career. Even the great Helen Hayes noted that at twenty-one, she was a "little bag of tricks" and had to put herself through difficult study to emerge as an actress, although at twenty-one she was already famous and successful.

Actor training does not refer to a specific kind of study or to a set period of time. Acting is taught in hundreds of colleges and universities, for example, and degrees in acting are granted by many of them, but the chronological length of such programs and the granting of degrees does not mean that the actors are through training when the degrees are given. In the final analysis, every actor's training is special to him or her, and its length will be different from the training periods of other actors.

There are a number of actor-training systems. The most influential in the United States and Canada are those based on the ideas of Konstantin Stanislavski (see p. 148). Other systems in use have very different foundations, such as the psychological theory of transactional analysis, the theatre games and improvisations of Viola Spolin, and the rigorous religiosity of Jerzy Grotowski. Different as all these are, they are helpful in varying degrees to different actors. *No one system is best for everybody.* The important thing about these systems is that they organize the work of the actor's consciousness, instrument, and imagination. Without a workable system, the would-be actor makes progress only randomly, repeating mistakes and often making his bad habits worse. With a workable system, the actor finds the way out of this self-destructive cycle.

A good system trains all three parts of the actor and enables him to act to the fullest extent of his potential. A poor system neglects one or even two parts of the actor and cripples him accordingly.

Preliminary Training

There was a time when would-be actors "came up" through a provincial and repertory system, moving from small roles in minor companies to larger roles and more important theatres. They learned by imitation and they learned by taking hints from experienced actors. Nowadays most professional actors have had formal training, either in a college or in one or more private studios. Each such institution uses a system, but most of them require some kind of preliminary training. Many young actors have trouble recognizing this preliminary work as part of acting, although it is essential. (In a college, such work would usually come in the freshman year.) Without it, most actors would not succeed. Partly, it is a process of *un*learning mistaken notions and bad habits, and partly it is a process of training mind and body to adapt to the conditions of the theatre instead of the conditions of life (by learning, for example, that behavior that is considered ridiculous in life is sometimes essential in rehearsal and performance.)

It is usually thought to be unwise for beginning actors to go directly into the rehearsal and performance of plays or parts of plays—so-called scene work. Instead they are given preliminary training in the following areas.

Relaxation. Surprisingly many people who want to learn to act are so tense that they are quite literally unable to act; that is, muscle tension inhibits or totally prohibits any creative use of the instrument. Physical tension causes sudden, random, or pathological movement (shaking, trembling) and dangerous misuse of the vocal mechanism. The tense actor may think of himself as *in*tense and not tense, and without training he has no way of telling the difference. He will see himself as "really into" a role, when his teacher or his audience will see nervous, confusing, and uncontrolled movement.

Relaxation exercises cover a broad range from disciplines as different as modern dance and Yoga. All are intended to cause the consciousness to let go of the body, to return it to its natural state of receptiveness and awareness, and to make the body itself supple and loose.

Contact or Awareness. The relaxed body, freed from the tyranny of tension, becomes aware of itself and its environment. The consciousness no longer hurries it along toward some rigid goal; it has time, as it were, to stop and enjoy the scenery (including its own internal scenery). The coming and going of the breath, the comfortable positions of the body in standing, sitting, kneeling, and lying, the sense of the nearness and farness of objects and people—these things and many more can be explored. Sensory awareness is raised, and exercises are given that can be repeated (throughout the actor's life, if necessary) to maintain or renew that awareness.

Contact with others can also be taught at this stage so that the beginning actor learns to relate to the other people working with him, to help them and to accept the help that they offer him or her. The accepting of such help is, perhaps surprisingly, very difficult for many beginners, probably because not asking for or accepting help is a habit brought in from life. Most of us are taught to be "self-reliant" and "independent," and our society prizes these qualities. However, the *self*-reliant actor is a menace. *Taking* and *giving* are the bases of good performance.

An early exercise in contact is the "mirror game." Facing a partner, the actor copies the other's simple gestures and expressions as if he were the reflection in a mirror. On command from teacher or coach, the two switch roles, the leader now becoming the mirror. The beginner quickly learns to copy accurately and simply (to accept help) and to perform gestures that can be easily copied (to offer help). The exercise is one that even experienced actors can use to break down personal barriers.

Centering. Many disciplines, among them Eastern meditative religions and some schools of modern dance, emphasize exercises that focus on a bodily center—a core of balance and physical alignment, a place from which all movement and energy seem to spring. This idea of a center concerns both the body (balance, weight, placement) and the voice (breathing, sound making). In Yoga, the abdomen below the diaphragm is such a center; in the dance of Martha Graham, the center is slightly above the pelvis.

Centering for the actor is "a unity of *energy source/energy flow,*" according to Robert L. Benedetti *(The Actor at Work).* The "feeling of centeredness is

Figure 9–9. Contact and Concentration. Sharing with other actors and with the audience is vital to the actor. *The Imaginary Invalid* as performed by the Clarence Brown Company at the University of Tennessee. *(Directed by Julian Forrester, designs by Robert Cothran and Marianne Custer. Photo by Jonathan Daniel.)*

a *total* experience of the *total* self." Such a statement should probably be taken metaphorically, not literally. Centering leads the beginning actor away from the mistaken idea that the physical self is located in the head and face, that the voice is located in the mouth and the throat, and that the physical relationship to the rest of the world is located, through gravity, in the feet; rather, the actor finds his center somewhere near the crossing point of an X of arms and legs—a center of gravity, a center of balance, a center of diaphragmatic breathing.

Play. Dramas are "plays"; actors are "players." Yet, when a well-meaning beginner begins to act, he is often anything but playful. A terrible intensity and a terrible seriousness rule the work. To counter this tendency, much of early training is spent reteaching people how to play, in the sense both of teaching them to play games and in the sense of teaching them to approach the creative act joyously, in the way that the poet Yeats said that even tragedy was "gay." Because children often have this sense of playful theatricality in their own pastimes ("Let's pretend"), many theatre games are versions of children's games or of adult "parlor" games that are noncompetitive fun. Competitive games are poor, even counterproductive for such exercises, because competition tends to emphasize ego and to divide, rather than unify, the members of a group.

Kinds of games would include *act-and-guess* games like charades, *let's pretend* games, and *join-in* games that involve the whole group—playing dodge ball with a nonexistent ball or making sandcastles or clay figures with nonexistent material.

Training the Instrument

"Stage movement" and "voice production for the stage" sound like titles of academic courses. They suggest that the subject matter can be learned and that then, like familiarity with Shakespeare's plays or a knowledge of the calculus, they can be forgotten or assimilated. In actuality, the training of the instrument is never such a brief process.

Both body and voice use complicated sets of muscles put into action by the brain, sometimes consciously, sometimes unconsciously and habitually (for example, few of us have to remember to breathe). The actor has to be made aware of the muscles being used; he has to improve the condition of the muscles; he has to unlearn or relearn or learn a new pattern of use of those muscles; he has to repeat such patterns so often that they, in turn, become habits; he has to learn precisely what muscular actions will produce what results (in terms of sound or movement), under what orders from the brain; he has to learn what combinations of orders and muscular sets will provide new, unusual, and effective sounds or movements. As well, he has to learn the "proper" application of certain kinds of voice (singing) and movement (fencing, dancing). Such a learning process takes years, and no single course in voice or movement is going to begin to approximate it.

Body and Movement. The actor's body need not be heavily muscled like an athlete's, but it should be flexible, strong, and responsive. Long, well-toned muscles are achieved through exercise; flexibility is attained through stretching, calisthenics, and practiced movements designed for that end. As with any physical activity, it must be maintained, for without proper exercise, muscles atrophy.

The actor would be in error if he tried to train like an athlete (one set of muscles would be developed at the expense of others); instead he wants *resistance to fatigue, quick responsiveness,* and *adaptive ability* (that is, the ability to imitate other kinds of posture and movement or adapt his own movement to, for example, aged posture and movement or the posture/movement of a body much heavier, and so on). In addition, the actor should learn the following:

1. *Body language and nonverbal communication.* We all express our emotional states and our basic psychic orientations through *body language,* with great emphasis on our *centering.* The actor, his own centering under control, learns how to "move" his physical center to match that of his character, for example, to embody that person whose center is always protected (by bent posture, folded arms, crossed legs when sitting, and so on) or the person who forces his center on the world (belly carried well in front of him, arms behind

Figure 9–10. The Trained Body. Especially when using masks, the actor must be able to express himself and to create theatrically with his body. *The Cat and the Moon* at the Project Arts Centre, Dublin, Ireland. *(Directed by James W. Flannery, masks and costumes by Nicole Kozekiewicz.)*

the back) and so on. The actor also learns how all of us communicate without words, through such simple gestures as the waving of a hand ("hello" or "come here" or "no thank you") to complex "statements" of posture and gesture that say things completely different from the words that pass our lips. Such training takes two forms: study of the subject (much of it still in the fields of psychology and anthropology) and application to his own body.

2. *Rhythmic movement.* Ballroom dancing, simple modern dance, disco dancing, and the like have the double advantage of being enjoyable and of helping the actor to move to an external rhythm. Such learning is adaptable to the more complex rhythms of his own voice and dramatic lines.

Figure 9–11. The Trained Body. This photograph will reward study of the actors' uses of their bodies to express situation and character, as well as to create an effective picture of their inter-relationships through line and gesture. The "closet" scene from *Hamlet* at the Stratford Shakespearean Festival, Canada, 1957. *(Christopher Plummer as Hamlet.)*

3. *Period movement and use of properties.* Historically accurate, and theatrically effective, use of fans, canes, swords, shawls—the list is endless.

4. *Movement in costume.* Theatrically effective movement and gesture in wigs, capes, hoop-skirts, boots—again, the list is a long one.

5. *Movement onstage.* Traditional interior settings do not have walls that meet at the same angles as rooms, and so stage furniture in such settings is rarely angled as real furniture is. As a result, "crosses" (movements from one point onstage to another) take unreal routes. On the proscenium stage, actors must learn to "curve" crosses so that they end up on a line parallel to the curtain line with another actor (in this way, neither winds up speaking upstage into an acoustical well). On thrust and arena stages, the actor learns to play to all of his audience, to adapt his posture and movements so that each section of the audience is treated fairly. Too, there are ways of bending, sitting, and standing that are appropriate to the stage in that they are not awkward or comical, although training in these "correct" ways of doing things is becoming more appropriate to training in period movement.

Voice Production. The human voice is a product of controlled muscular work (breathing and sound shaping in the mouth and throat) and chamber resonance (head and chest). Its shaping and control are not simple. Nonetheless, we make sounds and shape them all the time—only to find that our everyday sounds are inadequate for the theatre because they cannot be heard, they cannot be understood, and they are unpleasant. Unlearning and relearning are necessary for most actors.

The human voice is produced when air is forced over the *vocal folds* or *cords*, causing them to vibrate and to set a column of air vibrating, producing sound. This sound induces vibrations in *cavities* in the head and in *bones* in the head and chest. The sound is shaped in the throat and mouth, primarily with the *jaws* and *tongue* and is further shaped into the sounds we call words by: *initiation* of sound; *interruption* of sound by the interaction of lips, tongue, and teeth; and *placement* of sound through action of the lower jaw and of the tongue. Thus, for example, the two-letter word *it* is sounded by rather abruptly initiating sound with the lips and teeth parted, the tongue slightly arched but not touching the roof of the mouth to make the vowel sound, which may be extended at will (an important element of any word to the actor); the consonant *t* is made by ending the sound and simultaneously touching the tip of the tongue to the roof of the mouth and then moving it rapidly forward toward the teeth. The consonant *t* sound is "unvocalized"; its vocalized sibling is *d,* which is made in the same way, but with throat-produced sound continued until the tongue releases from the roof of the mouth. (Other such vocalized/unvocalized pairs are *v* and *f, g* and *k.*) To the actor, the process of producing the word *it* is not a casual matter but is one of primary importance, and he must train and train to develop the muscular control to *initiate* sound at precisely the desired moment, *maintain* it at the desired, regular pitch for the desired length of time, and end it crisply with tongue, jaw, and lip muscles. Further control will allow him to exaggerate or dampen the potentially explosive consonant, creating an affected aftersound with the *t* ("it-tuh") or even to end the sound without recourse to tongue movement, cutting it off in the throat with the "glottal stop" (familiar from dialect pronunciation of a word like *bottle,* which comes out as "bo-//-le").

The actor trains his vocal mechanism for maximum control of *every word that is uttered,* as well as for production of sounds that are not "words."

Other voice and voice production training covers:

1. *Breath Control.* The principal source of the pressure that pushes air over the vocal folds is the *diaphragm,* a large muscle curved up under the lungs. When it flattens (downward), air is pulled in; when it releases (upward), air is pushed out. Lesser muscles along the ribs and upper chest are not so important to proper breathing; many untrained people, however, are "chest breathers" whose diaphragms are little used. Chest breathing, without effective use of the diaphragm, limits capacity and control and, under the stress of making loud and extended sounds in a theatre, often tenses muscles and transmits that tension into the throat. *Diaphragmatic breathing* is as essential for the actor as for the singer. It gives him increased

capacity and maximum control. A training exercise and a diagnostic one for use of the diaphragm is to sound a given note and to hold it for an extended time—ten to fifteen seconds, for example—and to do so without any wavering of pitch or intensity. This can be done up and down the scale at greatly varying intensities.

2. *Throat relaxation.* Tightness in the throat and lower jaw are a source of common and severe voice problems. Muscular tightness there "chokes" the sound, restricting the vocal folds and closing up resonating chambers. The actor learns to produce enormous volumes of sound without ever allowing the muscular effort in voice production to affect throat and jaw at all.

3. *Tongue and lip dexterity.* "Lazy tongue" is a common ailment; it produces slurred consonants and sloppy speech. Tongue twisters and other exercises tone the muscles and force the actor to listen to the sounds he makes.

4. *Sound placement.* Like singers, actors learn to "aim" sound at different resonating elements in their heads. Sounds may be more or less nasalized; they may make more or less use of deep "chest resonance."

5. *Correction of habits and defects.* Few actors come to training without vocal defects. Early diagnosis is essential. Some of the problems that are discovered will be the result of habit or acculturation: nasality, regional accents, lazy tongue. Some will be peculiar to the actor's body: adenoids (which cause denasalized sound), poor dental structure (lateral lisp), vocal nodes (hoarseness of voice). Each case must be treated individually, and in extreme cases, medical advice and care may be needed.

6. *Dialects.* The idea of a "stage speech" that is radically different from "standard English" is disappearing, and the day of the actor who talks like an English nobleman is past. Nonetheless close and accurate knowledge of the way that different ethnic groups speak is essential. Untrained actors have remarkably vague ideas of what southern or midwestern American speech is like, not to mention the affects on American English of a French, German, Scandinavian, or East Indian accent. In learning the specific characteristics of each variety of speech, the actor will probably make use of the *phonetic alphabet,* a system for recording sounds rather than spellings.

Training the Imagination

Perhaps the word *training* is slightly inaccurate here. The actor goes through a process in a training atmosphere and is *encouraged* to discover and remain aware of his own imagination. Whether or not the imagination itself can be "trained" remains open to question, and many psychological data suggest that what we have called *imagination* is a capacity of the brain and the mental/emotional self that is always at work but that rarely surfaces. Still, if one can teach the rational brain mathematics, perhaps one can teach the nonrational brain imagination. Most certainly, one can try to encourage the nonrational brain to speak up and make itself heard.

Creative Exercise. In the belief that we all have imaginations and that we are all "creative" (as children are creative), we devise exercises for the

Figure 9–12. Imagination and Instrument. Seated, center, the actor William Hutt as Lady Bracknell in *The Importance of Being Earnest.* Such a performance as this one is a consummate example of the actor's art, of the work of imagination through the instrument, of the climax of years of training, of the artful blend of acting and performing. Others pictured are Nicholas Pennell as John Worthing, Tom Kneebone as Rev. Chasuble, Pat Galloway as Gwendolen Fairfax. Foreground: Richard Monette as Algernon Moncrieff, Marti Maraden as Cecily Cardew. *(Photo by Robert C. Ragsdale, F.R.P.S., courtesy of the Stratford Shakespearean Festival, Canada, at the Stratford Festival's Third Stage in 1975.)*

actor that will free him from both the conscious embarrassment of being "sensitive" and from the unconscious inhibition of the nonrational. There are several ways to do this; two that readily suggest themselves are to send the actor's mind to those places where we know he is or has been in contact with his imaginative self: his dreams and his childhood. Writing down dreams as a regular part of his daily preparation is remarkably helpful to many, especially those who insist that they "never dream" or "dream nothing interesting." The very fact of causing themselves to remember and write down dreams leads to an acceptance of the idea of dreaming and hence to a greater willingness to "listen to" their dreams. Dreams are vibrant proof of the ability of our minds to imagine, for they are made up of images, metaphors, and puns; they are often playful in their structure and their language; and they have both content and form that our rational minds would never think of. Because they are so close to the psychological heart of the dreamer, however, they represent a ready danger. An instructor who insists on analyzing the actors' dreams is invading privacy and may be endangering psychological health. *The object of dream exercises is to make the actor aware of his imaginative potential, not to probe his inner self.*

Childhood memory can be turned to good account in the same way. Student actors are asked to take a comfortable, neutral position, usually lying down—the Yoga's "dead man" position is a good one—and to begin to remember a pleasant (sometimes an unpleasant) childhood experience. Piece by piece, they are told to particularize the memory—to remember what they wore, what the air was like, what the sounds were. Although this is an exercise in memory, it becomes an exercise in imagination as the actor finds how much detail the mind is capable of holding and of using. A variation of this exercise is to have the student elaborate on a memory of a childhood fantasy or game—its participants, its "costumes," its plot, its literal and its fictional setting, and so on.

Other exercises in sensitivity or creativity use group participation in building a story or a moment. Lying again in relaxed and neutral positions, the group develop a story, usually around a beginning sentence like "There was a woman who lived by the sea whose name was . . ." Each actor in turn builds on the story. It is of utmost importance that no member of the group be allowed to protect himself through nonparticipation expressed by laughter or by additions to the story that are silly or sarcastic. It is for precisely this kind of exercise that all student actors will earlier have gone through work in relaxation and contact, so that they will have shucked off the tendency toward nonparticipation that is the nonactor's approach to imaginative effort.

Image Exercises. The creative mind probably works, at least a good deal of the time, in images rather than in words (although many words are themselves images). Image exercises encourage the actor to grasp the mental pictures that part of his brain offers to him. The parlor game—also a psychological testing device—in which each one writes down "the first thing that comes into his head" after a word is said or a picture is shown is useful. At a more sophisticated level, simple character-creation around pictures, objects, or sounds can be beneficial. An actor is given an object and told to perform a related character for the group. For example, a knife is set out; the actor bends forward, walks with difficulty, his body held to protect its center greedily. Why? From knife, the actor went to "sharp," sharp in business, a miser; he added the element of "a cutting wind" that he had to struggle against. (Note that this is not an exercise in storytelling. If the knife had suggested a murderer, the exercise would have been marginally successful, for here the association is not one of image but of literal use.)

Visualization. Again, group exercises are useful. In a relaxed and neutral position, members of a group build a scene as previously they had built a story. It is important that all *see* the scene as fully as possible; to do this, they must hold the scene in their minds in all its details. One may begin, "A lake, a summer's day," the next may add, "There are houses around the lake, with wooden docks sticking out into the water, people swimming from them," and so on. The group should go on until the picture is as complete as it can possibly be—sizes, shapes, numbers, colors—a totality. Such an exercise is useful in touching the actor's sense of creativity, in sharpening his concentration and sense of detail, and in preparing him for

Figure 9–13. Imagination and Instrument. Vigorous and effective use of the instrument comes from creative use of the imagination. *The Italian Straw Hat* as performed by the Acting Company. *(Bert Andrews Photo, courtesy of The Acting Company.)*

those times in rehearsal and performance when he must "see" for the audience:

> HORATIO: But look, the morn in russet mantel clad
> Walks o'er the dew of yon high eastward hill.

Sense Memory. Like the group storytelling, individual recounting of the "picture" around a memory encourages a sense of detail and of visual memory. As many senses as possible should be incorporated. Such memories need not come from childhood; they may come from the day before, even moments before. The purpose is to cause the actor to capture a sensory moment in all its fullness and, through both remembering it *and* recounting it, to cause him to be able to create such sensory reality around moments that come not from memory but from the theatre.

Improvisation. No single word and no single tool has been more used and misused in the last several decades than improvisation. Improvisation— the creation of quasi-theatrical characters or scenes or plays without the "givens" of drama—has been used to create theatre (without a playwright), to enlighten an actor about his character (the so-called etude, or improvisation based on material in a dramatic script), to structure theatre games, and to teach many aspects of acting. As a tool for training the imagination, it is an application of the techniques already mastered. In a sense, it is the basis of some of the other techniques; having an actor create a character around an image is such a use of improvisation. At this stage of actor training, it can be used to apply the imagination, to stimulate it, or to supply raw materials not within the actor's experience. (That is, an improvisation focused on a frightening event may help the actor who has never experienced fear to know it.)

In order to work at this level, however, improvisation must be kept simple and must be carefully focused by the instructor. At best, improvisations can quickly develop along unwanted lines, especially with actors who want to "tell stories" (create theatrically interesting situations); when that happens, there will probably be so many processes going on that the student actor will not understand what he is doing. For the purposes of the imagination, it may be enough to create, for example, a scene of the sort discussed under "Visualization" and then to have the group improvise their participation in the scene—feeling the air, wading into the water, setting up a picnic on the beach. To do more risks complete loss of the imagined setting and a departure into other areas altogether.

When all this is said, however, we have to remember that there are people for whom imagination exercises are not very stimulating. To say that they will never be good actors would be incorrect. To say that they may have trouble—lots of trouble—with some aspects of acting would probably be accurate. There will always be those who respond like the woman in *A Chorus Line* who sings the song about such exercises in her acting class— "And I felt nothing."

Training the Consciousness

Certain areas of the actor's conscious work can be taught through example and through guided participation in production work. These include discipline, concentration, theatrical analysis, observation, and script analysis.

Discipline. Some things are so simple and obvious that beginning actors seem not to think of them. Ideally, the actor is *prompt;* when a rehearsal is called for seven-thirty, he shows up no later than that time. The actor is *alert* and *ready to work;* he gets enough sleep, avoids alcohol and drugs when working, and comes in a frame of mind and a set of clothes that will permit maximum work. The actor *prepares;* he does not forget the script, does not forget a pencil with which to make notes; he has done whatever homework on the play has been requested. The actor is *constructive,* not destructive; he does not make comments about other actors, does not break out of character while another actor is working, does not indicate in any way that another actor's experiment with a character is wrong or comical or foolish. The actor is *respectful;* he talks to the director about problems, not to other actors or the costume designer or the playwright.

Concentration. The habit of concentration comes from work. In many cases, student actors whose acquaintance with mental work has been limited

Figure 9–14. The Star. Leading actors who performed a starring role with stock companies, which they visited only long enough to perform, often acted in a kind of isolation. Abuses of the system led to a loss of contact, a lack of spontaneity and variety, sometimes the suppression of the most important creative elements of acting. Here, the great French actress Sarah Bernhardt as L'Aiglon.

to the classroom will have difficulty at first with the level of concentration that is needed. Not only the length of time but also the depth of the concentration that is required may seem unreasonable. Yet it is only through remarkable efforts of concentration that progress is made. An actor who cannot attain such concentration may need to return to exercise in relaxation and contact; he may need to find what is distracting the mind. Where a severe problem continues to exist, there may be a psychological difficulty that a nontheatrical expert will be needed to resolve.

Theatrical Analysis. It should be a goal of the actor's training to make him aware of his place in the theatre in each production he undertakes. This does not mean merely that the actor must understand his role; it means that the actor must grasp how he relates to the entire complex of the performance, including:

1. *Spatial understanding,* which includes the actor's awareness of each setting in which he appears, its shapes and proportions, as well as an understanding

of the relationship of the setting to the size and shape of the theatre and its audience. To reach this goal, actors in many theatre training programs are required to study design, lighting, and costume and to work on productions in nonacting jobs.

2. *Research resources,* for which the best preparation is usually a study of the history of the theatre. His own knowledge will then become a resource, and formal study in this discipline will include a working knowledge of resources in the field.

3. *Dramatic appreciation,* for which the best preparation is usually a study of dramatic literature and a broad reading in the field. Formal courses in criticism are probably less valuable, except for the very advanced student, who is less likely to get bogged down in intellectual processes. Every actor should be expected to know the classics of each period and to know how he relates to roles in those plays.

Observation. As distinct from imagination and visualization, *observation* is a conscious perceiving and recording of sensory data. For the actor's purpose, it is limited mostly to the seen and the heard. Observation can be taught through a variety of devices that require attention to detail, such as talking through or writing highly detailed descriptions of objects (a specific chair, a dead fish). It can be encouraged by requiring the keeping of a notebook with daily or weekly entries of sounds and sights (people). The goal is to cause the actor to build a "library" of people upon which he can draw in building character.

Observation is one of the two sources of character externals; imagination is the other. Insofar as the actor wants to be authentic or truthful in his externals, observation is of huge importance. Perhaps surprisingly, relatively few beginning actors make much use of it, however. They seem to believe naively that creativity and the imitation of real people are opposed.

Script Analysis. The dramatic script is the foundation of the actor's work. It is his starting point and the point to which he returns. *Imagination* and *instrument* are the means through which he bodies forth the character on the stage, but it is the playscript that inspires and shapes their work.

Training in script analysis has three principal goals:

1. *An understanding of the entire drama.* On his first reading, the actor will be making judgments and sorting out impressions from the time the first page is turned. Because he is trained in the theatre, the actor will read the script more appreciatively as a "notation" for a performance than an untrained person would; the potential for production will be grasped, at least in part. Likes and dislikes (sometimes vague ones) will form. An awareness of the play's *totality* will take shape. Of particular importance to the actor on first reading will be the *style* of the play, its main *impact* on its audience, and its overall *shape.* Under style, he will understand the degree of abstraction of the script; the kind of language, whether poetic or mundane; and the historical period. The *impact* will be comic or serious and will be expressed most importantly through language or action, through idea or spectacle. The *shape* will describe the play's gross structure and its overall rhythms,

Figure 9–15. **Understanding through Analysis.** Each actor functions best by analyzing and understanding the entire play, not merely his own role; from that understanding comes group, or ensemble, playing. *Charley's Aunt* at the University of South Carolina. *(Directed by James A. Patterson.)*

whether it builds slowly or quickly to climaxes, whether it relaxes gradually from them or drops abruptly. This first contact with the totality of the play will also give the actor a first indication of what demands it will put on its actors—the size of the cast, special requirements of their instruments, the size of the major roles, the relative degree of intensity of the emotions to be embodied.

2. *An understanding of the place of the character in the whole drama.* A first reading will give the sensitive and trained actor a sense of the play; a second reading may be needed to begin to illuminate the function of his own character. By *function,* we mean the way in which the character contributes to the action. The actor must be trained to resist one question—*What makes my character stand out?*—and to ask another one instead—*How does my character contribute to the whole?* We have already pointed out that a critical judgment of character tries to assess precisely how successful the function of a character is; the actor, although not a trained critic, must also grasp this point. He may not express it in the same way, however; the actor thinks of performance and is likely to answer the question in terms of "ensemble," the acting together of the cast. *How does my performance fit into the performance of the entire cast?* may be the actor's way of asking the critic's question. It is a large question, because it takes into account the physicalization of all the roles and the rhythms of performance.

The actor must be trained to note what happens while his character is absent from the action. Dramatic action means change; when a character is offstage, changes are taking place, and when the character returns, those

Figure 9–16. Playing the Character. Stacy Keach as Buffalo Bill in *Indians* at the Arena Stage, Washington, D.C. *(Roland L. Freeman photo.)*

changes must be noted. The actor must, in his reading, learn to balance two lines of development, his own and the play's. He must never make the egotistical mistake of thinking that because he is not on, nothing worth noting is taking place. (There is an apocryphal story told of an English actress who never learned how Shakespeare's *Macbeth* ended, because she always played Lady Macbeth—who died before the play was over.)

3. *An understanding of the details that comprise the character.* As he reads the play again and again, not only a deeper understanding of the play and the character's part in it emerges but also a more and more detailed sense of just what the character is. The actor is trained to keep a notebook in which ideas about the character are written down, as well as all those things in the script that indicate the nature of the character. These include:

What the character does. We have called this the character's *function* in the dramatic action.

What the character decides. Decision illuminates character; in most plays, *nothing* is done without reason, and each reason for action is represented by a decision or choice. In a sense, dramatic character is a sum total of choices.

What is said about the character. The other characters often talk about the actor's character. In *Hamlet,* Polonius says that Hamlet is mad; in Eugene O'Neill's *Long Day's Journey into Night,* the mother says that her son Edmund was "always frightened." The actor must take careful note of such statements and judge their truth or falsity. Is Polonius a good judge of madness? Does the mother have a reason for wanting to pretend that her son is a coward? The actor will make tentative decisions about such matters, but their real resolution lies in the give-and-take of rehearsal and in conferences with the director.

What the character says about himself. Many characters talk about themselves. At the very opening of Chekhov's *The Seagull,* one character says to Masha, a young woman, "Why do you always wear black?" She replies, "Because I am in mourning for my life." What an enormous line for an actor to deliver! Not only is it a line weighted very heavily with meaning, but it also comes so early in the play—virtually at the curtain—that there can be no build to it. The actor must look at this piece of self-characterization very carefully, every bit as carefully as he would look at a line delivered by another character about Masha. Is she wrong about herself? Is she lying? Self-deluded? Crazy? Witty? What? The answers lie elsewhere in the play, among the other clues to character that the whole play provides.

What the playwright says about the character. Stage directions are not always very helpful to actors. Frequently they represent an after-the-fact description of how a given actor played a role in the initial production; sometimes they represent the playwright's ideal vision of the role. Most often, they do not take into account the particularization of character in a production. Actors are trained to read stage directions with skepticism, especially those that describe line readings ("sternly," "bitterly," "with emotion," and so on).

What behavioral traits are revealed. Behavioral traits are the specifics of character—the body language, the details of gestures and voice, the quirks. In Tennessee Williams's *Eccentricities of a Nightingale,* one character describes the "facial contortions" of Alma, the protagonist; another says that her voice has gone up "two octaves." These are not clues to deep character; they are clues to surface behavior. They are very useful to the actor in creating the character at the moments to which they apply.

It is essential for the actor, as for all other theatre makers, to look at the play in terms of its theatricality—artistic, sensory, intellectual, and human values. Such a breakdown will give him a grasp of the play's entirety and of its theatrical potential. It should not, however, dictate the actor's character. Grasping a play's idea, for example, must never suggest to the actor the reason for the character's existence, nor should the actor worry about how he might "play the idea," or, worse yet, how he might *be* the idea. The actor who says something like "In this play, I represent goodness," simply has not done the proper homework. Except in pure allegory, characters do not represent abstract ideas; they represent persons (who may embody or apply certain ideas).

In the same way, script analysis should teach the actor to avoid moral

Figure 9–17. The Actor's Life. Despite its occasional glamour and its professional satisfaction, the working actor's life is often hard. Travel, constant change, uncertainty, and the psychological demands of acting are among its problems. Here, the French actor Jodelet escaping a theatre fire, 1634.

value judgments. Characters in a play are not "good" or "bad" *to themselves.* Few real persons say, "I am a villain." The actor does not, then, play a villain; he plays the representation of a person whose actions may be judged, after the fact, as villainous—by others. Even as dangerous and damned a man as Claudius in *Hamlet* cannot productively be played as pure villain. In fact, his evil behavior takes on dramatic importance because he is convinced of its necessity; and later in the play, it takes on tragic weight as he admits, but cannot undo, his own guilt.

Put most simply, training in script analysis is training *to read.* It is training to understand what is *on the page*—not what might have been put on the page but was not, and not what the actor might prefer to find on the page. Script analysis deals with a very limited amount of information and tries to squeeze every drop from it; it neither invents nor guesses. Most of all, it requires that the actor read *every* word and understand it in clear detail;

from that clarity and that detail will come an objective understanding of the script that can be returned to again and again when acting problems arise.

After the actor learns to attend properly to the script and to understand what is there, he learns to apply the specific details of analysis that are peculiar to modern realistic acting, which continues to dominate the work of most American actors. Basically these are ideas originated or articulated by Konstantin Stanislavski, modified by the American Method and subsequent theories.

The actor is trained to analyze character for:

1. *Given circumstances.* These are the undeniable "givens" that the actor must accept: age, sex, state of health, social status, educational level, and so on. Often they are contained within the script, either in stage directions or in dialogue; sometimes they must be deduced or even invented. (How old is Hamlet? Was he a good scholar at the university? Is he physically strong or weak?)

2. *Motivation.* Realistic theatre believes in a world of connectedness and cause. All human actions in such a world are caused or motivated. To play a character in such a world, the actor looks for the motivation behind each action.

Some teachers have their students make notebooks for each character with a column in which a motivation can be noted after each line or each gesture. It is important that the student actor understand that, in this system, *all* behavior is motivated—every word, ever movement, every inflection. All action results from choice. "Not this, but that" was an expression used by Bertolt Brecht that has its uses even in non-Brechtian acting, because it helps the actor to understand that everything that his character does has a decision or a choice behind it. (Some choices or decisions may be defined by the actor as unconscious ones; he may then have the more difficult problem of embodying an unconscious motivation and a conscious substitute for it.)

3. *Objective.* Like motivation, the objective is part of a system of causality. It is the goal toward which an action strives. Motivation leads to action; action tries to lead to objective. The actual reaching of many objectives, however, is blocked. Often two characters will have mutually blocking objectives; when people say that "drama is conflict," they are describing such a situation.

4. *Superobjective.* "Life goal" might be an equivalent of the superobjective if a dramatic character were a real person. The superobjective must include all objectives pursued by a character and must exclude all improperly defined objectives. For example, we might say that Hamlet's superobjective is "to set the world right again"; his objective in the first scene with his father's ghost might be "to listen to this creature from Hell and put it to rest" (thus setting the world right by quieting the ghosts in it). In this case, the objective and the superobjective agree. If, however, the superobjective were defined as a Freudian "to take my father's place in the world," and the objective in the ghost scene were defined as "to listen to the ghost out of

love for my father," there would be a severe problem, and the two would have to be brought into sympathy. It is by defining the superobjective that the actor is able to check on the validity of all objectives.

Both the objective and the superobjective must be active. We have expressed them here as infinitives—"to set," "to listen"—but the actor does better to express them in active terms beginning with "I want," so that their strength and vitality are clearly visible to him.

5. *Through line.* If motivations and objectives are seen as beads, they can be strung on a through line that runs consistently through the character's entire presence in the play. The through line (sometimes called the *spine*) may also be seen as the line that runs through all objectives toward the superobjective. The actor learns to recognize that he has made an error in analysis when a motivated action does not fit on the through line. Such an action was what Stanislavski called a "tendency." It leads to poor acting because it takes the character away from pursuit of correct objectives and leaves him in a limbo of vagueness and contradiction, which an audience finds confusing and finally annoying. Much of what we call bad acting is, in fact, the playing of tendencies rather than the playing of a strong through line.

Only by careful study over an extended time does the actor learn to identify and work productively with motivation, objective, superobjective, and through line. Like all systems, this one can do more harm than good if it is improperly understood or if it is applied with a fanatical rigidity. Not too long ago, there was considerable resistance to this system by actors and directors trained in an older system that did not take causality so seriously (a conflict, in a sense, between an older "artificial" style and a newer "natural" one); older actors found Method actors overserious and sometimes difficult to work with. The story is told of a director who was working with a young Method actor who asked, "What's my motivation?" about every smallest thing he was asked to do. At last, the director, unable to stand it any longer, shouted, "Your job!"

Audition, Rehearsal, and Performance

The actor's training goes on long after he begins to take an active part in performance. Most actors continue to work on their instruments throughout their careers, and many return to professional workshops to refresh and sharpen their inner work. After the initial period of actor training, however—college, sometimes graduate school, an independent studio or teacher—the actor begins to look for roles and, having found one, begins the work of building and performing a character. Each step in the process has its special conditions, and for the professional actor, these steps will be repeated over and over throughout his life.

Audition

As a student, the actor is taught to develop audition materials. These are short scenes or monologues that best show his abilities. Although most auditions use scenes from the work to be performed, the actor is often asked if he wants to do something already prepared (on the theory that it will best show the actor's sense of his own strengths).

Most auditions are done for the director of the production. Usually the stage manager is there as well, along with someone representing the producer. A well-conducted audition takes place in a comfortable space where the actor can see the people for whom he is auditioning, where there are no acoustical problems, and where actor and director can talk conversationally, if necessary. Somebody should be there, as well, to read with the actor if a scene with another character is being read. (Usually, the stage manager does this.)

The most important things an actor can show in an audition are basic abilities and the capacity to work creatively with the director and other actors. One of the director's problems in auditions is to try to sort out the creative actors from the "radio actors"—those who have the knack of reading well on sight but who lack the ability to improve much beyond that reading. Thus cleverness in a first reading is not necessarily an advantage for the actor. What may count more is the capacity to work creatively and interpersonally, a capacity that the director may test for by asking actors to do simple improvisations, exercises, and games (like the "mirror" game and more complex ones) in which selfish, nonparticipating people can be spotted quickly.

Unfortunately auditions cannot always be a good indicator of how well an actor will perform, and they can have heartbreaking results. Imperfect as they are, however, auditions remain one of the most important elements of casting until a more objective, less flawed device is invented.

Rehearsal

Once cast, the actor begins to apply all that he has learned. Acquired discipline will, it is hoped, assure promptness, courtesy, respect for other actors and support of others' work. The instrument should be ready. Preliminary script analysis should be done, and the actor will undoubtedly arrive at the first rehearsal with many questions. It is one of the functions of the rehearsal process to answer those questions and to turn the answers into an exciting performance.

Trained and talented actors often work with surprising slowness. An outsider coming into a rehearsal after, let us say, two weeks of work might

Figure 9–19. Externals of Characterization. Costume and makeup can greatly help or inhibit the actor's creation of character. Two sketches of the actress Irene Vanbrugh in different roles. *(From the Collections of the University of Rochester Libraries.)*

well be dismayed by the apparent lack of progress that can be seen. Actors may still be reading some lines in flat voices, and, except for bursts of excitement, the play may seem dull and lifeless. This situation is in part intentional, however. Many actors "hold back" until they are sure that things are right. They do not want to waste energy on a temporary solution to a character problem. Temporary solutions have a way of taking on a life of their own: other actors become accustomed to hearing certain lines delivered in certain ways and to seeing certain movements and gestures; they begin to adapt their own characters to them. The actors begin to commit themselves to a pattern. To avoid this, many find it productive to withhold commitment for a good part of the rehearsal period. (Such slowness assumes, of course, a long rehearsal period. For much of educational theatre, which is on a strict schedule, as well as summer stock and repertory, short rehearsal periods and rigid calendars do not allow for delay.)

The actor experiments. Some of this experimenting is done away from the rehearsals; homework takes up a lot of the actor's time. Much of it takes place in rehearsals. Again and again, an actor will say, "May I try something?" Or the director will say, "Try it my way." *Try* is the important word—experiment, test. The good actor has to be willing to try things that may seem wrong, absurd, embarrassing. Because many acting problems cannot be solved by thinking or talking, he must be willing to solve them by doing.

Most importantly, the rehearsal period is a time for building with other actors. In a well-chosen group, nothing happens in isolation. Actors use the word *give* a lot: "You're not giving me enough to react to," or "Will it help you if I give you more to play against?" Such giving (and taking) symbolizes the group creation of most performance.

At some point during rehearsals, the creative and lucky actor may have a "breakthrough." This is the moment when the character snaps into focus. Motivations and actions that have been talked about and worked on for weeks may suddenly become clear and coherent. The breakthrough, like the second wind of the distance runner, may be partly a psychological trick, but its reality for the actor is very important: his creative imagination has made the necessary connections and has given usable instructions to the instrument. The character is formed.

The rehearsal period, then, is not merely a time of learning lines and repeating movement. It is a time of creative problem-solving, one in which the solving of one problem often results in the discovery of a new one. It is a time that requires give and take, patience, physical stamina, and determination. It frays nerves and wearies bodies. The intensity of the work may cause personal animosity. (For actors with good working methods, however, it is not necessary to like another actor to be able to work creatively with him.)

Most of all, the rehearsal period is the time when the actor joins with others to create. *The good actor creates a character; the outstanding actor creates a scene.*

Performance

For many actors, performance is the reward for the work of rehearsal. Others actually prefer rehearsal and find performance a necessary but less satisfying part of the process. In terms of creativity, it is, of course, best if the actor does not separate rehearsal from performance too strongly, although it is natural that the pressures of performance, because it is a public appearance subject to a very vocal judgment, cause some separation. Our society gives actors an overblown image of "opening night" and "being in the spotlight" that makes performance unnaturally stressful. Even worse, instant stardom (which can be followed by instant oblivion), rave reviews, the fantasy of the actor's name in lights, standing ovations—these are spin-offs of performing that do more to cripple young actors than to help them. Few actors, in fact, achieve stardom or standing ovations, and it is a sad mistake for any actor to think that such things are the only meaningful reward for performing.

Performance causes emotional and physical changes in the actor that are associated with stress. Some change, of course, is helpful; it gets the actor "up" so that his energies are at a peak, ready for the concentrated expenditure of energy that rehearsal has made possible. Too much stress,

Figure 9–20. Rehearsal and Performance. The prompter sat in his box at the front of the stage during nineteenth-century performances to help under-rehearsed actors—the antithesis of what the good actor aims for.

however, cripples the actor, and he may be afflicted by sleeplessness, headaches, diarrhea, and similar unpleasant symptoms. "Stage fright" and psychosomatic voice loss are very real problems for some. Ideally, good training and effective rehearsal will have turned the actor away from the root cause of stress (dependence on outside approval of his performance); where this does not happen, the actor may have to return to relaxation work or find outside therapeutic help to discover why he cannot cope with stress.

Opening nights raise energy levels because of stress and excitement. As a result, second nights are often dispirited and dull, because when the tension of opening is removed and the energy has been expended, a feeling of dullness, even of depression, often results. The wise actor expects this pattern. Again, preparation is a help—complete understanding of the role and the total performance, creative rehearsal work, open lines between consciousness and imagination. Before the second and subsequent performances, the prepared actor reviews his character work, goes over notes, reaffirms motivations and objectives. Never does he say, "Well, we got through the opening; the rest will take care of itself."

Once in performance in an extended run, the actor continues to be aware of a three-pronged responsibility: to himself; to the other actors; to the audience. Those responsibilities cannot end with the reading of the reviews.

In developing his system of acting, Stanislavski was interested both in actor training and in the problems of performance. His work cannot be viewed as merely a study of how the actor prepares; rather, it is also a prescription for the continuing refreshment of the performing actor. Stanislavski's own early performance was with the long runs of the commercial theatre, and it was to the problem of the extended run that he addressed himself. The result was a system that helps the actor to create what the English critic William Archer termed the "illusion of the first time" again and again. Put most simply, this means that the actor is able to capture the freshness and immediacy of the "first time" (both for his character and for his audience) by going back each time to the mental/emotional roots of the truthfulness of his performance—a process that is possible only if that performance is grounded in truth to begin with.

Continued performance for the trained actor, then, is not merely a matter of repeating rehearsed sounds and gestures night after night; it is a matter of returning to internally satisfying truths (motivations, objectives) and satisfyingly effective externalizations of them. Such a system may not be perfect, but it is far better than the repeated performance that grows tired and dull with repetition and that leaves the actor disliking both himself and the audience because of maddening boredom.

Finally, performance itself becomes a medium for the continuing creativity of the actor. He continues to shape character and scene. Audience response sometimes suggests where a performance is effective or poor, and the actor can work at correcting errors as the performance period continues.

The creation of a character must seem completed by opening night, and yet it is never truly finished.

The Personality of the Actor

The personality of men and women who act has been a source of fascination for centuries. The actor has long been seen as a special sort of person; even before the Romantic interest in odd and exotic individuals, actors were studied because of their ability to interpret human psychology and because of their apparent ability to balance both halves of the "paradox of the actor." Too, a number of traditions came to surround the acting profession, and if they were not always accurate, they came to seem accurate as actors themselves believed in them: "all actors have to be crazy"; "all actors are immoral"; "theatre men are homosexual"; "the theatre attracts misfits and oddballs"; "actors like to show off," and so on. Such ideas are no better than gossip until they are proven by objective standards, and for every

Figure 9–21. The Actor: Molière. Molière, because he was actor, playwright, manager and, in a sense, director, was a true "man of the theatre." He balanced the difficulties of the actor's life, but paid a great physical price for his work.

immoral actor, homosexual theatre person, and show-off, there is an opposite to disprove the stereotype. Nonetheless, some of these old ideas persist.

Because of a lack of hard data and the persistence of stereotypes, we cannot describe accurately the "personality of the actor." We might note the following, however:

The actor's profession puts him outside the mainstream of most lives because he works odd hours, works at a very high level of energy and concentration, and lives a life of extreme job and financial peril.

Part of the actor's reward is applause and other forms of audience approval, and a personality geared toward applause may be an insecure one— yet to face tryout after tryout, opening after opening, show after show after show takes stamina and a courage unknown to men and women in secure careers.

The actor's personal relationships are easily threatened by unusual hours, job insecurity, and the need to be able to move geographically on short notice.

Because his is a high-stress life, the actor is as subject to the allure of drugs and alcohol as the rest of the population, and perhaps more so.

The ability and desire to act, like all creative work, is "different," and the committed actor may be judged an outsider by the rest of society.

Thus, although we cannot draw a profile of a typical actor, we can point out some qualities that frequently occur. What must be clearly understood, however, is that the qualities that make a good actor—creativity, concentration, determination, stamina, access to the imagination, playfulness, the ability to cope with rejection, nonrational thinking, detailed emotional memory—should be kept separate from qualities that may appear because of the profession of acting and its stresses; in other words, the nature of the profession in our society may bring out behavior that is not typical of the art of acting but of our society's use of it. Thus the "personality of the actor" has to be a composite of those qualities that make up talent and those qualities that appear in response to the environment in which talent is used.

Acting History

Because we live in a time when realistic theatre is still dominant in the West, it is tempting for us to think that realistic acting is the culmination of a progression that began in the art's distant past. This idea will not stand up to close examination, however. The history of acting, like the history of the theatre itself, is a history of changes but not necessarily a progression. The Stanislavskian system has been productive for three quarters of a century, but before it was developed there were other systems that were equally useful for the actors of their times and that produced equally satisfying results for their audiences.

We do not know when acting began. That human beings have a mimetic or imitative urge is surely true; it is something that we share with many other animals. It is equally true that this mimetic urge is joined, in many primitive societies, to a desire to "body forth" natural forces in order to cause or to prevent certain natural events—rain, seasonal change, earthquake. But at what point this mimetic/ritualistic urge became historically an artistic one—at what point, that is, it was indulged for its own sake and not to accomplish an end—we do not know.

When, then, acting and actors were listed in historical records at the time of Thespis (c. 534 B.C.), the art of acting had probably already been in existence for some time and was already distant from its primitive roots in magic and ritual dance. And from that moment when history took note of it, acting began to take many forms; yet those forms varied between two poles we have already talked about: the artificial and the natural. Varieties of these two extremes could and can coexist in the same age, although, at any given moment, one or the other may dominate. Neither, as we have tried to show, is better than the other. Their historical fluctuations represent a tension within the art of the theatre and a tension between the theatre and the society of which it is a part.

Some of the important historical periods in which these changes can be seen are described in the following sections.

Ancient Greece and Rome

Just as the first important Western theatre was the Greek, so the first identifiable actors were those of Athens of the late sixth century B.C. The evidence of the plays and of archaeological remains tells us that Greek tragic actors were more "artificial" than "natural" for several reasons: they acted in masks; their costumes did not imitate real clothes but were abstract, almost priestly garments; women's roles were taken by men; the plays in which they appeared were highly conventionalized. It would appear that into the Hellenistic age, tragic acting grew increasingly abstract while comic acting became less so. Greek "new" comedy and Roman comedy became more imitative of real life, and data about acting suggest a shift in the same direction. Declamation became the tragic actor's keystone (rather than an imitation of natural speech), whereas the comic actor began to imitate types.

In some of the minor comic forms, however, comic acting took a somewhat different direction, becoming more rather than less abstract, and placing a strong emphasis on the grotesque rather than on the "real"; farce characters on vase paintings, for example, are shown with grotesque masks, oversized

Figure 9–22. Hellenistic Actors. *(Courtesy of the Metropolitan Museum of Art, Rogers Fund, 1903.)*

phalluses, and twisted bodies—all indicators of an abstract ("artificial") acting style that was, perhaps, more like our idea of what clowns do than of what comic actors do.

The Middle Ages

Early medieval theatre was liturgical—performed in the choir of the church in Latin, sung or chanted rather than spoken, fitted into the religious service, and always performed by men and boys. The acting, such as it was, must have been severely "artificial." Liturgical drama and liturgical acting continued on an abstract level throughout the medieval period; in the great civic pageant theatre, however, it appears that occasionally it was far more natural. God and his angels were "artificial," but some men and many devils were far less so. The devils, in particular, present an interesting contradiction. Although masked and fantastically costumed, and although representing nothing real in nature, they were frequently an imitation of human behaviors like greed, fear, and revenge. It was with the devils that medieval threatre gave an imitation of the seamier side of real life.

The Middle Ages generally lacked systematized acting or any strong sense of acting as an art, and the strong sense of artificiality about many roles may derive from the traditional aspect of the craft among untrained performers who "passed down" gestures, movements, and line readings almost as dogma.

Elizabethan England

Professional acting began to appear widely in the sixteenth century. It had its roots in medieval theatre but was strongly influenced by the Renaissance interest in oratory. Elizabethan acting was a strongly *vocal* art. Too, just as Elizabethan drama was influenced by the popularity of Roman models, so Elizabethan acting was probably influenced by an idea of how Roman plays must have been acted. The concept of "heroic" acting—absent in the Middle Ages—began to appear, and one of the important early Elizabethan tragic actors, Edward Alleyn, was evidently a powerfully vocal, physically rather stilted figure on the stage, yet one who could convincingly portray kings, villains, and divine madmen for his audience. This acting was comparatively "artificial"; that of his successor, Richard Burbage (who originated Shakespeare's Lear and Othello), was considered by his contemporaries more natural, although it is unlikely that he was "natural" in the modern meaning of that word. "Whatsoever is commendable in the grave Orator, is most exquisitely perfect in him," a contemporary wrote of such actors. "By his action he fortifies moral precepts with example, for what we see him personate, we think truly done before us. . . ."

Elizabethan comic acting can be seen as diverging into low and high comedy, the one clownish, the other playful, both artificial in that the use of the actor's instrument was dictated more by the demands of the stage than the demands of imitating life or society. Masks were not used; costumes were contemporary with the clothes of the audience, for the most part; boys played women's roles, but with an attention to mimetic detail probably unknown in the Middle Ages.

The Renaissance Commedia dell'Arte

The Italian comedy of the sixteenth and seventeenth centuries known as *commedia dell'arte* is one of the most fascinating to students of the theatre. Partly improvised, partly scripted, *commedia* often presented stories that centered on the *innamorati,* the young lovers. They were usually elegant in language and delivery, handsome to look at, images of upper-class love for the audience. Women played the female lovers and some became famous both as actresses and for their songs and verse. Around these only slightly abstract romantic figures, however, were a group of highly artificial gro-

Figure 9–23. Commedia Ac-tor. A Pantalone of the seventeenth century.

tesques who played in masks (the *innamorati* did not): old Pantalone, the bombastic Dottore, the cowardly but boastful Capitano, and a host of male and female tricksters, the *zanni*. Theatrical conditions encouraged artificiality: playing in masks; playing one role for a lifetime; developing comic "bits" and routines that were of value of themselves and could be used in many plays by many characters. This, then, is an example of a comic acting style that went strongly toward artifice, yet mixed with a much more natural style in the *innamorati*. This mixture of styles influenced the French playwright–actor Molière, in whose plays and in whose acting company the same dichotomy can be seen.

The Eighteenth-Century English Theatre

Women appeared on the English stage after 1660. By 1670, a very strong natural impetus had moved the acting of farce and comedy much farther toward the natural than Molière's acting of the same period. Tragic acting remained highly artificial, bounded by the rules of propriety that rather strictly dictated the use of the instrument. By the mid-eighteenth century, however, successive tragic actors began to diverge from this artificiality,

Figure 9–24. Eighteenth-Century Actress. The tragedienne Mrs. Yates as Electra.

none more than David Garrick. A contemporary wrote an account of his acting at a time when he was appearing with one of the stars of the old school, James Quin:

Quin presented himself . . . in a green velvet coat embroidered down the seams, an enormous full-bottomed periwig, rolled stockings, and high-heeled square toed shoes: with very little variation of cadence . . . accompanied by a sawing kind of action, which had more of the senate than of the stage in it, he rolled out his heroics with an air of dignified indifference . . . but when after long and eager expectation I first beheld little Garrick, then young and light and alive in every muscle and in every feature, come bounding on the stage . . . heavens, what a transition!—it seemed as if a whole century had been stept over in the transition of a single scene.

Yet, for all that it appeared to a contemporary that a great step had been taken, we have to remember that David Garrick's acting had its artificialities: he played Shakespeare in eighteenth-century costume; his movements were extreme and overstated, to judge from contemporary evidence. Yet Garrick best expressed the idea of natural man for the eighteenth-century audience, which was increasingly bourgeois, increasingly practical, and increasingly rational, and which was moving away from the aristocratic, snobbish proprieties of an earlier day.

The Romantic Theatre in England and America

If reason guided the eighteenth century, inspiration guided the Romantic early nineteenth century. If restrained utterance and idealized gesture were the models of the eighteenth century, passion in both voice and movement were the models of Romanticism. "From Nature doth emotion come," Wordsworth wrote; "Genius . . . finds in her His best and purest friend." The idea of "natural" man had changed radically, and natural acting changed to match it. No actor symbolized this shift more clearly than Edmund Kean (1787–1833), of whom the poet Coleridge said that watching him was "to read Shakespeare by flashes of lightning." Kean was passionate and "inspired": "Kean's face is full of light and shade, his tones vary, his voice trembles, his eye glistens, sometimes with withering scorn, sometimes with a tear. . . . Kean we never see without being moved, and moved too in fifty ways—by his sarcasm, his sweetness, his pathos, his exceeding grace, his gallant levity, his measureless dignity." The essayist William Hazlitt said of Kean's Richard III, "His pauses are twice as long as they were, and the rapidity with which he hurries over other parts of the dialogue is twice as great as it was. In both these points, his style of acting always bordered on the very verge of extravagance . . . Mr. Kean's *bye-play* is certainly one of his greatest excellences."

In America during the same period, major actors displayed the same tendencies, causing Walt Whitman to warn against imitators of the style:

We allude to the loud mouthed ranting style—the tearing of everything to shivers. . . . It does in such cases truly seem as if some of Nature's journeymen had made men, and not made them well—they imitate humanity so abominably. They take every occasion . . . to try the extremest strength of their lungs. . . . If they have to enact passion, they do so by all kinds of unnatural and violent jerks, swings, screwing of the nerves of the face, rolling of the eyes, and so on. . . . For there is something in real nature which comes home to the "business and bosoms" of all men.

But Whitman was speaking for an age that was growing increasingly practical-minded and grounded in contemplation of itself rather than of ideals, either rational or Romantic; the burgeoning industrial age would find the "natural" acting of Kean artificial in the extreme.

Modern Realistic Acting

The industrial age that followed the enormous technological advances of the early nineteenth century not only altered the idea of human nature yet again, but it also gravely changed the role in society of the theatre itself. The mind of the industrial age focused on function: people, ideas, or institutions without function were immoral and indefensible. The function of art was to reproduce the real world in order to hold it up for examination (and, presumably, for betterment). As a result, the function of acting became the literal reproduction of mannerisms and behaviors of industrial-age men and women.

The principal theorist of this new and aggressive step toward the natural was Konstantin Stanislavski. As we have seen, Stanislavski's acting system emphasized causality and connectedness (motivation and objective) and literal imitation of behaviors (given circumstances, sense and emotional mem-

Figure 9–25. American Realistic Acting. Before Stanislavski and the American "Method," American acting was "natural" in a way that we no longer recognize.

ory). Motivational psychology—itself a product of the industrial age—became the keystone of acting; inspiration was thrown out. The results were, in their way, brilliant. Stanislavski's genius is unassailable. He has influenced actors as superb as Laurence Olivier and Marlon Brando. For as long as the audience wanted to see its own world held up for examination, this modern natural style predominated—and it has lasted a comparatively long time. No truly artificial acting style has survived along with it, except in a museum atmosphere—Neoclassical comedy and tragedy at the Comédie Française, the Japanese Kabuki and No theatres, traditional opera.

With a shift away from industrial-age values, however, we find a tendency to move away from the natural in acting. The ideas of Bertolt Brecht on the one hand and of Jerzy Grotowski on the other have given impetus to widely different kinds of acting, but kinds of acting that have a common bond in their rejection of the natural and their thrust toward artificiality. It is pointless to discuss whether these developments are good or bad; the important thing is that they are happening. The age-old tension between the artificial and the natural continues and will continue long after any of these practices has been discarded.

CHAPTER 10

The Director

The director is a relative newcomer in the theatre. To be sure, there have always been people who have exercised a strong, central influence on productions, but in the sense that the word has been used for the last hundred years, *directing* is a phenomenon of the nineteenth and twentieth centuries.

If we look at the period when this practice began and flourished, we may be able to deduce what its importance is and why it appeared at that time; that is, we may be able to deduce something about directing by recognizing that it appeared when illusionism became important in the theatre and when industrialism was important in Western society. The era of the director is also the era of the pictorial illusionist and of the industrial manager, and we may deduce that directing is concerned with illusionism and picture making, and with management and organization, in a way or ways that had not concerned the theatre before.

Directing, like any artistic practice, has changed since its beginnings. Directing may continue to change, but we cannot say with any certainty in what direction; what we can say is that a hundred years after his first important appearance, the director is the dominant figure in theatrical production.

A few theatres now function without directors, most notably those organized around cooperative or communal principles (see pp. 99–102). With

Figure 10–1. The Emergence of Directing. As a separate part of performance, directing is a relative newcomer. This is a fairly early (1898) example of the work of the director on the English stage—*Julius Caesar* in London.

those exceptions, however, theatres at every level now have directors: in high schools and colleges, it is the director who organizes and oversees all productions; in many community theatres, it is the director who oversees the selection and mounting of plays, and it is a director who is the paid professional on the staff, with a paid business manager or technical director; and in the professional theatre, in Europe as in North America, it is the director whose stamp goes most clearly on every production.

Filmmakers talk of the *auteur* theory of film—that is, the idea that a film is dominated by a single intelligence, its director's. The concept is true of much of our theatre, as well. Where a single figure stands out, it is not usually the actor or playwright or designer who will be that figure, but the director. In essence, the director now does things that were either done by several people before the modern period or were not done at all. Put more briefly, it may be said that what the director does is to *unify*. Thus, if a single difference could be noted between a modern and an older performance, all question of styles aside, it would be this binding of all the elements of performance into a unity—a unity of meaning in the interpretation, a unity of visual effect in the designs and staging, and so on. Because of our way of looking at things, we tend to see this unity as desirable and even inevitable, and we would find the *pluralism* (multiplicity of effects) of an older performance confusing or even comical. A theatregoer in another age, however, would accept pluralism as quite natural to the theatre and he might find modern directorial unity puzzling, or even oversimple and boring.

The Function of the Director

The director unifies within two main categories, *interpretation* and *presentation.* By *interpretation,* we mean not only the analysis of the dramatic text but also the evaluation of the nature of the audience and the assessment of the abilities and potentials of the other theatre artists. By *presentation,* we mean the whole process of embodying the interpretation in the form that will be most effective for the audience. The director, then, is the crucial person who stands between the theatre's potential and the audience's enjoyment; the director is the person who is most responsible for realizing that potential.

Before the appearance of the director, interpretation was done by the other theatre artists themselves: the dramatic text by the playwright, the roles by the actors, the scenes and spectacle by a painter or machinist. Presen-

Figure 10–2. The Undirected Actor. Before the nineteenth century, other theatre artists did much of what we now call directing. Leading actors often "directed" themselves, or worked in relative isolation against a background of minor actors.

tation was done by actors and technicians who were organized by a manager or a theatre owner or patent holder, but without that artistic unity that we now almost take for granted; that is, there was always somebody to "put the show together," but in the eras before the director appeared, that someone was a businessman or a religious or civic leader (as in classical Greece or medieval Europe), and the goal was not aesthetic unity but efficiency. Of course there were people in those earlier eras who selected plays, cast the actors, rehearsed them, and made sure that everything was ready by opening night (or day); however, those jobs were often parceled out among several people, and none of them was profoundly concerned with making the finished product all of a piece. To cite a single historical example: when members of the French court visited Dover, England, in 1670, both of the companies presented plays. For the occasion, the plays were newly costumed with expensive clothes donated by the English king and members of the nobility. The two licensee–managers of the English companies made sure that the plays went well and that the actors were sober, well rehearsed, and properly cast, but so far as we know, not the slightest thought was given to integrating the color, cut, and sumptuousness of those costumes into some overall interpretation of the plays and the performances. If there was any attempt at unity, it was a unity of *the occasion*—the best actors in their best plays in the best costumes that could be provided—and in no sense a unity of meaning or of illusion.

In doing the jobs that formerly may have been done by many people, as well as in doing a job that had only rarely been done before—unifying the performance—the modern director finds that he must be effective in more than one area. Of primary importance are skill in *organization, human relations,* and *decision making.* Organization includes the director's ability to put his own ideas into order and to combine them with the ideas of other people, as well as the ability to order rehearsals, schedules, and budgets; human relations includes both the ability to inspire other artists and the ability to work directly with people of quite different kinds, imposing his own wishes only when absolutely necessary and working creatively with other people on group solutions to complicated problems; and decision making requires the clear-headedness to define problems and to see the conditions under which they must be solved (including limitations of budget, time, available talent, and so on) as well as the self-knowledge that will allow him to make decisions (or postpone certain decisions) under often stressful conditions. To put these skills to greatest effective use, the director needs *stamina* and *concentration* as well as artistic talent.

In some theatre organizations, of course, some of the director's jobs are done by another person, especially in the professional theatre. Most likely, business matters will fall to a business manager or producer in this situation, while artistic matters will belong to the director; however, as one moves away from the high-powered organization of Broadway, more and more responsibilities fall into the director's lap, until, in many community, school, and university theatres, it is safe to assume that the director is aware of and actively engaged in every aspect of production.

The following, then, will comprise the director's functions and responsi-

Figure 10–3. The Directed Production. This photograph of Chekhov's *Three Sisters* at Wayne State University shows many signs of the director's work, in an overall consistency, in picturization and composition, and in textual interpretation. *(Directed by Joan Hackett, designs by Russ Smith, James R. Essen, and Audley Grossman, Jr.)*

bilities: The *artistic* functions of (1) script selection or approval (including work with the playwright on an original script); (2) script interpretation; (3) design approval and coordination (sets, lighting, sound, and costumes); (4) actor coaching; and (5) staging (including pictorial creation, orchestration of voices, stage movement, and performance rhythm), as well as the *managerial* functions of (1) production coordination and planning; (2) casting; (3) rehearsal scheduling and conduct; (4) performance coordination, including timing; and (5) liaison among management, actors, and designers.

Play Selection

Directors in community, school, and university theatres most often select the plays they direct; in the professional theatre, they at least approve the scripts (if they are staff directors) or find themselves "matched" to a new play by a producer. Never, if it is at all possible, does a director take on the task of directing a play he does not like. The demands are too great, the depth of involvement too extreme; the dislike would ruin the production.

Directors choose to do plays because the plays excite them. Of the elements of theatre, idea and spectacle are probably the most common ones to prompt directorial interest. Ego certainly enters in, as does the desire to exercise his own artistry. However, if theatrical elements conflict, the director sometimes finds that he has made a bad choice; that is, the director may love the idea of the play but may overlook the fact that he does not know how to make the music of the language exciting or does not know how to compensate for a lack of spectacle, and so on. As directors gain self-knowledge through experience, they learn what they do well or badly, and they learn to make wise script choices. Most important, perhaps, is the acquired knowledge of learning to study the script in great depth—not to be led astray by enthusiasm for a single element, only to find to one's sorrow later that serious problems were overlooked.

With the script chosen, the director begins to translate that early enthusiasm into the stuff of performance. To do so, he needs a "springboard," a taking-off place from which to make a creative leap. The terms *concept* and *directorial image* are also used, but *concept* implies rational thought, and *image* implies picture making, and the director's process at this stage may be neither rational nor pictorial. Certainly very few directors *begin* their creative work with a reasoned, easily stated idea, and those who are drawn to a script because of (for example) its music or because of the opportunity it gives to display the artistry of an actor will probably not *begin* with images. On the contrary, what many directors begin with is a seemingly random, sometimes conflicting medley of ideas, impressions, and half-formed thoughts whose rational connections may still be hidden. It is then the director's task—and an exercise of his special talent—to sort all these out and to find their connections and to see which can be given theatrical life and which cannot. Thus much of the director's early work is not the definition and application of a "concept," but the establishment of a jumping-off place, the sorting out of raw materials from a whirlwind of impressions.

Seldom—perhaps never, except in the most perfunctory sort of work—is the springboard merely "to do the play." A director who sets out merely "to do the play" is like the actor who sets out to learn the lines and not bump into the furniture; he is going through the motions without ever confronting the real task. This is as true of a classic play as of the most avant-garde script. It might seem that classic plays would be an exception because, supposedly, so much is known about them and so many other productions can be drawn upon—the director would simply stage the play's established greatness. Such an approach is a guarantee of dullness, at best. A play will not be exciting in performance simply because other audiences have found other productions of it exciting; it must be made exciting all over again every time it is staged.

A good director takes nothing for granted. Most of all, he does not take for granted the presence of the audience. Everything that is tried will be measured against an idea of how the anticipated audience will react—with the qualification that every director knows that mere reaction is not in itself a good thing; the *proper* reaction is what is wanted.

Figure 10–4. The Directed Production. Shaw's *You Never Can Tell* at Wayne State University. *(Directed by Robert Emmett McGill, designs by Russell Smith, James A. Hatfield, and Daniel Thomas Field.)*

In early readings, the director usually has both positive and negative thoughts about the play and its audience impact. Two lists could be made, one of strengths and one of weaknesses. These two lists *taken together* would show how the director's ideas were forming. It is important to remember that weaknesses as well as strengths are included. Just as artists in any form are inspired by obstacles, so the director is inspired by script problems (as, for example, the poet finds inspiration in the problem of rhyme).

Let us suppose, for example, that the director is considering a realistic nineteenth-century play. The play is a classic of its kind and so has established merit; on the other hand, it is also old enough to seem dated to a modern audience in language and some plot devices. Thus, after early readings, the director could list some strengths and weaknesses:

Plus	Minus
Strong subject matter	Creaky structure—melodramatic
Excellent central character	Dated language
Great third-act climax	Some "serious" stuff now funny
Good potential for probing Victorian attitudes	Soliloquies, set speeches very hard to make convincing today

To the director who is excited by the play and is setting out to do it, these two columns might better be titled "Potentials" and "Challenges." From the realization of the one and the solution of the other will come the director's best work.

The Director and the Play: Text or Pretext?

The play is chosen; the first identification of strengths and weaknesses is made. The work of interpretation begins. It is an open-ended process, and, like the actor's, it never really finishes; it merely stops. If the director does more than one production of the same play, he may create quite a different production the second time: the process of interpretation has gone on and has changed as the director and the world have changed.

But a serious question arises: What is the director's responsibility to the dramatic text? Is it the director's job to put the play on the stage with utmost fidelity, or is it the director's job to create a theatrical event to which the script is merely a contributing part? Can the director cut lines or scenes, transpose scenes, alter characters? Can the director "improve" the play, or is it his responsibility to treat it as a sacred object?

Directors vary widely in the way they answer such questions. Their views range from veneration of the text to near indifference; the play is seen as a holy object on the one hand and as a merely useful artifact on the other.

The Worshipful Director's Approach. "The play is the only permanent art object in performance; it is a work of art in its own right, to be treated with respect and love. Because it has stood the test of time, it has intrinsic value. By examining it, we can know its creator's intentions—what meanings he meant to convey, what experiences he meant his audience to have, what theatrical values he meant to celebrate. The playwright is a literary artist

Figure 10–5. The Director and the Text. The director's possible approaches to the text range from "worship" to "heresy." Where does this production lie? Shakespeare's *Richard III* at the University of South Carolina. *(Directed by Stuart Vaughan.)*

and a thinker, and his work is the foundation of theatrical art. It is the director's job to mount the playwright's work as faithfully and correctly as is humanly possible.

"Historical research and literary criticism are useful tools for the director; they illuminate the classic play. Quirky modern interpretations are suspect, however: to show Hamlet as a homosexual in love with Rosencrantz and/ or Guildenstern would be absurd and wrong because we know that such a relationship would never have been included in the tragic view that Shakespeare held.

"Negative personal responses to a play mean that the director should not do the play: if he finds the conventions of Racinian tragedy laughable, he had better never direct *Phèdre* than mount a production in which his own taste turns it into a modern black comedy.

"The director's job is not primarily to create theatre; it is to cause the play to create theatre. The difference is crucial. The director says quite properly, 'I must allow the play to speak for itself and not get in the way.' To do otherwise is to betray the play, and I will not do it *even if the 'betrayal' is great theatre.*"

The worshipful director views his opposite with something like horror; at best, the other's productions cause him to laugh derisively. What the worshipful director knows of Peter Brook's *Midsummer Night's Dream* or Grotowski's *The Constant Prince* (modern productions of classics that drastically altered the originals) causes him offense and grief. Most often, a single word is used by the worshipful director to describe such productions: *wrong.* Because they are not faithful to their classic originals, they are *wrong.*

The Heretical Director's Approach. *"Interpreting the text* means *making a theatrical entity of it for an audience.* Not making *the* theatrical entity of it, and not 'finding its meaning' or 'doing it correctly.' There is no single interpretation of a play that is 'correct.' There are only interpretations that are right for a given set of performers under a given set of conditions for a given audience.

"How, then, can a director judge the rightness of the production? He does not, any more than a painter judges the rightness of a painting. The director's final criterion is the satisfaction of his overall goal: Is it good theatre?

"It is foolish to think that the director's task is to stage the play according to some other standard. Fidelity to some 'authorized' or time-honored view of the play is not, simply in and of itself, a good thing. It is foolish to say that the director did the play 'wrong' unless what the director did was make bad or dull theatre. The director has to be faithful to his own vision, not to tradition or academic scholarship or propriety; only when that vision fails can he be said to be wrong.

"Does this mean, then, that the director has no responsibility to the 'meaning' of the play? Yes, in the sense that the director's responsibility is to the meaning of the performance, of which the play is only a part. Are we, then, to have homosexual Hamlets and comical Phèdres? Yes, if such extreme interpretations are necessary to make the plays into effective

Figure 10–6. The Director and the Text. The scene between Arsinoe and Celimene in Molière's *The Misanthrope.* What is the director's attitude toward the text? *(Courtesy of the American Conservatory Theatre. With Kitty Winn and Michael Learned. Photo: Bill Ganslen, San Francisco.)*

theatre and if they are entirely consistent within their productions. Are we, then, to have productions of classics that are directly opposite to their creators' intentions? Yes, because it is finally impossible to know what somebody else's intentions were and because an intention that was dynamite in 1600 may be as dull as dishwater in 1980; and anyway, theatre people have always altered classics to suit themselves: *Macbeth* was turned into an 'opera' in 1670, and *King Lear* had a happy ending in the eighteenth century."

The extremes of the heretical director's views can lead to results that many people find offensive or meaningless; on the other hand, this view can also lead to innovative and truly exciting productions. Generally both sorts take a risk: the heretical director takes the chance of making himself ridiculous, the worshipful director of making himself vapid. At their best, however, both can create productions that thrill audiences, the one with revelations of familiar material, the other with a brilliant rendition of the strong points of the classic.

Script Interpretation

No matter what his orientation toward the text, the director must now work to analyze it: take it apart, reduce it to its smallest components, "understand" it. (To *understand* does not mean to "turn the script into a rational description of itself"; it means, rather, to make the director's consciousness capable of staging it.) The job of interpretation has many aspects, which are often explored simultaneously, both before and during rehearsals.

Tone and Audience Impact

Funny/serious, cheerful/sad, light/heavy—the possibilities are many and must be identified for each act, each scene, and each line, as well as for the entire play. The director looks both for the play's intended effects—funny lines, frightening moments, spectacular events—and for the ones where he may impose a quality of his own invention. Neither laughter nor powerful emotion necessarily belongs unchangeably to parts of many scripts, especially when realistic acting and the concept of *subtext* are applied; the director will spend a good deal of time deciding what he will do. Even when the proper tone is found for the play, the lines alone will not deliver that tone to an audience. Laugh lines must be carefully set up and "pointed," with both business and timing; moments that have a wonderful potential for powerful emotion can easily be lost without careful, intense study and work by the director.

Of particular interest in this aspect of interpretation is *mood*—the emotional "feel" that determines tempo, pictorial composition, and tempo—and *key*—(as in "high key" and "low key"), the degree to which effects are played against each other or against a norm for contrast. High-key scenes may even go to *chiaroscuro* ("light/dark") effects that use the darkest darks and the lightest lights, as in dramatic painting; such a technique is of great value in setting the mood for a play like *Dracula* (and equally true in films—note, for example, the uses of strong lights and darks, sudden shocks, abrupt changes of tempo, and startling entrances or appearances in films like *Frankenstein, Psycho,* and other horror/mystery classics.)

Relative Importance of Elements

Modern directors try to work carefully with all elements of theatre, although the director of modern realistic plays is often limited in his work with spectacle and sound. The director must study the play to find which elements are most important and which he can use most creatively to serve the play. Spectacle (including the pictures created by the actors' movement and by scenery) and sound (including music, sound effects, and language) are often elements that the director can manipulate and can bring to the play as

Figure 10–7. Mood. Emotional "feel" of a scene grows out of the director's careful interpretation of the text. *Abelard and Heloise* at Centenary College. *(Directed by Robert R. Buseick, designs by Debra Hicks, Barbara Acker, and David Pellman.)*

"extras" that the playwright has not included. Character, idea, and story, on the other hand, are usually more integral to the script itself, although subject to considerable interpretation and "bending" by director and actors. Many directors annotate their scripts in great detail for these three elements, some marking every line of dialogue for its contribution to character, idea, or story. Such annotations give the director both an overall sense of the play's thrust and specific instances of that thrust at work.

This area of interpretation is critical. An element misunderstood at this stage can mean a moment lost in performance, or even an important thread through the whole play; to miss a major emphasis can mean a failed production. For example, a play that depends heavily on the beauty and intricacy of its language (sound) will usually suffer if directed to emphasize story or character, with the language overlooked or ignored (a not infrequent problem in productions of Shakespeare's plays); a play of character, if directed for its story, often has incomprehensible spots and long stretches where "nothing seems to happen." Thus, the director must not only pick the element or elements that he can give theatrical life to; *he must also pick the element or elements that the script gives theatrical life to.* This means knowing *which* element(s) is most important; *where* in the play each has its heights and depths; and *how* the director will give theatrical excitement to each.

Action and Progression

Performance is active and most plays have progressive actions; that is, they occur through time (audience time) and they must at least seem to increase in intensity as time passes (as, that is, the audience is led from preparation through complication to crisis and resolution). There is a trap here for every director, however, in that it is the very nature of audience perception to need greater stimulation as time passes—a familiar enough situation to all of us, who can become bored after a time with something that entertained us at the beginning. Thus it is part of the director's problem to counter the apparent drop in intensity that occurs as time passes by using every device possible to *increase* intensity, that is, to support theatrically the progressive intensity of the script. An audience's responses may be compared to a parabola when it enjoys a performance: they start at a low point, rise higher and higher as time passes, and usually fall off after a climax. The director wisely structures the performance to serve this perceptual structure (or another equally satisfying one of his own invention). *The director cannot allow a performance to become static,* or it will seem to fall off rather than remain still. He must serve the needs and the desires of that parabola—audience suspense.

It is not enough, then, to find the important elements and to know where the script emphasizes them. The director must now find how each element grows in interest as the performance progresses. The word *progression* must

Figure 10–8. Progression. Each scene and each *beat* is part of a performance-long progression and must be located on that progression by the director. *The Three Sisters* at the Minnesota Theatre Company. *(With Jessica Tandy, Hume Cronyn, Michael Levin, and Ellen Geer. Directed by Tyrone Guthrie.)*

be used again and again: What is this character's progression? What is the progression of the story? Is there progression in the spectacle?

If the progression is missed, the audience will become confused or bored. They may say things like "It went downhill" or "It got dull after the first act" or "It went nowhere." Theatre people, seeing such a performance, often say that "They played the last act first," which is a way of saying that the high points of the important elements were so much in the director's mind that he directed the entire play to emphasize them, thus destroying progression.

The reverse of the question "What is the progression?" is "What can I save for the climax?" In other words, how can the director emphasize the highest point of the performance (usually toward the end, coincident with story's climax) by contrast or by saving effects for that moment? Preparation and contrast are important; equally important is saving something—the final high pitch of emotion, the most exciting tempo, the loveliest visual effect.

Environment

As the actor determines "given circumstances," so the director determines environment: place, time of day, historical period, and so on. Much of this is given in the script, although if it is given only in the stage directions, the director may choose to ignore it. Some directors cross out the stage directions before ever reading them, believing either that they were written for some other director's production (usually, in the United States, for Broadway) or that they were written simply to make the play more readable for armchair theatregoers. Modern realistic plays usually have highly detailed descriptions of settings and costumes; classic plays often have none at all (many directors prefer the latter).

It has become common directorial practice to change the period of classic plays. Shakespeare's *Troilus and Cressida*, for example, has been done in the costumes and accents of the American Civil War. The play is about the Trojan War, but the director may have wanted to stay away from classical Greek costumes and settings because of what they say to the modern mind; he may have wanted to stay away from Shakespearean costume and setting because they say something quite different (and something that might seem more comic than anything else). Setting the play in the American Civil War, then, not only had the advantage of novelty, it also identified the play with a conflict real to Americans and yet slightly distant, one that is viewed both romantically and cynically (applicable to a play that is both romantic and cynical), and it had the added advantage of separating the often confusing warriors of the opposing sides by their Americanized accents (northern and southern).

Questions of tone, mood, and key influence the director's thinking about environment. There are excellent reasons for putting a murder mystery in a country house on a stormy night, just as there are excellent reasons for putting a brittle comedy in a bright, handsome city apartment. It is not only the rightness of the environment for the characters that the director

Figure 10–9. Environment. The director's physical sense of the play will greatly influence the setting, the lighting, and the selection of props. *The Visit* at Centenary College. *(Directed by Robert R. Buseick, design by Tommy Serio.)*

thinks of (i.e., if they are rich they should have a rich environment, if Russians they should have something Russian, and so on) but the rightness for the indefinable subtleties of mood: the laziness of a warm day, the tension of an electric storm, the depressing gloom of an ancient palace.

Idea

As we have already pointed out, idea is the element of theatre that gets the most attention after the audience has left the theatre and the least while it is enjoying the performance. Paradoxically idea is an important criterion in play selection, many directors being committed to plays because of enthusiasm for their subject or approach. Idea may continue to influence their interpretation and their work; however, they are careful *not* to direct the play so that it is "about the idea." The other elements will usually determine the shape of the production, and idea will inhere in all of them but be blatant in none. Even an impassioned "idea" speech at the most thrilling moment of the play must spring from action and character and must exist *because* of action and character. If it exists because the playwright or the director wants to make a statement, it will leap out of the performance and the performance will suffer.

Idea, in fact, does not inhere in individual speeches or in literal statements that can be neatly extracted from the play. The very word *idea* describes not a single, literal statement but a body of matter that we have called "meanings" in another chapter (see pages 428–432). It is woven into the texture of the performance, embodied in the actors' creations of their roles and the director's creation of mood, among other things. The director does not spell out the idea for the audience; where the idea excites him, it becomes something to be embedded in the entire performance.

Design Oversight and Inspiration

After he begins the work of interpretation, and well before rehearsals begin (where such a thing is possible), the director begins to meet with the several designers. When feasible, this process may actually begin months before rehearsals, but the practicality of production in many theatres means sometimes that it comes within short weeks or even days of casting. Communication with the designers is best started early. Many directors have approval of the hiring of designers and so can begin almost as soon as they agree to direct.

Depending on the theatre itself, the director and the designers (sometimes with producer, playwright, technical director, costume foreman, and so on) hold *production meetings* weeks or months before the actors are cast. These meetings have three principal goals: *artistic coordination,* so that direction and designs are in harmony; *managerial efficiency,* to coordinate budgets, schedules, and personnel assignments; and *communication,* to encourage the complete exchange of creative ideas.

Within this framework, the director works on the following areas.

Design Mood and Meaning

The director is rarely a designer, but he knows the practical needs and the aesthetic values of both play and production. Communicating feelings and ideas about play and production is an important directorial skill, especially when it is done without crippling the designers with restrictions instead of inspiring them with creative interpretation. The designers will have made their own interpretations of the play, and they will often be different from the director's. Bringing them all into a single focus is the director's task.

The director has to be careful at this stage that his ideas are not so rigid or so narrow that they cause the designers to make a single statement over and over. Unity *and* variety (or variety within unity) must be stimulated, and the potential for progression must always be inspired in the designs.

The visual potency of lighting, set, and costume are very important determinants of mood. The director must be clear about his interpretation and must be sure that the designers share that vision. Inconsistency here leads to severe weakening of the performance.

Ground Plan

In a realistic interior, the director may almost design the entire acting space simply by setting down his needs in detail. The number and location of entrances, the number and location of seating elements, the number and location of objects that will motivate behavior and movement (for example, stoves and refrigerators, fireplaces, closets, and bookcases) are important to the way many directors think about realistic plays and may be determined by such directors even before they meet with their designers. Some directors even give their set designer a ground plan, complete except for minute matters of dimension. Others may remain open until the designer has created a ground plan around a more general statement of needs.

In the nonrealistic play, or sometimes in the realistic play with exterior scenes, directors may have less rigorous requirements. Still, for variety, mood, and emphasis, the director will probably specify differences in level, separation of playing areas, the location of seating elements, and so on. An effect created by the director may strictly require certain things: one director's production of *Macbeth,* for example, had the witches shift magically from a ledge far above the stage to stage level (two sets of actors were used to play the witches); here, obviously, the designer had to provide precisely the levels demanded by the director.

As well, other design elements may be suggested or required by the director; for example, the size and shape of the space where a crowd is used, or where a sense of the isolation of a single figure is wanted, or where a feeling of cramped oppression is sought.

It is no matter whether the designer or the director finally creates the ground plan(s). Once they are established, they become the basis for all staging. Drawn to scale, they can be used with scale cutouts of furniture and actors to plan movement and picturization. They are also the basis for the three-dimensional model of each setting that the director usually provides, and they are also useful to the director in planning the staging.

Costumes, Lights, and Sound

As with the ground plan, so with the other design areas: both the practical and the aesthetic must be considered. The kind and amount of movement wanted by the director influences costume design; the costume designer's knowledge of dress influences movement (as when, for example, the tight corset of the late nineteenth century or the very broad skirts of the eighteenth century are used). So, too, with colors: bright pastels may be suitable for a comedy, both in costumes and in lighting (as well as setting); dull colors and heavy fabrics under gloomy light may match a tragic interpretation.

Figure 10–10. Environment and Costume. The director's sense of space, mood, and movement determines much of setting, props, and costume. *The Three Sisters* at the Minnesota Theatre Company. *(Directed by Tyrone Guthrie, design by Tanya Moisiwitsch.)*

Practical considerations influence other decisions: certain areas will have to be brightly lighted so that the action can be seen; certain actors will have to be in strong colors or outstanding costumes so that they will gain focus. Lighting colors must be carefully coordinated with the colors of sets and costumes so that they do not wash out those colors or turn them to undesirable colors; the location of lighting instruments has to be coordinated with the location of set pieces and rigging to avoid casting shadows or creating actual physical interference.

As the production meetings continue and rehearsals near, these and many other matters will have been considered: budget, shifting of scenery, time for costume changes, location of offstage storage space. As decisions are made final, each designer provides the director with a detailed plan of his own work in the form most appropriate to it: color renderings and fabric swatches for costumes; ground plans, scale drawings, renderings, and models for sets; light plots with gel colors for lights. The sound designer (where one exists) may work with an annotated script and lists of sound materials (music, sound effects). These renderings, plans, and other materials represent the culmination of the designers' work with the director: detailed, readable plans for a total production, all in harmony with each other and with the director's interpretation of the text.

Actor Coaching

Most modern directors involve themselves closely with their actors' creation of their roles. It is a very rare director who does not. The influence of Stanislavski, in particular, has led to a collaboration between actor and director that has developed, in some cases, into a great dependency on the director, a dependency that is sometimes fostered by the teacher–student relationship at universities where acting is taught. Just as there are now playwrights who expect to have their plays "fixed" by the director (a relationship that grew primarily from the Broadway playwright–director collaborations of the twentieth century), so there are actors who expect to have their interpretations "fixed," or even given to them whole by their directors. Particularly in educational and community theatres, great trust is put in the director by the actors, and many interpretations are virtually handed down entire from director to actor.

When the actor–director relationship works as a productive collaboration, however, the director functions as a coach who advises, inspires, and encourages the actor. Significantly the director works in such a relationship with questions rather than with statements ("Why do you think the character says it just that way?" instead of "What the character means is . . ."). The director will have mastered the actor's vocabulary and, using it, can ask those questions that the actor may not yet be able to phrase for himself. The director is the sounding board and the artistic conscience of the actor, mentor and interpreter, bringing to the actor's work another dimension, another voice, another view of the whole play and all the characters.

The Director–Actor Relationship

The director and the actor have had to learn to need each other, for there is no reason to suppose that early directors were warmly welcomed by actors, who, until then, had been independent. There is still much in the relationship to make it difficult for both. The actor is worried about himself, the director about the entire performance; the actor works from a narrow slice through the play, the director from the whole thing; the actor risks everything in front of an audience, the director does not; the actor naturally resents commands, the director sometimes has to give them. Add to these differences the natural indifference or apathy of people brought into a working situation by professional accident rather than affinity, plus the stressful atmosphere of rehearsals, and the relationship can be strained indeed.

Perhaps surprisingly, then, most directors and actors work quite well together. Credit for much of this goes to the director's human skills, although some of it must go to the patience and determination of the actor. The most potent factor may be, in the end, the knowledge that both are engaged in a creative enterprise whose success benefits both.

The director–actor relationship takes several forms.

Figure 10–11. Ensemble Work. Actors achieve ensemble playing through sharing and concentration; a director helps them greatly through his relationship with them. *The Waltz of the Toreadors* at Wayne State University. *(Directed by Don Blakely, designs by James Knight, Helen Markovitch, and Daniel Thomas Field.)*

The Director As Parent. "Do it my way because I say so." The authoritarian director gets results early and keeps control of the production. He risks alienating or stifling the creative actor. He often lectures at considerable length and takes the role of a professor with students.

The Director As Guru. "If you do it my way, it will demonstrate our spiritual sympathies." A product of the 1960s, the guru is as much spiritual cult leader as stage director. His vision is a vision of existence, not merely of performance, and the actors are acolytes and members of a spiritual community. Brilliant work sometimes comes from devoted followers—innovative, revealing, revolutionary. The uncommitted may find it puzzling, silly.

The Director As Therapist. "Trust me; tell me your problems." In the psychologically oriented theatre of the 1940s and 1950s, the director/therapist functioned well. He is still effective with actors trained in that tradition, especially when the actor's self and the character are made to dovetail. The director/therapist is somewhat of a mystery, if not a nosy busybody, however, to actors who work in another way.

The Director As Seducer. "You're wonderful; we're going to do great things together." Sexual seduction is not really a directorial technique, although it is not unheard of; rather, emotional attachment and even dependency is the object. This approach often succeeds in binding the actors to the director with great affection and loyalty. The difficulty lies in the lack of correspondence between affection and creative work, in the loss of perspective through noncritical, "global" attitudes on both sides.

The Director As Victim. "Do I have to do *everything?*" The director/victim suffers a lot. The weight of the production, the stress of rehearsals, the emotional demands of each scene seem to reduce him to tears. He pleads, begs, cajoles, often gets remarkable results from sympathetic actors, and succeeds in touching their own emotional selves, but suffers from a loss of authority.

The Director As Playground Director. "Let's have *fun* with this show!" Buoyant and youthful, the playground director tries to make everything fun, funny, cute, or touching. Much of theatre is work, however, and many plays have other qualities. This kind of director is good with children and probably an inspiration to beginners and amateurs but is too one-sided for serious actors.

The Director As Green Thumb. "I think we have something growing here." Totally organic, he puts little or nothing down on paper, seldom seems to prepare, and always waits for things "to develop." Such directors, if inexperienced, have been known to ask when the actors were going to start to move around. With gifted and experienced actors, the director/gardener can build a profoundly creative situation, but the method—or lack of it—causes frustration and anger in many actors.

The Director As Lump. "Be better." He mostly sits there, a lump in the rehearsal hall, occasionally complaining to the stage manager. His directions are so vague that the actors despair: "Sort of drift to the left a little way" or "Kind of give him a love–hate look." The actors, forced to shift for themselves, may either work it out or quit.

The Director As Director. He is an amalgam of all the above—occasionally authoritarian, sometimes seductive, organic when his prepared solutions do not work, fun-loving when there is genuine fun in a scene or a situation. The complete director is multifaceted, even many-faced, all things to all people and all plays. What he tries to avoid is being limited, because a strictly limited approach inevitably antagonizes at least some of the actors.

Actors depend on their director. Therefore the more precise and sure the director can be, the better. Precision and sureness come from *preparation,* and so the basis of the most productive actor–director relationships is the director's own work in advance of rehearsals.

The Director and the Characters

Many directors are themselves actors and/or acting teachers. They understand actors' approaches and vocabularies. Only rarely do they try to impose a new system on their actors, and then only if they are gurus or director/teachers. Thus their work on character will be adapted to the system used by the actor playing the role.

Basically the director does the same character homework as the actor. He keeps a notebook, with pages or columns for each character. The director focuses, however, not on the objectives and motivations of a single character (except when working with the actor playing that character) but on shifting patterns of objectives that conflict, part, run parallel, and conflict again. It is not merely that the director maintains an overview of the terrain that the actors travel; it is that the director finds the heart of the play in the coexistence and conflict of character lines.

Figure 10–12. External Signals. The director must concern himself with the "signals" that communciate all aspects of the performance to the audience—style, mood, tone, genre—and the visual devices that call attention to those signals. *The Inspector General* at the University of Northern Iowa. *(Directed by Thomas Carlisle, designs by Harvey Sweet and Kathleen G. Runge.)*

Too, the director is profoundly concerned with the "outside" of the performance. The director is a master communicator, interested almost obsessively in *things that signal to the audience*. His is the art of external signals, both visual and auditory. The actor devotes time and energy to the inner reasons for giving signals; the director works on those inner reasons only to help the actor, saving his own creative energy for the signals themselves.

As the director plans his schedule, attention is given to how each actor will build his own character. Some actors make great progress early, and one or two may never do so. Still, the director knows that by a certain date, "inner" work must be well under way. By some later date, the director must let go, "sit farther back," work more externally and more comprehensively. The closer the date of the first performance, the less attention the director will be able to give to detailed actor-coaching, which is only one aspect of the modern director's total job.

Staging

"Blocking," "staging," or "traffic direction," as some people wryly call it, is one of the director's inescapable responsibilities. No matter how much the actors and even the director are devoted to inner truth and to characterization, the time must come when the director must shape the actors' moves and timing, must give careful attention to *picturization* and *composition* and to *movement*. It is in the very nature of modern theatre that the visual details of the stage have significance, and the director must make that significance jibe with his interpretation.

For significance is the crux of the matter. We live in a world where movement and visual arrangement signify: they give signals. In the realistic theatre, the same things signify that do in life; in the nonrealistic theatre, these things can be kept from signifying or can be made to signify differently only with careful control and effort.

Before the appearance of the director, audiences seemingly found less significance in stage movement, gesture, and picture—or, more accurately, they found a *theatrical* significance in them: the star took center stage, facing front, with other actors flanking and balancing him; a hero's movement pattern and posture was heroic; the heroine moved so as to show herself off and to divide or punctuate her speeches. We cannot say with certainty what the audiences made of what they saw, but we can say with certainty what they did not see: modern staging, with its meticulous attention to visual symbolism (picturization), beauty (composition), and movement.

Much of what is taught about directing today is devoted to these matters. By and large, what is taught has been established by tradition and extended by popular theory, little of it having been tested objectively. Much of the theory of picturization—especially the supposed "meanings" of various stage areas—derives from traditional use of the proscenium stage and probably has less relevance for thrust and arena staging. Indeed, as realistic plays

Figure 10–13. Movement. Movement has many purposes for the director, and he must make a single movement serve many of them. *A Flea in Her Ear* at the University of Nevada, Las Vegas. *(Directed by Jerry L. Crawford. Designs by Fredrick L. Oslon and Pat Crawford.)*

exert less influence on the theatre, and as new theories of theatre evolve, many of these traditional theories of directing will probably fade.

Movement

As actors are aware of and exploit "body language," so the director is aware of and uses "movement language." Stage movement is more abundant than real-life movement; in a real situation, people often sit for a very long time to talk, for example, while on a stage characters in the same situation will be seen to stand, walk, change chairs, and move a good deal. Partly this abundance of movement results from the physical distance of the audience—small movements of eyes and facial muscles do not carry the length of a theatre; and partly it results from the director's need for variety, for punctuation of action and lines, for the symbolic values of movement itself, and for the changing symbolic values of picturization.

Stage movement is based partly on the received wisdom of statements like "Face up to it," "She turned her back on it," "He rose to the occasion." Too, it serves to get characters into positions with which we have similar associations—"at the center of things," "way off in the blue," "out in left field."

The director is concerned with *speed, amount,* and *direction* of movement. Direction includes both motivation and human interaction; speed shows strength of desire or strength of involvement (impassioned haste, for example, and ambling indifference); amount shows much less than the other two and is perhaps most useful for contrast (a character making a very long movement after several short ones or in contrast with the small moves of several other characters).

Movement also *punctuates* the lines. It introduces speech: the character moves, catches our attention, stops and speaks; it breaks up speech: the character speaks, moves, speaks again, or moves while speaking and breaks the lines with turns or about-faces. (Pacing is frequently used for this reason. In life, we associate pacing with thought, and so a pacing character may seem thoughtful, but his turns are carefully timed by the director to mark changes in the speech itself.)

Movement *patterns* have a symbolic value much like that of individual movements and can be derived from the same figures of speech: "twisting him around her finger," "winding her in," "going in circles," "following like sheep," "on patrol," and many others suggest patterns for characters or groups. They are used, of course, to underscore a pattern already perceived in the play or the scene.

Pictorialism

Pictorialism—the exploitation of the stage's potential for displaying pictures—is not entirely limited to the proscenium theatre but does have its greatest use there. From the late nineteenth century through the middle of the twentieth, the proscenium was seen literally as a picture frame, and the audience sat in locations that allowed it to look through the frame at its contents. With the advent of thrust and round stages, however, this "framing" became impossible, and audiences were located on three or all four sides of the stage, so that each segment of the audience saw quite a different picture. Thus only certain aspects of pictorialism have universal application, and of these the most important by far is picturization.

Of considerably less importance, except on the proscenium stage, is the symbolic value of *stage areas.* These areas (on the proscenium stage) are Down Center, Right, and Left (*Down* meaning toward the audience, *Right* meaning to the actor's right and thus the audience's left) and Up Center, Right, and Left. Down Center is unquestionably the most important (or "strongest") area, followed by Down Right and Down Left. (Traditional wisdom has it that Down Right is more important than Down Left and that it has a "warmth" that Down Left lacks. The point is questionable.) The Upper areas are weaker and Up Left is the "coldest," hence appropriate for scenes of menace and the supernatural and inappropriate for love scenes, or so traditional wisdom has it. The real value of identifying the stage areas is in creating *variety* and *identification,* variety because it is tedious if the audience has to watch scene after scene played in the same area, and identification because the association of an area with a character or a feeling is an important

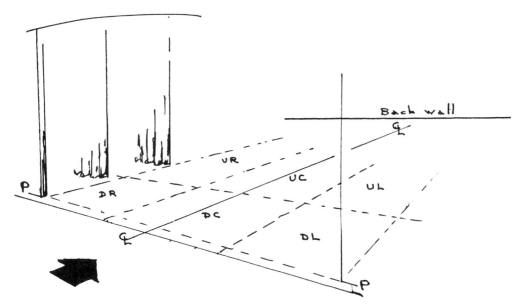

Figure 10–14. Stage areas as seen from the audience (arrow).

tool for conveying emotional meaning to the audience. And, unquestionably, the matter of "strength" does have some importance, if only because common sense tells us that the downstage areas are stronger because we can see the actors more clearly there—and, as a result, we want to play our most important (but not all) scenes there.

Picturization. Puns and traditional sayings give us a clue to how picturization works—and also suggest to us how the mind of the director works as it creates visual images of the sort that communicate to us in dreams. "Caught in the middle," "one up on him," and "odd man out" all suggest strong pictorial arrangements of actors. When a director combines them with area identification, for example, they become richer and more complex. The additional use of symbolic properties or set pieces—a fireplace, associated with the idea of home ("hearth and family"), for example—gives still greater force to the picture. Thus a character who "moves in" on the hearth of a setting while also moving physically between a husband and wife ("coming between them") and sitting in the husband's armchair ("taking his place") has told the audience a complicated story without saying a word.

Sometimes as in Shakespeare's *Richard II* (Act III, Scene iii), the playwright's own symbolism creates a rich texture of both picture and movement.

"King Richard appeareth on the walls," (First Quarto), "Enter on the walls," (First Folio):

North: *My lord, in the base court he doth attend*
            To speak with you; may it please you to come down?

Richard: *Down, down I come, like glist'ring Phaeton . . .,*
            Wanting the manage of unruly jades.
            Is this the base court? Base court, where kings grow base . . .

[Richard comes down to stage level; the usurper Bolingbroke kneels to him, as is evident from omitted material]

Bolingbroke: *Stand all apart,*
And show fair duty to his Majesty. ("He kneels downe." First Quarto.)
My gracious lord.

Richard: *Fair cousin, you debase your princely knee*
To make the base earth proud with kissing it. . . .
Up, cousin, up; your heart is up, I know,
Thus high at least, although your knee be low.

The scene begins with Richard "on high" while his enemies are in the "base court" at stage level. (A base court was a part of a castle, but *base* means "common" or "unworthy," as well as "low" in both the physical and the social sense.) Richard says he will come "down, like glist'ring Phaeton," that is, like the young man who drove the chariot of the sun too near the earth because he could not control the horses that pulled it ("wanting the manage of unruly jades."). But the audience already knows (from earlier reference) that the sun is Richard's emblem, and the director has probably

Figure 10–15. Picturization. The director's creation of a stage picture "tells the story of the scene," as in this scene from Molière's *The Miser* where relationships and situation have been made clear. *(Courtesy of Wayne State University, Directed by N. Joseph Calarco, designs by Norman Hamlin, Michael L. Seiser, and Tom Bryant.)*

made sure that it is visible on Richard's costume and may even be suggested by the shape of his crown, so the sun is being *debased,* brought down, even as Richard physically moves down to stage level. There, the usurper tells everyone else to "stand apart," that is, to give them room, but the word *stand* may be ironic and the director may use it to make an ironic picture, because they should kneel to the king. Bolingbroke himself does kneel (stage direction, First Quarto), but the gesture is a mockery, as Richard notes, "You debase your princely knee/To make the base earth proud. . . . ./Up, cousin, up . . . ," reminding the audience that Richard himself was, only moments ago, "up" on the higher level. And Richard goes on: touching his crown (a traditional bit of business), he says, "Up, cousin, up/Thus high at least. . . ." That is, he will raise himself high enough in the presence of his king (though he should be kneeling) to seize the crown.

Thus, in a quick sequence of moves and gestures, the symbolic flow of the scene is given to the audience. With a scene of this richness and detail, the director need only follow its lead; few modern scenes are this explicitly symbolic, however, and the director usually has to create his own picturization to match his interpretation.

Focus. A stage is a visually busy place, with many things to look at; therefore the audience's eyes must be directed to the important point at each moment. There are a number of principal devices for achieving *focus: framing* (in a doorway, between other actors, and so on); *isolating* (one character against a crowd, one character on a higher or lower level); *elevating* (standing while others sit, or the reverse, or getting on a higher level); *enlarging* (with costume, properties, or the mass of a piece of furniture); *illuminating* (in a pool of light or with a brighter costume); and *indicating* (putting the focal character at the intersection of "pointers"—pointing arms, swords, eyes, and so on.)

Focus is largely a mechanical matter, but it is an important one that affects both movement and picturization.

Composition and Balance. Most stage pictures that are picturized and focused are also rather well *composed,* or good to look at, but directors are often careful to study the production with an eye to improving the aesthetic quality of the scenes. What is *not* wanted is easier to say than what is: straight lines, lines parallel to the stage front, evenly spaced figures like ducks in a shooting gallery, and so on. *Balance* is also sought so that the stage does not seem heavy with characters on one side, light on the other. Composition is, finally, an irrational matter and a highly subjective one; directors who concern themselves with it in depth learn much from the other visual arts, especially traditional painting.

Mood. Mood is established most readily with lighting and sound and with the behavior of characters. However, certain visual effects of character arrangement contribute, as well: horizontals, perhaps, for a quiet, resigned scene from Chekhov; looming verticals and skewed lines for a suspense

Figure 10–16. Focus. The director has several devices by which he can focus the audience's attention on a single part of the stage picture. This photograph shows effectively divided visual focus or "pointing," which achieves variety without destroying the focus on the two principal characters. *As You Like It*, the wrestling scene. *(Courtesy of Wayne State University. Directed by Richard Spear, designs by James A. Hatfield, Gary M. Witt, Daniel Thomas Field, and Helen Markovitch.)*

melodrama. Mood values are as subjective and irrational as those of composition, however, and as hard to describe. In reality, what the director remains watchful for are clashes of mood, where movement and picturization conflict with other mood establishers.

Directorial Rhythm

Rhythm is repetition at regular intervals. The elements of rhythm in the theatre are those things that regularly mark the passage of time: scenes, movements, speeches, words. For the director, rhythm includes *pace* and *timing*, as well as one aspect of *progression*. The director is concerned, then, not only with the interpretation of character and the visual signals of interpretation but also with *the rate(s) at which things happen*.

We have seen that speed of movement is important to movement meaning. Now we may say that it is also important to intensity and rhythm. We associate quickness with urgency, slowness with relaxation; perhaps more importantly, it is the change in speed that is most important of all. We may compare this phenomenon with the beating of a heart: once the normal heartbeat (base rhythm) is established, any change becomes significant. The director establishes his base rhythm with the opening scenes of the play and then creates variations on them, and the shortening of the time (cues) between moves, between lines, and between entrances and exits becomes a rhythmic acceleration that gives the audience the same feeling of increased intensity as would a quickening of the pulse.

Pace is the professional's term for "speed," but it is not merely a matter of tempo. Much of what is meant by *pace* is, in fact, emotional intensity and energy, and the director who tries to create a feeling of intensity by telling the actors to "pick up the pace" or "move it along" will probably succeed only in getting his actors to speak so fast that they cannot be understood. Pace has to grow naturally out of understanding and rehearsal of a scene, not out of a decision to force things along. Indeed, the scornful dismissal of such an attempt as "forcing the pace" and "pumping it up" suggests how futile it is.

Timing is complicated and difficult, something felt rather than thought out. *Comic timing* is the delivery of the laugh getter—a line or a piece of business—after exactly the right preparation and at just that moment when it will most satisfy the tension created by a pause before it; it also describes the actor's awareness of the timing that has produced previous laughs and of how each builds on those before. The timing of serious plays is rather different and depends far more on the setting of (usually) slow rhythms from which either a quickening tempo will increase tension or a slowing will enhance a feeling of ponderousness, of doom. For example, at the end of *Hamlet,* Fortinbras has the following speech (Act V, Scene ii):

> *Let four captains*
> *Bear Hamlet, like a soldier to the stage;*
> *For he was likely, had he been put on,*
> *To have prov'd most royally; and, for his passage,*
> *The soldier's music and the rights of war*
> *Speak loudly for him.*
> *Take up the bodies: such a sight as this*
> *Becomes the field, but here shows much amiss.*
> *Go, bid th' soldiers shoot.*
>
> (A dead march. Exeunt, bearing off the bodies;
> after which a peal of ordnance is shot off.)

This follows an active scene of dueling, argument, and violence, and a short, less active scene of Hamlet's and Horatio's final words to each other, with the arrivals of ambassadors and Fortinbras. Fortinbras' speech is jumpy and uneven, effective because it *lacks* regular rhythm, but it finally settles down into the firm, regular rhymed couplet, "Take up the bodies . . ."

that sets the final rhythm of the play. The rest could be timed on a metronome, taking the base rate (the pulse) from the couplet. *Go* is a long sound, followed (in one director's view) by a pause of two beats. The words that remain have but a single stress among them, on *shoot.* After this one-beat word there is another pause of as long as three beats (in the major rhythm of which *Go* and *shoot* are major units). Then the drum ("a dead march") starts its slow beating on the same tempo; a measured number of beats later, the cannon sound ("a peal of ordnance"); another measured number of beats later, the lights begin to dim or the curtain to close, still on units of the original rhythm.

This control of a scene may seem unnecessarily rigid, and controlled rhythm of this kind works only when it is carefully planned and rehearsed, because there is no such thing as a timing that is "almost rhythmic." The rhythm is either exact or it is nonexistent, and it is in the control of stage effects like the drum and the cannon that the director can most carefully control it. (It is partly because of the need for control of such effects, in fact, that the director came into being.)

The Director As Manager

Although we have separated the director's artistic from his managerial functions so that we could talk about them, there is actually no clear line between the two. A strong element of the manager is needed in the execution of all artistic decisions, and managerial abilities are always needed in the director's work with people. The director has to be both artist and manager in almost all of his work, and he is unique among professionals precisely because of this unusual combination of traits—on the one hand, the often solitary consciousness of the artist, and on the other, the gregarious organizational intellect of the manager. Within the same person, then, the artist proposes and the manager disposes, sometimes at widely different times and sometimes simultaneously.

Insofar as the director-as-manager can be separated, however, he will work in the following areas.

Production Preparation and Coordination

In a Broadway production, many managerial functions are performed by the producer or the producer's office; in community and school theatres, the director performs most or all of them. *Scheduling, budgeting, personnel selection, research,* and some aspects of *public relations* all fall to the director's lot. Scheduling includes the overall flow of production work from inception to performance, including production meetings, rehearsals, and the coordination of design and technical schedules, at least for purposes of information (including costume fittings for actors, clearing of the stage for construction work, and

Figure 10–17. Pictorialism. Strong focus, effective picturization, and a questionable balance and composition are shown in this photograph of *Five On the Black Hand Side* at Wayne State University. *(Directed by Martin Molson, designs by Blair Vaughn Anderson, Benjamin F. Levenberg, and Denise DeYonker.)*

so on). These schedules are kept by the director or his stage manager on some easily read form like an oversized calendar.

Budgets are rarely initiated by a director, who does not hold the purse strings of the theatre, but the director must be able to keep his own staff's budget and, far more importantly, to understand and honor costume, setting, and other budgets so that he will not ask for more than can be paid for. In many college and university theatres, the director functions as producer and has budget control over the design areas (that is, the production money is budgeted as a single figure, which can be carved up as the director wishes).

Personnel selection (not including the actors) covers the director's own staff, most particularly the stage manager and his assistants. In many situations, it will extend to the choreographer and the music director, with whom the director must work closely; it may include selection or at least approval of designers. The guiding principal is that the director must, if at all possible, be surrounded with people whom he respects and with whom work is congenial.

Research is carried out by a director on virtually any aspect of the production. Designers do their own research, to be sure, but such matters as the actors' accents, social mores, manners and mannerisms, the traditions surrounding the staging of a classic, historical conventions associated with it, critical comments on it, and the work of other actors and directors in other productions of it concern many directors. It is not their aim to steal ideas from other productions; rather, it is their aim to learn from them, to honor traditions, and to build on what has been done before. This is particularly true in the staging of something like Gilbert and Sullivan, for example, where audiences are very familiar with the work and the traditions of performance are very strong.

Public relations is not usually a directorial responsibility, but as a matter of taste and even of self-protection, the director often wants at least advisory approval of graphic and written material. He is always aware that "mediation"—the nonperformance communciation that surrounds a play—is an important factor in an audience's perception of it. Staging publicity photos, providing historical material from his research, and appearing on interview shows to publicize the show are only a few of the things that a director may do to give his production the best possible mediation.

Casting

"Style is casting," director Alan Schneider said some years ago. The remark underlines the enormous importance of casting to the director; its success or failure indelibly stamps the production.

The producer or director puts out a *casting call* and schedules *auditions* or *tryouts.* In New York, much casting is done through agents and private contact, although union contracts require that an *open call* be held at which all Actors Equity members who want to can be interviewed; in university and community theatres almost the opposite situation holds true, because maximum participation is wanted and closed or private auditions are frowned on. In repertory theatres, of course, where the company are under contract, the director must work rather differently to make the company and the plays mesh, and casting and play selection have a good deal of influence on each other.

The director's conduct of a casting session is a trial of his tact, patience, and humanity. Such auditions exist for the director, but would-be actors often believe that the sessions exist for them, and directors disabuse them of this error as gently as possible. Both good and bad actors try out, and there will be good actors who are wrong for the play and poor actors who may have a quality that somehow seems right. The director wants to hear and see each one, but he wants to see and hear only enough of each one

Figure 10–18. Casting. Talent, variety, appropriateness, certain special qualities are sought by every director in casting—a crucial moment in every production's creation. Here, the cast of the Acting Company's production of *The School for Scandal. (Photo by Stephen Aaron.)*

to know what he can do; the director has no unwritten contract with those trying out to sit patiently while they go on and on. Consequently, tactful as the director tries to be, a few people may wind up believing that they were not given an adequate trial. Such is rarely the case—for the logical reason that it is to the director's own benefit to hear everybody; but what many actors, especially inexperienced ones, fail to understand is that experienced directors learn to make sound preliminary judgments on the basis of less than a minute's audition. It remains the director's task, however, to be considerate, positive, and polite and to see that his staff is the same. The goal is to relax tense actors, to help rid them of nerves that obscure talent by strangling good voices and tensing flexible bodies.

The director or an assistant keeps notes on each aspirant, often in the form of a checklist with headings for physical characteristics, voice, and so on. "Type" may also be indicated—the range of given circumstances that the individual's voice and body would suggest in the realistic theatre. Abilities and outstanding characteristics are noted in enough detail so that the notes themselves will both recall the individual to mind and serve as a basis for later judgment. (Not to be emulated is the practice of the director of an outdoor historical drama who purportedly noted only three possibilities on his tryout sheets: "White," "Indian," and "Unusable.")

In a tryout, the director is looking not for a finished performance but for a display of potential. He may use script readings, performance of prepared materials, and improvisation and theatre games. Aspirants may be asked to work singly or together or with a stage manager. Some will be called back one or more times because the director feels that they have more potential than was shown the first time; and as a final decision nears, the director will want to compare the "finalists" very carefully.

The actual selection of a cast is complicated and, finally, irrational. It is partly a creative act—the creation of the artistic unit that will bring life to the play. Feelings and hunches are important; so, unfortunately, are personal prejudices. Above all, the director wants to be sure in his choices, for replacing an actor after rehearsals have started severely upsets the creative process.

When the cast is chosen, the director posts the cast list. In some situations, he will notify actors personally or will have them notified through agents. Each person who tried out but was not cast should have been thanked. If the whole process has been conducted well, there will be inevitable disappointment among those not cast, but no sense of bitterness or injustice.

Rehearsals

Every director has his own pattern in rehearsal, and every pattern has to be adaptable to the special needs of each cast and each play. In general, however, a structure like the following is used.

First Rehearsal. The cast gathers, a trifle nervous and unsure. Many are strangers to each other. The director plays the role of host at a party, of sorts: making introductions, breaking the ice, moving these individuals toward cohesion. (Even when the playwright sits in, it is the director who is the "host" because of his position.) The play will probably be discussed at some length, the director explaining in general what his ideas are and in what direction he intends to move; the designers may be asked to show and discuss models and/or sketches. Certain practical matters are got out of the way by the director or the stage manager (signing of necessary forms, resolving of individual schedule conflicts, and so on).

Then the play is read, either by the entire cast or by the director or the playwright. Some directors interrupt this first reading often, even on every line, to explain and define; others like to proceed without interruption so that the actors may hear each other. Either way, once the books are open and the lines are read, the rehearsal period is truly under way.

Rehearsal by Units. Rehearsing entire acts is often not the way to do detailed work, and so the acts are further broken down into *French scenes* (between the entrance and exit of a major character) or *scenes* (between curtains or blackouts), and then further into *beats* or *units* (between the initiation and end of an objective). These short elements are numbered in such a way that, for example, all the appearances of a major character can be called by listing a series of numbers, for example, 12, 13, 15, 17, meaning Scenes 2, 3, 5, and 7 of the first act. By scheduling detailed rehearsals this way, the director often avoids keeping actors waiting for long periods while they are not in the scenes; that is, they can be called for another day or night.

Figure 10–19. The Product of Rehearsal. *Marat/Sade* at the University of Iowa. *(Directed by Evzen Drmola, design by Hermann Sichter.)*

Or this same number system can be used to call scenes that need extra rehearsal.

As a very general pattern, it can be said that many directors move from the general rehearsal of early readings into increasingly detailed rehearsals of smaller and smaller units, and then into rehearsals of much longer sections when the units are put back together with each other.

Run-throughs. A *run-through* is a rehearsal of an entire act or an entire play; it gives the director (and the actors) insight into the large movements and progressions of the play. After run-throughs, the director will probably return to rehearsal of certain small units, but as performance nears, more and more run-throughs are held.

Technical and Dress Rehearsals. As production coordinator, the director cannot forget that the integration of lights, costumes, sound, and scenery into the performance is also his responsibility. *Technical rehearsals* are devoted to any or all of these elements, normally done with the actors but sometimes without them, when cue-to-cue or dry-run technical rehearsals are held. In either case, it is normally the stage manager who takes over the management of the script and the cues in preparation for running the show during performance; the director makes the thousand and one decisions affecting the look and sound of the production and conveys them to the stage manager.

Dress rehearsals incorporate costumes into the other technical elements, and final dress rehearsals are virtually performances in all but their lack of an audience. Nothing is now left to chance: actors must be in place for every entrance well in advance of their cues; properties must be in place, with none of the rehearsal substitutes now tolerated; costumes must seem as natural to the actors as their own clothes (achieved by giving them, weeks earlier, rehearsal costumes of cheap materials); every scene shift and light cue must be smooth, timed as the director wants it.

And then, for the director, it is over. To be sure, he may continue to call polishing rehearsals even after opening night, or full rehearsals if the play is a new one that has gone into *previews* (full performances with audience in advance of the official opening) and needs fixing; but as a rule, when the play opens, it belongs to the actors and the stage manager, and the director is a vestige of another era in its life. He may continue to check the production regularly, even for months or years if it is a Broadway success, but in effect, after opening night, the director is a fifth wheel. Until the next play, of course.

More than one director has compared his work to that of a parent, his child being the production. The director rears it from birth to maturity and then pushes it out into the world. It is a paradox of the craft—as it is, perhaps, of parenting—that the proof of one's success is the loss of one's function.

Directing History

Before 1850

As we have already seen, the modern director appeared in the second half of the nineteenth century, a product (by a process we do not yet entirely understand) of the parallel developments of stage realism and modern industrial consciousness. However, it would be a mistake to pretend that nobody before 1850 had ever performed the director's functions, for it is clear that many people in many ages in fact did so.

In fifth-century B.C. Greece, the playwrights themselves staged their plays and undoubtedly had a strong voice in such matters as casting. We know too little of just how costumes and scenes were executed to say with any certainty just what part the playwrights took, but they undoubtedly exercised some control. Apparently what they did not do was to unify each production aesthetically or to make some personal statement through the production itself.

The "master of secrets," keeper of the register, and other figures of the medieval European theatre were at least analogous to directors, although they may have combined the roles of designer, technician, and stage manager more than they directed in a modern sense. A certain amount of actor coaching was done by these men, especially with amateur actors, but medieval accounts and pictures suggest that it was as managers more than as artists that such people were wanted.

With the rise of professional acting companies, *actor–managers* appeared,

Figure 10–20. Before Directing: Molière. As man of the theatre, Molière performed many of the functions of the modern director.

combining the roles of producer and director-as-manager. Molière was the supreme example of the type in France, and his play *The Versailles Impromptu* shows him rehearsing his troupe as both playwright and acting coach. His position as the troupe's playwright gave him much added authority, of course, both within the company and in Paris and at the court. There is no reason to believe, however, that his "directing" ever included such matters as picturization or the introduction of personal statements or effects or theories of theatre. As well, Molière exercised virtually no control over scenery and costumes, and much of his work for the court (the great *comédies–ballets,* for example, like *Le Bourgeois Gentilhomme*) was under someone else's supervision. Still, Molière represents one line of what we have come to recognize as a two-pronged evolution of directing, that of the experienced and practical theatre person who seeks to improve his company's work. (Significantly, many such people were playwrights.)

The tendency shown by Molière continued in the work of people like David Garrick during his years as actor-manager at London's Drury Lane (1747–1776), when he banished spectators from the stage, perfected his own "natural" style of acting, and brought the stage designer De Loutherbourg to London. Garrick's tendency, like that of Molière and other people working in the mainstream theatre, was to improve what already existed, not to innovate. Garrick sought to get the best out of the best people of his time, to perfect what was already being done. This effort, however, has to be compared with that of another early "director," the German author–critic Johann Wolfgang von Goethe. During his "Weimar Classicism" period (c. 1796–1807), Goethe was a dictatorial protodirector, setting down rules for stage action and acting, picking scripts, controlling stage movement, business, and line readings. He represented the other view that would eventually appear in modern directing, that of the theorist who distrusts the variable and unpredictable talents of others, especially of actors, and who seeks to unify and improve them by locking them into rigidly planned and rehearsed performances.

In France, from the late 1790s on, a tendency toward directorial control of production appeared in the boulevard theatres and especially in the work of the playwright Guilbert de Pixérécourt. Here, for perhaps the first time, a change in theatre production encouraged the appearance of a director; Pixérécourt's plays, which he staged himself, depended heavily on precise timing and the carefully rehearsed use of stage effects and three-dimensional properties. Only through the assertion of a single, central control could such timing and effects work properly, and Pixérécourt seized that control to guarantee the success of his plays.

The First Modern Directors: Wagner and Saxe-Meiningen

Richard Wagner composed large, "mythic" operas that are still important in the world repertory, such as *Tannhäuser,* the *Ring Cycle, Parsifal.* The Duke of Saxe-Meiningen governed a theatre company that toured Europe from 1870 to 1890. Wagner was a theorist as well as a composer, and his "master artwork" represents the theorist's attempt to cope with the unpredictability of actors by completely dominating them; Saxe-Meiningen came closer to a Garrick or a Molière in his comparative trust of his actors, although he, too, was nearly dictatorial in his actual work with them. Between these two, Wagner and Saxe-Meiningen, the role of the director and the impact of his work was brought to the attention of the world; and, after them, most Western theatres would want—and would have—a director.

Wagner's work in his own theatre at Bayreuth, Germany (1876–1883) was monumental, total in its control over the performance, and of enormous European influence because of Wagner's reputation. He oversaw every aspect of each production. The opera house itself was a revolutionary building designed according to his theories. Although not a "realist" in the theatre, Wagner was a believer in illusionistic theatre, and his work as a director at Bayreuth was of immediate use to directors elsewhere.

The Duke of Saxe-Meiningen's troupe specialized in historical and poetic dramas in which realism and historical accuracy of costume and setting were important and in which group composition, balance, movement, and individual posture were given great attention. Saxe-Meiningen's was a highly pictorial directing style (the duke himself was a painter) that emphasized focus and composition. Famous for its crowd scenes and its ensemble acting, the Saxe-Meiningen company gave Europe an outstanding example of a detailed visual realism of the kind that the new theatre was seeking; more lastingly, it gave it an example of the result of a dominant director working to bring a unified style to a large company.

Twentieth-Century Directing: Eclecticism and Monomania

The impact of Saxe-Meiningen's work was to be seen almost immediately in the practices of such early directors as Antoine (the Théâtre-Libre, Paris, 1886), Stanislavski (the Moscow Art Theatre, 1898), Shaw (after c. 1898), and others. Although Wagner's work did not have the same direct influence, his theories did, and his concept of the "master artist" was carried even farther by the English designer–theorist Edward Gordon Craig (after 1902). Craig's "supermarionette," a puppet or robot to be controlled by the master artist, was his solution to the variability and unpredictability of the actor; the idea remained unrealized, however, and Craig's own work as a director was far from successful. Nonetheless his and Wagner's distrust of the actor and their demand for a solution to the problem of the actor (as they saw it) has continued in one line of modern directing theory. (It is significant of the shift in values in the theatre that the actor had usually been considered

Figure 10–21. After Saxe-Meiningen: Antoine. *Monsieur Vernet* at the Theatre Antoine, 1903.

Figure 10–22. Early American Directing: Belasco. David Belasco's own play, *The Girl of the Golden West,* 1905. *(Courtesy of the Theatre Collection of the New York Public Library.)*

central to theatre art.) It was taken up by, among others, Vsevolod Meyerhold, whose "biomechanics" and "constructivism" combined with this dictatorial direction to render his actors little more than puppets. It is with Meyerhold, too, that we begin to see clearly the director's tendency to wrest control of the play text from the playwright, a tendency already visible in Craig's stage designs. Thus, by the first quarter of the twentieth century, some directors had already sought to establish themselves at the very center of the theatre in place of the actor and the playwright.

Other directors, however, followed the more pragmatic example of Saxe-Meiningen. Although equally autocratic in their methods, in many cases, they saw their role as that of interpreter or organizer of the play-as-performance, especially in the realistic theatre. Within a decade of Antoine's staging of realistic plays in Paris, other realist directors were at work all over Europe; by 1900, the word *director* was in wide usage even in the popular press. In America, the illusionistic staging of Steele MacKaye in the 1880s was carried forward by one of his assistants, David Belasco, who became the preeminent example in America of the practical director. Also a producer and a playwright, Belasco did popular plays in a strictly commercial atmosphere, duplicating some of the earlier realists' experiments (the use of a real restaurant with real food, for example) both for their spectacle and for their public relations potential. In a very real sense, Belasco was the first of the *eclectic* American directors, one who would draw on any tradition, *ism,* or practice if it would serve his own ends.

The most important eclectic director, however, was not Belasco but the German Max Reinhardt. An authoritarian, Reinhardt was not at all a rigid theorist, and his productions covered a spectrum from the grandiose *The Miracle* (early 1920s) to an intimate production of Frank Wedekind's *Spring's Awakening* at the Berlin Kammerspiele to a circus-ring production of *Oedipus Rex*. Reinhardt had no one style, no one theory; if he experimented, it was not along a theoretical line but along a practical one to find what would work best with each play for its audience. From his work and its reputation came the methods of the eclectic directors who dominated the theatre until the 1960s: Tyrone Guthrie in England, Canada, and the United States, for example. It is, in fact, these eclectic directors who have dominated most mainstream European and American theatre, and it is their methods and practices that are taught in the hundreds of theatre programs in the United States and Canada, which seek to train directors capable of staging a wide variety of plays in a wide variety of styles.

In the United States, realistic staging took a more extreme course after about 1940 with the work of a group of psychological realists, of whom none was more successful or more famous than Elia Kazan. A product of the Group Theatre, Kazan represented the culmination of the American interest in Stanislavskian "inner" work, with its incorporation of theories of psychology and with the director functioning more than ever before as an acting coach. Kazan's work with the playwrights Arthur Miller and Tennessee Williams on plays like *Death of a Salesman* and *A Streetcar Named Desire* shows another side of this development: the American director who has placed himself at the theatrical center and who works as mentor and critic of the playwright as well as coach and therapist of the actor. Kazan withdrew from the theatre about 1965 and is now a novelist, although he is likely to be best remembered as a great director of plays and films.

The late 1960s brought what seemed to be a new kind of director into the theatre. Not an eclectic but a theoretician, he may yet prove to be but a variation of the Wagner–Meyerhold type; however, these directors to date

Figure 10–23. American Eclecticism. Experiments and avant-garde techniques quickly move into the mainstream of eclectic American directing, as in this production of Aristophanes' *Lysistrata,* where elements of *Hair* and the experimental direction of the nineteen-sixties can be seen. *(Kenyon College production. Directed by James A. Patterson.)*

have shown significant differences in their willingness to trust the actor (although skeptics have pointed out that they tend to surround themselves with actors who are psychologically and spiritually dominated by them). Their work seems to be based on an idea of group art—not of an ensemble in the Molière or the Saxe-Meiningen sense, but of a cooperative creating body, often working within a quasi-religious framework. Seminal to such directors have been the writings of Antonin Artaud (or, rather, the small portions of Artaud's writings available in languages other than French). These directors include Jerzy Grotowski, Peter Brook in his more recent work, Julian Beck and Judith Malina of the Living Theatre, and Richard Schechner. Each is bound to his theatre by strong ideological ties, even by idealism, as the actors are bound by a commitment and a discipline that is spiritual as well as artistic. Although each shows some eclecticism of styles, they are radically unlike the earlier eclectics in their inability or their unwillingness to confront traditional texts on their own terms. They often invent new theatre pieces or combine and alter old ones. Like most experimental directors, they are already seeing some of their innovations coopted by the eclectic directors of the mainstream.

.

CHAPTER 11

The Design Team: Scenery, Lighting, and Costumes

The Design Team

Sitting in the modern theatre, one sometimes takes the presence of scenery so much for granted that it is almost easy to forget that theatre does not have its roots in either spectacular effects or localizing settings. We have become acculturated to the presence of physical environments that so closely suit the mood and meanings of each play that we may lose sight of the fact that the theatre for a very long period used little more than the architectural details of the theater building itself as environment and that for centuries after that, it was satisfied with stock settings that could do for many plays: a room in a palace, a garden, a forest. We live in a period of magnificent settings and superb designers; however, stage design has not always been considered fundamental to theatre or its performance.

Much the same thing is true of costume designers, although it seems likely that their art (extended to include the making of masks) is a very, very old one, whereas sound designers are so recent an innovation that most theatregoers over forty are still surprised to see them listed in the program. Creators of lighting effects may be said to go back to the Renaissance, but it is probably more helpful to think of the art of stage lighting as coming into its own when a controllable means of illumination was invented: gaslight (about 1830).

Figure 11–1. The Work of the Designer. Detail, "authenticity," and other elements of the realistic theatre brought forward a theatre artist who had been less important in some earlier theatres. *Orpheus Descending* at the University New Orleans. *(Directed by William Harlan Shaw, set design by Lane Halteman, costumes by Barbara R. Alkofer, lights by Robert Hardison. W. A. Hunt, III, photo.)*

Actors, directors, and playwrights work with life as their material. Theatre designers, however, work with the *environment* of human life, and their materials are the materials of our world—light and shadow, fabric and color, wood and canvas, plastic and metal and paint. Because their materials are of this kind, the designers are far more vulnerable to shifts in technology than are actors, playwrights, or directors. In fact, advances in technology inevitably change the way in which theatre designers practice their art, and, in the case of both light and sound, technology virtually created the arts. Thus, theatre designers stand in both the world of the artist and the world of the artisan or the mechanic, and they usually must be expert in both.

What Is Theatre Design?

Because the designers derive their materials and their subjects from the real world, it should be easy to understand that their art is the creation of worlds on the stage. These worlds are sometimes imitations of the real world,

Figure 11–2. Costume Design. Dressing the actor probably pre-dates dressing the theatre. Here, a nineteenth-century costume design.

Dolorès. Acte I.

Croquis d'un costume de M. Paul Steck

Velours uni

Velours

Soie avec application passement mat.

fourrure

Nœuds soie

Passementerie perles ivoire

Caractéristique du costume

Costume en soie & velours blanc, unie, soie unie broché, garnie de petite passementeries fourrures du même ton aux manches. les doubles manches bien amples.
Tablier de dessous, dessins appliqués sur fond de soie unie. Le petit col de ruche posé sur un double col uni & solide. les souliers de même nuance & unis

sometimes not; in either case, they use familiar materials, but often in unfamiliar ways. The scenic and costume designers know that their products will be seen under colored light and so will look quite different on the stage from the way they look in sunlight; the lighting designer knows that he must satisfy the needs of the audience—to see the actors, most simply—as well as provide mood, color, and emphasis, while illuminating surfaces that are quite different from the things they imitate; the sound designer may be asked to create sounds that never existed in life or to amplify and distort real sounds to match the needs of a bizarre world.

The world that the designers create is the world of the play, which is not at all the same thing as a literal copy of the real world. Each designer

Figure 11–3. The Designer's World: Technology and Art. Designer Lee Simonson said that "technology is the tail to the poet's kite," meaning that it must be mastered by the designer for his art to be successful. The Madison Square Theatre, 1884, with then-new technological innovations, including an elevator stage.

goes about his or her task differently in creating that world, but each shares a common goal: to create a world within which the actors can create convincing life. This goal means that the designers must work as a team and that they must work in concert with the director, so that a compatible world is created by all of them.

This world begins with the play. There are cases, of course, where designers have made sketches and labeled them "Setting for a tragedy," or something of the sort, but these are exercises. Contemporary design is tied inescapably to the dramatic text. The world that it creates has its roots deep within that text—*not* merely in the stage directions, but in the lives of the characters. It should be easy to see, for example, that the "Rome" of *Julius Caesar* is not the same as the "Rome" of the musical comedy *A Funny Thing Happened on the Way to the Forum.* The stage directions of both may say "Rome," but the tragic action of one and the comic helter-skelter of the other demand utterly different worlds; and the designers will create quite different worlds, where people wear quite different clothes and walk about in quite different kinds of light and shadow and hear quite different kinds of sound.

Several factors, all to be found in the play, govern how the designers create their world.

Tone and Mood

We could say "genre," rather than "tone and mood," but it would be inaccurate. Designers pay close attention, of course, to the vast differences between comedy and tragedy, but these two categories are simply not enough. Every play is its own category and must be approached through the range of tones that it contains. If the play is Henrik Ibsen's *A Doll's House,* the designers must be aware of both the light-heartedness of several early scenes and the great seriousness of the last act; if the play is Tennessee Williams's *The Glass Menagerie,* they must sense both the romantic quality of Tom's recollections and the fragility of his sister's life; if the play is Neil Simon's *Chapter Two,* they must be ready for both Simon's funny gags and the real sadness of the central character's dilemma. *And* they must express these subtleties in settings, costumes, lights, and sounds that are required by the scripts: a middle-class Scandinavian drawing room, a St. Louis apartment, a New York City high rise.

Figure 11–4. Tone and Mood. Visual elements of costume and setting are combined here into a strong visual statement that sets tone and mood. *The Eiffel Tower Wedding Party* at the University of Wisconsin–Rock County. Directed by Felicia Hardison Lordré. Designed by Gary J. Lenox.

Figure 11–5. Level of Abstraction. Plays with specific locales need not be specifically located by the designs. *Exit the King* at the University of Missouri, Columbia. *(Directed by David Jones, design by Christian Cooper.)*

Level of Abstraction

The designers are faced with a very wide spectrum of possibilities, from literal realism to fantasy to almost pure abstraction. At one extreme, for example, could be the setting for a play like Eugene O'Neill's *Desire Under the Elms,* where the decision might be made to create a literal replica of a house in New England down to the last detail of the patterns in the wallpaper. At the other extreme might be one of the "space stage" settings of the 1920s and after, abstract constructions of stairs, ramps, and levels on which some of the plays of Shakespeare were staged. In costuming, we might find real clothes, purchased from actual stores and dyed to represent sweat and dirt; at the other extreme, we might find the costumes of the dancers in the Alwyn Nikolais Dance Theatre, which use elastic fabric, extension of limbs, and various kinds of padding to change completely the outline of the human body.

In part, the decision as to how abstract the designs will be comes from the designers' and director's interpretation of the script; in part, it comes from a decision as to how much the abstraction or literalism of the play itself will be emphasized. In *Desire Under the Elms,* for example, the decision to create literal settings and costumes is not an inevitable one; with equal justification, the designers might decide to create a mere suggestion of the house. In the same way, the designers of a play of Shakespeare's may decide that an abstract setting is inappropriate and may go to quite literal, realistic settings (although such decisions are fairly rare today).

Figure 11–6. Historical Period. In both setting and costume, this production has sought to catch an abstraction of the medieval, although the levels of abstraction of setting and costume do not seem the same. *Once Upon a Mattress* at Centenary College. *(Directed by Robert R. Buseick, sets by David Pellman, costumes by Barbara Acker.)*

Historical Period

As we have indicated elsewhere (see p. 354), the shifting of classical plays from one period to another has become a fairly common practice. Certainly designers are confronted constantly with plays that do not have contemporary settings, costumes, and sound. The look and the "feel" of other periods become important aspects of design, then (and even the lighting designer is affected by historical period, for he may derive ideas about direction and quantity of light and the quality of shadow from looking at paintings and engravings of the period). In setting and costume, some of the implications of historical period are obvious; the kinds of problems that they raise are most often handled by careful research by the designers. Sound, too, may be affected if period music is used or if certain kinds of sounds are called for—footsteps, for example, echoing from the stone walls of an old corridor instead of from modern materials; or the sound of a trumpet flourish; or the sound of Hamlet's "peal of ordnance," and so on.

Historical period contains a trap for the designers. The trap exists in the perceptions and the knowledge of the audience: the designers must consider not only what things looked like in the period but what the audience *think* they looked like. What we know of the 1920s, for example, is conditioned by what we have seen in cartoons, old movies, and magazines—but did all women really bob their hair, and did all men really wear knickers and high collars? In the Elizabethan period, were all houses made of plaster-and-timber fronts, and did all men wear puffed-out breeches and hose? Did warriors in the tenth century wear plate armor? Or, to reverse the calendar, will all people in the distant future wear tight-fitting clothes of unisex design?

And there is still another trap: contemporary fashion. Audiences are greatly influenced by their own ideas of beauty. As a result, a hairstyle that is supposed to be of 1600 and was designed in 1930 will often look more like a 1930 hairstyle than one from 1600; or, to take a familiar example from the movies, cowboys' hats in the movies of the 1940s look far more like 1940s ideas of what was becoming to men than they ever looked like the actual headgear of Westerners of the frontier period.

So designers must think of several things at once when confronted with historical period. It is not enough to go to a book and copy literally what is there.

Geographical Place

As with historical period, geography greatly influences design, unless the decision is made to abandon it altogether (that is, to be abstract instead of literal). The whitewashed houses of the islands of the Mediterranean are vastly different in color, texture, and scale from the adobes of Mexico or the balconied houses of New Orleans; the traditional clothes of Scotland, Morocco, and Scandinavia are distinct; the quality of light in Alaska and the Texas Panhandle is very different. Sound and light are quite different outdoors from in. Even at considerable levels of abstraction, differences in geography inform some design definitions. A recent French production of Molière's *Scapin*, for example, used as its design base an abstract interpretation of Naples, Italy, an idea carried out in its bright, hot lighting and in its setting, which consisted almost entirely of steps and of washing hung out to dry on lines. This setting was very far from literal, but it captured an essence that designer and director thought important.

Socioeconomic Circumstances

The clothes and house and furniture of a Roman emperor are different from those of a servant; the same elements have certain special characteristics

Figure 11–7. Beauty. Costumes, settings, and lighting can create beauty in their own right. The sculptural masks and the abstract costumes do that here. There is sometimes a danger, to be sure, that a beauty that calls attention to itself will actually detract from the performance. *The King of the Great Clock Tower* by William Butler Yeats at the University of Ottawa Drama Guild. *(Directed by James W. Flannery, designs by Jacques Camothe.)*

for the family in *The Glass Menagerie.* As with the other considerations, a decision may be made to ignore such matters, but *a decision must be made.* The matter itself cannot be ignored. And the more realistic the level, the more important these considerations become. In doing *Desire Under the Elms,* for example, it is probably important that the characters' economic level be accurately portrayed. In doing a play like Maeterlinck's impressionistic *The Intruder,* it is very unimportant.

Historical period greatly complicates social and economic matters. As with other historical elements, audiences may have general or inaccurate ideas about what constituted the look of wealth or position or power or poverty in a distant era. What, for example, did a wealthy merchant wear in the seventeenth century that a nobleman did not? What furniture did the nobleman own that the merchant did not? What separated serf from artisan in the Middle Ages?

Again, designers (with the director) may decide to go against audience expectation by confusing the signs of class and wealth. The 1974 film version of *The Three Musketeers,* for example, spread dirt and sweat around pretty evenly among its characters, so that its noble and romantic musketeers were not always distinguishable from their servants or the populace at large. Such a design scheme has to be the product, like all others, of a decision.

Aesthetic Effect

Put most simply, every designer hopes that his designs will have beauty. That beauty is a variable should be clear—the romantic loveliness of a magic forest cannot be compared with a construction of gleaming metal bars and white plastic plates—but that every designer aims at a goal of aesthetic pleasure seems true. Intentional ugliness may occasionally be aimed at, but even then we are tempted to say that the result is beautiful *because* its ugliness is artfully arrived at.

Composition and balance enter into aesthetic consideration just as they enter into the considerations of the director. Teamwork is again essential, as setting, costumes, and lights are inevitably seen by the audience as a whole. Thus unity is also an aesthetic aim, and one achieved through constant sharing of ideas by all the designers.

The Designers at Work

Although many of their decisions are reached in concert (at production meetings), the designers do most of their work in solitude or with the technicians who execute their designs—the scene designer with builders and painters, the costume designer with people in the costume shop, and so on. At this distinct stage of their work, each specializes and proceeds in a way appropriate to his concern.

The Scene Designer

It is the scene designer's job to create a performing space for the actors and a physical environment for the play's action; he makes decisions subject to the considerations already outlined. The result is the setting, which normally has the added function of supplying the audience with clues about the play's locale.

Other important questions are the *number of settings* (Can the entire play be played in one set, or must different sets be designed and changed for each scene, or can some sort of *unit set* serve for all scenes?); the *shape and size of the stage* (Will the audience surround it or look at it through a proscenium arch? If it is small, how can it be kept from seeming cramped? Will the actors play within the setting or in front of it?); the *sight lines* of the theatre (What peculiarities of the theatre's architecture demand that the settings be built in special shapes so that every member of the audience can see?); the *means of shifting the scenery* (Is there overhead *rigging* so that scenery can be "flown," or is there an elevator stage or a turntable stage for bringing new settings in mechanically?); the materials from which the scenery will be built (Is it better to use traditional *flats* of wood and canvas, or will built-up details of wood or plastic be better, or will such special materials

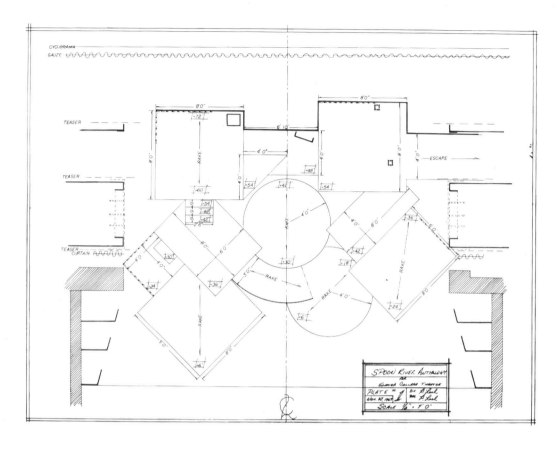

Figures 11–8 and 11–9. Designer's Plan and Sketch. *Spoon River Anthology,* Elmira College. *(Directed and designed by Peter Lach.)*

as poured polyurethane foam or corrugated cardboard or metal pipe be better?); any *special effects* that make special scenic demands (Are there vast outdoor scenes in a proscenium theatre that require large painted *drops,* or will such unusual events in the play as earthquakes, explosions, and so on require special solutions?); any decision to imitate *historical scenery* that creates special requirements (That is, if a seventeenth-century play is to be done with Italianate scenery, what will the effects be?); and the demands of *budget* and *schedule.*

All of these matters may influence the designer before he ever puts pencil to paper, although preliminary doodles and sketches may attempt to catch the "feel" of the play long before any practical matters are dealt with. These early impressions will spring from early readings of the play, and they will eventually be incorporated in some form into the *rendering* of the settings that the designer gives the director. Together, they will have worked out the ground plan of each setting (see p. 357), and the ground plan will form the basis of both renderings and three-dimensional models. If the renderings are acceptable, the designer will proceed to elevations and scale drawings of all scenic pieces, and these, with all instructions for building and painting, will go to the production's *technical director,* the man or woman in charge of executing the scenic designs.

In addition, the scene designer is normally in charge of the design or selection of all *properties,* the things used by the actors that are not part of the scenery (furniture, flags, hangings, and so on), as well as such "hand props" as swords, cigarette cases, guns, and letters. Where such things must be designed, as in a period play, the designer creates and the technical staff executes (as in the Stratford, Ontario Festival theatre, where magnificent period properties are made); where they are acquired from outside sources, the designer haunts stores and antique shops and pores over catalogs of all sorts. In plays done with minimal scenery, as in arena staging, the large properties take on added importance, and their design and selection are carried out with great care.

The Costume Designer

The costume designer clothes both the character and the actor, creating dress in which the character is "right" and the actor is both physically comfortable and artistically pleased. This double responsibility makes the costumer's a difficult job, for he must consider all of the matters already discussed as well as deal directly with the actor and his body. It is never enough to sew up something that copies a historically accurate garment; that garment must be made for a character, and it must be made for an actor. The actor must be able to move and speak; he should also feel led or pushed by the costume to a closer affinity with the character and the world of the play. Generally actors want costumes to be becoming to them personally, and costumers need tact in dealing with people who feel that their legs or their noses or their bosoms are not being flattered.

In designing for the character, the costumer must keep firmly in mind

Figures 11–10 and 11–11. Costume Styles. Peasant dress as interpreted for the stage in the early eighteenth and the mid-nineteenth centuries; the realistically-conceived Irish peasant is the playwright Dion Boucicault, in costume for one of his own plays, the other a dancer. Level of abstraction is very important here, as is the aesthetic consideration of line, silhouette, fabric draping, and ease of movement. *(Boucicault photo from the collections of the University of Rochester Libraries.)*

the *given circumstances* of the character, such as age, sex, state of health, social class, and so on, as well as the focal importance of the character in key scenes (Should he form part of a crowd or stand out?), and most importantly of all, those elements of character that would express themselves through clothes. Is he cheerful or somber? Simple or complex? Showy or timid? Majestic or mousy?

Other important matters are *silhouette* (the pleasing or homely mass and outline of the costume as worn); *the costume in motion* (Does it have potential for swirl or billow or drape or curve as it moves? Does it change with movement? Will it encourage, even inspire, the actor to move more dynamically? What aspects of it—fringe, a scarf, coattails, a cape, a shawl—can be added or augmented to enhance motion?); *fabric texture and draping* (Does the play suggest the roughness of burlap and canvas or the smoothness of silk? What is wanted—fabrics that will drape in beautiful folds, like velour, silk, jersey, or fabrics that will hang straight and heavily?); *fabric pattern* (all-over, small, repeated patterns as opposed to very large designs on the fabric, or none at all); *enhancement or suppression of body lines* (the pelvic V of the Elizabethan waist, or the pushed-up bosom of the French Empire, the pronounced sexuality of the medieval codpiece, or the body-disguising toga; and, for the individual actor, are there individual characteristics like narrow shoulders, skinny calves, or long necks that must be disguised by padding or by control of costume?); and, where necessary, *special effects* (animal or bird costumes, fantasy creatures, and so on).

In addition, the costumer must consult with both scene and lighting designer fairly constantly to make sure that the costumes will look as they are designed to under stage light and against the settings. Practical considerations like budget and deadlines are, of course, always important.

The costumer's designs are usually presented as color renderings, normally with swatches of the actual materials to be used attached and with detailed notations indicated for the *costume shop foreman.* From these, patterns are made where needed; the costumer selects fabrics and usually oversees their cutting and the construction of the costumes themselves. Most theatre companies of any size keep a stock of costumes from which some pieces can be pulled for certain productions, thus saving on both time and money. Costume support areas of any size usually include, besides the stock, fitting rooms, cutting tables, sewing machines and sewing spaces, and tubs for washing and dyeing.

The Lighting Designer

When stages were lighted by candles, attempts to control the light were very crude and seldom very successful. In those days, the lighting designer's work was largely confined to special effects, such as fire. With the introduction of a controllable light source, however, and with the demand in the nineteenth century for more and more realistic imitations of phenomena like sunrise and moonlight, the designer's task became far more challenging and his creation far richer. Very shortly, the possibilities of stage lighting expanded enormously from simple imitation of natural effects, and lighting became a design element as important and as potent as scenery itself.

The possible uses of theatre light are enormous. Through manipulation of intensity and direction, for example, a designer can change the apparent shape of an onstage object. Through manipulation of intensity and color, he can greatly influence the audience's sense of mood and tone. Through manipulation of direction and color, the designer can create a world utterly

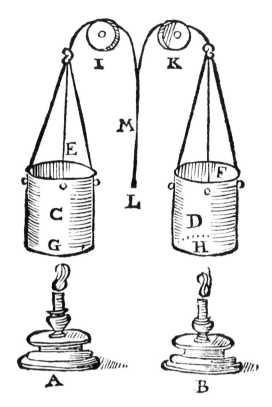

Figure 11–12. Early Lighting.
Candles with a crude "dimmer"
from Sabbattini's *Practica,* 1638.
*(Courtesy Rare Book Division, The New
York Public Library, Astor, Lenox and
Tilden Foundation.)*

unlike the one in which the audience lives, with light coming from fantastic angles and falling in colors never seen in nature.

Modern equipment has made theatre lighting more flexible than early designers ever dreamed. Small, easily aimed *instruments* (lighting units) and complex electronic controls, sometimes with computerized memories, have made possible a subtlety in stage lighting that was unknown even twenty years ago.

The lighting designer works with three fundamentals: *color, direction,* and *intensity* of light. These are partly interdependent because of the nature of the light source, an incandescent filament. *Color* is changed physically by the placement of a transparent colored medium (usually called a *gel*) in the beam of light; these are not usually changed during a performance. *Direction* is a function of the location of the lighting instruments, of which there may be as many as a hundred and fifty in a contemporary production; each instrument is plugged into an electric circuit individually or together with a few others chosen ahead of time to illuminate the same scene. The location of instruments is rarely changed during performance, and so designers are limited by the number of instruments and the number of electrical circuits available to them. (Advanced systems that allow for the mechanized movement of lighting instruments during performance are very flexible, indeed.) Light *intensity* is controlled by changes in the electrical current supplied to the instrument; this process is called *dimming* and is done by manipulating the levers on dimmers, of which several fundamentally different kinds are in use. All have the same goal of changing the amount of light coming from the instrument from zero to full intensity, with the capability of stopping at any point in between.

The lighting designer's plan is called a *light plot.* It shows the location and direction of each instrument, as well as showing what kind of instrument is to be set at each location—usually either a *floodlight* (softedged and wide-beamed) or a *spotlight* (hardedged and narrow-beamed). The locations chosen are over and around the playing area, so that light falls on the actors and the acting space at an angle, both vertically and horizontally. (Light that falls straight down or comes in parallel to the stage floor gives very unusual effects, although both have their uses.) In addition, such subsidiary instruments as *light borders* or *strip lights* (rows of simple lights without lenses, suspended overhead for general illumination), *footlights* (at floor level along the front of many proscenium stages), and *follow spots* (very powerful spotlights that swivel so that their bright beam can constantly illuminate a moving performer) are sometimes used.

The lighting designer is usually responsible for projected scenery or projected shadows, clouds, and similar effects.

The lighting designer has the special responsibility of making everyone else's work accessible to the audience. What he does determines, quite simply, what the audience will see. Light creates depth, for one thing, and it can make an actor's eyes seem to sink into deep sockets or vanish in a bland, flat mask. Light gives or takes color, and it can make costume colors glow with vibrancy or fade into dirty gray. Light is selective, and it can show the audience precisely what is to be seen or it can obscure all manner of things.

In making the other artists' work accessible to the audience, the designer has to consider all three elements: intensity, direction, and color. There are no hard-and-fast rules here; rather, there is need for a manipulation and an experimentation that is like putting colored paint on canvas. Although much of the lighting designer's work is done in production meetings and at the drawing board, much more of it is done in *technical rehearsals,* when, with the director, he experiments with colors and intensities and, frequently, makes decisions to change the locations and the plugging of instruments. Because of this experimental work that comes very late in the production period (often only days before opening), the lighting designer's work is crammed into a short time, and he or she works then at great intensity.

The Sound Designer

Sound became a theatre art with good stereo equipment and related amplification, blending, and tuning equipment. To be sure, sound was used in theatres before that time, and as long ago as Shakespeare's Globe, someone had to be responsible for rolling the cannonballs that simulated thunder, but a sound that could be shaped dimensionally and controlled in pure, correct tones was not possible until very recently. To the regret of many,

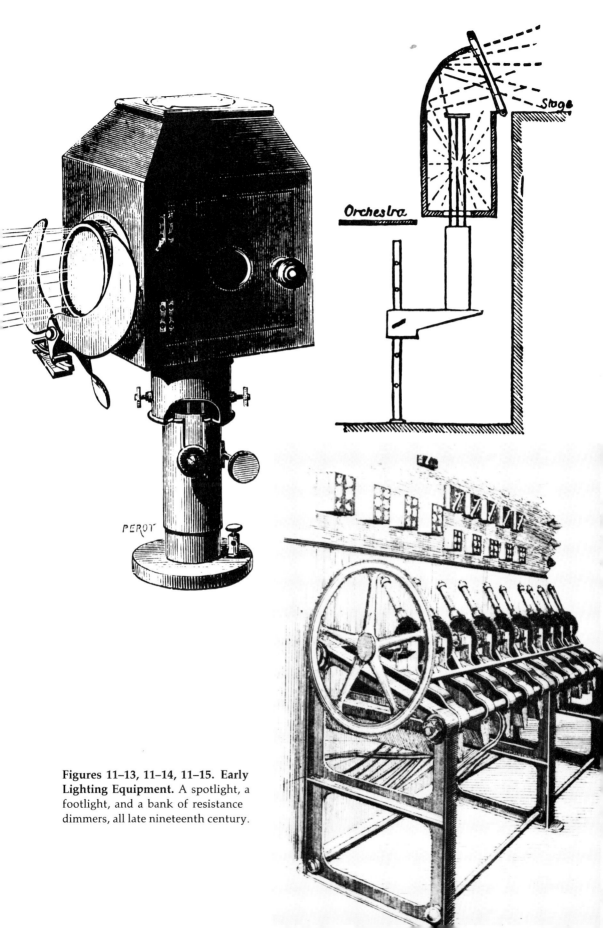

**Figures 11–13, 11–14, 11–15. Early
Lighting Equipment.** A spotlight, a
footlight, and a bank of resistance
dimmers, all late nineteenth century.

Figure 11–16. Lighting Design. Such effects as luminescence and translucency are the lighting designer's work, as well as control of mood, color, and effective illumination of actors and costumes. *A Little Night Music* at Centenary College. *(Directed by Robert A Buseick, design by Clifford L. Holloway.)*

including more than one New York theatre reviewer, the sound designer's job has been expanded on Broadway to the "miking" of performers, so that today many Broadway actors are heard through speakers rather than directly. As good as modern equipment is, it is not yet good enough to allow the effect of several speakers to imitate in range, vibrancy, and direction the natural voice of the actor. It has proved a benefit, however, to actors who lack sufficient voice to be heard in large theatres.

As equipment becomes still more sophisticated and as expertise increases, the work of the sound designer may become as important and creative as that of the lighting designer. Limited at present to concepts of "sound effects" and "background music," the sound designer will one day be able to wrap the audience in sound as the lighting designer wraps the stage in light, and to play as flexibly with sound as the other plays with light. Rock concerts and sound-and-light shows are already pointing the way.

History of Design

Before the Renaissance

Anyone who sets out to build a theatre is, in a sense, a scene designer. This was especially true in those theatres (in Greece and Rome) where the theatre facade itself served as the background for most performances. We have evidence of the use of scenic devices like *periaktoi* and *pinakes,* but we know nothing of the people who designed and executed what went on their surfaces. Costumers, including mask makers, remain mysterious to us, and no examples of their work survive; yet in sculpture and wall paintings we have good examples of what their work looked like.

In the medieval theatre, both scenic and costume design became far more important. Few names of individual designers survive, but the "masters of secrets" on the Continent were both scene designers and master machinists, just as the English and Continental craftsmen who fashioned the ornate devils' costumes seen in illustrations of the period—as well as such special costumes as the close-fitting leather garments of Adam and Eve and the opulent robes and crowns of the Magi—were costumers of high order. Little attention was paid to any unified concept of design that would run through an entire production, but theatre design did attract artists of very high quality; the painter and miniaturist Jean Fouquet, for example, whose *Martyrdom of St. Apollonia* is one of the great visual records of medieval production (see p. 246), was in overall charge of at least two major medieval productions that we know of.

The Renaissance and the Neoclassical Periods

With the Renaissance revival of classical (mostly Roman) ideas, theatre design moved into entirely new areas. On the one hand, the construction of theatre buildings, which were unknown in the Middle Ages, made the use of a new kind of scenery possible (besides requiring the talents of skilled architects); on the other, the introduction into the theatre of single-point perspective made the employment of a scenic designer essential. Technical mastery carried over from the medieval period made spectacular effects possible, and their planning was absorbed into the designer's work, although master machinists were charged with their execution. Artistic skills brought in from painting and drawing provided the base for the creation of scenes having three dimensions on surfaces that had only two. Early designer–architects like Sebastiano Serlio (sixteenth century) and Joseph Furttenbach (seventeenth century) moved the new art along very quickly, from the heavy scenery of Serlio, with its built-up three-dimensional detail and its painted wings and returns, through various methods of changing scenes quickly with the use of painted flats, wings, drops, and borders. In Elizabethan England, Inigo Jones brought this Italianate staging to the court theatre and

Figure 11–17. Renaissance Costume. Royal entries and masques, as well as the theatre, called for lavish costume design throughout the Renaissance.

executed for it both superb settings and lavish costumes. By the time of Giacomo Torelli (later seventeenth century), the designer's art was a very rich one indeed, and one that Torelli carried to heights thought magical through his control of effects and rapid changes.

Costumes, unlike settings, had not been affected by any such fundamental change as the introduction of perspective, and they were a logical development of the skills of the Middle Ages and the early Renaissance. In both scenery and costumes, specific imitation was not in the least aimed at; generalized settings (a room in a palace, a garden) and emblematic costumes (a noble in the Roman manner, a Turk) were the object. Both setting and costumes could be lavish on occasion, as in the great masques of the several courts, but in the commercial theatre, both scenes and costumes were made to serve many plays without much attention to their specific rightness.

In the eighteenth century, Italianate design was carried to its ultimate development by the Bibiena family, whose complex interiors in multiple-point perspective were truly magnificent embodiments of their audience's fantasies.

The Eighteenth-Century Through Realism

Between 1750 and 1900, two important changes took place: costume and scenery shifted from the generalized to the specific, and theatre lighting first came under artistic control. David Garrick initiated both these changes in London when he imported the artist Phillippe de Loutherbourg, a scenic designer of great skill and an experimenter with colored and controlled light. De Loutherbourg was not an innovator of scenic practice—in a very real sense, the shape of theatrical scenery did not change until the box set was introduced in the mid-nineteenth century—but he was an important innovator in the way he used scenery and in the things he took as scenic subjects. "Local color" became his concern in many scenes, so that the replication of actual places and of actual historical periods was attempted, and to accomplish this relative accuracy, he began to break up the symmetrical wing-and-border arrangement of traditional scenery. *Relieves* that had cutouts through which deeper scenes could be observed, flats with curved and broken edges, and wings placed asymmetrically and at angles became common. Upon these were scenes painted in a style that was beginning to approach the pictures painted by the pre-Romantics. De Loutherbourg also supervised his own settings and created all the settings for most of his productions, and thus *unity* became a real concern of the designer.

In the Romantic period, de Loutherbourg's example was continued by many designers; in London, the outstanding artist was William Capon. If a single word defines his work, it is *specificity*, for with Capon, the concern with real places and correct historical reproduction, based on research, became important. The same broken scenic lines and asymmetry of de Loutherbourg continued, as they were joined, as the nineteenth century progressed, by elaborate stage machinery to satisfy an audience hungry for spectacle.

Figure 11–18. The Scene Painter. Romanticism and Realism both put a premium on artistic scene-painting. This is a nineteenth-century artist's view of a scene-painting studio, examples of which still exist wherever large painted settings are used.

Figure 11–19. Unified Costume Design. The same impulse that led to historically accurate settings created an appetite for accurate costumes that were unified across a production. This is a costume for the London production of *Julius Caesar* seen in Figure 5–9, designed by the Academy painter Alma-Tadema. It is "accurate"—but it looks like a late Victorian gown.

Melodrama demanded spectacle and specificity; design and technology kept pace, or tried to, until moving pictures abruptly made them irrelevant by giving the mass audience a form in which a much more convincing spectacle and a much more detailed specificity were possible.

Gaslight came to some metropolitan theatres by 1830; the box set was introduced about the same date. The Romantic scenery of Capon was adaptable to realistic uses, especially to the historically accurate productions of Shakespeare that highlighted the second half of the century in London, and it was this scenery by and large—highly complex, often asymmetrical, but still painted on two-dimensional flats—that dominated much of the mainstream of scenic design well into the twentieth century. The box set was structurally different, of course, and was far more suitable to the realistic interiors that were demanded by both realism and naturalism, yet the basic design approach was the same: reproduction of specific kinds of locale through the application of techniques and concepts of reality brought over from painting.

In costume, unified design was impossible until the practice of having actors provide their own costumes was changed. To be sure, developments toward the specific were made in the Romantic period—more accurate Roman costumes, Macbeths in Scottish garb, ancient Greeks with bare arms instead of the sleeves of an eighteenth-century coat—and as the century moved forward, the increasing interest in local color and historical reconstruction led to greater attention to costume detail. When the English actor–managers were able to organize entire productions with entirely unified designs, the modern concept of the costumer's art became prominent. The same development was taking place on the Continent in the productions of the Duke of Saxe-Meiningen and in the French state theatres. By 1900, many individual artists were being brought into the theatre to create entire productions; the use of the English academic painter Sir Lawrence Alma-Tadema to design the settings and costumes of Sir Herbert Beerbohm Tree's *Julius Caesar* (see p. 342) is simply an example of a trend.

After Realism: Toward the Modern Theatre

Electric light reached commercial theatres in the 1880s; the American Steele MacKaye experimented with it from that time until his death, although the rather primitive instruments and dimming equipment made creative lighting difficult.

The potential of electric light was seen almost immediately, however, and the great prophet of light as a new design medium appeared in the person of Adolphe Appia before the turn of the century. Appia used music as a metaphor of theatrical art and light as an embodiment of that metaphor, to be orchestrated, played with, and treated as melody, *leitmotif,* and theme with variations. But in espousing the use of the new technology, Appia (who was followed by the much more vocal Gordon Craig) was also espousing a change in the basis of theatrical scenery: instead of two dimensions with a third dimension suggested by painted perspective, there would be architectural mass in three dimensions. It was a shift from the flat surface to the cube. In design after design, Appia and Craig showed great masses broken by stairs and planes, upon which light fell in mysterious and magical patterns. Ideologically they had moved theatre design from realism to symbolism and impressionism; artistically they had moved it from the techniques of the painter to the techniques of the architect.

By World War I, the Appia–Craig approach had radically influenced the work of many designers. Even realistic design was affected, and "selective realism" became common, with the ultrarealistic stage picture giving way to clusters of realistic objects within the playing area: furniture backed by partial walls, for example, and houses suggested by skeletal structures, as if their joists and studs had been stripped bare. The result was a cross between the symbolic and the realistic, and it had a romantic and "poetic" quality that persists in much American scene design right up to the present. For example, the use of shutters and doorways and rooflines suspended in space against cycloramas suggestive of infinite distance has an emotional softness that has proved effective for the plays of dramatists like Tennessee Williams. American designers from Lee Simonson and Norman Bel Geddes to Jo Mielziner adapted the Appia–Craig approach to American realistic drama to achieve this selective realism, Bel Geddes in the 1920s and 1930s going far toward symbolism with the "space stages" of his Shakespearean productions (assemblages of ramps, steps, and platforms to provide many acting areas for large-cast plays, but with no specific locales).

Contrasted with this eclectic American design is the highly theatrical design approach espoused by the playwright–director Bertolt Brecht and executed for him by the designers Teo Otto and Caspar Neher. Here, instead of cutaway objects, houses seen against infinite space, or romantic groupings of realistic objects, entire but undersized houses were used, with properties of such realism that they were actually usable (real armor with real dents; real pots and pans; real, not painted, dirt), all seen against backgrounds that suggested the theatre and not poetic infinitude—flat hangings or projected slogans on the wall of the theatre. Lighting instruments were hung in view of the audiences, and this epic scenery was designed to dovetail perfectly with Brecht's epic direction and drama.

The shift from painterly to architectural scenery and the new emphasis on light went hand-in-hand with new ways of seeing theatre space. When, for example, the designer Jo Mielziner wanted to move beyond the proscenium arch with the setting for Arthur Miller's *Death of a Salesman* in 1947, the move was thought very daring, but in 1950, the first American arena stages began to appear, and by the mid-1960s, thrust stages were the focus of theatres at Stratford, Ontario, and elsewhere. With the waning of emphasis on perspective and two-dimensional painting, the proscenium arch became less and less important; the playing space in new theatres moved out into

Figure 11–20. Costume for Dance. This "lily" costume for Loie Fuller (1900) is a superb example of a costume designed to be in motion, a prime requisite of dance costume design and one that led to the abstract designs of modern dance.

Figure 11–21. Nonrealistic Costume. Alice and the Dormouse, from *Alice in Wonderland,* 1887.

the audience, and designers moved architectural setting and three-dimensional lighting along with it. After the invention of the transistor in the late 1950s, lighting controls became rapidly smaller and more flexible, resulting in a rapid increase in the number of instruments that a designer could effectively use; and lighting instrumentation (itself greatly helped by the introduction of the smaller and lighter quartz lamp in the 1960s) multiplied. The difference is symbolized by the comparison of a small professional theatre of 1950, which used twenty-three instruments to light its 20-foot by 20-foot arena stage, and a university theatre of 1978 that used over a hundred instruments to light its 27-foot by 27-foot arena.

Again, no fundamental shift in costume design paralleled the change in scene design, and no new technology appeared to change it as lighting had changed scenery. Innovations in the field of dance did move one branch of costume toward abstraction, and from Isadora Duncan through Alwyn Nikolais, dance creatively exploited an antirealistic costume that the narrative theatre rarely dared try. New materials were introduced (nylon, mylar, and stretch fabrics), but they changed only the price and some details of sewing. Costume designers were affected by the sudden changes in stage lighting,

Figure 11–22. **Costume As Commentary.** Costume (including makeup) can sometimes be designed to make a satirical point, as in this production of *Cabaret*. (Courtesy of Florida State University. Directed by Richard Fallon.)

and they could pay new attention to both color and fabric because those things would be seen in new ways. Ideological matters also affected costume: epic theatre costumes had the same reality and lack of "prettiness" as epic scenery and epic acting; American selective realism, on the other hand, accepted the glamorization of the actor and the character (or of certain actors and certain characters) as inevitable; and only in experimental, nonrealistic theatres were costumes and masks used as symbolic statements or outright labels (in, for example, street theatre, the exaggerated elements of groups like the Bread and Puppet Theatre, or the political grotesques of El Teatro Campesino).

Theatre design in the last quarter of the twentieth century has become diverse in its approaches and its ideologies, and national styles are discernible;

nevertheless design of the contemporary period is so different from that of a century ago that its individual examples have far more in common with each other than with any historical antecedent. The change from painted flats to three-dimensionality was important; the change from candlelight and gaslight to electricity was profound. Perhaps most important of all, the incorporation of design into theatre training at all educational levels has led to the acceptance of a common denominator: the unification of all design into a single, overriding scheme consonant with the dramatic script.

CHAPTER 12

The Playwright and the Critic

It may seem odd to pair two people as unlike in many ways as a playwright and a critic; certainly many playwrights and many critics would themselves think it very peculiar. They have, however, a number of things in common: both are profoundly concerned with performance, but neither takes a part in it; both focus on the play text, although both concern themselves with the work of actors, directors, and designers; both do a much higher proportion of their work away from the theatre than other theatre makers.

There are, of course, profound differences between them, for all that some critics have also written plays and some playwrights have also ventured into criticism. That there is a difference in psychology and in temperament between them seems clear. Many people would insist that there is an essential difference in the basic nature of their activities, one being creative and the other not so much creative as technically proficient. Often actual playwrights and actual critics are bitter enemies: the playwrights believe they have been cruelly and unfairly handled by critics, while the critics (actually reviewers, more often than not) feel that playwrights and other theatre people ascribe motives and powers to them that they do not have.

Thus the playwright and the critic are both related and distinct. They are two sides of a coin, two sides with quite different faces but a common substance. Their real concern is with the nature of dramatic art and its extension to the stage.

The Playwright

"Good playwrights begin as bad poets," a writer (not himself a good playwright) is alleged to have said. What he meant was that playwrights show much of the poet's concern with language but finally lack the poet's control of it. Many literary people (by whom we mean poets, novelists, book critics, literary and academic historians, and so on) consider it a bad thing that playwrights "start out as bad poets"—that they do not enshrine the word above all else. In fact, to see this quality as "bad" is to overlook what the playwright's task is all about.

Wright means "maker." As a wheelwright used to be a maker of wheels

Figure 12–1. The Playwright: Ibsen. The nineteenth-century dramatist Henrik Ibsen—a creator of dynamic theatre, a figure of controversy, a man whose work spanned several forms and styles during a career that was dedicated to perfecting his craft.

and a shipwright used to be a maker of ships, so the playwright is a "maker of plays"—not a *writer* of plays. At least, not basically and primarily.

The playwright is a writer because writing—the setting down of a set of symbols—is the best way we have to describe certain kinds of events. It is partly an accident that what the playwright does looks like what the poet does and like what the novelist does—setting down words on paper. If playwrights had a set of symbols like mathematical notation or musical notation, we might be less tempted to think of them as literary artists (i.e., people who started out as "bad poets"), for nobody thinks of mathematicians or composers as literary artists gone wrong. In addition to his use of language to describe dramatic action, of course, the playwright also deals in the language of his characters, and because they speak with the same words in which poems and books are written, the playwright "writes" dialogue for them, and so is a "writer."

It is a common misconception that any writer who writes good conversation "ought to write a play." Novelists and short-story writers often write excellent conversation in their works. Is it a clue to their potential to write plays? Not really. The connection between fictional conversation and stage dialogue is a very thin one, more one of accidental resemblance than of real substance. The novelist's conversation is praised for its truth to life, for example; so is the playwright's sometimes—but the playwright's dialogue is a much more terse, loaded, *active* thing than the novelist's, because it has to serve the needs of the stage and not of the page, and those needs are different, involving character motivation, density of information, and rhythm.

To say categorically that playwrights are not "writers" would be foolish. To say that they are not literary artists would be silly. Playwrights join novelists and poets in various academies of arts and letters; their works are studied in literature courses; people who call themselves literary scholars write books about them. They are not, however, *primarily* literary artists; they are primarily artists of the theatre who leave a literary record (the play) of their work behind. In trying to remember this distinction, we should keep in mind a critic's observation that "Molièr saved French comedy from literature"—that the man of the theatre triumphed, as he always must, over the purely literary artist.

This is not to say that writing plays somehow disables one from writing other things. On the contrary, some poets and novelists have been excellent playwrights: W. H. Auden and T. S. Eliot both wrote for the theatre, as did Byron; people who have been artistically successful with both the novel and the play include the Nobel Prize–winner Samuel Beckett and, two centuries ago, Henry Fielding. We could amass a far longer list of names, however, of literary artists who have failed as playwrights: the novelists Henry James, Ernest Hemingway, and John O'Hara; the poets Edna St. Vincent Millay, Shelley, and Wordsworth, among many. Thus, the playwright is an artist related to literary artists but separable from them—by the nature of the thing he creates, by the nature of the materials in which he works, and probably by temperament and impulse.

Why Playwright?

Why somebody becomes a playwright instead of a novelist or a poet is something of a mystery. There is a germ of truth in the idea that playwrights often start out to be something else. But then, many theatre people start out as something else—directors as actors or stage managers, agents as designers or actors. Perhaps there is a difference in that so often playwrights start out to be something quite outside the theatre. It has often been observed that much of the vitality of new movements in theatre comes from the entry into it of people from entirely outside the theatre who then write a play or plays. The germ of the mystery is why they decide to write that play.

The answer lies in the nature of the playwright's craft: creating replicas of human action rather than records of it (novels) or responses to it (poems).

Outside the mainstream, the theatre has long been very tolerant of forms, length of plays, and styles radically different from those in vogue in the mainstream; that is, what would be "bad plays" by mainstream definition may be welcome outside it. In fact, a case can be made for saying that the newcomer's strength lies in his ignorance; lacking knowledge of the "rules" of mainstream playwriting, he writes in a seemingly new and refreshing way. The first plays of playwrights as widely different as Molière and Edward Albee illustrate this "strength of ignorance," and it is no accident that in both cases the early plays were very short, for the newcomer is unwittingly innovative when he creates what is there to be created and then stops, without regard for the so-called full-length entertainment of mainstream practice. It is when, then, a newcomer has an idea for what we have called a "replica of human action," however slight and however short, that a playwright is in the making. When the newcomer is brought by luck or design into contact with a theatre and theatre people, plays get written.

It is not an accident that new playwrights often appear in bunches. Whether they are the University Wits of the Elizabethan period or the Off-Off-Broadway playwrights of the early 1960s, they are drawn to playwriting by the same theatrical conditions at the same time—in the case of the University Wits, the explosion of theatrical interest in Oxford and London; in the case of the Off-Off-Broadway playwrights, the explosion of theatrical excitement in the cafés of New York City.

Other factors are, of course, important. A dying or dead theatre rarely attracts new playwrights; a vital one does—and, paradoxically, a vital commercial one attracts them both to itself and to its avant-garde opposite. Money is often an important factor, as is social status. It is sometimes argued, for example, that the English theatre did not attract would-be playwrights in the eighteenth century because the licensing laws made the craft financially unattractive, and many turned to the novel instead. When, on the other hand, a theatre offers large financial rewards, as the American theatre has since the 1920s, many new writers are drawn to it.

But only rarely does somebody sit, like a cartoon character, with a light bulb over his head and the words "Aha, I'll be a playwright!" coming out

Figure 12–2. The Play in the Making. The playwright's work does not end with the completion of the script, but continues at least until the first performance and sometimes long after. Here, the first read-through of a new play with actors, playwright, and director—*Getting Off* by Lee Thomas. *(Courtesy of the Eugene O'Neill Theatre Center. Photo by Jon Brandeis.)*

of his mouth in a balloon. Most often, there are early tries at other kinds of creativity, a sense that something needs to be got out of the self and into a form but that the form is unclear, until the often accidental connection with the theatre comes about, and the first play takes shape.

Training and the Craft

Playwrights are neither born or made; they happen. Unlike actors and directors, they do not, as a rule, go through structured periods of formal training to perfect their art. To be sure, there are playwriting programs in American universities, but their record of producing playwrights who write plays of recognized quality is not comparable with their impressive records in acting, direction, and design. Courses in playwriting often familiarize theatre students with the problems of the playwright and give an enriching new slant on other areas of theatre work; advanced degrees in playwriting are frequently combined with scholarly work in such a way that playwriting becomes an adjunct of critical study. Playwriting as an academic discipline, however, suffers from the same problems as creative writing, in general, and when it seems to produce results it is because the same factors are at work: teachers who are themselves artists and who teach as much by example as by precept; constant encouragement of creativity itself, so that the student is surrounded by other writers and playwrights; and strong professional links with agents, producers and publishers, so that entry into the mainstream is greatly eased.

This is not to say that playwriting can neither be learned nor taught. Certain supposed "rules" can always be taught. And when a theatrical style remains in vogue for a long period, playwrights can be "taught" the hallmarks of that style, meaning really that they can be taught how to imitate the plays that have already succeeded in that style. Thus, in the realistic theatre, would-be playwrights could be taught to put exposition into the mouths of characters who had a reason for explaining things; they could be taught to prepare for the third-act resolution by planting information about it in Act I; they could be taught that taxi drivers and duchesses do not speak in the same way; and so on. In so far, then, as playwriting is a craft, such teaching was and still can be effective. Its limitations lie in the difference between the craft and the art of writing for the theatre and between the imitation of an existing style and the innovation of a new one (the newcomer's "gift of ignorance").

As well, when imitation of an existing style has been wanted, playwrights have frequently come from within the theatre. They are "people of the theatre" who are "theatre-wise." What is really meant is that they have familiarity with a particular style. Thus the Restoration actor Thomas Betterton could become a playwright when he wanted a vehicle for himself in the mode of the day; the producer David Belasco could write plays to suit the realistic style of which he was already a master as producer.

When imitation of an existing style has not been the principal object, however, playwrights have often come from totally unexpected directions, and their practice of the craft has been radically different (and has been much pounded by critics; indeed, the work of such newcomers is most often called "not really a play" by reviewers, which is often a way of saying that the work in question is not an imitation of the dominant style). Most often, when newcomers have a very strong impulse to say something in the theatre, however, they do not take kindly to an imitation of the existing style, because styles that have dominated for a long time become increasingly drained of their potential for saying anything. Consequently, we sometimes find newcomers doing really remarkable things—flying in the face of established practice, writing "nonplays," being viewed with derision by mainstream professional and critic alike. In our own time, this has been spectacularly true of both black and feminist playwrights. Both groups have been deeply committed to a view that by its very nature rejected some aspects of mainstream practice, and both groups have been made up of people who feel personally rejected and who, more often than not, *are* rejected by the mainstream. The black plays of the 1960s, therefore, were called "crude," "naive," and so on, just as were the feminist plays of the 1970s. Both groups of playwrights found audiences, however—obviously an essential for any new playwright—and their successes with those audiences, being noted by the mainstream, caused some of the playwrights to be adopted or coopted into the mainstream. As a result, what had been "crude" and "naive" and "not a play" became "experimental" and "new." In such a way are some playwrights' careers shaped; others find success by careful adherence to tradition and established form.

Playwright and Audience

"The drama's laws/The drama's patrons give," Samuel Johnson wrote in the eighteenth century. The remark illustrates, for one thing, a distance between the playwright and the critic, for the playwright usually listens to the audience whereas the critic listens to abstract theory. It illustrates, too, the uneasy relationship between the playwright and his audience, for to the playwright, the audience is a fickle monster that can either make him rich and loved or humiliated and poor. Between playwright and audience exists a relationship that is often ambivalent in the extreme. "The aim of comedy is to make decent people laugh," Molière said, but finding and keeping the attention of those "decent people" was a task that occasionally eluded even him.

Johnson's remark should remind us, too, that the playwright and the critic not only take a quite different view of the "laws" of the drama but also are frequently indifferent to each other. Not all critics, to be sure, set about to define the "laws" of the drama, but many do; yet while they are doing so, the playwrights are listening not to them but to themselves or to the audience. In fact, if we look at the material set forth above, we see that innovative playwrights frequently work apart from or even in opposition to the "laws" of the moment, and that what they write is written according to a set of "laws" that are yet to be discovered. Thus it is a mistake to think that playwrights pursue their craft by listening to critics. Very few do. Probably they often should, but most do not. Many playwrights would insist that they do not because they are themselves the makers of the drama's laws. In fact, they are not. They are artists, who neither make rules nor observe them; they make windows, as it were, through which the landscape of dramatic law can be glimpsed.

The relationship between playwright and audience is rather different. Audiences do not care for the laws of drama either. They care for their own entertainment. They are, however, often conservative and even more cautious. When they go to a theatre, they want to get their money's worth, and they do not want to be lectured at, shocked, frightened, or bored. They do not want to suffer either heart attacks or fits of yawning. As a result, they look with enthusiasm on any novelty that is an imitation of what they are familiar with.

This attitude leaves many playwrights in a quandary. They are all right if they are content to do hackwork—but few are, and even those who are successful hacks dream of one day having an artistic hit. Consequently the majority of playwrights find themselves caught between their own urge to create and their audience's demand that they imitate what has already been done.

As in so many aspects of theatre, the situation is resolved by compromise.

Figure 12–3. Playwright and Director. In the contemporary American theatre, the director often has great influence on the final form that a play will take. Here, director and playwright watch a rehearsal at the Eugene O'Neill Theatre Center, where many new playwrights first see their plays come to life. Left, director Tony Giordano; right, playwright Lee Thomas. *(Photo by Jon Brandeis.)*

The playwright creates early plays that attract a small and sympathetic audience—perhaps made sympathetic by an affinity of situation or of lifestyle, as was the case with the audiences for the early efforts of black, feminist, and Off-Off-Broadway playwrights. After these initial successes, the playwrights move toward the mainstream and the audience moves toward the playwrights, accepting new language, new ideas, new forms, sometimes with a rapidity that is startling. We need only look at the radical changes in the American theatre from 1964 to 1970 to see how very quickly such a shift can be made.

Once established, the playwright enjoys one or more years of acceptance and then, more often than not, begins to lose his audience. Yesterday's innovator is often tomorrow's has-been. Rare is the artist who continues to innovate throughout his life; most reach a plateau and then seem to imitate themselves or, in some cases, to "experiment" with manner rather than with substance (seemingly true in the cases of Tennessee Williams and Edward Albee, for example). A few hold their audiences and grow with them—a Molière, a Shaw, an Ibsen, a Brecht. They are the masters of their art—playwrights of lasting power in secure theatres.

The Playwright's Compromise

In the realistic theatre, playwrights had to strike a balance between their own impulse to expand the meaningful aspect of the theatre and the stage's impulse to limit meaning to the same role that it plays in life. For a Shake-speare or a Molière, who were not limited by considerations of realism, language was the primary means of theatrical communication. Even in the late nineteenth and early twentieth centuries, realistic plays about upper-class life could be heavily verbal because the people they were about were (or so it was believed) articulate and literate. However, as the theatre focused more on inarticulate protagonists in a democratized theatre, verbalism be-came a less useful tool and playwrights found themselves trying to find a compromise between their own impulse to "say" things and their characters' inability to say much of anything.

This example illustrates the kind of compromise that playwrights have always made. In the early nineteenth century, it was a compromise with the pyrotechnical needs of Romantic acting and the needs of Romantic scen-ery; for Molière, it was a compromise with the moral and literary proprieties of a rigid society; for Euripides, it was a compromise with tradition and established, even ritualized, form. No playwright escapes the awareness that there must be a compromise between his own creative impulse and the conditions of the theatre of his time.

For the theatre has two characteristics that do not belong to other arts (except, perhaps, film—whose compromises are often even more severe). First, it is an art where the need to provide a frame for the arts of acting and design must be met; and second, it is a public art, subject to both a legal and a social censorship that the novel, the poem, and the essay do not know. Satisfying the first of these requirements—providing a structure for actor and designer—is not a compromise but a basic quality in writing plays. Satisfying the second—whether it is meeting the stylistic demands of realism or the moralistic demand of censorship—requires a compromise that playwrights make only with reluctance.

The Playwright in the Real World

Plays begin as a great variety of things: a story overheard, a chance remark, a note jotted down on a slip of paper. There are as many beginnings of plays, probably, as there are playwrights—some begin with an idea, some with a character, some with a situation, some with a story. And from that beginning, different playwrights take widely different tracks: some write detailed outlines, some write none; some write hundreds of pages of dialogue, some put down on paper no more than will appear in the finished play. One way or another, however, the play is written—over a period of days, months, or even years—and then its real life begins, for a play on paper is only a long step toward a theatre performance, holding the promise of life instead of life itself.

Getting the Play Produced. In recent years, the number of theatres in which new plays can be produced in the United States and Canada has increased noticeably. The multiplication of regional repertory theatres in the 1960s has led to a reversal of the old situation in which New York produced all new plays and small theatres around the country then picked them up. Many plays now begin their lives in theatres like New Haven's Long Wharf and then move to Broadway or Off-Broadway; in addition, organizations like the National Playwright's Conference of the O'Neill Theatre Center give first productions to a wide spectrum of scripts, many of which are later produced elsewhere. New York, however, and most especially Broadway, remains the goal of most playwrights. There are two reasons: money and status. Broadway royalties are far higher than anywhere else, and Broadway production, with the best actors, directors, and designers, and subject to the best journalistic criticism, is the most prestigious.

Plays are not produced at any of these theatres by accident. Nor are many new plays that attract widespread attention (except at an institution like the O'Neill Center) scripts that come out of nowhere. Most are submitted to regional theatres or Broadway or Off-Broadway producers by agents. Far less often, a play may reach a producer by way of an actor or a director. In any case, the playwright's first high hurdle is finding that first production, whatever the medium he uses to reach a producing organization.

The Playwright and the Theatre. Producers have readers who read scripts and make comments. When a script is accepted for production, it already has an accompanying list of such comments as well as the producer's own views; added to these will be the ideas of the director when one is chosen. Each principal actor will add ideas, and each of these people—producer, director, actors—may have still other ideas that have come from friends, wives, lovers, and relatives. The playwright having his first play done is tempted to try to please everybody, usually under the mistaken notion that he should be grateful for such attention. By the time the playwright has had several plays done, he may be downright rude about suggestions coming from any source at all. Between these two extremes lies the kernel of the playwright's work during the production period: accepting ideas for changes that are wisely based in the unique circumstances of the production. Perhaps regrettably, in the modern American theatre the director is assumed to have considerable critical skill and to be an expert in everything from dramatic structure to dialogue. Changes in a script, however, are rarely simple; as the Broadway playwright William Gibson said some years ago, altering a play is like taking bricks out of a wall: for every one that is taken out, half a dozen others have to be put back. At times, playwrights wonder what it was about their play that ever caused people to want to do it, because they have asked for so many changes that nothing seems to be left of the original. Confronted with this situation, the playwright may throw a temper tantrum, go home, or stiffen his back and say, as more than one successful Broadway playwright has, "Do it as it is!"

The Economics of Playwriting. Broadway playwright Robert Anderson was quoted as saying that he couldn't make a living in the theatre; all he could make was a killing. A few playwrights do make livings, especially as the number of regional theatres has multiplied, but the hit-or-flop life of Broadway still prevails; the playwright can still make only a killing,

Figures 12–4 and 12–5. Rehearsal and Performance. Many changes are made before the new play reaches performance, most of them coming during rehearsal to meet the needs of the actors, the perceived weaknesses of the script, and the creativity of the artists involved. Here, *The Funniest Joke in the World* in an early rehearsal and in performance. *(Anstie's Limit, the University of South Carolina.)*

rarely a living. Standard Broadway contracts, under the aegis of the Dramatists Guild, give the playwright a percentage of the theatre's weekly gross,
a percentage that climbs as the gross climbs past certain plateaus. On a
hit, these figures can be impressive—well over five thousand dollars a week.
On a modest success, they can be a thousand a week or less. On a flop,
nothing. Considering that few playwrights have a successful play every
year, we can easily see that the income from even a hit must be spread
over several years, and after an agent's commission and professional expenses
and taxes are taken out, the prorated remainder may be less than many
upper-level businessmen take home. There are, of course, the significant
additional income of film and television sales—and perhaps most importantly, there is the secondary income of amateur and stock production.

Amateur rights are handled mostly by two organizations, the Dramatists
Play Service and Samuel French, Incorporated. They collect royalties on
productions by amateurs (community, school, and university theatres) for
the life of the play's copyright—since the Copyright Law of 1977, the author's
life plus fifty years. Although the royalty on a single performance of a
play is small, the collective royalty per year on a play that is popular with
the nation's several thousand community and college theatres can be large,
and even plays that fail on Broadway can become staples of amateur theatre
and go on providing income for decades.

Yet, with all this, relatively few people make a living as playwrights.
It is a difficult craft that requires special talent, and it is made far more
difficult by the conditions under which plays must find production.

The Critic

Critics generally have a bad name in the theatre and, indeed, in the
world in general, where "to criticize" means to speak harshly of something.
One writer called critics "crickets" because of their supposed chirps and
annoying, insectlike attacks; the eighteenth-century satirist John Swift wrote
of "The vermin critic . . . With harpy claws and pois'nous tongue." Oliver
Wendell Holmes, the nineteenth-century American author, said, "Nature,
when she invented, manufactured, and patented authors, contrived to make
critics out of the chips that were left." These negative senses of *critic* and
criticize should be put aside, however; in a theatrical context, a critic is a
person who evaluates, knowledgeably and fairly and from a defined set of
standards. "A man skilled in the art of judging literature" was Samuel Johnson's definition more than two hundred years ago; for all its narrow-minded-
ness of gender, it does emphasize the ideas of skill, art, and judgment, which
are still important to the act of criticism. The judgment itself, however, is
not a yes–no, good–bad one, but an analytical process that tries to measure
a particular (a play or a performance) against a standard based on other
particulars. The act of critism may also be the measurement of the standard

Figure 12–6. The Playwright and a Critique. At the O'Neill Center, the playwright gets feedback from knowledgeable theatre people after presentation of his play. Here, playwright Keven Morrison, right, meets with (left to right) dramaturg Marilyn Stasio, director Tony Giordano, and Artistic Director Lloyd Richards. *(Photo by Roger Christiansen.)*

itself against the particular; indeed, in the activity of a good critic, the two are always being tested against each other.

There are very few critics in any age, although there are usually a good many people who are mistakenly *called* critics. Just as the playwright seems to be a writer because he appears to engage in the same act as literary writers, so many journalists are called critics because they appear to engage in the same acts as critics. Thus we must distinguish among three kinds of function.

The Reviewer. Reviewers are familiar to most people from daily newspapers. They also appear on television and radio. They review films, TV programs, plays, books, and so on. The most common vision of the reviewer (thought of popularly as a vision of "the critic") is a person rushing from the theatre at the final curtain to write a review before the deadline for the newspaper's morning edition. There is some accuracy to this notion, and it explains in part why reviewers are seldom critics: they have too little time for the exercise of judgment, art, or skill. About all they have time for is the exercise of personal reaction. There is nothing inherently wrong in this, except that what the reviewer is most often saying is "I liked/disliked this," a statement that is not an exercise of analytical judgment but a personal response. The trained and experienced reviewer knows that it is a personal response and has trained himself to recognize the response and to be able to turn it into interesting, often witty prose; the very experienced reviewer will be able to compare it with other responses and other plays and make comparisons that are sometimes quite revealing. Reviewers who write for weekly or monthly journals may have the time to exercise judgment instead of reaction and may function as critics, although the type is rare. Walter Kerr of the New York *Times,* for example, sometimes reaches this level. At the opposite pole are journalists with no theatre knowledge who write a species of "gee-whiz" feature story that has nothing at all to do with real criticism. Although well-meaning, such people (and they abound on small-circulation daily newspapers) can be harmful if their writing consistently blurs the distinction between good and bad performance (often in the name of not hurting anybody's feelings) and consistently blurs the distinction between the *play* and its *performance.* Such a reviewer may say that Susie Smith was wonderful as Blanche Dubois when what he means is that Blanche Dubois is a great character in an exciting play.

The Theorist. Perhaps all true critics aspire to be theorists, and it may fairly be said that in order to criticize one must be possessed of a sound theory. To initiate a theory is quite an undertaking, however, and the people who have successfully done so in a clearly stated, well-reasoned way are few indeed: Aristotle, Sir Philip Sidney, Gothold Ephraim Lessing, et al. In our time, Artaud, Brecht, and Grotowski may be said to be theorists of the theatre, but there is a vagueness to Artaud and a mysticism to Grotowski that may disqualify them, and Brecht's theory may prove to be merely a temporary deviation from other modern theory.

Many sound critics function by using theories set down by other people, most often by Aristotle or one of his interpreters. However, when a critic sets out to propound his own theory, we ask several things before we will accept it as a basis for analytical judgment: that it be *general,* that is, that it be applicable to many cases and not merely a few; that it be *internally consistent;* that it be based on known *examples,* as scientific theory is based on the observation of phenomena; and that it be *useful,* that is, that it have relevance for dramatic criticism generally. But by *usefulness,* we do not mean that it should assume or suggest that drama itself has any given purpose; rather the opposite is taken as true, for a "theory" that bases itself on a specific purpose (that plays must make one proud to be black, that plays must make real life better) is not a theory but a persuasive argument.

A dramatic theory remains, of course, unproved, hence the word *theory* rather than *law.* The theorist is aware of this and spends his life preparing to accept (at some cost) proof of the theory's weakness.

The Critic. We have already said what a critic is, and even what he is not. Most of all, what he is not is someone who uses *I* a lot. Indeed, it may be said that a function of theory is the short-circuiting of *I:* it is not "my" emotions or "my" beliefs that enter into judgment, but an intelligent analysis based on an accepted theory. Among modern critics, none shows

Figure 12–7. New Play in Performance. The American College Theatre Festival offers a unique opportunity for student playwrights to have their work performed in national competition. Here, *Round Trip Ticket* by Bruce Jones at Mankato State University. *(Directed by Bruce Jones, design by Robert Cohn.)*

this clarity and lack of egoism more than H. D. F. Kitto, whose critical analyses of Greek tragedy are models of their kind.

What we do expect from the critic, even while we reject his ego, is a clear statement of theory: we want to know what his basic assumptions are. The reason is that no single theory covers all cases. A Brechtian critic will be hampered in dealing with medieval drama, an Aristotelian in dealing with Romantic drama. It is always to our benefit to know this and to learn about *both* theory and drama by testing the exceptions against the rule.

The Criticism of Performance

In brief, there is no criticism of performance, because, at this stage of the art, there is no theory of performance. Modern critics would certainly argue with this statement, because they are actively trying to evolve a theory of performance. A great part of the difficulty at the present, however, lies in our lack of a way of talking about performance. That is, we have theories of acting, direction, and design, but we do not have a language for talking about all those things in combination *while the performance goes forward.* Performance is a process; processes are difficult to describe. The critic wants to make them hold still so he can study them; they simply will not hold still, and if they are made to hold still, they cease to be performances. Of almost equal concern is the problem of the intervention of the critic himself: the act of criticism changes the perception of what is going on. Finally, there is the difficulty of saying just what we are watching and how it is happening (so that, for example, the dramatic idea of "an action" is insufficient to describe the actor-playing-character-in-costume-making-decision at a moment that is the focus of hundreds of other such moments). Some critics have suggested comparisons with computers or electronic circuits to describe the complexity of this process, but at this time, there is no clearly reasoned and stated theory of performance that allows anyone to criticize it.

How do we deal with performance, then? Haphazardly, and according to ego, instinct, and received wisdom. We have not critics but reviewers of performance, some of them quite good, like Walter Kerr and Kenneth Tynan. The more theatre experience they have, the better they usually are. Kerr has taught acting and directing and is himself a very experienced director; thus he can talk about acting and directing in terms of their theories and their practices (and to a large degree, he can talk about plays as a critic). Thus the reviewer of performance is the best we have right now. He cannot tell us how performance works or what his theory of performance is, but he can tell us how elements of performance support or hurt each other and how the play is distinct from each element of performance.

How to Read a Play

Having said this much about theory and criticism, we must now backtrack a bit in order to deal with the way in which most of us can confront a script. Not being critics, not having vast experience, not having carefully formulated theories, we cannot be as systematic and as skilled as a critic. This does not mean, however, that we must abandon all system, nor does it mean that we are free to rely on our own instincts. "I liked it" is an acceptable response to a candy bar, but not to a dramatic text: even a responsible beginner must be expected to read a play and make a judgment that is reasoned, orderly, and defensible.

Students are sometimes inclined to look upon analysis of drama as a "my-reactions-are-as-good-as-yours" situation in which all that is needed is a more or less clear statement of feelings. In fact, nobody cares about those feelings; not even the student should much care about them, although he should cetainly be aware of them, if only because of their negative influence. Such feelings belong in the same category as the old line "I don't know anything about art, but I know what I like," because, knowing nothing, one *cannot* know what one likes; one can know only what one happens to react to—quite a different matter.

Figure 12–8. Beneath Criticism? Enormously popular plays like *Mazeppa* may have been trash by the standards of dramatic criticism, but they succeeded because of strong performance values. *(Courtesy of the Theatre and Music Collection, the Museum of the City of New York.)*

What follows is a series of questions that may serve as a first approach to reading plays. It is designed only to get around "gut feelings" and go to more or less rational analysis. It is not founded in a theory, and anyone who wishes to move into actual criticism will do so by studying dramatic theory and espousing that which best matches his own basic assumptions.

1. *What are my basic assumptions about the nature and the purpose of theatre?* For example, it is important to find out if one is prejudiced against or for one particular style. Many people have an undefined prejudice in favor of realism, and so they find themselves saying something like, "I didn't really like Shakespeare's *Julius Caesar* because people don't really talk that way." Self-analysis will show that this is a statement of prejudice, a prejudice in favor of realism. Admitting the prejudice does not mean that one has to get rid of it; it does mean that one will now be able to work with the prejudice in mind, putting it into a box and setting it aside, as it were. The same thing is true of one's ideas of theatrical purpose; if one believes that the purpose of theatre is entertainment, then one is likely to say something like, "I just hated *Macbeth* because it was so depressing." This statement actually contains both a prejudice and a confusion: first, a prejudice against serious matter in drama; and second, a confusion about the difference be-

Figure 12–9. Group Creativity. Not all plays have playwrights. Some are improvised, some are written but are group creations. This is a street theatre group performing an antinuclear power play of their own making.

tween events that would be depressing in life and the effect of the same events on the stage.

The beginner may want to read several plays and jot down immediate responses: "I liked," "I disliked." Careful and honest analyses of these emotional reactions will show where prejudices and assumptions lie.

2. *What, exactly, am I reading when I read this play?* Far too often, people confuse what they *might* read or what they *would rather* read with what they actually *do* read. *The analysis of drama is limited to what is actually in the dramatic text.* It has no interest in how many children Lady Macbeth had or what her relationship with her father was (although these matters may be of interest to an actress playing Lady Macbeth). It is not concerned with what might have "happened" before the play begins or what might "happen" after the play ends. It concerns itself with the words that are written down between the title of the play and the final curtain, and nothing more. Given this all-important limitation on the scope of inquiry, then, the reader goes on to ask:

a. *What are the most important elements in the play?* Plot? Character? Idea? Spectacle? And then, as a corollary, *How do these elements relate to each other?* And then, *Are there inconsistencies in any of them?* (For example, in Eugène Scribe's *Adrienne Lecouvreur,* a character pursues chemistry as a hobby, although the hobby violates his other traits of character; the hobby is needed so that, late in the play, another character will have access to poison—inconsistency of character is demanded by the requirements of plot.) It should be obvious from the way that these questions are asked that inconsistency in any element is a symptom of dramatic weakness.

b. *What gives the play coherence and inner consistency?* This is another way of asking, "What ties the play together?" In a strongly plotted play, the coherence is usually causality; where causality is lacking (as it is, for example, in some of Samuel Beckett's plays), we must look for another cohesive element. A play that lacks cohesion would be a collection of random events, tied together only by the fact that they are happening within the framework of the play itself (like a happening, in fact). A lack of coherence, like a lack of consistency within an element, is a sign of poor dramaturgy.

c. *What are the meanings of the play?* We do not ask, "What is *the* meaning?" and we reject works like *theme* and *statement.* Plays do not generate a single, simple statement of idea; after all, if they are good, they are themselves total statements of an idea and are not reducible to simple prose statements. Perhaps, more important than knowing what such statements might be is understanding how meanings are generated: how plot generates meanings, how relationships among characters generate meanings, how the "meaningful" statements of characters generate meanings. *No play is without meanings.* Even the silliest of farces gives meaning if only because it gives an imitation, however distorted, of human action and social organization. A bedroom farce may be fairly rich in meanings that have to do with how people view sex and marriage and love, how people view age and youth, how they view the differences between men and women. A play need not be heavy with big, intellectual speeches to offer meanings—and it is the job of the careful reader to recognize those meanings and to explain how they operate.

d. *What are the systems behind the play?* That is, what are the systems—moral, political, social, and poetic—of the author and his real world? Put a little differently, What are the author's prejudices? Every playwright has them, if only because he lives in a certain place and time. Thus, it is important to know that Shakespeare was a Christian and Sophocles was not, that Brecht was a Marxist and Williams is not, that Myrna Lamb is a feminist and Lillian Hellman is not. To an extent, one can find these things out from reading the plays, but it is more efficient and often more accurate to learn them from outside sources. Such knowledge illuminates the systems of the plays themselves; it also keeps the reader from wasting time pursuing false leads, like the generation of critics who tried to fit the Greek tragedians into a Christian framework.

Note that the reader is not being asked to evaluate the systems behind the play. Shakespeare is not a better playwright than Sophocles because his system is a Christian one; Brecht is not a worse playwright than Williams because his political system is Marxist. The analytical reader of drama is not in the business of evaluating systems; he is only in the business of identifying them.

5. *What are the special strengths (or weaknesses) of the play?* Many plays have special values that lift them above others that are, in all other respects, equal. Particular beauty of language, for example, may compensate for weakness of plot or character; this is certainly true in some of Shakespeare's plays. Extraordinary potential for spectacle will at least explain why a play

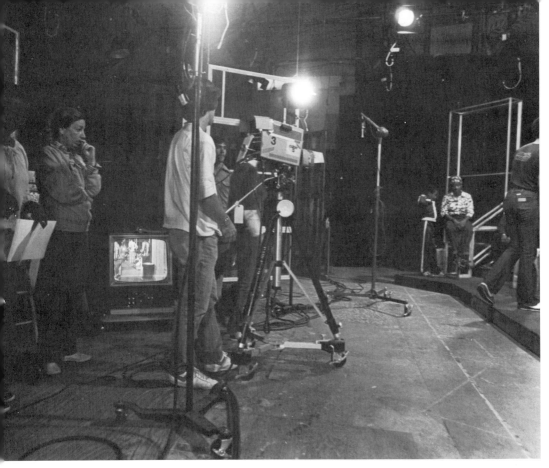

Figure 12–10. New Outlets for Playwrights. The O'Neill Center also encourages new scripts for television, increasingly an attractive outlet for theatrical playwrights. Here, the taping of Lee Hunkins' *Hollow Image* at the Center. *(Photo by John Brandeis.)*

was or is performed with great success. An abundance of laugh-getting lines or situations may lift an otherwise mundane comedy to a high level: several of Neil Simon's plays are crippled by weak plots and/or characters but are saved by brilliantly funny lines. However, where a play shows this kind of characteristic, the reader must take very careful note of it, for these are nondramatic or extradramatic elements that contribute little toward building a systematic way of evaluating plays.

History of Theory/Criticism

To offer a history of criticism or critics would be futile because it would be a history of specific cases. What follows, then, is a very brief history of dramatic theories and their applications by a few critics.

Aristotle and His Interpreters. Aristotle's *Poetics* (335 B.C.) represents at once the foundation of Western dramatic theory and the source of its most maddening controversies. The work is not entirely clear and it sets out to deal *only* with tragedy, not with comedy or mixed forms; its examples are taken, of necessity, from classical Greek and Hellenistic drama and could hardly be expected to anticipate the shifts in style and thought that were to follow; and it deals almost exclusively with drama and not theatre, so that the very concept of audience response is foreign to it. Nevertheless its system is the basis of much dramatic theory—some of it, regrettably, illinformed theory that mangles Aristotle's words and ideas.

Remembering, then, that the *Poetics* sets out to define only tragedy, we have the following:

"Tragedy . . . is an imitation of an action that is serious, complete, and of a certain magnitude . . . in the form of action, not of narrative. . . . [A]n action implies personal agents [characters], who necessarily possess certain distinctive qualities both of character and thought; for it is by these that we qualify actions themselves, and these—thought and character—are the two natural causes from which actions spring. . . . Hence, Plot is the imitation of the action—for by plot I here mean the arrangement of the incidents. By Character I mean that in virtue of which we ascribe certain qualities to the agents. Thought is required wherever a statement is proved, or it may be, a general truth enunciated. Every tragedy, therefore, must have six parts, which parts determine its quality—namely, Plot, Character, Diction, Thought, Spectacle, Song. Two of the parts (Diction or language and Song or music) constitute the medium of imitation, one (Spectacle) the manner, and three (Plot, Character, Thought) the objects of imitation.

. . . The incidents and the plot are the end of tragedy; and the end is the chief thing of all. . . . [W]ithout action there cannot be tragedy; there may be without character. . . . [T]he most powerful elements of emotional interest in tragedy—Reversal and Recognition scenes—are parts of the plot. . . .

The Plot, then, is the first principle, and as it were the soul of a tragedy: Character holds the second place. . . . Third. . . . is Thought—that is, the faculty of saying what is possible and pertinent in given circumstances.

Fourth . . . comes Diction; by which I mean . . . the expression of the meaning in words; and its essence is the same both in verse and prose.

Of the remaining elements Song holds the chief place. . . .

The Spectacle has . . . an emotional attraction of its own, but . . . it is the least artistic, and connected least with the art of poetry. For the power of tragedy, we may be sure, is felt even apart from representation and actors. Besides, the production of spectacular effects depends more on the art of the stage machinist than on that of the poet.

Aristotle went on to discuss "wholeness" of the work (having a beginning, a middle, and an end, connected by causality); unity of plot (so that if any part is removed, the whole is disturbed); the arousal and catharsis of feelings, usually translated as "pity and fear"; structural elements like reversal, surprise, and recognition; the nature of the tragic protagonist and his action; and other matters. None of what he said was directed toward any form other than tragedy of the kind Aristotle knew, but his *Poetics* has been haggled over for two thousand years and more by people trying to make it fit quite different works. It is, perhaps, a measure of the *Poetics'* greatness that it is revealing as applied to other work, at least when the critic applying it is thoroughly knowledgeable and very careful.

SPIRITS of the BRITISH DRAMA, or the legitimate GHOSTS horrified

Figure 12–11. Legitimate versus Illegitimate. Traditional theatre, based on critical theory and dramatic precedent, is often distinct from popular forms that escape formal criticism. When the two compete for the same audience, theatrical "battles" erupt; sometimes, such a battle is actually one between mainstream and experimental forces. *(Courtesy of Prints Division, The New York Public Library, Astor, Lenox and Tilden Foundations.)*

In the twentieth century, Aristotle has come in for strong attack—by Brecht, for example, who lambasted him for things he had not said and tarred him with the same brush as neo-Aristotelians of the early years of the century.

It is true that Aristotle makes a splendid critical whipping boy. As the first on the ground, he was and always will be in a vulnerable position. His ideas, however, persist both despite and because of such attacks, for they represent a clear statement of a very fundamental position on one view of the drama: the primacy of action, and hence of plot; the importance of organic unity, and perhaps of causality; the hierarchical ranking of plot, character, and thought, and the relegating of spectacle to a low and seemingly almost extraneous position; the emphasis on kinds of incident—reversal, surprise, recognition; and, partly by implication (because he said very little about comedy), an emphasis on the division between tragedy and comedy and an apparent elevation of tragedy.

Aristotle's ideas remain vital today in the critical writing of men like

Gerald Else and the so-called Chicago school, as well as that of several eminent English critics. His ideas were also of direct influence on the Roman critic Horace, whose *Art of Poetry* (20 B.C.) was a more rigid, more authoritarian interpretation of many of the same points, with added attention to comedy.

Renaissance and Neoclassical Theory. Medieval dramatic theory was scarce, to say the least, and had little carry-over into the age that followed.

Critics of the Renaissance, however—like Renaissance playwrights and designers—were quick to discover their classical antecedents and quick to apply them. Aristotle and Horace both became models for Renaissance theory, with the distinction that Renaissance theory moved from a consideration of the intrinsic value of the dramatic work of art to a consideration of the work in terms of a set of rules. These rules had a much more narrow application of the idea of unity (the so-called three unities of time, place, and action) to distinctions of genre and to the five-act form. For example, the Englishman Philip Sidney in *The Defense of Poesy* (1583) stated that the goal of poetry, both comedy and tragedy, was both to delight and instruct, that "the stage should always represent but one place, and the uttermost time presupposed in it should be, both by Aristotle's precept and common reason, but one day."

Nowhere does the impact of Renaissance theory show more clearly than in the controversy surrounding Corneille's play, *Le Cid* (1636). French drama, much more than English, was strongly influenced by Italian Neoclassical theory; yet *Le Cid*, for all its author's insistence that he had followed the rules, and for all its enormous popular success, was vigorously attacked by the then-new French Academy. The academy's judgment, written with all the care of a legal brief, found the play faulty on several points: its plot was defective because it lacked verisimilitude (even though, as the judgment admitted, the plot was based on historical fact, but "not all actual occurrences are suitable for the theatre"); it was overcrowded with incidents because the author, having accepted the twenty-four-hour rule of the unity of time, tried to make too much happen in that period "for the mind to encompass"; the unity of place was not honored, "for the stage represents more than one locale"; and consistency of character was violated when a "virtuous daughter" fell in love with her father's murderer.

This adherence to an ideal of dramatic laws, although far from universal, remained dominant through much of the eighteenth century.

By mid-century, however, both the authority of the rules and the preeminence of Aristotle and Horace were being questioned; a "battle of the ancients and the moderns" was fought among conservative and liberal English critics. In Germany, Gotthold Lessing's *Hamburg Dramaturgy* (1767–1769) questioned many of the tenets of Neoclassicism: he advocated what he called "domestic tragedies" and attacked those older plays whose protagonists were noble by station because it was assumed that tragic heroes should be noble by nature. "The names of princes and heroes can lend pomp and majesty to a play," he wrote, "but they contribute nothing *to our emotion*" (our italics, to emphasize the change from regard for rules to regard for the responses of the audience.) Of the unities, he wrote that "physical unity of time is not sufficient; the moral unity must also be considered," and "unity of action was the first dramatic law of the ancients; unity of time and place were mere consequences of the former." In short, Lessing represented a reaction against Renaissance and Neoclassical absolutism, a dramatic theory based as much on common sense and on fatigue with the artificiality of Neoclassicism as on any powerful new belief.

Romanticism. Aristotelian theory had placed the value of the dramatic work of art within the work itself, discernible by a study of its parts and its inner consistency; Renaissance and Neoclassical theory had placed the value of the dramatic work of art in a set of external rules and authorities. At the end of the eighteenth century, a new dramatic theory saw the locus of value shift again, this time from the rules to the inner self of the observer. Lessing anticipated this, but now it became a standard in its own right, expressed eloquently by Friedrich Hegel in the 1820s:

> *In modern romantic [drama] . . . it is the individual passion, the satisfaction of which can only be relative to a wholly personal end . . . that forms the subject-matter of all importance. . . .*
> *Modern tragedy accepts in its own province from the first the principle of subjectivity of self-assertion. It makes, therefore, the personal intimacy of character . . . its peculiar object and content.*

In the same vein, the English poet Samuel Taylor Coleridge dismissed both the Neoclassical concern with genres and the idea of verisimilitude. Of generic criticism, he wrote, "[We] must emancipate ourselves from a false association rising from misapplied names, and find a new word for the plays of Shakespeare. For they are . . . neither tragedies nor comedies, nor both in one, but a different genus. . . . They may be called romantic dramas, or dramatic romances." In place of Neoclassical verisimilitude, Coleridge substituted the "willing suspension of disbelief," a measure of dramatic reality defined *by the audience* when it knowingly accepts the dramatist's goal.

To Romantic theory, then, the subjective sensibility was the measure of the drama, and adherence to rules was foolish when compared to the primacy of individual feeling and poetic creation. As might be expected, a theory based on subjectivity and feeling was not, in the hands of most critics, an actual, rationally stated theory; it was instead a point of view, a place from which to survey the landscape.

Toward the end of the nineteenth century, a more carefully defined set of theories, quite different in kind, replaced the Romantic; however, the Romantic *viewpoint,* as a place from which to begin critical operation, was retained. It persists, even to the present in the work of Freudian critics, whose profound concern with dramatic character as abnormal psychology shares the Romantic's interest in the subjective individual; and it seems to persist in the so-called archetypal critics of the mid-twentieth century, like Northrop Frye, who have given particular attention to dramatic works as embodiments of archetypal patterns (rituals and myths) that speak to the audience's unconscious (certainly in keeping with Romantic ideas of audience subjectivity and irrationality). Finally, the ideas of Antonin Artaud may

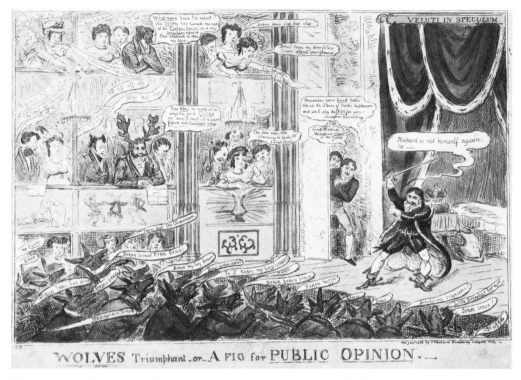

Figure 12–12. Criticism? Organized audience response is usually displayed by "claques," which are still seen at some performances of opera. Claques do not represent a real response, however, but a pre-determined pressure; their members are neither audience nor critics, but demonstrators. Shown here is the actor Edmund Kean, c. 1825, with his supporters and detractors. *(Courtesy of Prints Division, The New York Public Library, Astor, Lenox and Tilden Foundations.)*

be seen as Romantic in their extreme subjectivity and irrationality, in their utter rejection of rules and precedents ("No more masterpieces!"), and in their passion for the grotesque. One must be very cautious, however, in using the expression "dramatic theory" in speaking of Artaud, for he was neither a critic nor a theorist but an evangelist for an idea of theatre about which other people are still trying to create rational theories.

Industrial Age Functionalism. The novelist and critic Émile Zola pointed out in the 1870s that it had been the accomplishment of Romanticism to wipe out the theories of preceding ages: Romanticism was a revolution, bloody in its way, but not necessarily one that substituted one system for another. When the smoke of that revolution had cleared, there was no single theory to take the place of Neoclassicism. Perhaps the difficulty lay in the widespread acceptance of the shift to the Romantic viewpoint: when the subjective individuality of the audience becomes the standard of excellence, universal theory becomes a contradiction in terms.

At the same time, however, two other shifts were taking place: the Industrial Revolution was changing the place of human beings in society, and

the scientific revolution was changing the place of human beings in the world. Social and economic humanity was now linked to all other humanity through productivity and complex economics; natural humanity was linked to nature and to other organisms through evolution. Darwin's *On the Origin of Species* appeared in 1859; the flow of populations into factory towns was a flood by the same date; and by the 1870s, popular ideas of "bettering" people and society were leading to such new movements as the setting aside of tracts of land for public parks—Yellowstone and the Adirondack Park in America, for example. Nature was competitive, science said; the individual was a productive cog in an industrial machine, economics said; but life could be made good by providing for the betterment of one's fellows, philosophy said.

The theorist Hippolyte Taine posited an art that was "functional"—to be judged on the basis of its contribution to the betterment of humanity. In the theatre, Zola said, this meant using the drama as a species of scientific case study, to reveal social evils so that they could be improved. The rules had been smashed by the Romantics and were not even worth Zola's attention; verisimilitude had given way to the "willing suspension of disbelief," which now gave way in turn to scientific observation of scenes exactly like life. Romantic observation and creativity were replaced by scientific logic. Zola argued, "Naturalistic playwrights will rid us of fictitious characters, of conventional symbols of vice and virture, which have no value as human data. . . . [The] surroundings will determine the characters, and characters will act according to the logic of their own temperament."

The English playwright and critic George Bernard Shaw wrote of a play's "doing its work in the world," by which he meant its making a statement that would effect change. An apologist for the plays of Ibsen, Shaw expounded his theories in a long essay called *The Quintessence of Ibsenism:*

The action of [certain modern] plays consists of a case to be argued. If the case is uninteresting or stale or badly conducted or obviously trumped up, the play is a bad one. If it is important and novel and convincing, or at least disturbing, the play is a good one. But anyhow the play in which there is no argument and no case no longer counts as serious drama.

Bad plays and inferior dramaturgy were improved by a "healthy dose of realism"; twists of plot would give way to twists of argument; stage kings and queens would give way to people just like those in the audience. The stage would share a goal with the pulpit and the speaker's platform: to argue and to convince—for the betterment of humanity.

Functionalism persists in dramatic theory, although naturalism has faded. The Marxist theory of Bertolt Brecht is functional, above all else; his whole idea of theatre rests on the performance's making didactic points for its

Figure 12–13. New Play in Performance. De Ray Carver's *Side Show* at the American College Theatre Festival, produced by Angelo State University, San Angelo, Texas. *(Photo credit C. Maier.)*

audience, on its putting them into a frame of mind to judge and to effect change. Functionalism even persists in its opposite in the twentieth century, because it was a distaste for the dominant theory that led T. S. Eliot and others to evolve the so-called New Criticism in the 1930s and after, a theory that tried to deal with the work of art distinct from all consideration of its goals, its sources, and its place in history or society. New Critical theory, although important in poetry and the novel, was less so in the drama, where it was never fully articulated.

In the last third of the century, dramatic theory appears to have splintered. Versions of Artaud's nihilism dominate popular theory (some of them more anti-theory than theory), while academic critics labor at forging ideas with labels like structuralism, phenomenology, and semiotics. Reviewers appear to work mostly from a Romantic viewpoint—"my responses are my criticism"—while applying often conservative ideas of language, nudity, subject matter, and other details in the name of hazy functionalism (i.e., obscenity is bad because it does not do good). No single critic and no single theory dominates, and perhaps this is as it must be in an age where almost instantaneous communications have made it possible for everyone to have equal access to all ideas.

Nevertheless, with all the changes that have happened in the world of ideas, in science, and in communications, and with all the shifts in critical ground that have taken place, many contemporary critics have the sometimes uneasy feeling that dramatic theory has still one solid anchor in the tide—Aristotle.

Glossary

(Discussion will be found on the page or pages indicated, where appropriate.)

A-Effect. See *Alienation*. (174)

Absurdism. A style of drama popularized in France after World War II that viewed human existence as meaningless and treated language as an inadequate means of communication. Major authors include Samuel Beckett and Eugène Ionesco. (171)

Academy. A group formed to further a specific artistic or literary end; for example, the French Academy and the rhetorical academies of the Renaissance. (239)

Action. According to Aristotle, a causally linked sequence of events, with beginning, middle, and end; the proper and best way to unify a play. More popularly, the single and unified human process of which a drama is the imitation. To some modern critics, an interaction (between dramatic protagonist and others). (433)

Actor–Manager. A starring actor who surrounds himself with a company of which he is head and nominal artistic director; for example, Sir Henry Irving in the late nineteenth century in England. (377)

Actors Equity. See *Unions*. (80)

Actos. Very short, politically significant playlets. Term associated with Chicano theater, particularly the work of El Teatro Campesino. (112)

441

Agit Prop. Short for *agitation propaganda.* A kind of political drama popular in the 1920s and 1930s in America. Phrase subsequently used to describe all didactic drama whose social stance was unusually militant.

Agon. Debate. Specifically, that part of Greek old comedy customarily found at the conclusion of the first (Attic) portion of the play. (282)

Alienation. Customary, but perhaps misleading, translation of the German *verfremdung,* "to make strange." Term now almost always associated with Bertolt Brecht's epic theatre, which aims to distance the spectator from the play's action in order to force conscious consideration of the political and social issues raised by the play. Shortened often to A-effect. (174)

Angle Perspective. Multipoint perspective; results when several vanishing points are located away from the center of the stage so that vistas appear toward the wings. (244)

Angle Wing. Wings consisting of two parts hinged together, one rectangular flat placed parallel with the proscenium arch and one (called the return) placed at an angle to it in order to increase the sense of distance. (On a raked stage, the return is not a rectangle but a trapezoid.) (219)

Antiquarianism. The study of the details of past civilizations, often with a view to reproducing historically accurate settings onstage. Movement was popular toward the end of the eighteenth century and is viewed as a precursor to Romanticism. (202)

Apron. That part of a stage that extends in front of the proscenium arch. (235)

Arena Theatre. A theatre in which the audience completely surrounds the playing area. Also called *theatre in the round.* (408)

Atellan Farce. *Fabula atellana.* A short, rustic, improvised, and often bawdy play especially popular in Rome during the first centuries B.C. and A.D. Possibly the forerunner of the *commedia dell'arte* (see entry). (261)

Attic (Portion). That part of Greek old comedy that precedes the *parabasis.* Typically, it consists of a prologue, a *parados,* and an *agon,* each with distinctive metrical patterns. (282)

Audition. A session at which a theatre artist, usually an actor, displays his or her craft in order to secure a job. (326)

Ballad Opera. A "minor" form of musical drama especially popular during the eighteenth and nineteenth centuries in England and featuring political satire interlarded with familiar tunes for which new and topical lyrics were devised; for example, John Gay's *The Beggar's Opera.* (234)

Beat. A rhythmic unit in a play; defined variously by different actors and directors. (375)

Benefit. A performance, the profit of which is set aside for a particular actor, company member, or cause. In the eighteenth and nineteenth centuries, a primary means of supplementing an actor's annual salary. Now, any performance done for charity. (203)

Biomechanics. The concept and the complex of techniques devised by Vsevolod Meyerhold to train actors so that their bodies could be as responsive as a machine. (170)

Blocking. Stage movement for actors, given in rehearsal (usually) by the director. (363)

Body Language. Communicable emotional states understood from posture and other conscious and unconscious use of the body. See also *Gesture.* (308)

Book. 1. The spoken text of a play or musical; early musicals with stories and dialogue were called *book musicals;* 2. Several flats hinged together and folded together form a *book of flats;* 3. To *book* a production is to schedule a performance of it.

Border. Curtain, or less often flats or cutouts, suspended at intervals behind the proscenium arch to mask the overhead rigging. Particularly important in Italianate settings. (199)

Boulevard. Historically the permanent home of the old traveling-fair theatres of eighteenth-century Paris and later of the illegitimate houses where melodrama and comic opera flourished during the nineteenth century. Now refers to the district of the commercial theatres in Paris and means roughly what the word *Broadway* implies in the United States. (209)

Box. Historically the favored, and most expensive, seats in a theater. Made by sectioning off parts of a gallery, boxes were spacious and outfitted with armed chairs, in contrast to the crowded galleries, whose seats consisted of backless benches, and to the pit, where originally no seats were provided. (198)

Box Set. Interior setting represented by flats forming three sides (the fourth wall being the proscenium line); first used around 1830 and common after 1850. (151)

Breeches Role. Role in which an actress portrays a male character and dresses as a man, presumably adding sexual titillation to dramatic interest. (204)

Broadway. In popular parlance, that area of New York City on and adjacent to the street named Broadway where the commercial theatre of America is concentrated. (78)

Burlesque. In eighteenth- and nineteenth-century theatre, a form of "minor" drama popular in England and featuring satire and parody. In America of the late nineteenth century and the twentieth century, a kind of entertainment originally dependent on a series of variety acts but later including elements of female display (including striptease) in its major offerings. After moving to the fringes of respectability by the 1940s, burlesque disappeared in the United States by the late 1950s. (233)

Business. Activity performed by actor(s) at given points in a performance; for example, the *business* of lighting a cigarette or cooking a meal. See also *Lines of business.* (149)

Byplay. Business that takes place alongside the primary action and that is slightly different from it; for example, in *Tartuffe,* Orgon's behavior under the table while Tartuffe is trying to seduce Orgon's wife.

Catharsis. Aristotle cited as the end cause of tragedy "the arousal and catharsis of such emotions [pity and fear]," a statement popularly understood to mean that tragedy "purges" fear and pity from the audience; but alternative interpretations suggest that tragedy arouses and satisfies such emotions within its own structure and characters. Highly controversial and elusive concept. (433)

Causality. Belief that human events have causes (and therefore consequences); as a result, events are seen as joined in a chain of cause and effect.

Cavea. Audience area in a Roman theatre. Roughly equivalent to the Greek *theatron* or today's *auditorium.* (268)

Centering. Actor's term for localization of human energy source in the body, usually in the abdomen. (306)

Character. One of Aristotle's six parts of a play, the material of plot and the formal cause of thought; an agent (participant, doer) in the play whose qualities and traits arise from ethical deliberation. In popular parlance, the agents or "people" in the play. (286)

Chariot and Pole. An elaborate system for changing elements of the scenery simultaneously. Devised by Giacomo Torelli in the seventeenth century, the system involved scenery attached to poles that rose through slits in the stage floor from chariots that ran on tracks in the basement and depended on an intricate system of interlocking ropes, pulleys, wheels, and windlasses for their simultaneous movement. (219)

Choregos. Wealthy citizen of Athens who, in the Classical Age, provided money for theatrical productions at the festival. (284)

Chorus. In Greek drama of the fifth century B.C., a group of men (number uncertain) who sang, chanted, spoke, and moved, usually in unison, and who, with the actors (three in tragedy and five in comedy), performed the plays. In the Renaissance, a single character named *Chorus* who provided information and commentary about the action in some tragedies. In modern times, the groups that sing and/or dance in musical comedies, operettas, ballets, and operas. (273)

City Dionysia. The major religious festival devoted to the worship of the god Dionysus in Athens. The first records of tragedy appeared at this festival in 534 B.C., and so it is called the home of tragedy. See also *Festivals.* (283)

Classical. Specifically refers to that period of Greek drama and theatre from 534 B.C. to 336 B.C. (the advent of the Hellenistic period). Loosely used now to refer to Greek and Roman drama and theatre in general (a period dating roughly from the sixth century B.C. through the sixth century A.D., about twelve hundred years). (275)

Comedy. A kind (genre) of drama variously discussed in terms of its having a happy ending, dealing with the material, mundane world, dealing with the low and middle classes, dealing with myths of rebirth and social regeneration, and so on.

Comedy of Manners. Refers most often to seventeenth- and eighteenth-century comedies whose focus is the proper social behavior of a single class. (231)

Comic Opera. A "minor" form of musical drama popular first in the eighteenth century and characterized then by sentimental stories set to original music. Later used to mean an opera in which some parts were spoken (in contrast to "grand opera," where everything was sung). (193)

Commedia dell'Arte. Italian popular comedy of the fifteenth through seventeenth centuries. Featured performances improvised from scenarios by a set of stock characters and repeated from play to play and troupe to troupe. See also *Lazzi.* (220)

Community Theatre. Theatre performed by and for members of a given community, especially a city or town. Usually amateur, with sometimes professional directors, designers, and business staff.

Complication. Ascending or tying action. That part of plot in which the action is growing tenser and more intricate up to the point of crisis (turning point), after which the action unties and resolves in a section called the *denouement* (see entry). (286)

Composition. Arrangement of visual elements for aesthetic effect. (368)

Confraternity. In France, a religious brotherhood, many of which sponsored or produced plays during the Middle Ages. One, the Confraternity of the Passion, held a monopoly on play production in Paris into the 1570s. (254)

Constructivism. A nonrealistic style of scenic design associated with Vsevolod Meyerhold and marked by its view that a good set is a machine for doing plays, not a representation of familiar locales. Incorporated simple machines on stage and often revealed the method of its own construction. (170)

Continental Seating. First devised by Wagner in the late nineteenth century for his theatre at Bayreuth; eschews a central aisle in favor of entrances and exits at the end of each aisle. (143)

Convention. A way of doing things agreed on by a (usually unstated) contract between audience and artists; for example, characters' singing their most important feelings and emotions is a *convention* of musical comedy. (34)

Corpus Christi. A spring festival established in the fourteenth century in honor of the Christian Eucharist at which medieval cycle plays and cosmic dramas (see entry) were often performed. Also see *Festivals.* (253)

Cosmic Drama. Long dramatic presentations popular in the Middle Ages that depicted religious events from the Creation to the Last Judgment. Short plays were combined until the total presentation could last several days or weeks and occasionally a month or more. See also *Cycle play.* (254)

Court Theatre. A theatre located at the court of a nobleman. After the Renaissance, Italianate theatre, whose perspective was drawn with the vanishing points established from the chair of the theatre where the ruler sat, making his the best seat in the house. (218)

Criticism. The careful, systematic, and imaginative study and evaluation of works of drama and theatre (or any other form of art). (424)

Cue. Immediate stimulus for a line, an action, or an effect. (370)

Cycle Play. Medieval (especially English) dramas covering the "cycle" of history from the creation of the world to doomsday. See also *Cosmic drama.* (254)

Decision. In Aristotelian criticism, the most highly characterizing trait of a dramatic agent; the trait that translates idea into action and thus, in Aristotelian terms, unites thought with plot (in the sense here of action). See also *Plot* and *Action.* (320)

Declamation. A style of verbal delivery that emphasizes beauty of sound, speech, and rhetorical meaning rather than the realistic imitation of everyday speaking. (333)

Decorum. In Neoclassical theory, the behavior of a dramatic character in keeping with his or her social status, age, sex, and occupation; based on the requirements of *verisimilitude* (see entry). (214)

Denouement. That part of the plot that follows the crisis (turning point) and that includes the untangling or resolving of the play's complications. (286)

Determinism. Philosophical stance undergirding Naturalistic drama that asserts that human behavior and destiny are determined by factors, especially heredity and environment, largely beyond human control. (153)

Deus Ex Machina. Literally, "the god from the machine," a reference to a deity who flew in at the conclusion of some Greek tragedies (particularly those of Euripides) to assure the play's appropriate outcome. Popularly, any ending of a play that is obviously contrived. (278)

Deuteragonist. In classical Greece, the second actor. (279)

Diaphragm. Large muscle, located atop the abdominal cavity, that forces air into and out of the lungs and thus figures prominently in the proper production of sound. (311)

Diction. In Aristotle, one of the six parts of a play; the formal cause of music, the material of thought; the words of the play. Popularly the proper and clear formation of the play's words. (286)

Didacticism. "Teaching." In the theatre, plays are didactic when they emphasize ideological content rather than artistic form.

Didaskalia. In ancient Greece, records of dramatic competitions. (275)

Dimmer. Instrument for controlling the intensity of light by manipulating the amount of electricity that reaches individual lamps. (399)

Dionysia. A Greek religious festival in honor of the god Dionysus. The City Dionysia and the Rural Dionysia both included drama as a part of the celebration, but the city festival was clearly the dominant one of the two. See also *Festivals.* (283)

Diorama. Distant scene viewed through a cutout or other opening in scenery. Also, a three-dimensional arrangement of figures and painted scenes. (405)

Dithyramb. A hymn of praise to the god Dionysus, performed by a chorus of men or boys; a regular part of the religious festival of Athens after 509 B.C. (288)

Discovery Space. Permanent or temporary space in the Elizabethan (Shakespearean) playhouse that permitted actors and locales to be hidden from view and then "discovered" (or revealed) when needed. Location, appearance, and even invariable existence of the space are hotly disputed. (225)

Domestic Tragedy. A serious play dealing with domestic problems of the middle or lower classes. In the eighteenth century, a reaction against "regular" or Neoclassical tragedy. See also *Purity of genres.* (435)

Dominus. In Rome, head of an acting troupe *(grex).* (262)

Doric (Portion). The second part of Greek old comedy; that part that follows the *parabasis* and typically consists of alternating songs and episodes and concludes with a burst of comic revelry, often involving song, dance, and sexual celebration. (282)

Double. 1. To play more than one role. 2. *The Theatre and Its Double,* an influential book by Antonin Artaud, calls the Western theatre merely a shadow or *double* of the (to him) true and vital Eastern theatre. (176)

Downstage. That part of the stage closest to the front. In early Italianate theatres, the stage floor was raked (slanted) up from the front to the back; therefore to move forward on the stage was literally to move "down the stage." (365)

Drama. 1. In the eighteenth century, a serious play (*drame,* in France) that dealt with domestic issues and thus failed to conform to the standard Neoclassical definition of tragedy. 2. Any serious play that is not a tragedy. 3. The literary component of performance, the *play*—often contrasted with the *theatre.* (197)

Dress Rehearsal. A final rehearsal in which all visual elements of production, including costumes, are used. Typically a rehearsal that strives to duplicate, insofar as possible, an actual performance. (376)

Drop. Backdrop. Large curtain, usually of painted canvas, hung at the rear of the stage to provide literal and visual closure for the stage setting. (199)

Dual-Issue Ending. Double ending. Ending of a play when good is rewarded *and* evil is punished. Associated with melodrama particularly. (188)

Eclectic(ism). Gathering of materials from many sources; popularly a mixture of styles and methods. In twentieth-century theatre, the idea that each play calls forth its own production style. (381)

Educational Theatre. Theatre by and (in part) for students in an elementary, secondary, or collegiate setting. (126)

Ekkyklema. In classical Greece, a machine used to thrust objects or people (often dead) from inside the scene house and into view of the audience. Probably some sort of wheeled platform that rolled or rotated through the *skene's* central door. (277)

Ensemble. A performing group. Also, a group acting method that emphasizes unity and consistency of performances. (319)

Environmental Theatre. 1. Theatre whose performance is the audience's environment, so that the performance surrounds some or all of the audience and the line between performance space and audience space breaks down. 2. Theatre done in nontraditional space.

Epic Theatre. Term originated by Erwin Piscator and popularized by Brecht to describe a theatre where the audience response is objective, not subjective, and where such narrative devices as film projections, titles, and storytelling are used. See also *Alienation.* (173)

Epilogue. A short scene that comes at the conclusion of the main line(s) of action.

Existentialism. A philosophical system that lies at the root of absurdism (see entry) whose basic assumptions are the absence of transcendental values, the isolation of humans and their acts, and the lack of causality in the universe. (171)

Exodos. In Greek theatre, the final choral song that takes the chorus out of the playing area at the conclusion of the action. (283)

Experimental Theatre. Any theatre whose methods or goals depart markedly from the mainstream of its day; thus, in the eighteenth century, Romanticism was experimental; in the heyday of American Realism, Absurdism was experimental. (94)

Exposition. Necessary information about prior events, or a part of a play given over to communicating such information; because it is a "telling" and not an enacting of narrative, it is usually nondramatic.

Expressionism. A style of theatre popular in Europe after World War I and typified by symbolic presentation of meaning, often as viewed from the standpoint of the main character; distortions of time, space, and proportion are common. (169)

Fabula Atellana. See *Atellan farce.*

Fabula Crepidata. That kind of Roman tragedy written by Romans about the Athenian upper class. Actors were dressed as Athenians, thus the name of the form (after the Greek costume *crepidum*). (263)

Fabula Palliata. That kind of Roman comedy written by Romans about the Athenian middle class. Actors were dressed as Athenians, thus the name (after the Greek costume *pallium*). (264)

Fabula Praetexta. That kind of Roman tragedy written by Romans about the Roman upper class. Actors were dressed as Roman aristocrats, thus the name (after the Roman *toga praetexta*). (263)

Fabula Raciniata. The Roman mime, so named probably because of the popularity of the hood *(racinium)* as a costume element in this form. (267)

Fabula Togata. That kind of Roman comedy written by Romans about the Roman middle class. Actors were dressed as Romans, thus the name (after the Roman *toga*). (264)

Festivals. In Greece, religious worship took place in private and at major public festivals. In and around Athens, there were four festivals devoted to the god Dionysus. At three of these, records of drama appeared during the fifth century B.C. At the festival of no other gods can such records be found. See *City Dionysia, Rural Dionysia,* and *Lenaia.* During the Middle Ages, Christian festivals at which dramas were often produced. See also *Corpus Christi.* (283)

Flat. A structure upon which scenery is painted, consisting of a wooden frame and canvas covering; usually of a size to be carried by one or two persons for shifting. Used in both Italianate staging and box sets (see entries). (199)

Flying. Method of handling scenery for quick shifting by raising it out of sight over the stage with one of various systems of ropes, pulleys, counterweights, machines, and so on. Also, the illusion of flight in actors and properties through the use of concealed wires and the same system of ropes and pulleys. (394)

Focus. The point or object that draws the eye of the audience to the stage picture. (368)

Footlights. Light sources arranged along the front of a stage (between actors and audience) to throw light upward from stage level to eliminate shadows from harsh overhead lighting. Rarely used with modern lighting systems, but standard equipment with candle, oil, gas, and early electrical systems (c. 1650–1920). (200)

Forestage. That part of the stage in front of the scenery, especially in Renaissance stages, using a slanted floor for forced perspective in the scenic area. See also *Apron.* (235)

Formalism. 1. Strict adherence to established ways (forms) of doing things. 2. In scenic design, use of nonrepresentational shapes and forms as the design base. 3. In criticism, attention to matters of dramatic form and structure as distinct from philosophical and sociological issues, etc.

Functionalism. Aesthetic or artistic method that focuses on the function of objects (scenery, for example) instead of on prettiness. (437)

Gallery. The highest audience areas in nineteenth-century theatres (box, pit, and gallery), hence, the cheapest seats; the balconies. (198)

Genre. In dramatic criticism, a category of plays: comedy, tragedy, melodrama, farce. Popularly, any category.

Gesture. In one sense, any human act that conveys meaning (i.e., a speech is a gesture). In a more limited sense, a planned physical movement that conveys meaning, like waving a hand or pointing a finger. (308)

Given Circumstances. In Stanislavskian vocabulary, those aspects of character that are beyond the character's or actor's control: age, sex, state of health, and so on. (323)

Glory. In medieval and Renaissance art, a cloud or sunburst in which divinities appeared. In the theatre of those periods, a flown platform made to look like a cloud or sunburst. (254)

Graeco-Roman. That period in Greece and Greek lands when Roman domination had arrived, usually dated from c. 100 B.C. to the fall of the Western Roman Empire, c. A.D. 550. In theatre architecture, those Greek theatres that were remodeled to bring them in closer accord with the Roman ideals of beauty. (Not to be confused with Roman theatres built in Greek lands.) (286)

Grex. In Roman theatre, a group of actors. (262)

Groove. A shallow channel in the stage floor in which a flat rode, for quick scene changes; a bank of several grooves would allow one flat to be pulled aside while another was pushed on in its place, seemingly in the same plane. (235)

Ground Plan. The "map" of the playing area for a scene, with doors, furniture, walls, and so on indicated to scale. (357)

Ground Row. A piece of scenery at stage level, often used to hide stage-level machinery or lights or to increase the sense of distance. (199)

Guerrilla Theatre. Didactic political theatre done in nontheatrical spaces—streets, factories, subways—without previous announcement; hit-and-run performances like guerrilla attacks. (107)

Guilds. Religious and, sometimes, trade or professional organizations in the Middle Ages that became the producers of civic medieval theatre. (253)

Happy Idea. Term used to refer to the basic premise on which a particular Greek old comedy was based. For example, the *happy idea* in *Lysistrata* is that women can prevent war by withholding sex. (282)

Heavens. 1. Area above the stage: in the Elizabethan theatre, the underside of the roof that extended over the stage. 2. In the nineteenth century, the highest gallery. (224)

Hellenistic. 1. That period of Greek history dating from the coming of Alexander the Great (c. 336 B.C.) to the encroachment of the Romans on Greek lands (c. 100 B.C.). 2. In theatre architecture, those Greek theatres built during the Hellenistic period. (284)

Hero, Heroine. 1. A figure embodying a culture's most valued qualities (for example, Achilles in *The Iliad*) and hence the central figure in a heroic tragedy. 2. Popularly the leading character in a play or, more precisely, the leading male character in a play. 3. In melodrama, the male character who loves the heroine. See also *Protagonist.* (189)

Heroic. Of or relating to a hero; by extension, exalted. *Heroic* couplets are two lines of rhyming iambic pentameter, probably an English attempt to reproduce the French Alexandrine, the approved verse for Neoclassical tragedy. *Heroic acting* stressed the vocal and physical grandeur of the actor. *Heroic tragedy,* popular during the seventeenth and eighteenth centuries, customarily treated the conflict between love and duty and was written in heroic couplets. (233)

High Comedy. Comedy of intellect and language, usually emphasizing upper-class characters and concerns. See also *Comedy.*

Hireling. In professional companies of the Renaissance and after, an actor or technician hired by the shareholders to work for a set wage at a set task. (226)

Householder. Member of a professional company who owns a share of the theatre building itself. (226)

Humanism. That philosophy that believes that people should be at the center of their own deepest concerns. (212)

Idea. In Aristotelian criticism, the moral expression of character through language; more generally, the intellectual statement of the *meaning* (see entry) of a play or a performance. (286)

Identification. Audience attitude in which the audience member believes that important elements of himself are to be found in a dramatic character; the audience "identifies" with the character. A suspect theory. (58)

Illusion of the First Time. An expression used by an English critic (late nineteenth century) to describe the effect of good realistic acting: that is, the event seems to be happening for the first time *to the character.* (330)

Illusionism. Scenic practices (with analogs in acting, directing, and other theatre arts) that rely on a belief in the theatrical imitation of the real world. (200)

Imagination. In acting, inventive faculty of the actor. (See also *Instrument.*) More generally, that faculty of mind or feeling, usually thought to be nonlinear, imagistic, metaphorical, and playful. (301)

Impressionism. A style of art that sought truth in the fleeting moments of consciousness. Prevalent in the drama and theatre of the 1890s, Impressionism was noted for its moody and mysterious quality. Major practitioner was Maurice Maeterlinck. (167)

Improvisation. Acting technique or exercise emphasizing immediacy of response and invention rather than rehearsed behavior. (315)

Instrument. The actor's physical self. See also *Imagination*. (300)

Interlude. A kind of dramatic fare performed between other events, as between the courses of a banquet. Important during the Middle Ages and the Renaissance and connected with the rise of the professional actor. (259)

Intermezzi. Italian entertainments usually given at courts and presented between other forms of entertainment. See *Interlude*. (220)

Interregnum. "Between the kings"—that period of English history (1642–1660) after Charles I was removed from the throne and before Charles II was restored; with a Puritan government in power, theatres were closed. (230)

Italianate Staging. A kind of staging developed during the Renaissance in Italy and marked by a proscenium arch and perspective scenery arranged in wing and drop. (216)

Kinetic Memory. The body's retention of gesture, posture, or action, distinct from conscious orders from the brain.

Kothornos. High, platformed shoes worn by actors in Greece and Rome during the third century B.C. and later. Mistakenly attributed to the classical Greeks by early historians. (279)

Laughing Comedy. Specifically, comedy dating from the late eighteenth century and intended to restore the comic (laughing) spirit to the comedies of the age—in contrast to the then-popular sentimental or tearful comedies (See entry). (193)

Lazzi. Stock bits of business designed to provoke a particular response, usually laughter, from the audience. Associated particularly with the *commedia dell'arte* and the French farce of the seventeenth century. (220)

Lenaia. One of three major Athenian religious festivals devoted to the public worship of the god Dionysus at which drama was recorded. The home of comedy. See also *Festivals*. (284)

Lines of Business. A range of roles in which an actor would specialize for the major part of his or her acting career. Particularly important during the seventeenth and eighteenth centuries. (236)

Liturgical. Associated with the liturgy of the church; in drama, the kinds of plays that were done inside churches as part of the religious services and thus were performed in Latin, by the clergy, and were usually chanted or sung rather than spoken. (250)

Low Comedy. A kind of comedy that depends for its humor primarily on situation, visual gags, or obscenity. See also *Comedy*.

Ludi. 1. In Rome, festivals or *ludi* were given for public worship of a variety of gods and on various public occasions like military victories and the funerals of government officials. As drama was often included as a part of the festivals, they are important in a history of Roman theatre. **2.** Early medieval term for plays. (262)

Mansion. The particularized setting in the medieval theatre that, together with the *platea,* or generalized playing space, constituted the major staging elements of that theatre. Several mansions were placed around or adjacent to the *platea* at once—thus "simultaneous staging." See also *Platea.* (251)

Masque. Spectacular theatrical form, especially of the Renaissance and the Neoclassical periods, usually associated with *court theatres* (see entry) or special events. Emphasis was put on costumes and effects, with much music and dancing; amateur actors frequently performed. For example, Milton's wedding masque, *Comus,* and Ben Jonson's many court masques. (230)

Master Artwork. *Gesamtkunstwerk.* Both term and concept popularized by Richard Wagner, who argued that such a work would be the artistic fusion of all major artistic elements, including music, into a single work under the artistic supervision of a single master artist. (142)

Meaning. Intellectual content suggested or inspired by a play or a performance. All plays have meaning, however trivial, and most plays and performances have several meanings. Best thought of as "range of meaning" or "world of meaning." (431)

Master of Secrets. That craftsman/artist of the medieval theatre charged with the execution of special effects in the dramas. (254)

Mechane. Machine, or *machina.* In classical Greece, a crane by means of which actors and objects could be flown into the playing area (orchestra). (277)

Medieval. That period of world history dating roughly from the fall of the Western Roman Empire (c. A.D. 550) to the fall of Constantinople and the beginning of the Renaissance (c. 1450). In drama, the period between 975, the first record of drama in the church, and c. 1550, when religious drama was outlawed in many countries throughout Europe. (249)

Melodrama. Literally "music drama." A kind of drama associated with a simplified moral universe, a set of stock characters (hero, heroine, villain, comic relief), rapid turns in the dramatic action, and a dual-issue ending. Leading form of drama throughout the nineteenth century. (188)

Method. The American version of Stanislavski's "system" of actor training. (150)

Middle Comedy. That transitional kind of Greek comedy dating from c. 404 B.C., the defeat of Athens by Sparta, and 336 B.C., the beginning of the Hellenistic age. Less topical than Greek old comedy, middle comedy dealt more with domestic issues and everyday life of the Athenian middle class. (283)

Mime. 1. A kind of drama dating at least from the sixth century B.C. in Greece in which *unmasked* actors of both sexes portrayed often bawdy and obscene stories. The first *professional* performers appeared in the mime. In Greece, the form was never permitted in the religious festivals, but in Rome, it became the most popular kind of drama after the first century A.D. 2. Form of silent modern theatre, as popularized by Marcel Marceau and Mummenschanz. (267)

Mimesis. Imitation. (433)

Miracle Plays. Medieval plays treating the lives of saints. (258)

Monopoly. Legal control or exclusive domination of a theatrical locale; the courts of both France and England in the late seventeenth century, for example, granted licenses to a limited number of theatres that thus gained *monopolies*. (235)

Morality Plays. Allegorical medieval plays, like *Everyman*, that depict the eternal struggle between good and evil that transpires in this world, using characters like Vice, Virtue, Wisdom, and so on. (258)

Motivation. In Stanislavskian vocabulary, the dramatic justification for an action or a set of behaviors onstage. (323)

Music. One of Aristotle's six parts of a play: the material for diction. Popularly, the kind of art form having harmony and rhythm. (286)

Musical. An American musical comedy, a form traceable to the mid-nineteenth century and now typified by a spoken text or *book* (see entry) with songs and (usually) dances and a singing-dancing chorus. (81)

Mysteries. Medieval plays treating events based on the Bible or the Apocrypha and performed singly or in combination to produce the so-called cycle or cosmic dramas (see entries). (258)

Myth. Story with a religious or magical base, featuring a myth hero who typifies important features of the culture, for example, the myth of Oedipus (ancient Greece) or the myth of Skunniwundi (American Indian). In a less precise sense, some critics speak of the myth behind or imbedded in a work of narrative art and even of a dream, that is, the culturally important pattern that can be found there.

Naturalism. A style of theatre and drama most popular from c. 1880 to 1900 that dealt with the sordid problems of the middle and lower classes in settings remarkable for the number and accuracy of details. Practitioners included Émile Zola, André Antoine, and Maksim Gorki. See also *Determinism*. (147)

Neoclassical. A style of drama and theatre from the Italian Renaissance based loosely on interpretations of Aristotle and Horace. Major tenets were: verisimilitude, decorum, purity of genres (see all of these entries), the five-act form, and the twofold purpose of drama: to teach and to please. (213)

NeoRomanticism. Literally, "new Romanticism." A style of theatre and drama of the late nineteenth century that sought to recapture the idealism and exoticism of early nineteenth-century Romanticism. A reaction against the pessimism and sordidness of the Realists and the Naturalists. (167)

New Comedy. That form of Greek comedy dating from the Hellenistic and Graeco-Roman periods and treating the domestic complications of the Athenian middle class. A major source for Roman comedy. (285)

Noble Savage. A manifestation of *primitivism* (see entry) that depicted a romanticized view of primitive people and led to an artistic presentation of American Indians, African slaves, and so on as major figures in art. (183)

Obie. Awards given annually to performers, playwrights, designers, and productions that made significant contributions to the Off-Broadway theatre scene. Name comes from the first letters of *Off-Broadway*. (86)

Objective. In Stanislavskian vocabulary, a character's goal within a beat or scene; the goal of a motivation. (323)

Old Comedy. That form of Greek comedy written during the Classical period (see entry) and featuring topical political and social commentary set in highly predictable structural and metrical patterns. (283)

Off-Broadway. Popularly, those small, originally experimental but now often quite commercial, theatres that are located outside the Times Square/Broadway area. Contractually, those theatres with a seating capacity of fewer than three hundred that are authorized to pay lower wages and fees to union employees than are the larger, Broadway houses. (90)

Off-Off-Broadway. Popularly, the very small nontraditional theatres located in churches, coffee houses, and so on that fall considerably out of the commercial mainstream. Contractually, theatres with highly limited seating capacities that may be granted exemptions from a wide variety of union regulations and scales. (93)

Onkos. That high and ornate headdress worn by tragic actors beginning during the Hellenistic period in Greece and later Rome. Mistakenly attributed to classical Greek actors by early historians. (279)

Orchestra. 1. That area of the Greek and Roman theatre that lay between the audience area and the scene house. 2. Originally the circular space where actors and chorus danced and performed plays; later a half circle that was used as a seating space for important people and only occasionally as a performance area. 3. In modern times, the prized seating area on the ground level of a theatre and adjacent to the stage. (276)

Organic. Suggesting growth from a definable beginning; developing naturally.

Pacing. Apparent rate of performance; partly a matter of the speed with which the performance goes forward, but also related to intensity of action and complication and the artistic ways (actor's intensity, for example) that the action is realized. (370)

Pageant. In the medieval period, a movable stage, a wagon on which plays were mounted and performed in parts of England, Spain, and occasionally Continental Europe. By extension, the plays performed on such wagons. (255)

Pantomime. In the Roman theatre, a dance/story performed by a single actor with the accompaniment of a small group of musicians, particularly during the Christian era. 2. In the eighteenth and nineteenth centuries, a "minor" form of entertainment marked by elaborate spectacle and often featuring *commedia* characters and a scene of magical transformation. (234)

Parabasis. That section of Greek old comedy where the chorus or choral leader addressed the audience directly, often on matters of topical political or social interest. Separates the Attic from the Doric parts of old comedy. (282)

Parados. 1. In Greek theatre buildings, the alleyway that ran between the audience area and the orchestra circle through which the chorus made its entrances. 2. In Greek drama, that section of the play during which the chorus made its entrance. (276)

Paraskene. Those parts of a Graeco-Roman (and probably Classical Age) Greek theatre that extended from the ends of the skene toward the orchestra. Absent in Hellenistic theatres. (276)

Paratheatrical. Related to or parallel to the theatrical. Used to refer to activities tangential to theatre: circus, parades, and so on. (98)

Performing Arts. Those arts that depend on a live performer in the presence of a live audience, for example, theatre, dance, opera, musical concerts. (2)

Periaktoi. Stage machines in use by the Hellenistic period in Greece. An early method of scene changing that consisted of a triangle extended in space and mounted on a central pivot so that when the pivot was rotated, three different scenes could be shown to an audience. (268)

Period Movement. Actors' movements imitative or suggestive of the way people moved, or are thought to have moved, in another historical period. (310)

Perspective. Simulation of visual distance by the manipulation of size of objects. (216)

Phallus. Simulation of the male sexual organ. In Greek old comedy and satyr plays, phalluses were enlarged and otherwise made prominent for purposes of comic effect. (278)

Phonetic. Relating to the human voice and human speech; symbolizing (in letters or pictures, for example) precise human sounds, as in the phonetic alphabet. (312)

Pictorialism. Directorial use of the proscenium stage's potential for creating pictures, for both aesthetic and ideological ends. (365)

Picturization. Directorial creation of stage groupings ("pictures") that show or symbolize relationships or meanings; storytelling through stage pictures. (366)

Pinakes. Type of scenic unit dating from the Classical Age in Greece. Presumably resembled a modern-day flat. (277)

Pit. 1. Area of the audience on the ground floor and adjacent to the stage. Historically an inexpensive area because originally no seats were provided there and later only backless benches were used. By the end of the nineteenth century, a preferred seating area (now called the orchestra section). 2. Now refers often to the area reserved for members of the orchestra playing for opera, ballet, and musical comedy. (198)

Platea. The unlocalized playing area in the medieval theatre. See also *Mansion.* (251)

Plot. 1. In Aristotle, one of the six parts of a play and the most important of the six; the formal cause of character; the soul of tragedy; the architectonic part of play. 2. Popularly the story of a play, a novel, and so on. (286)

Pluralism. Toleration of several kinds of things in a category; theatrical pluralism in a community accepts, for example, professional and amateur theatre side-by-side, or high tragedy and low comedy and the circus, and so on.

Political Theatre. The kind of theatre devoted to achieving political and social rather than artistic goals. (107)

Poor Theatre. Phrase popularized by Jerzy Grotowski and referring to the kind of theatrical production that is stripped of all (to him) inessential elements (scenery, costuming, lighting, etc.) and focuses only on the relationship between actor and audience. (98)

Possession of Parts. During the seventeenth and especially the eighteenth centuries, the practice of leaving a role with an actor throughout his career once the role was given him. Under the system, a sixty-year-old woman playing Juliet in Shakespeare's tragedy was not unheard of. (236)

Presentational. Style of performance and design that lays emphasis on *presenting* a theatrical event to an audience. Contrasts with representational (see entry) which stresses the reproduction of life on stage for an audience that merely looks on.

Preview. Public performance given prior to the official opening of a play, often to test the audience's response. (377)

Primitivism. Interest in life and societies of primitive people; associated in particular with the Romantic movement of the late eighteenth and early nineteenth centuries. (183)

Private Theatre. In Elizabethan and Stuart England, indoor theatres that were open to the public but were expensive because of their relatively limited seating capacity. Located on monastic lands, these theatres were outside the jurisdiction of the city of London. Initially they housed children's troupes, but later the regular adult troupes used them as a winter home. (226)

Prologue. In Greek drama, that part of the play (*prologos*) that precedes the entrance of the chorus. In other periods, a short introductory speech delivered by an actor, either in or out of character, to set the scene, warm up the audience, defend the play, or entertain. (282)

Properties. Objects used on stage—furniture, cigarettes, dishware. (396)

Proscenium (Theatre). Theatre building in which the audience area is set off from the acting area by a proscenium arch that frames the stage, protects the perspective, masks the backstage area, etc. The audience views the onstage action from one side only. (216)

Protagonist. In Greek theatre, the first (or major) actor, the one who competed for the prize in acting. Later, the leading character in any play (the "hero"). (279)

Psychological Realism. A kind of theatre that relies on a view of human behavior as defined by late nineteenth-century and twentieth-century psychology. (149)

Pulpitum. In Roman theatre, the stage. (268)

Purity of Genres. Neoclassical tenet that elements of tragedy and those of comedy could not be mixed. The injunction was not merely against including funny scenes in tragedy but also against treating domestic issues or writing in prose, these elements being of the nature of comedy. (214)

Raked Stage. Stage slanted up from front to back to enhance the perspective. Stages began their rakes either at the front of the apron or at the proscenium line. (218)

Realism. The style of drama and theatre dating from the late nineteenth and early twentieth centuries that strove to reproduce on stage the details of everyday life with a view to improving the human and social condition. (136)

Regional Theatre. Theatre outside New York City in the United States and Canada; term usually restricted to professional, nontouring companies. (121)

Rehearsal. The practicing of plays, either whole or in part, in order to improve their performance. (326)

Renaissance. Literally, "rebirth"; refers to a renewed interest in the learning and culture of ancient Greece and Rome. Beginning in Italy, the Renaissance spread throughout Western Europe from c. 1450 to c. 1650. (211)

Repertory. A set group of performance pieces done by a company is its repertory. Also, the practice in such a company of alternating pieces so that they are done *in repertory*. Loosely a resident professional theatre company in the United States, called a *repertory theatre*. (123)

Representational. A style of performance and design that lays emphasis on re-creating onstage aspects of daily life; the audience members are thought of as passive onlookers. Contrasts with *presentational* (see entry), a style that stresses *presenting* an event *for an audience*.

Restoration. The period of English history that dates from 1660, when King Charles II was restored to the throne. (230)

Reversal. According to Aristotle, one of the three qualitative parts of plot: *suffering* (awareness, consciousness), *discovery*, and *reversal*. By extension, any rapid change in direction or fortune in a play, and thus a quality attributed to melodramas in particular. (286)

Reviewer. A person who views an artistic event and then writes his/her descriptive evaluation of it for immediate publication. (425)

Rhythm. Regular and measurable repetition. (369)

Rigging. The combination of ropes, lines, pulleys, pipes, and so on that permit the manipulation of scenic units backstage. (394)

Ritual. Any oft-repeated act that has a specific goal. *Ritual theory:* a theory that asserts that drama derived from religious rituals (in Greece, for example, religious rituals devoted to the worship of the god Dionysus). (287)

Roman. A period in theatre and drama dating from c. 364 B.C. to c. A.D. 550 and customarily subdivided into the Republican period (c. 364 B.C.– c. 27 B.C.) and the Empire (c. 27 B.C.–c. A.D. 550). (260)

Romanticism. A style of threatre and drama dating from c. 1790 to c. 1850 and marked by an interest in the exotic, the subjective, the emotional, and the individual. Began in part as a reaction against the strictures of Neoclassicism; grew out of the eighteenth century's sentimentalism (see entry). (183)

Royalties. Payments made to authors (and their representatives) for permission to reproduce, in text or in performance, their artistic products (plays, designs, etc.). (424)

Run-Through. A kind of rehearsal in which the actors perform long sections of the play (or the whole play) without interruption, usually for the purpose of improving the sense of continuity, shaping the whole, and so on. (376)

Rural Dionysia. One of three Athenian festivals devoted to the public worship of the god Dionysus at which drama appeared. See also *Festivals.* (283)

Satyr Play. A short, rustic, and often obscene play included in the Dionysian festivals of Greece at the conclusion of the tragedies. (283)

Scaena. Scene house in the Roman theatre. (268)

Scaena Frons. The facade of the *scaena.* Noted for its elaborateness, with niches, porticoes, statuary, and so on. (268)

Scaffold. In medieval staging in England, the localizing structure in or near the *platea.* See also *Mansion.* (251)

Scenario. In general, the prose description of a play's story. In the *commedia dell'arte,* the written outlines of plot and characters from which the actors improvised the particular actions of performance. (220)

Scrim. Mesh used in scenery; becomes transparent when lighted from behind, opaque when lighted from the front; useful for transformations, misty effects, and so forth. (200)

Script. Play text. See also *Text* and *Book* (318)

Secularism. Belief in the validity and importance of life and things on earth. Often contrasted with spiritualism, other-worldliness, or religiosity. The Renaissance period was marked by a rising *secularism.* (212)

Sedes. Also called *mansions* (see entry). The particularized locations of a medieval stage, any number of which could be shown simultaneously and arranged about the generalized playing space *(platea).* An older (Latin) term for *mansion* (French) or *scaffold* (English). (251)

Sense Memory. Recall of a sensory response—smell, taste, sound—with both its cause and the actor's reaction; important to the creation of a character's behavior in some theories of acting. (315)

Sententiae. Pithy, short statements about the human condition. Associated with the tragedies of Seneca and with those of his successors. in the Renaissance. (264)

Sentimentalism. Prevalent during the eighteenth century, sentimentalism assumed the innate goodness of mankind and attributed evil to faulty instruction or bad example. A precursor of the Romanticism of the nineteenth century. (181)

Sentimental Comedy. A kind of comedy particularly popular during the eighteenth century in which people's virtues rather than their foibles were stressed. The audience were expected to experience something "too exquisite for laughter." Virtuous characters expressed themselves in pious "sentiments." (193)

Shareholder. Member of a sharing company who owned a part of the company's stocks of costumes, scenery, properties, and so on. Sharing companies were the usual organization of troupes from the Renaissance until the eighteenth century (and beyond), when some actors began to prefer fixed salaries to shares. (226)

Shutter. Large flat, paired with another of the same kind, to close off the back of a scene in Italianate staging; an alternative to a backdrop; sometimes used for units at the sides. When pierced with a cutout, it became a "relieve" and showed a *diorama* (see entry). (218)

Sight Lines. Extreme limits of the audience's vision, drawn from the farthest and/or highest seat on each side through the proscenium arch or scenery obtruding farthest onstage. Anything beyond the sight lines cannot be seen by some members of the audience. (394)

Signature Music. Music associated with certain characters or certain types of characters, particularly in the melodramas of the nineteenth century. Stage directions indicate "Mary's music," "Jim's music," and so on. (188)

Simultaneous Staging. The practice, particularly during the Middle Ages, of representing several locations on the stage at one time. In medieval staging, several *mansions* (see entry), representing particular places, were arranged around a *platea*, or generalized playing space. (251)

Siparium. Curtain in the Roman theatre that hung at the rear of the playing area, perhaps to serve as a background for the action and as a masking for the offstage area. (268)

Skene. The scene house in the Greek theatre. Its appearance can first be documented with the first performance of the *Oresteia* in 458 B.C. Its exact appearance from that time until the first stone theatre came into existence (probably in the late fourth century B.C.) is uncertain. (276)

Slice of Life. Critical notion closely associated with Naturalism and used to describe plays that avoided the trappings of Romanticism and the obvious contrivance of well-made plays in favor of a seemingly literal reproduction of daily life on the stage. (148)

Soliloquy. An intensely emotional passage, often lyric, delivered by a person onstage alone.

Spectacle. One of Aristotle's six parts of a play, the part of least interest to the poet but of most importance in differentiating the dramatic form from the narrative and the epic. In everyday parlance, all visual elements of production and, by extension, particular plays, scenes, or events in which visual elements predominate. (286)

Spine. In Stanislavskian vocabulary, the consistent line that connects all elements of a character through a play. See *Through line.* (325)

Stage Left. The left half of the stage as defined by some one standing onstage facing the audience. (365)

Stage Right. The right half of the stage as defined by some one standing onstage facing the audience. (365)

Star. Dominant actor or actress whose name and presence draw an audience. (317)

Star System. Company organization in which minor characters are played by actors for the season, while central roles are taken by stars (see entry) brought in for one production; still common in opera, sometimes seen in summer theatres. (203)

Stichomythia. In classical tragedy, especially Seneca, the alternation of short, pithy lines by two or more characters. (264)

Stock Company. Theatre company in which actors play standardized roles and (originally) owned shares of stock in the company. (203)

Storm and Stress. *Sturm und Drang;* a theatrical movement in Germany during the 1770s and 1780s that was marked by its militant experimentation with dramatic form, theatrical style, and social statement. (195)

Story. Narrative; coherent sequence of incidents; "what happens." A general, non-technical term that should not be confused with *plot*. (55)

Street Theatre. Theatre, often political, that takes place outside traditional theatre spaces and without traditional theatrical trappings. (107)

Style. 1. Distinctive combination of elements. 2. In Aristotelian terms, the way in which the manner is joined to the means. 3. Particulars of surface, as distinguished from substance. 4. "The way a thing is done" in a time and place. (36)

Subtext. In Stanislavskian vocabulary, action "between the lines," implied but not stated in the text. (318)

Superobjective. In Stanislavskian vocabulary, the "life goal" of the character. (323)

Surrealism. A style popular immediately following World War I that rejected everyday logic in favor of a free expression of the subconscious (or dream) state. (171)

Symbolism. A style of theatre and drama popular during the 1890s and the early twentieth century that stressed the importance of subjectivity and spirituality and sought its effects through the use of symbol, legend, myth, and mood. (168)

Technical Rehearsal. Rehearsal devoted to the practice and perfection of the various technical elements of the show (lighting, sound, flying, trapping, and so on). (376)

Tendencies. In Stanislavskian vocabulary, aspects of an actor's performance that digress from the *through line* (see entry). (325)

Text. The written record of a play, including dialogue and stage directions; a playscript. (348)

Theatre of Cruelty. Phrase popularized by Antonin Artaud to describe a kind of theatre that touched the basic precivilized elements of people through disrupting normal "civilized" expectations about appearance, practice, sound, and so forth. (176)

Theatron. Audience area in the Greek theatre, the "seeing place." Roughly equivalent to today's auditorium ("hearing place"). (276)

Theory. In dramatic criticism, a consistent and cohesive idea of drama that explains all its elements. (426)

Through Line. In Stanislavskian vocabulary, a consistent element of character running through a scene or a play. (325)

Thrust Stage. Dominant kind of staging during Shakespeare's time in England that is being revived in many contemporary theatres. Also called *three-quarter round* because the audience surrounds the action on three sides as the stage juts into the audience area. (223)

Timing. Actor's sense of tempo and rhythm. (370)

Tiring House. The building from which the Elizabethan platform, or thrust, stage extended. A place where the actors attired themselves. (224)

Tony. Annual awards made by the directors of the American Theatre Wing in memory of Antoinette Perry to recognize outstanding contributions to the current New York theatrical season. (86)

Tragedy. In popular parlance, any serious play, usually including an unhappy ending. According to Aristotle, "an imitation of a worthy or illustrious and perfect action, possessing magnitude, in pleasing language, using separately the several species of imitation in its parts, by men acting, and not through narration, through pity and fear effecting a catharsis of such passion." At this point in theatrical history, almost indefinable.

Transformation. 1. Technique popularized in the 1960s whereby an actor portrayed several characters without any changes in costume, makeup, or mask, relying instead on changing voice and body attitudes in full view of the audience. 2. In medieval and Renaissance theatre, seemingly magical changes of men into beasts, wives into salt, and so on. (100)

Trap. Unit in stage floor for appearances and disappearances; varies from a simple door to complex machines for raising and lowering while moving forward, backward, and sideways. (208)

Tritagonist. The third actor in Greek tragedies. Typically played a series of minor and bit parts. (279)

Trope. An interpolation in a liturgical text. The medieval drama is believed to have been derived from medieval troping. (250)

Übermarionette. Super puppet. A mechanical substitute for the living actor, a robot. Term popularized by Gordon Craig. (380)

Union. An alliance of persons formed to secure material benefits and better working conditions. Major theatrical unions are USAA (United Scenic Artists of America, for designers); Equity (Actors Equity Association, for actors); IATSE (International Alliance of Theatrical Stage Employees, for theatre technicians). (87)

Unity. Cohesion or consistency. When applied to a text, it refers to the method of organizing: unity of plot, unity of character, unity of action. When applied to design, it refers to how well all the visual elements fit together to achieve an artistic whole.

Upstage. The sections of the stage closest to the back wall. Comes from a time when stages were raked, or slanted, from the front to the back, so that upstage meant quite literally walking *up* the stage toward the back wall. (365)

Unit Set. A single setting on which all scenes may be played. (394)

Vaudeville. 1. In America in the nineteenth and twentieth centuries, vaudeville was popular family entertainment featuring a collection of variety acts, skits, short plays, and song-and-dance routines. 2. In France in the eighteenth and nineteenth centuries, *vaudeville* referred to *comédie-en-vaudeville*, short satiric pieces, often topical, that were interspersed with new lyrics set to familiar tunes and sprinkled with rhyming couplets *(vaudevilles)*. The form in France is roughly equivalent to the *ballad opera* (see entry) in England. (193)

Velum. An awning introduced in the Roman theatre to protect audiences from the sun as they watched spectacles in the theatres and amphitheatres. (268)

Verisimilitude. Central concept in Neoclassical theory and criticism. Literal meaning is "truth-seemingness," but used historically, at a time when *truth* referred to the general, typical, categorical truth. Not to be confused with "realism." (213)

Versurae. Extensions of the scene house in Roman theatres that enclosed the stage at each end; roughly the equivalent of the *paraskene* in Greek theatres.   (268)

Via Negativa. "The negative path." Popularized by Jerzy Grotowski in actor training; the necessity to strip away all disguises, masks, or protections of the performer so that he may begin work at a very basic and truthful level. (98)

Villain. Character in melodrama who opposes the forces of good (represented by the hero and the heroine) and who, at the play's end, is punished for his evil ways. Typically the villain propels the action of a melodrama. (189)

Vomitoria. Corridors, entrances, and exits of a Roman theatre. Those nearest the stage corresponded roughly to the *paradoi* of the Greek theatres.   (268)

Vocal Folds. Tissue in the throat over which air passes to make sound; incorrectly called *vocal cords.* (311)

Well-Made Play. A play written by or in the manner of Eugène Scribe and marked by careful preparation, seeming cause-and-effect organization of action, announced entrances and exits, and heavy reliance on external objects or characters to provide apparent connections among diverse lines of action. Now often used as a term of derision. (195)

Wings. 1. Scenic pieces *(flats)* placed parallel to the stage front, or nearly so, on each side of the stage; combined with overhead units for "wing-and-border" settings. 2. The offstage area beyond the side units of scenery—"in the wings." (From which is derived *wing space*, the amount of room offstage at the sides.) (200)

Bibliography

ALBRIGHT, HARDIE. *Stage Direction in Transition* (Belmont, Calif., 1972).

ATKINSON, BROOKS. *Broadway* (New York, 1970).

BENEDETTI, ROBERT. *Actor at Work*. Rev. ed. (Englewood Cliffs, N.J., 1976).

BIEBER, MARGARETE. *The History of the Greek and Roman Theatre*. 2nd. ed. (Princeton, N.J., 1901).

BROCKETT, OSCAR G., and FINDLAY, ROBERT R. *Century of Innovation: A History of European and American Theatre and Drama Since 1870* (Englewood Cliffs, N.J., 1973).

BROCKETT, OSCAR G. *History of the Theatre*. 3rd ed. (Boston, 1977).

CAMPBELL, LILY BESS. *Scenes and Machines on the English Stage During the Renaissance* (Cambridge, England, 1923).

CLARK, BARRETT H., Ed. *European Theories of the Drama*. Rev. ed. by Henry Popkin (New York, 1965).

COLE, TOBY, Ed. *Playwrights on Playwriting* (New York, 1960).

COLE, TOBY, and CHINOY, HELEN K., Eds. *Actors on Acting*. Rev. ed. (New York, 1970).

_____. *Directors on Directing* (Indianapolis, 1963).

COREY, IRENE. *The Mask of Reality; An Approach to Design for the Theatre* (Anchorage, Ky., 1968).

CROYDEN, MARGARET. *Lunatics, Lovers, and Poets: The Contemporary Experimental Theatre* (New York, 1974).

DEAN, ALEXANDER, and CARRA, LAWRENCE. *Fundamentals of Play Directing*. 3rd ed. (New York, 1974).

Drama Review, The

ENGEL, LEHMAN. *The American Musical Theatre* (New York, 1967).

FERGUSSON, FRANCIS. *The Idea of Theatre* (Princeton, N.J., 1949).

FORD FOUNDATION. *The Finances of the Performing Arts* (Washington, 1974).

FRYE, NORTHRUP. *Anatomy of Criticism* (Princeton, N.J., 1957).

GOLDMAN, WILLIAM. *The Season: A Candid Look at Broadway* (New York, 1969).

GURR, ANDREW. *The Shakespearean Stage, 1574–1642* (Cambridge, England, 1970).

HARSH, PHILIP W. *A Handbook of Classical Drama* (Stanford, Calif., 1944).

HEWITT, BARNARD. *Theatre USA, 1668–1957* (New York, 1959).

————, Ed. *The Renaissance Stage: Documents of Serlio, Sabbattini, and Furttenbach* (Coral Gables, Fla., 1958).

HODGE, FRANCIS. *Play Directing: Analysis, Communication, and Style* (Englewood Cliffs, N.J., 1971).

HUGHES, LEO. *The Drama's Patrons: A Study of the Eighteenth Century London Audience* (Austin, Texas, 1971).

KRUTCH, JOSEPH WOOD. *"Modernism" in Modern Drama* (Ithaca, N.Y., 1953).

LANGER, SUZANNE. *Feeling and Form: A Theory of Art* (New York, 1953).

LAWRENSON, T. E. *The French Stage in the XVII Century: A Study in the Advent of the Italian Order* (Manchester, England, 1957).

MELCHER, EDITH. *Stage Realism in France Between Diderot and Antoine* (Bryn Mawr, Pa., 1928).

MOODY, RICHARD. *America Takes the Stage: Romanticism in American Drama and Theatre, 1750–1900* (Bloomington, Ind., 1955).

MORISON, BRADLEY G., and FLIEHR, KAY. *In Search of an Audience: How an Audience Was Found for the Tyrone Guthrie Theatre* (New York, 1968).

NAGLER, A. M. *A Source Book in Theatrical History* (New York, 1959).

New York *Times,* The.

NICOLL, ALLARDYCE. *Masks, Mimes, and Miracles* (New York, 1931).

PARKER, W. ORIN, and SMITH, HARRY K. *Scene Design and Stage Lighting.* 3rd ed. (New York, 1974).

SCHEVILLE, JAMES. *Breakout! In Search of New Theatrical Environments* (Chicago, 1972).

SHATTUCK, ROGER. *The Banquet Years: The Arts in France, 1885–1918* (New York, 1961).

SIMONSON, LEE. *The Stage Is Set* (New York, 1932).

SOUTHERN, RICHARD. *Seven Ages of the Theatre* (New York, 1961).

VARDAC, A. N. *Stage to Screen: Theatrical Method from Garrick to Griffith* (Cambridge, Mass., 1949).

Village Voice, The.

WICKHAM, GLYNNE. *Early English Stages, 1300–1660.* 2 vols. (New York, 1959–1972).

Illustration Sources. Illustrations for which no credit source is given in the captions are taken from the following works:

BAPST, GERMAIN. *Essai Sur l'Histoire du Théâtre,* 1893.

BESANT, WALTER. *London in the Time of the Tudors,* 1904.

[COMBE, WILLIAM]. *The Tour of Doctor Syntax,* 1828.

CRUIKSHANK, GEORGE. *The Comic Almanack* (various years).

————. *The George Cruikshank Omnibus,* 1842.

[DICKENS, CHARLES. ed.] *The Life of Grimaldi,* 1838.

DORPFELD-REISCH, W. *Das Griechische Theater.*

FITZGERALD, PERCY. *The Romance of the English Stage,* 1874.

GHERARDI, E. *Le Théâtre de Gherardi,* 1721.

GINISTY, PAUL. *La Vie d'un Théâtre,* 1898.

GRANT, JAMES. *Sketches in London,* 1838.

LOLIÉE, FRÉDÉRIC. *La Comédie-Francaise: Histoire de la Maison de Molière,* 1907.

The Percy Society. *Early English Poetry, Ballads and Popular Literature of the Middle Ages.*
. . . 1846.

POUGIN, ARTHUR. *Dictionaire Historique et Pittoresque du Théâtre,* 1885.

Scientific American, Supplement (various issues).

Le Théâtre (various issues).

The Theatre (various issues).

THORNBURY, G. W. *Old and New London,* 1881.

WIESELER, FREDERICH. *Theatergebaude und Denkmaler des Buhenwesens,* 1851.

Note: Pages in *italics* refer to illustrations.

A

Abelard and Heloise, 352
Abstraction, level of, 37, 390, *390*
Absurdism, 171–172, *172*
Acting
  being and pretending, 295, *296*
  history of, 332–39
  inner and outer, 295
  method, 99, 150, 158, 161
  modern realistic, 338–39, *338*
  natural, 153, 204, 206–207
    versus artificial, 204, 293–94
  performing and, 303–304, *304. See also*
    Performance
  realistic, 207
  Stanislavski on. *See* Stanislavski
  technique versus inspiration, 294–95
  see also Actor(s)

Action, 18–19, 353–54
Actor(s), 291–339
  audition, rehearsal, and performance
    by, 325–30
  Brecht on, 174
  coaching of, by director, 359–63
  definition of, 18
  in experimental theatres, 98–100, 102
  Greek, *278,* 279
  instrument of, 300–301, *300,* 308, *315*
  in late nineteenth century, 134
  naturalistic, 153. *See also* Acting, natural
  in Neoclassical era
    in England, 226, *227, 229*
    in France, 241–42
  paradox of, 292–304
  personality of, 330–32
  in Restoration theatre, 235–36
  in Romantic era, 202–207, *203*

Actor(s) (Cont.)
Stanislavski on training of, 149, 150
star. *See* Star system
training of, 304–25
women as, 204, *205*, 235–36
see also Acting
Adding Machine, The, 170
Adler, Stella, 150
Aeschylus, 52, 279–80
Ah, Wilderness, 157
Albee, Edward, 83, *84*, 93, 171, 172, 420
Alienation effect, 174
All My Sons, 161
Allen, Michael, 93
Alleyn, Edward, 334
All's Well That Ends Well, 65
Alma-Tadema, Lawrence, *406,* 407
American Hurrah, 100, 101
Analysis, by actor, 300, 317–18, *319*
Anderson, Maxwell, 158
Anderson, Robert, 86, 422, 424
Antigone, 109, 110
Antoine, André, 141, 152–55, *152,* 380, *380,* 381
Appia, Adolphe, 9, 144, 168–69, 407
Aristophanes, 282–83, *284*
Aristotle, 175, 266, 275, 286, 287–88, 298, 426, 432–35, 440
Arsenic and Old Lace, 57
Art(s)
during 1960s and 1970s, 76–78
performing, 3–22
definition of, 4
major, 6–13
theatre as, 13–22, 60–61, 142
Artaud, Antonin, 144, 172–73, 176–78, 383, 426, 440
As You Like It, 369
Assomoir, L', 154, 155
Athletic events, 12–13, *12*
Atkinson, Brooks, 157
Auden, W. H., 415
Audience, 23–45, 47–69
Artaud on spiritual awakening of, 177
Brecht on alienation and thoughtful participation of, 174–75
claques in, *437*
contract between artists and, 41–44, 68
definition of, 18, 24–26
director and, 351
diversity of, 5, *5*

in Greek theatre, 276–77
middle class, in Romantic era, 181–82
as participants, 107
perceptions of, 34–39
playwright and, 419–20
in political theatres, 107
reasons for attending theatre, 30–34
responses of, *20,* 25, *26,* 39–41, *40,* 63–68
negative, 66–68, *68,* 199. *See also* Riots
size of, 24, *26–28*
as spectator
Foreman's aims for, 104
Grotowski's interest in, 98–99
styles of, 39–41, *40*
Wagner on importance of, 141–42, 143, 144
Audition, 326
Augier, Émile, 144
Awards, drama, 85*t.,* 86

B

Bankhead, Tallulah, 54, 158, 160
Baraka, Imamu Amiri (LeRoi Jones), 115
Bayreuth theatre, 141–44, *143,* 379
Beaumarchais, Pierre, 193
Beaumont, Francis, 229
Beauty, changing standards of, 392, *393,* 394
Beck, Julian, 109, 111, 383
Beckett, Samuel, 54, 172, *172,* 415
Behrman, S. N., 157
Belasco, David, 381, *381,* 418
Bells, The, 134, *135*
Benedetti, Robert L., 306
Bentley, Eric, 78, 111
Berlin, Irving, 157
Bernhardt, Sarah, 131, *317*
Betterton, Thomas, 236, 418
Big Hotel, 105
Biomechanics, 170–71
Black Medea, 118
Black theatre, 113–18
Blacks, The, 114
Body, training, 308–10, *309, 310*
Boleslavsky, Richard, 150
Bologna, J., 121
Bonne Esperance, La, 151
Boorstin, Daniel, 31

Booth, Edwin, 135, *206*
Booth, Junius Brutus, 207
Boucicault, Dion, 132, *397*
Boys in the Band, The, 91, 93
Brando, Marlon, 161, 339
Bread and Puppet Theatre, 97, *97*
Brecht, Bertolt, 41, 109, 110, 171–76, 323,
    408, 420, 426, 431
Breeches roles, 204, *205*
Brig, The, 109, *110*
Broadway, 78, *79,* 80–90, 155–63
    business aspects of, 87–90
    comedy on, 86–87
    definition of, 28
    importance of, 80
    musicals of, 80–83
    from 1900 to 1960, 155–63
    plays of, 80–81
        serious, 83–86
    playwrights and, 422, 424
Brook, Peter, 83, 97, 383
Brown, Kenneth, 109, *110*
Bubbling Brown Sugar, 117
Bullins, Ed, 113, 117
Burbage, Richard, 334
Burlesque, 132, 133
Byron, George, 415

C

Cabaret, 410
Calm Down Mother, 100, 121
Camelot, 73, 81
Camille, 105
Capon, William, 405, 406
Carmines, Al, 93, 121
Carousel, 165
Caruso, Enrico, 294
Carver, De Ray, *438*
Casting, 373–75, *374*
Cat and the Moon, The, 309
Censorship, 153
Centering, 306–307, 308
Ceremonies in Dark Old Men, 117, *117*
Chaikin, Joseph, 94, 99–102
Character
    actor and, 297–98, *297,* 318–23, *327*
    director and, 362–63
    in theatrical performance, 58–60
Chariot-and-pole system, 219, *219*

Charley's Aunt, 319
Chase, Mary, 160
Chausée, Pierre Claude Nivelle de La,
    243
Chekhov, Anton, 146–47, *146,* 150, 161,
    169
Chekhov, Mikhail, 150
Chicanos, 112
Childress, Alice, 115
Choral drama of Greece, 273–75
Chorus Line, A, 81, 82, *83*
Christian, The, 137
Cibber, Colley, 236
Cid, Le, 238–39, 435
Cino, Joe, 93
Civic and religious theatre, 245–88
Clairon, Mademoiselle, 202
Claques, *437*
Clurman, Harold, 150
Coaching, by director, 359–63
Cohan, George M., *159*
Cold Storage, 88
Coleridge, Samuel Taylor, 337, 436
Comédie Française, 25, *29,* 37, *182,* 196–
    97, 202, *241,* 242, 244, 339
Comedy, 86–87
    French and Italian, in Neoclassical era,
        241, 243
    Greek, 282–83, 285–86
    laughing, 193–95, *194*
    after 1900, 156, *156*
    Restoration, 231–32, *232,* 234–35
    Roman, 264–66, *265, 270, 271*
    sentimental, 193
    well-made play as, 195
Comic operas, 132
Commedia dell' arte, 220, *221,* 222, 234, *234,*
    261, *292*
Commercial theatre, 78–90
    realism as
        from 1850 to 1900, 131–35
        from 1900 to 1960, 155–63
    see also Broadway; Off-Broadway
Concentration, by actors, 299, *299,* 316–
    17
Congreve, William, 232
Connelly, Marc, 114
Conquest of the Universe, or When Queens Col-
    lide, 104
Consciousness, of actor, 299–300, 316–25
Constant Prince, The, 99
Constructivism, 170–71

Contemporary theatre, 73–128
  commercial, 78–90. *See also* Broadway;
    Off-Broadway
  design in, 407–11
  educational, 126–28
  in 1960s and 1970s, 73–78
  nontraditional, 93–121
  regional professional, 121–26
Conventions, 34–35, *34*
Cook, George Cram, 93
Cook, Ralph, 93
Cooper, Thomas A., 206
Copyright Law of 1977, 424
Coquelin, Benoît Constant, 134
Corneille, Pierre, 238–39, 435
Costumes
  for dance, *408,* 409
  design of, *387,* 396–98, *397,* 406–407,
    406
  director and, 357–58, *358*
  Greek, 278
  historical accuracy in, 140
  modern, 409–10, *410*
  nonrealistic, *409*
  Renaissance, 404, *404*
  in Romantic era, 202, *203, 207,* 208,
    404–407, *405*
  unified design of, 406–407, *406*
  see also Design
Coterie theatres, *27*
Coward, Noel, 155, *156*
Craig, Gordon, 144, 168–69, 380–81, 407
Critics, 43, 413–14, 424–40
Cronyn, Hume, 53
Crowd scenes, realistic, 139, *139, 140*
Cryer, Gretchen, 121

D

Dadism, 171
Dance, 10–11, *11*
  costumes for, *408, 409*
  in musicals, 160
Davenport, William, 231, 235
De Mille, Agnes, 10, 160
Death of a Salesman, 58, 118, 161–62, 164,
  408
Decorum, definition of, 214
Design(ers), 385–411
  Brecht on, 174–75

costume, *387,* 396–98, *397,* 406–407,
  406
director and, 356–58
goals of, 386–94
history of, 403–411
at work, 394–402
see also Costumes; Lighting; Scenery
Deux Grossès, Les, 138
Devrient, Emil, 206
Diderot, Denis, 193, 197, 202, 292, 293,
  294
Directors(ing), 341–83
  coaching by, 359–63
  design oversight and inspiration by,
    356–58
  function of, 343–45
  history of, 377–83
  as managers, 371–77
  medieval, 254
  Meiningen as father of modern, 141
  play selection by, 345–50
  playwright and, *420, 422*
  rhythm used by, 369–71
  script interpretation by, 351–56
  staging by, 363–69
  Stanislavski as, 149, 150
Discipline, 18, 316
Doctor in Spite of Himself, The, 38
Domestic Manners of the Americans, 67
Drama. *See* Play(s); Theatre
Drama Critics Circle Award, 85*t.,* 86
Drama Review, The, 98
Drame, 197
Drexler, Rosalyn, 121
Dryden, John, 233
Du Bois, William E. B., 113
Dumas *fils,* Alexandre, 144, 195
Dumas *père,* Alexandre, 197
Duse, Eleonora, *144*

E

Eccentricities of a Nightingale, 321
Eclecticism, in directing, 381–82, *382*
Educational theatre, 126–28
Eiffel Tower Wedding Party, The, 389
El Teatro Campesino, 112–13
Elder, Lonne, 117
Eliot, T. S., 54, 415, 440
Elizabethan English theatre, 222–26, *223–
  25, 334–35*

Endgame, 172
English theatre
  eighteenth century, 336–37
  Elizabethan, 222–26, *223–25,* 334–35
  Neoclassical, 222–37
  Romantic, 337–38
Ensemble work, *360*
Environment, director and, 354–55, *355, 358*
Epic theatre, 171, 173–76, *173*
Equus, 18, 62–63, *324*
Ethelwold, Bishop of Winchester, 250–51
Etherege, George, 232
Euripides, 280, 282, *283, 287,* 421
Existentialism, 171–72
Exit the King, 390
Exoticism, *187,* 188
Experimental theatres, 94–107
Expressionism, 169–71, *170*

F

Fantasticks, The, 91, *91*
Farce, French, 238, *238, 241*
Fashion, contemporary, in design, 392
Federal Theatre Project, 159–60
Feminist theatres, 118–21
Ferlita, Ernest, *Black Medea* of, *118*
Festival theatres, 163
Feydeau, George, 131
Fichandler, Zelda, 122
Fiddler on the Roof, 81
Fielding, Henry, 415
Film, 6–7, *7*
Five-act form, 215
Five On the Black Hand Side, 372
Flea in Her Ear, A, 131, *300, 364*
Fletcher, John, 229
Floyd, Carlisle, *Susannah* of, *127*
Fonda, Henry, 89
For Colored Girls Who Have Considered Suicide/ When the Rainbow Is Enuf, 116, *116,* 117
Ford, John, 229
Foreman, Richard, 102–104, *103*
Forrest, Edwin, *33*
Fourth-wall realism, 166
France
  farce in, 238, *238, 241*
  Neoclassicism in, 237–44
  see also Comédie Française
Frankenstein, 109–10
Frivolity Music Hall, replica of, *32*
Frye, Northrop, 436
Funniest Joke in the World, The, 108, 423
Funny Girl, 81
Furttenbach, Joseph, 219, 403

G

Garrick, David, 204, 337, 378–79, 405
Gay, Addison, 115
Geddes, Norman Bel, 407–408
Gelber, Jack, 109
Genet, Jean, 114, *114*
Geographical place, design and, 392
Gershwin, George, 158–59
Getting Off, 417
Gibson, William, 422
Gielgud, John, 54
Gilbert, William Schwenck, 132–33
Gilbert and Sullivan, 132–33
Gin Game, 53, 88
Giordano, Tony, *420, 425*
Girl of the Golden West, The, 381
Glass Menagerie, The, 161
Godspell, 88
Goethe, Johann Wolfgang von, 195, 379
Goldsmith, Oliver, 193, 194
Gordone, Charles, 117
Gorky, Maksim, *147,* 148
Greek theatre, 271–86, *274*
  acting in, 333–34, *333*
  Classical period of, 275–84
  design in, 403
  Hellenistic period of, 284–86
Green, Paul, 114
Green, Robert, 222
Greenwood, Joan, 54
Grotowski, Jerzy, 97–99, 102, 178, 303, 305, 383
Group
  creativity of, *430*
  self-image of, of audience, 41
Group Theatre, 28, 150, 158
Groupings, 139, *139,* 140
Groupness, 27
Guerrilla theatre, 107
Guthrie, Tyrone, *4,* 122, 123–24

Guthrie Theatre, 122, 124
Gwyn, Nell, 236

H

Hair, 68, 81, 82, *82, 382*
Hamlet, 58, 59, 62, 63, *293, 302, 310,* 321, 322, 370–71
Hammerstein, Oscar, 157
Hammerstein II, Oscar, 160
Hansberry, Lorraine, 114
Hardy, Alexandre, 238
Hart, Moss, 156
Hauptmann, Gerhart, 148, 153
Hayes, Helen, 305
Hazlitt, William, 337
Hegel, Friedrich, 436
Hell set-piece, *252*
Hellman, Lillian, 86, 129, 158, 431
Hello, Dolly, 81
Hellzapoppin', 81
Hernani, 196–97
    riot after, 25, *26, 68,* 197
Heroic tragedies, 233–34
Historical period, 36–37, *37, 38,* 39
    appeal of, 59, *59*
    designer in, role of, 391–92, *391*
Holliday, Judy, 160
Hollow Image, 432
Horace, 266
Horowitz, Israel, 93
Houseman, John, 160
Howard, Sidney, 157
Hugo, Victor, 196–97
Humanism, 212

I

Ibsen, Henrik, 144–45, *144,* 153, 157, 169, 195, *414,* 420, 439
Idea, theatrical, 61–63, 355–56
Identification, by audience, 58–59
Imaginary Invalid, The, 307
Imagination, of actor, 301–302, *302, 312*–14, *313, 314*
Immediacy, 19, 21
Importance of Being Earnest, The, 313
Impressionism, 167–69, *168*
Improvisation, 315–16
    in Open Theatre, 100, 101

Independent theatre movement, 155
Indians, 320
Industrial Revolution, 437, 439–40
Inge, William, 129, *130,* 162
Innovation, 35–36, *36*
Inspector General, The, 362
International Copyright Agreement, 132
Interview, 101
Ionesco, Eugène, 172
Irving, Henry, 134, *135,* 141, *206*
Irving, Washington, 199
Italian Straw Hat, The, 315
Italianate theatre, in France, 239, *240, 241*
Italy
    commedia dell' arte of, 220, *221,* 222, 234, *234,* 261, *292*
    Italianate staging in, 216, *217,* 218–20, *220*
    Neoclassicism in, 213–15
    see also Roman theatre

J

Jefferson, Joseph, 134
Jodelet, 322
Johnson, Samuel, 419, 424
Jolson, Al, 160
Jones, Elinor, *A Voice of My Own* by, *120*
Jones, Inigo, 231, 403
Jones, LeRoi (Imamu Amiri Baraka), 115
Jones, Margo, 122, 163
Jonson, Ben, 229, 231
Julien, Jean, 153
Julius Caesar, 139, 342, *406*
Jumpers, 95

K

Kaiser, Georg, 169–70
Kanin, Garson, 160
Kaufman, George S., 156, 158, 163
Kazan, Elia, 161, 162, 382
Keach, Stacy, *320*
Kean, Edmund, 206–207, 337, *437*
Kemble, Adelaide, *203*
Kemble, John Phillip, 206
Kennedy, Adrienne, 117, 121
Kennedy, John F., 73–75
Kennedy's Children, 76
Kern, Jerome, 157

Kerr, Jean, 86, 163
Kerr, Walter, 90, 106, 426, 428
Kiley, Richard, 81
Killigrew, Thomas, 235
King of the Great Clock Tower, The, 393
Kirkland, Jack, 156
Kitto, H. D. F., 427
Kommissarzhevsky, Vera, 150
Kopit, Arthur, 93, 172
Kotzebue, August Friedrich von, 189
Kyd, Thomas, 222

L

Labiche, Eugène, 131
Lamb, Myrna, 121, 431
Lemaître, Frédérick, 207
Lessing, Gotthold Ephraim, 193, 195, 197, 426, 435–36
Lighting
  designer of, 398–400, *398, 401, 402*
  director and, 357–58
  electric, 407
  by gaslight, 406
  modern, 407–409
  see also Design
Lillo, George, 197, 234
Little Night Music, A, 402
Little theatres, *27, 28*
Liturgical theatre, 250
Living Theatre, 99, 100, 107, 109–12
Lodge, Thomas, 227
Lohengrin, 10
London Merchant, The, 234
Long Day's Journey into Night, 321
Loutherbourg, Phillippe Jacques de, 202, 405
Lowell, Robert, 93
Lower Depths, The, 147
Ludlam, Charles, 97, 104–107, *105*
Lully, Jean-Baptiste, 242
Lyly, John, 222
Lysistrata, 382

M

Macbeth, 56
MacBird, 91
McCullers, Carson, 114, 162, *166*
MacKaye, Steele, 381, 407

Macklin, Charles, 236
Macready, William Charles, 202
Maeterlinck, Maurice, 167–68, *168*
Magic, as spectacle, *52, 53*
Malcontents, Les, 209
Malina, Judith, 109, 110, 111, 383
Mame, 81
Man of La Mancha, 21, 81
Man and Superman, 57
Manager, director as, 371–77
Marat/Sade, 83, 376
March, Fredric, 160
Marlowe, Christopher, 222
Marshall, E. G., 160
Marx, Karl, 136
Masks
  Greek, 278–79, *278*
  Roman, 268, *270*
Masques, 230–31
Maugham, Somerset, 155
Mazeppa, 51, 429
Mediation, 43, *44, 48, 49*
Medieval theatre, *246,* 247–60
  acting in, 334
  design in, 403
  liturgical, 250–51
  outside Church, 256–59
  property in, *253,* 254
  secular, 259
Meiningen company, 140–41, 148, 149
  see also Saxe-Meiningen
Melodrama, 132, 133, *133,* 134, *134, 135*
  of Euripides, 282
  historical, 209
  in Romantic era, 188–89, 191–92, *191,* 209
Member of the Wedding, 166
Menken, Ada Isaacs, *51*
Merman, Ethel, 158, 303
Method acting, 99, 150, 158, 161
Mexican-Americans, 112
Meyerhold, Vsevolod, 170, 381
Midsummer Night's Dream, A, 83
Mielziner, Jo, 162, 407, 408
Miller, Arthur, 129, 161–62, 171, 382
Milner, Ron, 115
Mime
  Roman, 266, 267
  see also Pantomime
Minelli, Liza, 303
Minnesota Theatre Company, 122, 124
Miracle plays, 258

Misanthrope, The, 350
Miser, The, 367
Mod Donna, The, 121
Modern theatre. See Contemporary theatre; Realism
Molière, 38–39, 38, 239–42, 241, 242, 331, 336, 378, 378, 419, 420, 421
Monsieur Vernet, 380
Mood
  designer and, 389, 389
  director and, 351, 352, 368–69
Morality plays, 258, 259
Morrison, Kevin, 425
Moscow Art Theatre, 148–50
Mother Courage, 173
Movement
  by actor, 309–10
  stage, director and, 364–65, 364
Music
  emotional, 188
  in melodrama, 188
  signature, 188
Musicals, 81–83, 157–60, 159, 165
My Fair Lady, 81
Mystery Circle, The, 125
Mystery plays, 258
Myth, Wagner on, 141, 142, 144

N

National Endowment for the Arts, 124
Naturalism, 147–48, 147, 151
  in theatre, 150–55
Neal, Larry, 113, 117
Neher, Caspar, 408
Nemirovich-Danchenko, Vladimir, 148
Neoclassical theatre, 211–44
  design in, 403–404
  in England, 222–37
  in France, 237–44
  in Italy, 213–22
  theory in, 435–36
Nichols, Anne, 156
Nobel Prize, 85t., 86
Nonrecoverability, 19–20

O

Obie Awards, 85t., 86
Observation, teaching of, 318

Odd Couple, The, 89
Odets, Clifford, 158, 163
Oedipus Rex, 4, 49, 57, 279, 281, 284
Off-Broadway, 82, 90–91, 91, 92, 93, 103, 105, 109
Off-Off-Broadway, 93–94
Offenbach, Jacques, 132
Oh, What a Lovely War, 74
Oklahoma!, 160
Oldfield, Anne, 236
Olivier, Laurence, 49, 339
O'Neill, Eugene, 135, 157, 157, 163, 171
O'Neill, James, 135
O'Neill Theatre Center, 422, 432
Once Upon a Mattress, 391
Ontological-Hysteric Theatre, 102–104, 103
Open Theatre, 99–102
Opera, 9–10, 10
  comic, 132
Operettas, 132
Orpheus Descending, 386
Otto, Leo, 249, 408
Our Town, 160, 161
Owen, Rochelle, 121

P

Pace, 370
Pacino, Al, 89
Pageants, medieval, 255–56, 257, 258
Pantomime
  Neoclassical, 234–35
  Roman, 266–67
Papp, Joseph, 82, 84, 121
Paradise Now, 109, 111
Performance
  by actor, 303–304, 304, 328–30, 329. See also Acting
  criticism of, 427–28
  definition of, 18
  values of, 47–63
Phèdre, 240
Philosophical dramas, 195
Picnic, 129, 130
Pictorialism, in staging by director, 365–66, 372
Picturization, in staging by director, 366–68, 367, 372
Pinter, Harold, 54, 83, 86, 172
Pirandello, Luigi, 109

Piscator, Erwin, 171, 175
Pixérécourt, Réné Charles Guilbert de, 191, 379
Plautus, 264–65
Play(s)
  Broadway, 80. *See also* Broadway
  Greek, 279–83
  how to read, 428–32
  medieval, 250–51, 256–59
  realistic, 144–47
  Roman, 263–67
  selection of, by director, 345–50
  serious, 83–86, 158
  well-made, 195
Playwrights, 413–24
  audience and, 419–20
  compromise by, 420–21
  critic and, *425*
  income of, 422, 424
  as member of Open Theatre, 100
  in real world, 421–22
  theatre and, 422
  training of, 417–19
Polish Laboratory Theatre, 97–99
Political theatre, 107–21
Politics, theatre affected by, 73–75
"Poor theatre," 98, 99
Porter, Cole, 158
Primitivism, 183–84, 188
Prince, Hal, 83
Producer, search for, by playwright, 421–22
Production
  Greek, 277–79, *277*
  preparation of, role of director in, 371–73
  see also Costumes; Design; Scenery; Staging
Progression, director and, 353–54, *353*
Properties, 396
  medieval, *253, 254*
Psychological realism, 149–50, 382
Puccini, Giacomo, 131
Pulitzer Prize, 85t., 86
Purity of genres, 214–15
Pygmalion, 145

Q

Quin, James, 204, 236, 337

R

Rabe, David, 83–84
Racine, Jean, 239–40
Raisin in the Sun, A, 114
Randall, Bob, 87
Realism, 129–78
  alternatives to, 167–78
  in commercial mainstream
    from 1850 to 1900, 131–35
    from 1900 to 1960, 155–63
  design in, 404–407, *405, 406*
  in drama, 144–47
  emergence of, 136–47
  fourth-wall, 166
  in modern acting, 338–39, *338*
  naturalism and, 147–48
    in theatre, 150–55, *151, 152*
  problems with, 163–67
  psychological, 149–50, 382
  selective or simplified, 158, 161, 407
  of Stanislavski, 148–50
Recruiting Officer, The, 296
Regional theatres, 121–26, 162, *162,* 421–22
Rehearsals, 326–28, *329,* 375–77, *376*
Reinhardt, Max, 381–82
Religious and civic theatre, 245–88
Renaissance, 211, 212–213
  commedia dell' arte of, 220, *221, 222,* 234, *234,* 261, *292*
  theatre of, *248, 249, 266*
    acting in, 335–36, *335*
    criticism and theory in, 435–36
    design in, 403–404, *404*
    Roman influence in, 263–64, *265, 266*
Restoration comedy, 231–32, *232,* 234–35
Reviews
  by critics, 413–14, 425–26
  reading of, by audience, 43
Rhoda in Potatoland, 103, 104
Rhythm, directorial, 369–71
Rice, Elmer, 157, 158, 159, *170*
Richard II, 366–68
Richard III, 348
Richards, Lloyd, *425*
Ridiculous Theatrical Company, 104–107, *105*
Rights, amateur, 424

Riots
  Astor Place, 40, *40*
  Hernani, 25, *26,* 68, 197
  after Living Theatre performances, 111
Rip Van Winkle, 299
Rodgers, Richard, 160
Roman theatre, 260–71, *262, 263, 265*
  acting in, 333–34
  design in, 403
Romanticism, 181–209
  characteristics of, 183–88, *182, 184, 185, 186*
  commercialized, *138*
  costumes in theatre during, 202, *203, 207,* 208
  design during, 404–407, *405*
  in English and American theatre, 337–38
  plays in theatres during, 188–97
  practices of theatres during, 197–209
  theory during era of, 436
Romeo and Juliet, 16
Rosmersholm, 144
Round Trip Ticket, 427
Royalties, 132, 424
Ryskin, Morrie, 158

S

Sabattini, Niccolo, 219
Saint Joan, 123
Sardou, Victorien, 15, 131, 195
Sartre, Jean-Paul, 171
Saxe-Meiningen, Duke of, 138–41, 378–79, *380*
  see also Meiningen company
Scenery
  designer of, 394, *395,* 396
  limitations and advantages of, *21,* 22
  Neoclassical, 216–19
  Restoration, 235
  Romantic, *196,* 199–200, *199, 201,* 202, 404–407, *405*
  Serlian, 216, *217,* 218
  see also Design
Schechner, Richard, 93, 97–98, 178, 383
Schiller, Friedrich, 195–96
Schisgal, Murray, 93
Schneider, Alan, 372
School for Scandal, The, 194, *194, 374*
Schumann, Peter, 97

Science
  Neoclassicism and, 212
  realism and, 136–37
Scott, George C., 89
Scribe, Eugène, 144, 195, 430
Script
  analysis of, 318–25
  Artaud on substitutions for, 177
  interpretation of, by director, 351–56
Seagull, The, 321
Seascape, 84
Seating
  classless, 142
  continental, 142, *143*
  in theatres in Roman era, 198–99
Secular theatre, medieval, 259
Secularism, 212
Selective realism, 158, 161, 407
Selectivity, by actor, 299–300
Self-awareness
  artistic, 17–18
  group, of audience, 25
Seneca, 263–64
Sentimental comedy, 193
Sentimentalism, 181, 232–33, 234, 243
Serlian scenery, 216, *217,* 218
Serlio, Sebastiano, 403
Serpent, The, 100
Setting
  modern, proscenium arch less important in, 408–409
  in Romantic era, 200
  see also Scenery; Staging
Shaffer, Peter, 62
Shakespeare, William
  on audience responsibility, 42–43, *42*
  Gielgud's performances of, 54
  Globe of, *42*
  "illustrating," 134
  Kean in performance of works by, 337
  modern, *230, 237*
  in Neoclassical England, 222, 226–29, *227, 229,* 236
  problem of realism and, 164, 165–66
  reading, 429–31
  in Romantic era, *192,* 193, 202, 204, *206,* 207
  on theatre, 14
  various performing arts and, 16
  see also names of plays
Shange, Ntozake, 117, 121

Shaw, George Bernard, 31, 57, 131, *145, 146*, 157, 420, 439
Sheridan, Richard Brimsley, 193, 194, *194*
Sherwood, Robert, 158
Siddons, Sarah Kemble, 206
Side Show, 438
Sidney, Philip, 426, 435
Siegfried, 142
Sills, Paul, 97
Simon, Neil, 86, 89, 163, 432
Simonson, Lee, *388*, 407
Slade, Bernard, 87
Slave Ship, 115
Sleuth, 58
Smith, Maggie, 54
Social aspects
    of design, 392–93
    of epic theatre, 173–75
    of realism in theatre, 136–37
    of Romanticism, 182–85
    style of theatre related to, 37–38
    of theatre of cruelty, 176–78
    of Wagner's theatre, 143
    see also Society
Society
    art as response to and expression of, 5, 23, 25
    in 1960s and 1970s, 75–76
    see also Politics: Social aspects
Sophie, 102
Sophocles, 280, *281,* 431
Sound
    designer of, 400, 402
    director and, 357–58
    importance of, 53–54
Special effects
    in medieval drama, 254–55
    in Romantic era, *190, 191,* 200
Spectacles, *50,* 51–53, *51, 52*
    aquatic theatre as, *132*
    equestrian theatre as, *136,* 189
    in melodramas, 189
    Neoclassical, 220
Spolin, Viola, 305
Stage Blood, 105
Staging, 363–69, *364, 366, 367, 369*
    fourth-wall, 154
    Italianate, in France, 239, *240*
    medieval, fixed and movable, 255
        liturgical, 251–52
        outside Church, 255–56, *256*
        simultaneous, *256*

naturalistic, 151, 153, 154
Neoclassical, *214*
    in France, 243–44
    Italianate, 216, *217,* 218–20, *220,* 239, *240*
        for Shakespeare, 228–29, *229*
    realistic, 137–38, 140, 151
    Roman, 268, *269, 270*
    in Romantic era, 202, 208–209
Stallings, Laurence, 158
Stanislavski, Konstantin, 148–50
    on acting, 149, 298, 338–39
    influence of, 99, 305, 359, 382
    influences on, 141
    "method" acting based on ideas of, 158, 323
    Meyerhold and, 170
    Moscow Art Theatre and, 148–50
Star system, 139–40, 203–204, *317*
Stasio, Marilyn, *425*
Stewart, Ellen, 93, 97
Sticks and Bones, 84
Stock companies, 124, 203
Stoppard, Tom, *95,* 172, 298
Storm and Stress movement, 195
Story, value of, 55–58
Strasberg, Lee, 150
Streamers, 84
Street theatre, 107, *108*
Streetcar Named Desire, A, 58, 161
Streets of New York, The, 133
Strindberg, August, 148, 153, 157
Style
    of audience, 39–41, *40*
    in performing arts, 36–39, *37, 38*
    standards of beauty and, 392, *393,* 394
Sullivan, Arthur, 132–33
Summer and Smoke, 91
Surrealism, 171
Susannah, 127
Sydney, Phillip, 227

T

Talma, 206
Tarleton, *227*
Taylor, Rose, 121
Technology
    innovation influenced by, 35, *36*
    see also Science
Television, 7–9, *8*

Terence, 265–66
Terry, Megan, 100, 121
Theatre
  as artistic event, 16–22
  contemporary, 73–128. *See also* Contemporary theatre
  legitimate versus illegitimate, *434*
  little, *27, 28*
  modern, realism in, 128–78. *See also* Realism
  origins of Western, uncertain, 286–88
  as performing art, 3–6, 13–22
  "poor," 98, 99
  theory on, 432–40
Theatre of cruelty, 176–78
Theatre Guild, 157, 158
Théâtre-Libre, 152–55, 304
Theatres
  "classless," of Wagner, 143
  Elizabethan, 223–26, *223–25*
  Greek, *273, 276,* 277–79, *277,* 285, *285*
  innovative, by Wagner, 142–43, *143*
  large and small, 27–28
  modern, proscenium arch less important in, 408–409
  for naturalistic plays, 151
  Restoration, 235
  Roman, 267–68, *269*
  in Romantic era, 197–209
    architecture of, 197–98, *198*
Thomas, Lee, *420*
Thompson, Lydia, 133
Three Sisters, The, 146, *146, 345, 353, 358*
Three unities, 215
Through line, 325
Ticket sales, computerization of, 89
Timing, 370
TKTS, 89, *90*
Toffler, Alvin, 32, 76
Tolstoy, Leo, 153, 157
Tom Payne, 59
Tonight at 8:30, 156
Tony Awards, 85*t.,* 86
Torelli, Giacomi, 219, 239, 404
Tosca, 15
Tragedy(ies)
  acting in, 336–37, *336*
  Aristotle on, 433
  emotions in, 65, *66*
  Greek, 280, 282–86, *283*
  heroic, 233–34

in Neoclassical era, 240, 243
  Roman, 263–64, 266
Trial by Jury, 304
Troilus and Cressida, 354
Trojan Women, The, 63
"Turkeys," 156
Tynan, Kenneth, 428

U

Uncle Tom's Cabin, 133, *134,* 191–92, *191*
Uncle Vanya, 146

V

Valdez, Luis, 112
Values
  artistic excellence, 60–61
  human, 54–60
  intellectual, 61–63
  of performance, 47–63
  sensory, 51–54
Van Itallie, Jean-Claude, 93, 100, *101*
Vanbrugh, Irene, *327*
Vanities, 92
Vardac, A. Nicholas, 45
Vaudeville, 133
Verne, Jules, 33
Versailles Impromptu, The, 38
Versimilitude, 213–14, 215
Via negativa, 98
Viet Rock, 100, 101, 121
Vietnam War, *74, 75, 84,* 111
Villiers, George, 233
Violence, in 1960s and 1970s, 74–75
Visit, The, 355
Vitruvius, 216, 218
Voice, of actor, 53–54, 311–12
Voice of My Own, A, 120
Voltaire, 208, 243

W

Wagner, Richard, 104, 141–44, 175, 379, 380
Waiting for Godot, 68, *77,* 172
Waltz of the Toreadors, 360
Ward, Douglas Turner, 115
Warhol, Andy, 77

CAMROSE LUTHERAN COLLEGE
LIBRARY

Webster, John, 229
Wedekind, Frank, 382
Well-made play, 195
Welles, Orson, 160
West Side Story, 16
Whitman, Walt, 337, 338
Wilde, Oscar, 66
Wilder, Thornton, 160, *161*
Williams, Tennessee, 54, 86, 91, 129, 161,
    169, 382, 420, 431
Williams, William Carlos, 109
Wilson, Robert, 97, 104
Wiz, The, 117
Woffington, Peg, *54*
Women
  in "breeches" roles, 204, *205*

in Restoration theatre, 235–36
  see also Feminist theatre
Wood, William, 203
Wycherley, William, 232

Y

Yates, Mrs., *336*
You Never Can Tell, 347

Z

Zindel, Paul, 87
Zola, Émile, 148, 153, 437, 439